OXFORD STUDIES IN
MODERN EUROPEAN HISTORY

General Editors : SIMON DIXON, MARK MAZOWER,
and
JAMES RETALLACK

After Empires describes how the end of colonial empires and the changes in international politics and economies after decolonization affected the European integration process. Most studies on European integration have focused on the search for peaceful relations among the European nations, particularly between Germany and France, or examined it as an offspring of the Cold War, moving together with the ups and downs of transatlantic relations. But these two factors alone are not enough to explain the rise of the European Community and its more recent transformation into the European Union.

Giuliano Garavini focuses instead on the emergence of the Third World as an international actor, starting from its initial economic cooperation with the creation of the United Nations Conference for Trade and Development (UNCTAD) in 1964 up to the end of unity among the countries of the Global South after the second oil shock in 1979–80. Offering a new—less myopic—way to conceptualise European history more globally, the study is based on a variety of international archives (government archives in Europe, the US, Algeria, Venezuela; international organizations such as the EC, UNCTAD, and the World Bank; political and social organizations such as the Socialist International, labour archives and the papers of oil companies). It not only traces the reactions and the initiatives of the countries of the European Community, but also of the European political parties and public opinion, to the rise and fall of the Third World on the international stage.

Giuliano Garavini teaches International History at Roma Tre University in Rome. His main research interests include European integration, decolonization, and global struggles over natural resources. He has taught classes at various universities and institutions, including the Graduate Institute in Geneva, the European University Institute in Florence, and NYU Abu Dhabi. He has published on the interconnection between European integration and decolonization (*After Empires*, 2012), and on the global history of petroleum and of energy, in particular on the origins and significance of the 1973 'oil shock' (*Oil Shock: The 1973 Crisis and its Economic Legacy*, 2016) and on the 'counter-shock' in 1986 (*Counter-Shock: The Oil Counter-Revolution of the 1980s*, 2018). His last book is "The Rise and Fall of OPEC in the Twentieth Century" (OUP, 2019).

T0323373

ALSO PUBLISHED BY OXFORD UNIVERSITY PRESS

The Plough that Broke the Steppes
Agriculture and Environment on Russia's Grasslands, 1700–1914
David Moon

Enlightened Metropolis
Constructing Imperial Moscow, 1762–1855
Alexander M. Martin

All this is your World
Soviet Tourism at Home and Abroad after Stalin
Anne E. Gorsuch

Russia's Own Orient
The Politics of Identity and Oriental Studies in the Late Imperial and Early Soviet Periods
Vera Tolz

Model Nazi
Arthur Greiser and the Occupation of Western Poland
Catherine Epstein

The German Myth of the East
1800 to the Present
Vejas Gabriel Liulevicius

Sorrowful Shores
Violence, Ethnicity, and the End of the Ottoman Empire 1912–1923
Ryan Gingeras

After Empires

*European Integration, Decolonization, and
the Challenge from
the Global South 1957–1986*

GIULIANO GARAVINI

Translated by Richard R. Nybakken

OXFORD
UNIVERSITY PRESS

OXFORD
UNIVERSITY PRESS

Great Clarendon Street, Oxford, OX2 6DP,
United Kingdom

Oxford University Press is a department of the University of Oxford.
It furthers the University's objective of excellence in research, scholarship,
and education by publishing worldwide. Oxford is a registered trade mark of
Oxford University Press in the UK and in certain other countries

Originally published in 2009 as *Dopo gli imperi. L'integrazione europea
nello scontro Nord-Sud* © Giuliano Garavini
Richard Nybakken's English translation © Oxford University Press 2012

The moral rights of the author have been asserted

First published 2012
Reprinted 2013
First published in paperback 2021

Published in the United States of America by Oxford University Press
198 Madison Avenue, New York, NY 10016, United States of America

British Library Cataloguing in Publication Data
Data available

Library of Congress Cataloging in Publication Data
Data available

ISBN 978–0–19–965919–7 (Hbk.)
ISBN 978–0–19–886771–5 (Pbk.)

Contents

Figures and Tables

Chronology

1955	*April*	Twenty-nine African and Asiatic nations meet in Bandung
1960	*October*	Birth of OPEC
1961	*September*	First conference of the Non-Aligned countries in Belgrade
1962		Economic conference of the Non-Aligned countries in Cairo
1963		Signature of the Yaoundé Association
1964	*March*	First UNCTAD conference in Geneva and institutionalization of the G77
1965		Failure of the "Second Bandung"
1966	*January*	Tricontinental conference in Havana
1967	*June*	GATT's "Kennedy Round" without concessions to LDCs
	October	The G77 approves the "Algiers Charter"
1968	*February*	Second UNCTAD conference in New Delhi
1970	*September*	Third meeting of the Non-Aligned countries
1971		The EC approves its Generalized System of Preferences scheme
1972	*April*	Third UNCTAD conference in Santiago, Chile
	October	European Summit in Paris: EC leaders approve a global cooperation and development policy
1973	*September*	Fourth meeting of the Non-Aligned countries in Algiers
	October	Arab oil producers (OAPEC) approve embargo and production cuts
	December	OPEC decided new posted price for oil
1974	*April*	Sixth UN General Assembly (adoption of declaration on the NIEO)
	December	UN adopts the Charter of Economic Rights and Duties of States
1975	*February*	Lomé Convention between EC and forty-six ACP countries
	April	Failure of consumer–producer meeting in Paris
	November	First meeting of the six most industrialized countries in Rambouillet
	December	Beginning of the Conference for International Economic Cooperation (CIEC, North–South dialogue)
1976	*May*	Fourth UNCTAD conference in Nairobi
	June	G7 Summit in Puerto Rico
1977	*May*	Conclusion of the North–South dialogue in Paris
	September	Launching of the Brandt commission
1978	*July*	G7 in Bonn and application of "locomotive theory"
1979	*May*	Fifth UNCTAD conference in Manila

	September	Conference of the Non-Aligned Movement in Havana
1980	*February*	The Brandt Commission report is published
1981	*October*	North–South meeting in Cancun ends phase of global talks
1986	*February*	Signature of the Single European Act establishing a Single Market
		Oil price collapse: "oil countershock"

Introduction

Alexis de Tocqueville, that noble and liberal Frenchman of inexhaustible curiosity who had studied the rise of American democracy and the energy of its people with great insight—and not without fear—rediscovered his faith in Europeans around 1840, when they demonstrated themselves capable of crushing Chinese resistance during the first Opium War:

> So at last the mobility of Europe has come to grips with Chinese immobility! It is a great event, especially if one thinks that it is only the continuation, the last in a multitude of events of the same nature all of which are pushing the European race out of its home and are successively submitting all the other races to its empire or its influence. Something more vast, more extraordinary than the establishment of the Roman Empire is growing out of our times, without anyone noticing it; it is the enslavement of four parts of the world by the fifth. Therefore, let us not slander our century and ourselves too much; the men are small, but the events are great.[1]

After decades of such "submission," an epochal change brought the countries of Africa and Asia their political independence; the Great Divide that once separated the "enslaved" peoples from their imperial masters has been challenged and in many places overcome. Today the results of the process that goes by the controversial name "decolonization" are visible to even the most casual observer of the contemporary world. In 2006 an Indian company, Mittal Steel, acquired Luxembourg's most important industrial concern, Arcelor, giving birth to the largest steel conglomerate in the world. This was an event of clear symbolic significance, if one recalls that the steel industry was considered of such strategic importance to western Europe after the Second World War that in 1951 it was at the very heart of the continent's first efforts at integration: The European Coal and Steel Community (ECSC). At the dawn of the third millennium, the summit of the leaders of the seven most important economies—the G7, four members of which were European—has been overtaken in importance by the G20, which includes regional and emerging global powers, thus leading to speculation that the "West" has been matched and could possibly be surpassed by the "Rest."

This book is not a history of the European continent from the Atlantic to the Urals, nor can it be taken as a complete account of the main political, economic, and cultural events in western Europe during the years under consideration. Rather,

---

[1] Alexis de Tocqueville to Henry Reeve, April 12, 1840, in Roger Boesche, ed., *Alexis de Tocqueville: Selected Letters on Politics and Society*, trans. James Toupin (Berkeley: University of California Press, 1985), pp. 141–2.

it is a history of the postwar process of western European integration that focuses on the retreat from empire, the alternative order established by decolonization, and the cultural, political, and economic challenges faced by empires first and nations later. Europe's identity has been inextricably linked to its rule over the rest of the world, and this was no less true during the Cold War era than it had been a century earlier.[2] This suggestion, regrettably in large part disregarded until only very recently, was imparted by Geoffrey Barraclough to students and historians of current affairs at the height of the struggles for African and Asian independence:

> Between 1945 and 1960 no less than forty countries with a population of 800 millions—more than a quarter of the world's inhabitants—revolted against colonialism and won their independence. Never before in the whole of human history had so revolutionary a reversal occurred with such rapidity. The change in the position of the peoples of Asia and Africa and in their relations with Europe was the surest sign of the advent of a new era, and when the history of the first half of the twentieth century—which, for most historians, is still dominated by European wars and European problems, by Fascism and National Socialism, and by Mussolini, Hitler and Stalin—comes to be written in a longer perspective, there is little doubt that no single theme will prove to be of greater importance than the revolt against the west.[3]

Predictions of the crisis of Eurocentrism were already in the air during the *Belle Époque*, of course, and were later discussed with even greater urgency after the First World War, when they led to ominous treatises on the inexorable decline of Western civilization. Most thought, however, that the peril would come from the Anglo-Saxon nations—those whom the Italian historian Emilio Gentile has called the *europeidi*, the "children of Europe"—or from an Eurasian power like Russia. Asia itself did not yet disturb the sleep of a continent "whose power in arms and wealth allowed it to keep such ghosts at bay, so as not to disturb its faith in progress and the hope of new conquests and new triumphs."[4]

But by the early 1960s the emergence of the "darker nations" could no longer be ignored as, one after another, African and Asian nations obtained their independence and Latin American countries resumed their battle for political and economic emancipation. Following closely on the heels of political experiments such as the Non-Aligned Movement, the creation in 1964 of the United Nations Conference for Trade and Development (UNCTAD) confirmed the arrival of the Global South—or Third World, as it was called at the time—on the international stage, and embodied their quest for political and economic cooperation.[5] Through UNCTAD, for the first time the developing nations were able to harness the power

---

[2] On the links between Europe and the rest of the world in the long eighteenth century, see C.A Bayly, *The Birth of the Modern World 1780–1914: Global Connections and Comparisons* (Malden: Blackwell Publishing, 2004).

[3] G. Barraclough, *An Introduction to Contemporary History* (London: C.A. Watts, 1964), p. 164.

[4] E. Gentile, *L'apocalisse della modernità. La Grande Guerra per l'uomo nuovo* (Milan: Mondadori, 2008), p. 81.

[5] I use the terms Third World and Global South interchangeably, although the latter has a more nuanced meaning than the former. While the origins of the name "Third World" are well known—it was used for the first time in 1954 to distinguish this from the industrialized capitalist and Communist worlds—the "Global South" is still used today to refer to those countries and social movements that in one way or another are either opposed to, or are struggling to be more involved in, oversight of the globalization of the international economy.

of collective action in order to push for a reform of the rules of the international economy and of international law, selecting as the primary target first the former colonial empires and later "imperialism."

While it was not always successful in achieving its goals, the Global South should not be seen merely as a collection of desperate, starving peoples, its leaders awaiting salvation from the coffers of the industrialized world or its charitable organizations—the stuff of the straw man manipulated by international communism.[6] Nor should it be dismissed, as often occurs even in the best critiques of decolonization, as the passive victim of a process that simply transferred control of empires from European into American hands, or that gave birth to a new form of neocolonialism exercised through free trade and indirect economic and political control.[7] Rather, the story addressed in this book is that of proactive cooperation among nations with often divergent political regimes, which nevertheless managed to forge a common strategic vision, and of dynamic statesmen with a strong understanding of the global economy and the vagaries of international public opinion: From the first head of UNCTAD, the Argentine Raúl Prebisch, to the Algerian revolutionary leader Houari Boumedienne.[8]

In the first two chapters, readers will find a broad account of the parallel births and initial interaction (or lack thereof) between the Global South and the European Economic Community—or European Community (EC) as it would later be called, which included the EEC—created in 1957. The book's primary argument, developed in the subsequent four chapters, is that the common cause made by the countries of the developing world to change their position in the international economy, the partial success of their efforts—especially following the 1973 "oil shock"—and the subsequent collapse of their united front after the twin oil and monetary shocks of 1979–80, were developments that had a profound impact on the nature of western European integration itself. Alan Milward, in his pioneering works, has identified the significance of European integration up to the 1960s as a process primarily directed at the "rescue of the nation-state."[9] If the EC eventually become something more complex and permanent than a free market area, if it even seemed to emerge as a possible new international actor, this has much to do with the changing international environment in which it operated.

As much as possible in such a broad portrait, I have tried to attribute the appropriate weight to the influence of individual personalities, the action of the

---

[6] Pankay Mishra traces the origins of the intellectual alternatives to the European domination in Asia back to the very beginning of the twentieth century; P. Mishra, *From the Ruins of Empire. The Revolt Against the West and the Remaking of Asia* (London: Allen Lane, 2012).

[7] John Darwin argues that, "far from heralding a 'world of nations', decolonization's unexpected course seemed to have set the scene for new kinds of empire." J. Darwin, *After Tamerlane. The Rise and Fall of Global Empires 1400–2000*, (London: Penguin, 2008) pp. 476–7.

[8] The Third World has been defined by scholars like Vijay Prashad as a political and cultural project that was potentially capable of generating a new form of internationalism in competition with the established cooperative mechanisms of both Communism and liberal democracy. See V. Prashad, *The Darker Nations. A People's History of the Third World* (New York: The New Press, 2007). Odd Arne Westad, in contrast, views the history of the Third World, itself the product of European ideology and the Cold War, mainly as the story of a failure and of errors to be avoided in the future. As he argues, "what is needed is a hard-nosed understanding of the Third World idea in order to avoid repeating its mistakes."O.A. Westad, "The Project," (2008) 30(2) *The London Review of Books* 30.

[9] A. Milward, *The European Rescue of the Nation-State* (Berkeley: University of California Press, 1992).

European institutions in Brussels, the pressures of societal movements, and to the turning points brought about by changes in the western European political and cultural spectrum. It was possible to react in many different ways to the changes in international politics and economics after decolonization. The outcome of the 1980s, that is the decision to identify European integration with a regional and introverted project centered on increased competitiveness through the creative forces of the Single Market, was not in fact a foregone conclusion. Up until the end of the 1970s, and even into the first years of the 1980s, other paths were still open, and here are given prominent attention.

In an essay written amidst the smoking embers of the Second World War, Arnold Toynbee, the historian and diplomat with a precocious vision for grand ideas, described the nations of western Europe as the battleground of non-European powers and spoke of the "destructive recoil of European influence abroad upon Europe herself." It is worth citing the passage in which Toynbee makes reference to the possibilities of European unification soon after the Second World War:

> But is "union" the right name for the constellation of forces that we are forecasting? Would not "partition" be a more accurate word? For if Eastern Europe is to be associated with the Soviet Union under Soviet hegemony and Western Europe with the United States under American leadership, the division of Europe between these two titanic non-European powers is the most significant feature of the new map to the European eye. Are we not really arriving at the conclusion that it is already beyond Europe's power to retrieve her position in the world by overcoming the disunity that has always been her bane? The dead-weight of European tradition now weighs lighter than a feather in the scales, for Europe's will no longer decide[s] Europe's destiny. Her future lies on the knees of the giants who now overshadow her.[10]

Pessimism, fatalism, and a healthy dose of historical determinism dominate this analysis, which would ultimately bear little relation to the actual course of western European integration: Itself a story largely underestimated by the most recent, and otherwise valuable, syntheses on contemporary Europe.[11] The process of western European cooperation, however influenced by the logic of the Cold War from its very beginning, was at the heart of its leaders' response to the crisis of the nation

---

[10] A.J. Toynbee, *Civilization on Trial* (New York: Oxford University Press, 1948), p. 124.

[11] The most recent syntheses on the history of Europe after the Second World War pay a tribute to the success but also to the instability of European democracies, and to the "dark" influence exerted upon them by Fascism, racism, and other authoritarian tendencies: M. Mazower, *Dark Continent: Europe's Twentieth Century* (New York: Vintage, 2001). Alternatively, they spotlight the interconnection between events in western and eastern Europe, particularly the persistence of ethnic and national hatreds: see N. Davies, *Europe East and West* (London: Jonathan Cape, 2006). These works form a useful antidote to "institutional" histories which have focused only on western Europe and portrayed postwar European history as a period void of such tensions and marked instead by the inevitable reconciliation, peacemaking, and democratization leading to the creation of the institutions in Brussels. On the other hand, as argued by Holger Nehring and Helge Pharo, this prevalently Anglo-Saxon and Anglophone historiography is limited by considering Europe simply as a battleground of the Cold War, a region replete with ethnic and social conflict, but never as an active protagonist in the effort to construct a stable peace, either on the Continent or in the international sphere. See H. Nehring and H. Pharo, "Introduction: A Peaceful Europe? Negotiating Peace in the Twentieth Century," (2008) 17(3) *Contemporary European History* pp. 277–99.

state, helping to change their citizens' material wellbeing and mental world view, and certainly helping furnish a response to James Sheehan's recent query: "Where have all the soldiers gone?"[12] Even if it is has not been possible here to provide a detailed summary of the history of integration, its institutions, and its politics, the author owes a great deal to the growing of research compiled by a generation of young historians who are studying the phenomenon of European integration.[13]

The effort undertaken here simultaneously departs from a notion of western Europe as a purely passive community, the chessboard of the two superpowers, while attempting to outline the failures, the fateful shortsightedness, and the profound discontinuities in the evolution of the integration process. Even though there has been significant institutional stability since the creation of the ECSC in 1951, the EC was not—and is not today, in its new guise as the European Union—an irreversible or inexorable movement toward peace, justice, and happiness, as some of the propaganda coming from Brussels would have it; rather, it is an ever-changing entity deeply entwined with both international political and economic pressures, and changes in its internal political climate.

* * *

No book, much less a work of history that depends upon years of patient labor, is written in complete isolation. If it were so, I would long ago have missed two ideas that are central to the pages that follow, the importance of which was imparted to me by Antonio Varsori and Simone Paoli. The former taught me that European integration is not a phenomenon that began in 1951 and developed continuously to the present day; there have, instead, been so many different phases and ruptures that one might almost speak of several distinct "European integrations." I thus became convinced that the Europe of the Single Market in the mid-1980s had little to do with that of the Common Market in the 1960s and 1970s, and that it was necessary to understand what had happened between these two profoundly different moments. The latter brought my attention to the importance of 1968 as a *caesura*—in western Europe as much as if not more than in the rest of the world— and thus also as a turning point in the process of integration, if in no other way than for the obvious rupture in the political and cultural climate of the entire continent. I have broadened not a little the concept of 1968 as a *caesura*, applying it not only to questions of internal European affairs, but also to the relations between western Europe and the rest of the world.

Then there are those to whom I owe thanks for advice, for many small and not-so-small words of encouragement, who contributed valuable suggestions, proposed

---

[12] J. Sheehan, *Where Have All the Soldiers Gone?: The Transformation of Modern Europe* (New York: Houghton Mifflin Harcourt, 2008).

[13] For some recent work on the history of European integration see the volume based on the conference of the European Liaison Committee of Historians on the occasion of the 50th anniversary of the Treaty of Rome: W. Loth, ed., *Experiencing Europe: 50 Years of European Construction, 1957–2007* (Baden-Baden: Nomos, 2007); or W. Kaiser and A. Varsori, eds, *European Union History. Themes and Debates* (London: Palgrave, 2010). The main research topics of young historians of European integration may also be found online at the site of the International Research Network of Young Historians of European Integration (RICHIE): <http://www.europe-richie.org/>.

corrections or alterations, and gave me indispensable moral and material assistance during my research. In strictly alphabetical order, and shortening as much as possible what would otherwise be a very long list, I thank with all my heart: Daniele Caviglia, Mario Del Pero, Mark Mazower, Bernard Mommer, Mary Nolan, Francesco Petrini, Federico Romero, all my colleagues and professors from the doctoral program in the History of International Relations at the Università di Firenze and in the Department of International Studies of the Università di Padova. Lorenzo Ferrari has helped me with the maps. In the many archives I visited, some dusty and neglected, others spacious and heavily supervised, I was fortunate enough to encounter many willing and engaging interlocutors, among whom I would like to remember in particular Jean-Marie Palayret, who constitutes an indispensable point of reference for scholars of European integration in Fiesole (Florence). I would like to thank particularly Christopher Wheeler for the opportunity to publish at OUP.

This book was made possible by funding from the Dipartimento di Studi internazionali of the Università di Padova, by a semester research fellowship from LUSPIO, by funding from the PRIN 2005 "*Il Mediterraneo dalla crisi di Suez alla seconda distensione*" chaired by Professor Daniele Caviglia, by a research project (2008–10) coordinated by Professor Lorenzo Mechi of the Università di Padova, by the Short-Term Mobility program of the CNR, and by the Gerald Ford Foundation. I greatly benefited from participating in the "Decolonization Seminar" organized in Washington by the National History Center and directed by M. Roger Louis.

Finally, I would like to thank the staff of the Biblioteca di storia moderna e contemporanea and the Biblioteca del Senato in Rome, places where the writing of much of this volume was completed.

This book is a revised and updated version of the Italian "Dopo gli imperi. L'integrazione europea nello scontro Nord-Sud" (Le Monnier, 2009). While the structure of the book remains basically the same, sections have been rewritten, maps and bibliography have been added, and new archival research has been conducted.

1

The Third World and the Creation of UNCTAD

In the words of William Roger Louis, "the year 1956 is to 1882 as the end is to the beginning: Just as 1882 marks the start of the occupation, so 1956 severs the link and can be seen as the end of the colonial era in Egypt and the beginning of the new Scramble out of Africa and the Middle East."[1] Decolonization and the revolt against the West would lead to national independence for most countries in Africa and Asia by the early 1960s, while Latin American countries would resume their never-fully-abandoned drive for economic and political emancipation.

Nobody could predict then whether these nations—spread out across Asia, Africa, and Latin America; millions of peoples with different religions, languages, and traditions—would be willing to find common interests or the capacity for coordinated action. Indeed, there was a very real possibility that, once liberated from European colonial domination, these peoples would only find themselves subject to a new form of imperial tutelage by the two emergent superpowers, the United States and the Soviet Union, each endowed with competing global ideologies, ambitions, and military might.

In 1933, in his last letter from jail to his daughter Indira Gandhi, Jawaharlal Nehru wrote that "thought, in order to justify itself, must lead to action."[2] It should come as no surprise if, among the elites of the new nations torn between Wilson and Lenin, the virtues of free-market liberal democracy and the imperatives of social revolution under a planned economy, the practical need to make giant leaps forward through industrialization and higher prices for raw materials initially prevailed over protracted theoretical debates regarding the appropriate form of government. The titanic task of achieving development would be accomplished both by exploiting the military and economic assistance of any nation willing to provide it, and through a coordinated effort to reform the international trade system in their own favor. Antiwestern polemics and requests for some form of compensation for colonial "pillage" also offered an easy substitute for badly needed internal social and economic reforms.

The Third World was very soon to become the main arena for the competing visions of modernity and models of internationalism. But Third World countries did

---

[1] W.R. Louis, *Ends of British Imperialism: The Scramble for Empire, Suez, and Decolonization* (London: IB Tauris, 2006), p. 5.
[2] J. Nehru, *Glimpses of World History* (Delhi: Oxford University Press, 1980), p. 953.

not simply choose between these competing versions of modernity, just as they did not passively accept the logic of the Cold War as a fait accompli—even though many of the developing countries were forced to endure some of its devastating effects. As the most recent historiography on the Third World has confirmed, developing nations often struggled, both individually and collectively, to advance their own visions of modernization, more often than not characterized by high levels of state intervention and aspirations of fast-track industrialization,[3] just as they fought to promote their own priorities in the realm of human rights and international law.[4] This chapter will focus on the economic dimension of Third World internationalism, developed through the creation of the United Nations Conference for Trade and Development (UNCTAD) in 1964 and embodied by the slogan "trade not aid."

THE SPIRIT OF BANDUNG

Decolonization is a term widely used to describe the end of colonialism and the decline of European empires. It can suggest a course of planned or progressive abandonment of colonial possessions. The reality was both much crueler and less edifying. In the golden age of empires, the British Empire was spread across a territory 125 times larger than the United Kingdom; the Belgian Empire 78 times bigger than the motherland; the Dutch Empire 55 times bigger than the Netherlands; and the French Empire some fifteen times greater than its national territory. Even after the end of the Second World War, the European nations that had not lost the conflict clung tightly to their colonial possessions, which they considered an extension of the *metropole*, a central component of their prestige and national identity, and vital economic "living space," not to mention a strategic reserve of cheap labor.[5]

We shall see in the next chapter that western European governments were late in understanding the dimensions of the revolution under way in world politics. But not all European states, nor their leaders, reacted everywhere in exactly the same manner. It should be noted, for example, that the Labour government of Clement Attlee recognized very quickly that a peaceful resolution of the Indian question was fundamental to the preservation of financial resources for the construction of the welfare state in Great Britain. That very same Great Britain, however, conceded independence to Malaysia only in 1957, after aiding a brutal, decade-long repression of its communist insurrection.[6] That same year, in Kenya the British colonial

[3] D. Engerman and C.Unger, "Introduction: Towards a Global History of Modernization," (2009) 33(3) *Diplomatic History*.

[4] S.L. Hoffmann, "Genealogies of Human Rights," in S.L. Hoffmann, ed., *Human Rights in the Twentieth Century* (New York: Cambridge University Press, 2011).

[5] N. Davies, *Europe: A History* (New York: Harper, 2007), pp. 1068–9. Some recent syntheses of the history of decolonization include M. Shipway, *Decolonization and its Impact: A Comparative Approach to the End of the Colonial Empires* (Oxford: Blackwell, 2008); B. Droz, *Histoire de la décolonisation au XXe siècle* (Paris: Seuil, 2006).

[6] M. Thomas, B. Moore, and L.J. Butler, *Crises of Empire. Decolonization and Europe's Imperial States, 1918–1975* (London: Bloomsbury, 2010), pp. 82–4.

administration, after having tried to suppress the Mau Mau uprising through the use of concentration camps (in which allegedly more than 1 million Kikuyu were imprisoned), deployed its own version of a final solution, ironically named Operation Progress, based on the physical elimination of all opposition.[7] In at least twenty other cases, the process of liberation brought with it war or armed revolt.

During the 1950s and 1960s, the world witnessed the restructuring of a form of European commercial, military, and industrial colonization the distant origins of which lay in the sixteenth century, but which had become a predominant global force in the nineteenth-century Age of Imperialism.[8] The Netherlands was forced to concede independence to Indonesia in 1949, after having fought to the bitter end—sending as many as 150,000 soldiers to southeast Asia—to retain control of its oil resources, ultimately capitulating only before American threats of exclusion from NATO and the Marshall Plan.[9] France sustained two shocking military defeats, first in Asia and later in Africa, before relinquishing its colonial ties. The former, at the hands of the Vietnamese at Dien Bien Phu in 1954, was also "the first victory [by an Asian nation] over the West, except by Japan, in a battle fought by the two sides with equal weapons and on the same highly professional lines."[10] The road to liberation was even longer in Algeria: Only in 1962 did the French resign themselves to withdrawal, after enduring a seemingly endless string of terrorist attacks both in Africa and at home, finally overcome in the end by the Algerian FLN's international campaign to portray itself as progressive and to discredit the repressive measures of the French army in the eyes of world opinion.[11] In Egypt, the British Conservative government of Anthony Eden miscalculated the significance of an emergent Arab nationalism led by Gamal Abdel Nasser and, along with the French Socialist government, embarked on an ill-fated military venture to retake control of the Suez Canal.[12] The independence conceded to Ghana in 1957 and Guinea in 1958 paved the way for decolonization elsewhere in Africa, but in 1960 Belgium nevertheless still intervened in the Congo against the legitimate government of Patrice Lumumba, which appeared to threaten its economic interests.

Structural changes in three areas of international politics and economics also contributed to the end of European empires and aided the cause of the colonized peoples.[13] First, a spread of nationalist movements around the world was well under way after the First World War. Even though the United Nations was initially

---

[7] C. Elkins, *Imperial Reckoning. The Untold Story of Britain's* <r>Gulag</r> *in Kenya* (New York: Henry Holt and Company, 2005).

[8] D. Abernethy, *The Dynamics of Global Governance: European versus Overseas Empires 1415–1980* (New Haven, CT: Yale University Press, 2001).

[9] M. Michel, *Décolonisation et émergence du Tiers monde* (Paris: Hachette, 1993), p. 139.

[10] V.G. Kiernan, *From Conquest to Collapse: European Empires from 1815 to 1960* (New York: Pantheon Books, 1962), p. 217.

[11] M. Connelly, *A Diplomatic Revolution: Algeria's Fight for Independence and the Origins of the Post–Cold War Era* (New York: Oxford University Press, 2002).

[12] M. Ferro, *Suez 1956: naissance d'un Tiers Monde* (Brussels: Complexe, 1995).

[13] M. Ferro, *Histoire des colonisations. Des conquêtes aux indépendances XIII–XX siécle* (Paris: Seuil, 1994), p. 399.

created as a concert of Great Powers that included European imperial states, its General Assembly eventually became a stage for the international condemnation of colonialism and of racism.[14] A second change arose thanks to the intensification of commercial relations between the industrialized nations—an inversion of the tendency toward autarky and protectionism prevalent in the 1930s—and the perfection of transportation technologies, with their corresponding drop in shipping costs. These developments rendered direct control of colonies' raw materials both more expensive—in terms of military spending and related sacrifices in the development of national welfare states—and less necessary. Finally, there was the definitive recognition of the role of the two superpowers, and the knowledge that formerly colonized peoples could receive support from either of the two spheres of influence professing a universal ideology. Indeed, as Frederick Cooper has noted, the defeat of the European powers in southeast Asia at the hands of Japan had already allowed their former colonies in that particular region to taste the the flavor of national independence by the end of the Second World War.[15] Such territories would have to be *de facto* recolonized by former imperial masters, a much more difficult and unpopular task in the context of the Cold War than simply controlling revolts in long-established territorial possessions.

If these changes contributed to the end of direct European colonialism, that does not mean that the newly independent countries did not retain strong cultural and economic ties with their former *metropoles*. Mineral and oil companies operating in former colonies were still mostly based in London, New York, Paris, or Brussels, trade and migration was mainly directed towards the metropolitan areas, and the majority of the new elite had been educated in one of the languages of their former imperial masters. Nehru, though deeply influenced by the example set by the communist revolution, still evoked his youthful ties with Great Britain when dealing with the American ambassador John Kenneth Galbraith; the latter, in his memoirs, recalled how in his advancing age the Indian statesman enjoyed reliving, not the heroic period of Gandhi's nonviolent independence struggle but his formative years at Trinity College, Cambridge and his encounters with the extraordinary minds of scholars like R.H. Tawney or Sydney and Beatrice Webb.[16] The influence of European thought and practices helps to explain the strong desire of the new nations and their leaders to remain independent both of East and West, and their faith in their ability to develop autonomous national paths to economic and political modernization. This is clearly echoed by the Indian Marxist historian K.M. Panikkar:

> The period of maritime authority over Asia, beginning with Vasco da Gama's arrival and ending with the departure of the Western fleets from their bases on the Asian

---

[14] M. Mazower, *No Enchanted Palace. The End of Empire and the Ideological Origins of the United Nations* (Princeton, NJ: Princeton University Press, 2009), pp. 186–7.

[15] F. Cooper, "Reconstrucing Empire in British and French Africa," in Mark Mazower, Jessica Reinisch, and David Feldman, *Post–War Reconstruction in Western Europe. International Perspectives 1945–1949* (Oxford: Oxford University Press, 2011), p. 198.

[16] J.K. Galbraith, *A Life in Our Times: Memoirs* (New York: Ballantine, 1981), p. 408.

continent, covers an epoch of the highest significance to human development. The changes it directly brought about and the forces it generated in the countries of Asia in contact with Europe for a period of 450 years, and subjected to Western domination for over a century, have effected a transformation which touches practically every aspect of life in these countries. It is, therefore, not possible to survey them even in general outline. The social, political and economic conditions of Asian countries have undergone revolutionary changes as a result of these contacts and influences. Their religious and philosophical systems, the material set-up of their lives and their mental outlook have been affected to an extent which it is not possible for anyone to estimate now. Everywhere in Asia this prolonged contact has produced ferments, the possible effects of which cannot be foreseen.[17]

A rare exception among such widely used expressions, the origins of the term "Third World" are well known: The phrase was coined in 1952 by the French demographer Albert Sauvy in an article for the weekly magazine *L'Observateur* (renamed *Le Nouvel Observateur* in 1964):

> We speak often and willingly of two worlds and of a possible conflict between them, of their co-existence, etc. And all too often we forget that there exists a third world, the most important of all; chronologically speaking, it is that world which came first.[18]

The term itself was evocative, making explicit reference to the Third Estate from the years preceding the French Revolution, and its exclusion from political decision-making processes. But it was mute regarding the potential future of this gigantic mass of humanity that was imagining transnational or pan-continental federations but busily organizing itself into nation states. Vijay Prashad has in fact spoken of the Third World as a project for cooperation among "the darker nations."[19] And it is not a coincidence that it was a demographer like Sauvy that first used this neologism to define a part of the planet, largely confined to the southern hemisphere, the most noteworthy characteristic of which throughout the twentieth century was precisely its impressive population growth.[20]

The Third World would remain, at any rate, a primarily Western definition. The newly independent countries would determine their own identities, common interests, and autonomous political networks through their joint struggles on the international stage and their continued development of networks that had been

---

[17] K.M. Panikkar, *Asia and Western Dominance: A Survey of the Vasco Da Gama Epoch of Asian History (1498–1945)* (London: Allen & Unwin, 1953), p. 479.

[18] Y. Lacoste, *Unité et diversité du Tiers Monde* (Paris: La Découverte-Hérodote, 1984), p. 184.

[19] V. Prashad, *The Darker Nations: A People's History of the Third World* (New York: The New Press, 2007).

[20] For some considerations on Sauvy's seminal article see M. Connelly, *Fatal Misconception. The Struggle to Control World Population* (Cambridge: Belknap Press, 2008), pp. 153–4. Hobsbawm notes that while in 1900 peoples of European origin represented approximately one-third of humanity, the tragic period between the two world wars completely altered the demographic picture in favor of the colonized regions. The population of the member states of the OCSE at the end of the 1980s, in fact, represented no more than 15 percent of mankind. E.J. Hobsbawm, *The Age of Extremes: A History of the World, 1914–1991* (New York: Vintage, 1994), p. 345.

established after the first World War.[21] The first of these initial struggles, inevitably, was to avoid being transformed from colonies simply into pawns in the great game of the Cold War. A significant demonstration of their desire for autonomy and capacity for self-organization came in 1955 with the Bandung Conference, promoted by Nehru, Nasser, and the Indonesian leader Akmed Sukarno. The meeting was a major event watched closely by the international press; for the first time the governments of the "non-white" peoples had organized their own international event.[22] Often erroneously remembered as the foundation of what would become the Non-Aligned Movement (NAM), the meeting in Bandung was in reality motivated by tangentially related considerations: Halting Chinese expansion in Asia, thus avoiding potential conflict with the United States after the end of the Korean War; reacting to the "Pactomania" with which the US Secretary of State John Foster Dulles sought to contain Soviet expansionism (SEATO, the South-East Asia Treaty Organization, was signed in 1954); affirming their right to neutrality with respect to the two superpowers; and upholding the need to proceed with nuclear disarmament. Anti-imperialism and modernization to "catch up" with the West were the common ambitions voiced by Afro-Asian leaders.[23] The twenty-nine participants at the conference were primarily newly created Asian and African nations—the Asian representatives prevailed in both numbers and importance over their six African counterparts—but not all could be classified as neutrals: Pakistan, Japan, the Philippines, Thailand, Iran, and Turkey were tightly woven into the American sphere of influence, while the People's Republic of China was still closely linked to the Soviet Union. The Bandung Declaration included calls for universal access to the United Nations, but lacked precise claims for international economic reform.[24] Above all, the summit celebrated a growing spirit of "Afro-Asian" cooperation founded on a recognition of common desires for racial reparation and emancipation from the control of the superpowers.[25]

Midway through the 1950s the pace of decolonization had accelerated, as we have seen, tied in particular to the failure of Western military intervention during the Suez crisis. A significant role was played in this process by the pan-Arabism of

---

[21] M.P. Bradley, "Decolonization, the Global South, and the Cold War, 1919–1962," in M.P. Leffler and O.A. Westad, eds, *The Cambridge History of the Cold War: Origins, 1945–1962* (Cambridge: Cambridge University Press, 2012).

[22] G.P. Calchi-Novati and L. Quartapelle, *La conferenza afro-asiatica di Bandung in una prospettiva storica* (Rome: Carocci, 2007).

[23] C.J. Lee, "Between a Moment and an Era: The Origins and Afterlives of Bandung," in C.L. Lee, ed., *Making a World After Empires* (Athens: Ohio University Press, 2010), pp. 1–45.

[24] G. McTurnan Kahin, *The Asian-African Conference: Bandung, Indonesia, April 1955* (Ithaca, NY: Cornell University Press, 1956), p. 34: "It was further recognized that the assistance being received by certain participating countries from outside the region, through international or under bilateral arrangements, had made a valuable contribution to the implementation of their development programmes." The conference's promoters included: Ceylon, India, Indonesia, and Pakistan. Representatives of the following nations were invited to participate: Afghanistan, Cambodia, China, Egypt, Ethiopia, Côte d'Ivoire, Iran, Iraq, Japan, Jordan, Laos, Lebanon, Liberia, Nepal, the Philippines, Saudi Arabia, Sudan, Syria, Thailand, Turkey, the Democratic Republic of Vietnam (North), Vietnam (South), and Yemen.

[25] O. Guitard, *Bandoung et le réveil des peuples colonisés* (Paris: PUF, 1969).

Nasser, whose government, with its authoritarian undertones, promoted agrarian reform, undertook several economic experiments with a socialist flavor, expanded its influence in Iraq, Syria, and Yemen, and furnished diplomatic support to the Algerian liberation movement.[26] A similar influence was exerted in Africa by Ghana's Kwame Nkrumah, who broadcast appeals across the continent for economic independence and unity among the African peoples.

The year 1960 opened with British Conservative Harold Macmillan's important address at Cape Horn, known as the "Wind of Change" speech. Macmillan had perceived the significance of the coming challenge from the Third World—the "wind of change"—though he partially misunderstood its origins, reading it purely in terms of the conflict between East and West:

> As I see it the great issue in this second half of the twentieth century is whether the uncommitted peoples of Asia and Africa will swing to the East or to the West. Will they be drawn into the Communist camp? Or will the great experiments in self-government that are now being made in Asia and Africa, especially within the Commonwealth, prove so successful, and by their example so compelling, that the balance will come down in favour of freedom and order and justice?[27]

Sixteen new countries had already been admitted *en masse* to the UN in 1955. They were joined in 1960 by an additional fifteen decolonized states. In December of that year, in the glass palace of the UN in New York, the organization approved the "Declaration on the Granting of Independence to Colonial Countries and Peoples," a statement that heralded the numerical superiority of the newly independent nations in the General Assembly. Even more importantly, the Declaration signaled these countries' intent to take charge of the human rights agenda, and to impress on global public opinion the idea that the right to national self-determination would take precedence over the other universal rights listed in 1948 by the UN.[28] In the future, only a veto by one of the five major powers on the Security Council could block the will of the majority of Third World countries. A new axis of international conflict had been created, which intersected with that between East and West: The confrontation between North and South.

After a series of preparatory encounters among the Bandung nations under the active leadership of the Yugoslav president Tito—the organizer of the Brioni Conference in 1956, who early in 1961 sailed from Ghana to Egypt on his famous "peace ship" *Galeb* to persuade Third World leaders to convene a new meeting—the Non-Aligned Movement was formally launched in Belgrade in September 1961.[29] Its objective remained the easing of military tensions,

---

[26] G. Corm, *Fragmentation of the Middle East: The Last Thirty Years* (London: Hutchinson, 1988), p. 27.

[27] "The Wind of Change: Speech by the Rt. Hon. Harold Macmillan, Prime Minister, to both Houses of Parliament of the Union of South Africa, Cape Town, February 3, 1960," in *British Imperial Policy on Decolonization: 1938–1964*, vol. 2 (London: Macmillan, 1980).

[28] R. Burke, *Decolonization and the Evolution of International Human Rights* (Philadelphia: University of Pennsylvania Press, 2010), pp. 50–58.

[29] Marco Galeazzi, *Il PCI e il movimento dei paesi non allineati (1955–1975)*. Milan: Franco Angeli, 2011.

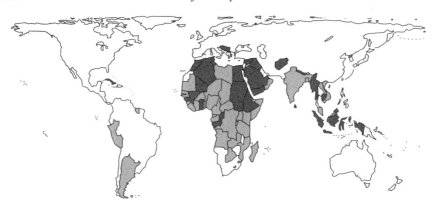

Founders of the Non-Aligned Movement (Afghanistan, Algeria (FLN), Burma, Cambodia, Ceylon (later Sri Lanka), Congo, Cyprus, Cuba, Ethiopia, Ghana, Guinea, Indonesia, Iraq, Lebanon, Mali, Morocco, Nepal, Saudi Arabia, Sudan, Tunisia, United Arab Emirates, United Arab Republic, Yemen (but see below), Yugoslavia)

Countries that joined the Non-Aligned Movement betweenits founding and 1976 (Angola, Argentina, Bahrain, Bangladesh, Bhutan, Botswana, Burundi, Cameroon, Cape Verde Islands, Central African Republic, Chad, Dahomey, Egypt, Equatorial Guinea, Gabon, Gambia, Guinea-Bissau, Guyana, India, Ivory Coast, Jamaica, Jordan, Kenya, Kuwait, Laos, Lesotho, Liberia, Libya, Madagascar, Malaysia, Malta, Mauritania, Mauritius, Mozambique, Niger, Nigeria, Nigeria, Oman, Peru, Qatar, Rwanda, São Tomé and Principe, Senegal, Sierra Leone, Singapore, Somalia, Swaziland, Syria, Tanzania, Togo, Trinidad and Tobago, Uganda, Upper Volta, South Vietnam, North and South Yemen (but see above), Zaire, and Zambia)

Figure 1.1. The Non-Aligned Movement (1961–1976)

offering alternatives to escape the blackmail and coercive compromises imposed by the Cold War.[30] The meeting, while upholding the Bandung principles, was also decidedly different from its predecessor. The presence of a country like Cuba broadened the alliance beyond its Afro-Asian origins, offering admission to a Latin America whose states had been considered to that point almost as culturally dependent arms of the Western powers. The exclusion of states like Pakistan or China, compromised by their presence in the military alliances of the Cold War, and the simultaneous refusal to include European neutrals like Ireland or Sweden, served to protect the autonomy and ex-colonial nature of the movement—with the notable exception of Yugoslavia, which hoped to

---

[30] 1961 was a year of heightened military tensions: Witness the French nuclear tests in the Sahara, the resumption of Soviet testing, the Bay of Pigs, the construction of the Berlin Wall, and the beginnings of conflict between China and the Soviet Union, as well as the emergence of open conflict between China and India. P. Calvocoressi, *World Politics Since 1945* (London: Longman, 1996), pp. 170–98.

play the role of bridge to the developed world.[31] Even though there was no clear provision for another conference after Belgrade, the birth of the Non-Aligned Movement thus marked an occasion to voice the demands of a more active and militant anticolonialism, also alert to economic concerns thanks to the influence of Nkrumah, who pushed for a follow-up meeting of the non-aligned the next year, centered exclusively on economic issues.[32] At the same time, the NAM quickly exposed the limits of the Afro-Asian project, in its attempt to construct a homogenous political ideology of non-European races and cultures based on confrontation and collective action in international politics. These limits emerged first during the standoff between India and China, two of the cornerstones of the Afro-Asian world, and again with even greater strength and clarity following the Sino-Soviet split of the early 1960s.[33] During Communism's Great Schism, in fact, China attempted to play the Afro-Asian card against the "European" Soviet Union in order to portray itself as vanguard of the colonized peoples; the USSR, in response, sought to invest in the concept of non-alignment to win the support of its most progressive elements, favoring an "active neutrality" that could help its fight against the capitalist West.[34]

Whatever its internal tensions, the birth of the Non-Aligned Movement confirmed the emergence of a new political actor. In his book *What is History?*, first published in 1961, E.H. Carr wrote that "it is only today that it has become possible for the first time even to imagine a whole world consisting of peoples who have in the fullest sense entered into history and become the concern, no longer of the colonial administrator or of the anthropologist, but of the historian."[35] If this was history in the making in the Third World, it promptly grabbed the undivided attention of the superpowers, which radically altered their foreign policies to accommodate the new scenario.

After Stalin's death in 1953, the Soviet Union had begun to shift its attention from the balance of forces in Europe, based on a notion of the USSR as a continental power and a strategy of waiting for the inevitable contradictions in Western capitalism to manifest themselves, to conceive also a more offensive and global strategic vision. The world was no longer interpreted according to the classic division into two armed camps; instead, new fronts appeared to be opening that could revitalize

---

[31] The twenty-five participants at the Belgrade meeting were: Afghanistan, Algeria (FLN), Burma, Cambodia, Ceylon, Congo, Cyprus, Cuba, Ethiopia, Ghana, Guinea, Indonesia, Iraq, Lebanon, Mali, Morocco, Nepal, Saudi Arabia, Sudan, Tunisia, United Arab Emirates, The United Arab Republic [the union of Egypt and Syria], Yemen, and Yugoslavia.

[32] D. Colard, "Le mouvement des pays non-alignés," (1981) 4613 *Notes et etudes documentaires*, p. 29.

[33] F. Fejtö, *Chine–URSS de l'alliance au conflit 1950–1972* (Paris: Seuil, 1973).

[34] Open Society Archives, Radio Free Europe Research, Slobodan Stankovic, *Tito and Non-Alignment*, December 6, 1967. F. Halliday, "The Middle, the Great Powers and the Cold War", in Yezid Sayigh and Avi Shlaim East (eds), *The Cold War and the Middle East* (Oxford: Clarendon Press, 1997), p. 19.

[35] E.H. Carr, *What is History?* (New York: Vintage, 1961), p. 199.

the international communist movement.[36] In the report of the Twentieth Congress of the Communist Party of the Soviet Union (CPSU) in 1956—when the Soviet leadership distanced itself, for the first time, from Stalinist "excesses"—a new attitude to the developing world was already emerging: "The new period in history which Lenin predicted has arrived, and the peoples of the East are playing an active part in deciding the destinies of the whole world, are becoming a new mighty factor in international relations."[37]

Stalin's successor as head of the Communist Party, Nikita Khrushchev, has been considered the most important reformer of Russian imperial foreign policy since the time of its formation.[38] He took a traditionally expansionist Eurasian power, accustomed to following western European initiatives in the Straits, the Mediterranean, and the Asiatic steppe, where it sought to check English domination in India, and attempted to transform it into a world power capable of pursuing a truly global strategy. The Soviet leader fueled these new ambitions by exploiting progress in the field of nuclear technology, which permitted Moscow to keep pace with Washington, and by publicizing the innovative capacity of Soviet scientific research—such as the launching into orbit of the first artificial satellite, Sputnik—which demonstrated the prestige and apparent productive efficiency of the planned economy. Beginning at the Twentieth Congress, Khrushchev gave a decidedly positive spin to decolonization, considering the new non-aligned states as Moscow's natural allies, and opening the USSR to the wind blowing from the East.[39] Indeed, it was precisely in 1956–7 that the Institute of World Economy and International Relations (IMEMO, in Russian) was created, with the intention of giving the Soviet leadership an instrument for strategic policy planning in the Third World.[40] This new course, which declared Moscow's desire to break out of the isolation to which Dulles and the discredit of the 1956 invasion of Hungary had helped to condemn it, was given concrete expression with an increase in financial and military aid distributed to the leaders of countries considered in the regional vanguard: Lumumba and Nasser in Africa, Nehru in Asia, and Castro in Latin America. Khrushchev ostentatiously declared his support for the UN Declaration of Independence of the Colonized Peoples in 1960, remaining in New York for an entire month during the preparations of the General Assembly—while President Eisenhower left to play golf—and resorted to exaggerated gestures, such as famously banging his shoe on the table, to draw attention to Soviet policy in the Third World and deflect attacks against its own imperial policy in eastern Europe. In

[36] A. Fursenko and R.S. Naftali, *Khrushchev's Cold War: The Inside Story of an American Adversary* (New York: W.W. Norton & Co., 2006), p. 314.

[37] C. Andrew, *The World Was Going Our Way: The KGB and the Battle for the Third World* (New York: Basic Books, 2005), p. 5.

[38] A.Z. Rubenstein, *Moscow's Third World Strategy* (Princeton, NJ: Princeton University Press, 1998).

[39] O.A. Westad, *The Global Cold War* (Cambridge: Cambridge University Press, 2005), p. 68.

[40] C.R. Dannehl, *Politics, Trade, and Development: Soviet Economic Aid to the Non-Communist Third World, 1955–1989* (Dartmouth: Ashgate, 1995), p. 33.

January 1961, in a speech at an academy for future party leaders, he gave a positively glowing evaluation of the future prospects for international communism:

> Our era… [is] an era of Socialist revolutions and national liberation revolutions; an era of the collapse of capitalism and of liquidation of the colonial system; an era of the change to the road of socialism by more and more nations; and of triumph of socialism and communism on a world scale.[41]

The great faith placed by the Soviet Union in the possibilities offered by the Third World was further demonstrated by the inauguration of the University of Friendship in Moscow, which opened its halls to students from Africa, Asia, and Latin America, preparing them for future socialist struggles.[42]

The reaction of the United States to decolonization was more conflicted. Notwithstanding its repeated reminders of the fact that the USA itself had been born in rebellion against a colonial empire, Washington assumed a much more ambiguous position regarding liberation movements, if for no other reason than that it was precisely those European "imperialists" that happened to be America's primary allies. With the emergence of the Cold War, the United States had turned its attention to western Europe out of the perceived necessity to rebuild the continent in order to avoid the risk of communist revolution. In Latin America, however, the USA soon demonstrated that it had not relaxed its iron grip over the region, overthrowing the government of Colonel Jacobo Árbenz Guzmán in Guatemala after it had attempted to pass radical agricultural reforms that would have entailed a massive expropriation of land from the United Fruit Company. The episode contributed to no small degree toward alienating Latin American leaders and eviscerating any anticommunist sympathies they may have harbored for the *gringos* from the north.[43] In Africa, meanwhile, Eisenhower was incapable of taking a firm stand to distance the USA from French repression in Algeria. On the chessboard of the Middle East, a joint action of the USA and Great Britain led to the 1953 coup against the Mossadegh government in Iran, guilty of having nationalized the country's oil resources, leading to the involvement of US oil multinationals in the previously British reservoir.[44] As a result, not even Dulles's condemnation of the Franco-British invasion of Egypt in 1956, coupled with the threat to expel the two countries from NATO, was enough to win African loyalties. At the UN in 1960, the USA could not bring itself to vote in favor of the resolution against colonialism: Broad segments of the American political class continued to view neutrality as an immoral concept in foreign policy, failing to comprehend the disquieting impact of a comment by a White House staffer (leaked to the media) that he was

---

[41] Cited in J.L. Gaddis, *We Now Know: Rethinking Cold War History* (New York: Oxford University Press, 1997), p. 183.

[42] Rubenstein, *Moscow's Third World Strategy*.

[43] W.R. Keylor, *The Twentieth Century World: An International History* (Oxford: Oxford University Press, 2001), pp. 311–12.

[44] In 1955 the Anglo-Iranian Oil Company renamed itself British Petroleum (BP) so where its allegiance lay could become more visible. See J. Bamberg, *British Petroleum and Global Oil, 1950–1975: The Challenge of Nationalism* (Cambridge: Cambridge University Press, 2000).

sick and tired of organizing Presidential meetings with all those *niggers*. Meanwhile, Washington prepared a military operation against Castro in Cuba, even when the latter had not yet openly revealed his preference for a pact of steel with Moscow.

A change of perspective arrived with the election of John F. Kennedy. The young Democrat began his term with an overture to the newly independent nations, "not because the Communists are doing it, not because we seek their votes, but because it is right."[45] In a 1960 speech at the University of Michigan he announced the creation of the Peace Corps, a project aimed at encouraging American students to volunteer their time working in the developing world (identifying Ghana by name as a destination for their youthful generosity), thus reaffirming the idea that the competitiveness of free societies depended on individual willingness to sacrifice for the national wellbeing.[46] We shall see later how Kennedy also launched the Alliance for Progress with Latin America, while simultaneously changing the terms and conditions of the economic aid furnished to less developed countries.

Internal factors also pressured the Kennedy administration to modify American attitudes, most notably the growing combativeness of the civil rights movement. With the emergence of the newly independent African nations came the need to avoid losing them to communism; it thus became ever more difficult to ignore the violent—and highly visible—discrimination against African-Americans in the US South, a contradiction that Fidel Castro ably manipulated by setting up his headquarters in the predominantly black neighborhood of Harlem while attending the UN General Assembly in 1960. African-American civil rights organizations actively sought direct ties with these new nations in order to gain a political edge in the fight for the betterment of the black people in the USA. In his memoir, John Lewis, one of the most prominent leaders of the National Association for the Advancement of Colored People (NAACP), recalled the epiphany of his experience touring Africa with other members of the organization:

> From Dakar we flew south aboard an Air Guinea jet piloted by two black men and staffed by black flight attendants. With all the flying I'd done in the United States, this was the first time I'd ever seen black pilots. And that was just the beginning. In every city I visited, I was struck by the sight of black police officers, black men behind the desks in banks, black people not just on bicycles but also behind the wheels of Mercedes. Black people in *charge*. Black people doing for *themselves*. I knew the situation over there, but knowing it was one thing; actually seeing it was another.[47]

Even Malcolm X, who accused the NAACP and Martin Luther King of timidity and collaboration with America's white elite, traveled to Cairo in 1964 for a con-

[45] L. Tosone, "Gli aiuti allo sviluppo degli Stati Uniti in Africa durante l'amministrazione Kennedy," in D. Caviglia and A. Varsori, eds, *Dollari, petrolio e aiuti allo sviluppo. Il confronto Nord-Sud negli anni '60-'70* (Milan: FrancoAngeli, 2008), p. 23.

[46] Online at <http://www.peacecorps.gov/index.cfm?shell=learn.whatispc.history.speech>.

[47] J.L. Lewis, *Walking with the Wind: A Memoir of the Movement* (New York: Harcourt Brace, 1998), p. 295.

ference of the Organization of African Unity in order to win support for a UN resolution against racism in the United States. In a letter from August of that year he remarked enthusiastically that his appeal had been a success and that "our problem has been *internationalized.*"[48]

The leaders of the civil rights movement were not the only ones calling for closer cooperation with the developing nations in order to transcend the logic of *Realpolitik* in US relations with the Third World. The voice of the nascent student movement also began to make itself heard, by distancing itself from a politics based exclusively on containment and the suppression of international communism. The 1962 Port Huron Statement of SDS (Students for a Democratic Society) openly denounced:

> American foreign policy [that] in the Fifties was guided by a concern for foreign investment and a negative anti-communist political stance linked to a series of military alliances, both undergirded by military threat. We participated unilaterally—usually through the Central Intelligence Agency—in revolutions against governments in Laos, Guatemala, Cuba, Egypt, Iran. We permitted economic investment to decisively affect our foreign policy: Fruit in Cuba, oil in the Middle East, diamonds and gold in South Africa (with whom we trade more than with any African nation) [...].
>
> Our pugnacious anti-communism and protection of interests has led us to an alliance inappropriately called the "Free World." It included four major parliamentary democracies: Ourselves, Canada, Great Britain, and India. It also has included through the years Batista, Franco, Verwoerd, Salazar, De Gaulle, Boun Oum, Ngo Diem, Chiang Kai Shek, Trujillo, the Somozas, Saud, Ydigoras—all of these non-democrats separating us deeply from the colonial revolutions.[49]

RECIPES FOR DEVELOPMENT

The emergence of the newly independent countries not only had an impact on the Cold War and international politics, but also allowed new voices to speak up that were critical of the organization of the international economy.

In 1950, the Western world once more accounted for approximately 57 percent of global production: The same percentage it had reached some 120 years earlier, when the productive capacities of the colonized world had begun to contract.[50] The economies of western Europe, like those of the communist East, were primarily driven by domestic reconstruction, which began to take off at a dizzying rate; industrial production in these countries grew at a rate of 6 percent a year from 1953 until 1975. International trade also witnessed a sudden surge, such that in 1957 the total value of commerce in manufactured goods surpassed that in

---

[48] Malcolm X, *By Any Means Necessary* (New York: Pathfinder Press, 1970), p. 132. [Italics in original.]

[49] Online at <http://coursesa.matrix.msu.edu/~hst306/documents/huron.html>.

[50] S.P. Huntington, *The Clash of Civilizations and the Remaking of World Order* (New York: Simon & Schuster, 1996) p. 87.

commodities.[51] The industrialized countries had begun to lay the groundwork for the "affluent society," a society founded, as we shall see, on a type of mass consumption that spread from the United States throughout western Europe. In 1959 a German paper could already speak of "our consumer society," where only a decade earlier Germany had been destroyed by the war and reduced to "Year Zero," its people without food, its buildings in a shambles, its spirit shattered.[52]

This productive revolution of the Western, industrialized world, which was not without its dark sides and internal contradictions, was accompanied and sheltered by international economic institutions. These new, multilateral institutions encompassed only a very limited part of the globe, however, leaving its most populous areas at the margins. The Pakistani writer Saadat Hasan Manto described how the meager affluence on display in many poorer countries at the outset of the 1950s was simply imported by foreign aid, which had been granted for strategic reasons and brought with it inevitable bonds of subordination:

> You will certainly ask me out of astonishment why my country is poor when it boasts of so many Packards, Buicks and Max Factor cosmetics. That is indeed so, uncle, but I will not answer your question because if you look into your heart, you will find your answer there (unless you have had your heart taken out by one of your brilliant surgeons).
>
> That section of my country's population which rides in Packards and Buicks is really not of my country. Where poor people like me and those even poorer live, that is my country.[53]

At the end of the Second World War the economic and social recovery of vast portions of the globe was simply not on the agenda of the victorious nations. The international economic institutions created at Bretton Woods included only a minority of the world's governments and peoples. The entire communist world was excluded owing to its hostility to the free market economy—including China, the largest Asian nation—as were the majority of colonized peoples, who only began to reacquire their independence in the 1950s.[54]

It was not just the territorial under-representation inherent in the Bretton Woods system that prevented it from taking into account the specific problems confronting the "underdeveloped countries," as they were called at the time. The attention of Anglo-Saxon economists centered on the internal reforms necessary for the most advanced nations, based on the conviction that for everyone else it would suffice merely to imitate their success. If a nation failed to achieve economic growth, whether European France or Latin American Colombia, independent of their relative level of development or geographic, social, historical, or educational conditions, economists of the age were quick to pin the blame on the poor performance of their political class. A UN report compiled in 1950 by a group of five

---

[51] P. Kennedy, *The Rise and Fall of the Great Powers* (New York: Vintage, 1989), pp. 347–437.

[52] V. de Grazia, *Irresistible Empire: America's Advance through Twentieth-Century Europe* (Cambridge, MA: Harvard University Press, 2005), p. 359.

[53] S.H. Manto, *Letters to Uncle Sam* (Islamabad: Alhamra, 2001), p. 21.

[54] P. Kennedy, *The Parliament of Man: The Past, Present, and Future of the United Nations* (New York: Random House, 2006), p. 117.

experts prescribed the following cure for the underdeveloped nations: Enact progressive economic and fiscal policy, control population growth, and invest in technology. As the prescription did not entail any consequent distribution of the necessary medicine, in either monetary aid or technological cooperation, it was a slippery slope from this view to the outright racism of attributing the inability to jump-start the motor of growth to the innate ethnic or cultural characteristics of a people. Theories abounded as to why poverty seemed endemic to certain areas of the world, most ascribing this to the stubborn lack of a work ethic among certain peoples: The "defensiveness" of the Indians, the "negativity" of the Cubans, or the "religious superstitions" that held back Ceylon.[55]

In his biography of John Maynard Keynes, Roy Harrod notes that the economist confided his plans for the postwar international economy in a 1943 letter to Sir Percival Liesching:

> As you know, I am, I am afraid, a hopeless sceptic about this return to nineteenth-century *laissez faire*, for which you and the State Department seem to have such a nostalgia.
>   I believe that the future lies with –
>   (i) state trading for commodities;
>   (ii) international cartels for necessary manufactures; and
>   (iii) quantitative import restrictions for non-essential manufactures.[56]

Like many of his earlier warnings, Keynes's ideas fell on deaf ears during the course of the Bretton Woods negotiations. In reality the Bretton Woods institutions—the International Bank for Reconstruction and Development (IBRD, later the World Bank), the International Monetary Fund (IMF), and what would become the General Agreement on Tariffs and Trade (GATT)—were built on a philosophy defined by John Ruggie as "embedded liberalism": Allow enough progress toward liberalization but also give space to governments to defend their social and political priorities.[57] The new multilateral institutions were certainly more sophisticated and less dependent on naked power than the trade and financial practices of the nineteenth century, defined in a seminal article by Gallagher and Robinson as "the imperialism of free trade";[58] but these institutions did not specifically take into account the peculiar necessities of the nonindustrialized world.

In the first draft of the World Bank statute, the word "development" does not appear even once. The immediate goal of the Bank was actually to finance European reconstruction. Only after the beginning of the Marshall Plan in 1948 did the Bank, seeing its principal *raison d'être* disappear, begin to search for new opportunities to invest in development, a circumstance which worried its then-president

[55] D. Kapur, J.P. Lewis, and R. Webb, *The World Bank: Its First Half Century* (Washington, DC: Brookings Institution Press, 1997), p. 146.

[56] R. Harrod, *The Life of John Maynard Keynes* (London: Macmillan, 1951), pp. 567–8.

[57] J.G. Ruggie, "International Regimes, Transactions, and Change: Embedded Liberalism in the Postwar Economic Order," (1982) 46(3) *International Organization* pp. 379–415.

[58] J. Gallagher and R. Robinson, "The Imperialism of Free Trade," (1953) 6(1) *Economic History Review*, pp. 1–15.

John McCloy (eventually to become the main exponent of US oil policy): "I think we are going to be driven into a very different field sooner than I thought, into the development field."[59] But the Bank's funds amounted to a fraction of those at the disposal of the Marshall Plan. In 1953 the Bank had granted loans for a total of some $1.75 billion—primarily throughout western Europe—while by mid-1951 the Marshall Plan had already transferred some $12 billion in aid to the participating European nations.[60] In contrast, the World Bank had sent less than $100 million to the poorest countries by 1950, because sufficient possibilities for investment were lacking. Until 1957 the majority of its investments remained in the developed nations. Only at the end of the 1960s did the Bank almost completely close shop in the industrialized world.[61] Bank loans were mainly granted for the creation or reconstruction of infrastructure and, because the funds for investment came largely from the private sector, these infrastructural improvements needed to be able to generate profits in order to repay the debt quickly and with interest. For at least the first decade of its existence the Bank shied away from loans for the creation of industry, still less those to help commodity producers: Such activities were deemed better left to private investment. Bank presidents tended to come from the upper echelons of Wall Street, a trend that granted the institution credibility and that allowed it to boast a positive balance sheet until the beginning of the 1960s. In short, the World Bank was able to extract some returns from its Third World investments, without yet providing a meaningful economic stimulus to those countries considered underdeveloped. The World Bank, however, was a relatively marginal international creditor, furnishing barely 5 percent of all development aid by 1957. The 1950s were instead a decade dominated largely by bilateral aid, in particular military aid from the United States, which comprised some 60 percent of the total, and that of the *metropoles* to their former colonies.[62]

The goal of the IMF, meanwhile, was to guarantee the stability of exchange rates, so far as this was possible in a system in which western Europe's most important currencies still were not fully convertible. At the end of the 1950s the scarce IMF loan funds available to Third World nations were tied to stabilization programs of such austerity that *The Economist*, in an article on the loan conditions applied to Latin American countries, called Per Jacobsson (then the IMF's managing director) "Mr. Khrushchev's secret weapon."[63]

The other pillar of global economic reconstruction, after the tragic results of the nationalistic and autarkic experiments of the 1930s, was supposed to be the

---

[59] M. Alacevich, *The Political Economy of the World Bank: The Early Years*, trans. The World Bank (Palo Alto, CA: Stanford University Press, 2009), p. 13.

[60] M.J. Hogan, *The Marshall Plan: America, Britain, and the Reconstruction of Western Europe 1947–1952* (New York: Cambridge University Press, 1987), p. 415.

[61] E.S. Mason and R.E. Asher, *The World Bank Since Bretton Woods: The Origins, Policies, Operations, and Impact of the International Bank for Reconstruction and Development, and the other Members of the World Bank Group* (Washington, DC: The Brookings Institution Press, 1973).

[62] R.E. Wood, *From Marshall Plan to Debt Crisis: Foreign Aid and Development Choices in the World Economy* (Los Angeles: University of California Press, 1986), pp. 70–1.

[63] H. James, *International Monetary Cooperation Since Bretton Woods* (Washington, DC: International Monetary Fund and Oxford University Press, 1996), p. 141.

creation of an International Trade Organization (ITO). Preliminary negotiations toward the creation of an ITO were held in Havana from 1947–8, under the auspices of the United Nations Conference on Trade and Employment. Frictions quickly developed, however, between the British, who wished to maintain trade preferences with the Commonwealth countries—preferences which Churchill himself admitted were of greater symbolic than economic value—and the United States, which sought to eliminate such preferences and all other customs barriers as far as possible.[64] A group of developing countries, led by Argentina, Chile, and Brazil, also played an active role in seeking to defend their levels of employment and industrial investment, managing to insert into the accords measures that would allow for the expropriation of foreign businesses, as well as a system of regional trade preferences.[65] In March 1948, the Havana Charter was approved by the UN, despite fierce resistance by the American delegation.[66] Ultimately, however, the agreement remained a dead letter, never ratified by the American Congress.[67] The Cold War had begun in earnest and the American government preferred to proceed down the path of liberalization and reinforce its transatlantic political and economic ties, rather than allow itself to be hamstrung by yet another international organization compromised by the presence of the communist countries.

Instead it was the GATT agreement, signed in 1947, that would long remain the primary instrument of international coordination on questions of commerce. In principle, the agreement was supposed to be of solely provisional value pending the creation of the ITO, and for at least a decade the plaque identifying the entrance to GATT headquarters in Geneva read "Interim Commission for the International Trade Organization." It was designed primarily to lower commercial tariffs among a restricted number of states—slightly more than forty in 1963—and operated according to a very basic principle: Extending to all "contracting parties" who signed the agreement the coveted "most favored nation" status, so that all signatories conceded to all other GATT members the same conditions offered to the nation with which it had the lowest trade barrier. In this way, GATT used a wedge of trade multilateralism to pry open a world which had been dominated since the 1930s by protectionism and bilateral trade relationships.

Midway through the 1950s, despite the creation of these three international economic organizations, optimism did not reign in Washington. This much is clear from the memoirs of Richard N. Gardner, a professor of economics and later a leading authority on international economic issues in the Johnson administration:

> The International Monetary Fund was then largely inactive, bypassed by belated efforts of postwar reconstruction. Sterling and the other major European currencies

---

[64] R.N. Gardner, *Sterling–Dollar Diplomacy in Current Perspective: The Origins and the Prospects of Our International Economic Order* (New York: Columbia University Press, 1980), p. 358.

[65] T.W. Zeiler, *Free Trade Free World: The Advent of GATT* (Chapel Hill: University of North Carolina Press, 1999), pp. 136–7.

[66] On the Havana negotiations see M. Hart, *Also Present at the Creation: Dana Wilgress and the United Nations Conference on Trade and Employment at Havana* (Ottawa: Center for Trade Policy and Law, 1995).

[67] M. Rainelli, *Le Gatt* (Paris: Editions La Découverte, 1993).

were still inconvertible; of the International Monetary Fund permitting exchange restrictions for a "transitional" period looked as if they might apply indefinitely. The Charter for an International Trade Organization had been withdrawn from the Congress; the General Agreement on Tariffs and Trade seemed too weak to organize an effective attack on trade barriers. The recipients of the Marshall aid were preoccupied with removing quantitative restrictions among themselves; the United States was undermining its commitment to liberal trade with a variety of protectionist practices; the outlook for substantial reductions in trade barriers on a global basis seemed highly uncertain. International economic cooperation was obstructed by a huge American trade surplus—the supposed chronic "dollar shortage"—and by divergent approaches to domestic planning and full employment.[68]

The Third World countries could count, it is true, on a certain consistency in their growth rates, but their overall weight in international trade was in steady decline. Their power in the governing institutions of the international economy was largely insignificant: If anything, the system was evolving from one in which only three countries—France, Great Britain, and the United States—decided everything to one in which the other western European powers, above all the Federal Republic of Germany, were making their presence felt. Changes in international economic regulation were clearly necessary to make democracy and market economy a more attractive proposition. But how, and to what end?

To answer this question we must take a step back and examine the ferment of new ideas brewing around questions of "development" and "growth" that would become the buzzwords among the elites of the industrialized Western economies during the 1960s. John Kenneth Galbraith, liberal intellectual *par excellence*, recalled that immediately after the Second World War he asked his university, Harvard, to institute a course on development. His request fell on deaf ears. Before long the Anglo-American academic world would change radically. The very same Galbraith noted that in the 1960s "no economic subject so quickly captured the attention of so many people as the topic of the liberation from poverty of the peoples of the poor nations."[69]

Certainly the memory of the Depression of the 1930s played an important role in the waning of classical liberal principles, demonstrating the weakness of the self-regulating market, as did the precariousness of an international monetary system based on the gold standard. Such views were largely due to the belated acceptance of the ideas of Keynes;[70] the Cambridge economist had predicted the inability of the self-regulating market to resolve the dilemma of a country faced with insufficient foreign investment and a weak domestic market—precisely the situation confronting the vast majority of developing countries. The point to note here is that a group of noncommunist intellectuals, though still a minority, had begun to seriously examine the question of growth

---

[68] Gardner, *Sterling–Dollar Diplomacy*, p. xvi.
[69] J.K. Galbraith, *The Nature of Mass Poverty* (Cambridge, MA: Harvard University Press, 1979), p. 19.
[70] F. Volpi, *Introduzione all'economia dello sviluppo* (Milan: FrancoAngeli, 1994), p. 30.

by the 1950s. These intellectuals understood that the underdeveloped countries found themselves in dire straits not because of the primitive nature of their culture and habits but for a variety of different reasons: Because they lacked capital; because more advanced industries had ever less need for some of their raw materials; because they lacked an entrepreneurial class; or because they found it difficult to make the transition from a primarily agricultural economy. Thus a segment of the intellectual and academic world, especially but not exclusively in the United States, began to consider the problems of Third World development a subject worthy of study. As Tony Killick notes, the 1950s was the decade of the great theories of economic growth:

> Rosenstein-Rodan's 1943 article perhaps marked the starting point and, of course, earlier writers, especially in the classical period, were also much concerned with development. Keynes and (as will be shown) Schumpeter were also particularly influential on later writers. But development economics "took off" in the fifties, beginning perhaps with the UN's *Measures for the Development of Underdeveloped Countries* (1951) and including major works by Nurske (1953), Lewis (1954 and 1955), Scitowsky (1954), Myrdal (1956, 1957) and Hirschman (1958). This period of "grand theorising", strongly marked by the boldness of its ideas, might conveniently be said to have concluded with Rostow's *Stages of Economic Growth* (1960), with Prebisch's 1964 UNCTAD document seen as a late entry into the field.[71]

Of all these theories—in the development of which, it should be noted, academics from the the continental European countries had a scant role—two would acquire lasting significance for their impact on international politics, because they were adopted as theoretical frameworks by leaders in either the developed or noncommunist developing world: Among the latter, the "structuralist" or "dependence" theory promoted primarily by the Economic Commission for Latin America (CEPAL, in the Spanish acronym used most frequently) based in Santiago, Chile, and headed by the Argentine economist Raúl Prebisch; among the former, the theory of "modernization" and "stages of growth" developed by economists at MIT in Boston and most commonly associated with the name of Walt Rostow.

Prebisch first rose to international prominence as the director of CEPAL, created in 1948 as one of the United Nations's regional economic organizations.[72] The choice of Prebisch to run the organization was a felicitous one, which immediately gave CEPAL global visibility. At age 25 he had already received a teaching appointment at the University of Buenos Aires, and by 29 he was made an economic advisor to the Argentine Prime Minister; he was later named Undersecretary of Industry, and at 34 was charged with reorganizing Argentina's Central Bank. A voracious

---

[71] T. Killick, *Development Economics in Action: A Study of the Economic Policies of Ghana* (London: Heinemann, 1978), p. 29.

[72] For an excellent biography of Prebisch, see E.J. Dosman, *The Life and Times of Raúl Prebisch, 1901–1986* (Montreal: McGill–Queen's University Press, 2009). One good work, based primarily on interviews with Prebisch himself, is N. Gonzalez and D. Pollock, "Del ortodoxo al conservador ilustrado: Raúl Prebisch en la Argentina, 1923–1943," (1991) 30(120) *Desarrollo Economico: Rivista de Ciencias Sociales*, pp. 455–86.

reader of classical economic theory, from Adam Smith to John Stuart Mill, but also of Marx, the most lasting impression on his thought would seem to have been left by the sad spectacle of the international monetary and economic conference held in London in 1933. On that occasion, the world powers had blocked Keynes's most innovative proposals and failed to halt the downward spiral of recession and economic protectionism, all while the smaller nations—among them Argentina, in whose delegation Prebisch took part—were invited as mere observers. One finds clear expression of the basis for Prebisch's thought in a short text, prepared in 1949 for the first conference of CEPAL in Cuba and published by the UN in April 1950 with the title *Economic Study of Latin America and Some of its Principal Problems*. Here, he wrote that the heart of the problem of underdevelopment lay in the fact that international commerce was based on an inequality of relations: On one side, the developed nations traded primarily manufactured goods produced by an oligopoly of large businesses, while on the other the developing nations exported raw materials on a highly competitive free market. This meant that, while innovation in the manufacturing sector translated into rising prices on the market and improvement in the living conditions of Western workers, a similar innovation of productivity for commodity producers resulted in a lowering of prices on the world market and the consequent impoverishment of its laborers. The logical conclusion was that international trade led to the systematic poverty of commodity-producing countries—hence the terms "structuralist" or "dependency" theory—to the advantage of the industrialized nations.[73] In the course of the 1960s and 1970s, scholars picking up on elements of Prebisch's ideas would push dependency theory to its logical conclusions, for instance in the work of Andre Gunder Frank, who argued that it was only thanks to the brutal exploitation of the South that the industrialized North could guarantee its elevated levels of economic growth. Dependency theory here slipped into a theory of imperialism, which carried an implication that Prebisch never raised and probably would have opposed: A revolutionary subversion of the world order.[74]

It should come as no surprise that Latin America produced the first criticisms leveled squarely at the mechanisms of the international economy. Latin American countries had been among the first to achieve political independence in the course of the nineteenth century, and while they had on occasion been able to leverage this position, they were well acquainted with the lack of bargaining power characteristic of countries, particularly exporters of raw materials, at the periphery of the international economy.[75] Latin American countries reacted to the crisis of the 1930s by investing in the growth of national industries capable of substituting for

[73] R. Prebisch, "Sobre desarrollo y politica commercial internacional," in *Justicia Economica Internacional: Contribucion al estudio de la Carta de Derechos y Deberes Economicos de los Estados* (Mexico: Fondo de cultura economica, 1975).

[74] For a brief discussion of the evolution of dependence theory, see G. Lundestad, *East, West, North, South* (Oxford: Oxford University Press, 1999); G. Rist, *The History of Development: From Western Origins to Global Faith* (London: Zed Books, 1997).

[75] C. Furtado, *Economic Development of Latin America: Historical Background and Contemporary Problems* (Cambridge: Cambridge University Press, 1976), p. 54.

imports from more developed countries.[76] As early as 1948, Venezuela became the first oil-producing country to impose a 50/50 profit sharing mechanism for oil concessions on the oil multinationals. In practice, this economic nationalism was rather successful: By the 1940s the majority of Latin American countries were highly urbanized, with one-fifth of their workers in the manufacturing sector—a level reached by the United States in 1890—and some (notably Argentina) had fully or partially nationalized their large industries and service sector.[77] The construction of Brasilia in a few short years from 1956 to 1960, a completely new and futuristic capital city (as evidenced by its visionary modernist architecture), provided ample evidence of this restless faith in modernity. Import substitution, it was thought, financed by the income from trade in commodities, would help stimulate further industrialization, which would in turn offer greater employment for new immigrants to the cities and promote modernization in all sectors, from transportation to distribution. For all this to be possible, however, it was necessary to improve the terms of exchange between commodities and manufactured goods in favor of the former.

The other major theory we have mentioned, that of "modernization," was conceived by a circle of economists known as the "Charles River group"—after the river that winds its way through Boston (home of MIT)—as a tool to halt communism's advance in the Third World. The two most important members of the group, Walt Rostow and Max Millikan, had been members of the Office of Strategic Services (OSS), the army intelligence service that was the predecessor of the CIA, during the Second World War. Until 1952 Millikan, in fact, had been the director of the CIA's International Economic Section, and the Center for International Studies, their intellectual base of operations at MIT, received direct financing from the Agency.[78] Rostow would go on to become National Security Advisor under President Lyndon Johnson, and one of the most tenacious defenders of military engagement in Vietnam. His most important work, *The Stages of Economic Growth*, which appeared in 1960 with the subtitle *A Non-Communist Manifesto*,[79] established the concept of "take-off": An explosive burst of economic growth that could only be made possible in the countries of the South by undertaking specific internal-structural reforms, which meant the opening of markets, freedom of competition, and, obviously, democratization. No mention was made,

---

[76] Discussions on industrialization were joined with the idea of internal social change directed primarily at the class of *latifondisti*, with little regard for investment or the necessity for a redistribution of wealth that would enlarge the middle class and, with it, the potential domestic market for industrially produced goods. M. Plana and A. Trento, *L'America Latina nel XX secolo* (Florence: Ponte alle Grazie, 1992), p. 101.

[77] J.A. Frieden, *Global Capitalism: Its Fall and Rise in the Twentieth Century* (New York: W.W. Norton & Co., 2006), p. 304.

[78] G. Rosen, *Western Economists and Eastern Societies: Agents of Social Change in South Asia 1950–1970* (Baltimore, MD: Johns Hopkins University Press, 1985).

[79] In Italy the book appeared without this subtitle, which would have rendered it extremely unpopular, in particular among the left-leaning readership of Einaudi, the Turin editing house that published it, many of whom were close to the Communist Party of Italy. W. Rostow, *Gli stadi dello sviluppo economico* (Turin: Einaudi, 1962).

for obvious reasons, of colonialism's role in contributing to the different stages of growth reached by empires and their former colonies. Translated around the world, this brief essay, which purported to explain the distinct historic phases of economic development, presented itself as an objective scientific analysis. In reality, of course, it was part of a precise foreign policy platform centered on peaceful persuasion rather than brute military force; indeed, the first version of the essay, published in 1957, carried the revealing title *A Proposal: Key to an Effective Foreign Policy*.[80]

By the end of the 1950s, economic growth had become the primary focus of the industrialized world and, considering the West's recent success in this regard, many of its most prominent economists began to believe they had discovered a magic formula. According to Mark Mazower:

> We can chart the development of the new creed fairly precisely. In the 1950s, the annual reports of the new OEEC (the Organization for European Economic Cooperation) spotlighted the need to improve productivity as the key to expansion. In 1956 it used the phrase "economic growth" for the first time. When the organization was refounded in 1960 as OECD, article I of its founding charter stated that the organization "aimed to achieve the highest sustainable growth and employment of standard of living in Member countries." In Walt Rostow's *The Stages of Economic Growth*…the growth creed acquired its gospel.[81]

With the election of John F. Kennedy, a president with strong ties to the liberal intellectual world, the "Charles River approach" became the unquestioned orientation of American foreign policy, as White House Special Assistant Arthur Schlesinger Jr. recalled:

> In this view foreign aid, instead of being a State Department slush fund to influence tactical situations, should aim at the strategic goals of stronger national independence, an increased concentration on domestic affairs, greater democracy and long-run association with the West.[82]

This new strategic direction, far from implying a diminishing importance for US military aid—which at the end of the 1950s was four times greater than civilian assistance—aimed to prove that economic growth and democracy could go hand in hand, and often resulted in an increase in aid "linked" to the import of American

---

[80] W. Rostow and M. Millikan, *A Proposal: Key to an Effective Foreign Policy* (New York: Harper and Brothers, 1957). On the way in which Rostow's thesis engaged the need to counter the influence of communist thought Gilbert Rist wrote:

> The problem was twofold: it had to be shown, mainly by reference to European economic history, how the recently decolonized countries might in turn promote growth leading to "development"; and it had to be explained why communism, far from making it possible to achieve this objective, was actually "a kind of disease which can befall a transitional society if it fails to organize effectively those elements within it which are prepared to get on with the job of modernization".

Rist, *The History of Development*, p. 94.
[81] Mazower, *Dark Continent*, p. 301.
[82] A.M. Schlesinger, *A Thousand Days: John F. Kennedy in the White House* (New York: Fawcett Premier, 1966), p. 468.

goods.[83] In 1960 the International Development Association (IDA) was created as a new World Bank tool to finance long-term development programs at more advantageous terms, a technique which would earn the name "soft loans." Until 1963 Eugene Black, the World Bank President, had refused to change the conditions for the Bank's loans, with the backing of the European executive directors who represented the Board's most conservative nucleus, despite an increasingly obvious lack of opportunities for investment. The new president nominated in 1963, George Woods, courageously declared that underdevelopment was not entirely the responsibility of the poor nations, that among its causes were low commodity prices as well as the trade barriers erected by the developed countries, and that it was absurd that an institution designed to support development should consistently run significant surpluses. The Bank slowly began to extend loans to the agricultural and industrial sectors, though initially concentrated primarily in Asia, and in particular India and Pakistan, where some 69 percent of all loans were allocated. The creation of the IDA also helped to dissuade Third World countries from continuing to call for the creation of a new development agency under the auspices of the UN, where they held a majority: SUNFED (Special United Nations Fund for Economic Development) remained in fact completely marginalized among the organizations charged with the allocation of aid. Bilateral assistance remained, at any rate, the primary tool by which aid was distributed from the industrialized world to the South, though by 1970 it had shrunk from 54.2 percent of the total to 38 percent.[84]

The other initiative launched by the Kennedy administration was the Alliance for Progress, unveiled at Punta del Este in 1960. This announcement committed the United States to investing $20 billion in Latin America over the course of the next decade to encourage a series of economic and social measures, primarily literacy and more equitable land distribution. The initiative was undertaken in part as a reaction to the failure of military intervention in Cuba, out of the fear that revolt could spread across the South American continent. The Alliance was, in retrospect, recognized even by Castro as an "astute" response to the Bay of Pigs fiasco:

> Kennedy proposed, after the defeat at Girón [the Bay of Pigs], an "Alliance for Progress," plus the Peace Corps, a very astute strategy for putting the brakes on revolution...
>
> In the end, many Latin American rulers stole all the money they could and the Alliance for Progress didn't solve a thing. Still, it was an intelligent reaction on Kennedy's part—he was a man of unquestionable intelligence.[85]

The Alliance was successful in temporarily isolating the Cuban socialist experiment, but failed to silence the criticism of those who had not forgotten Guatemala, or those who pointed out how the Alliance, by rewarding private capital, would in

---

[83] R.A. Packenham, *Liberal America and the Third World* (Princeton, NJ: Princeton University Press, 1973), p. 59.

[84] Wood, *From Marshall Plan to Debt Crisis*, p. 82.

[85] F. Castro and I. Ramonet, *My Life: A Spoken Autobiography*, trans. Andrew Hurley (New York: Scribner, 2008), p. 270.

essence only help to boost the investments of American multinationals in Latin America.[86]

Kennedy also echoed his message of "growth," "development," and "moderniza-tion" in his relations with America's transatlantic partners. In 1960, as we have seen, the creation of the Organization for Economic Cooperation and Develop-ment (OECD) was supposed to establish a mechanism for joint policy coordina-tion. Within the OECD, the Development Assistance Commission (DAC) was also supposed to guarantee greater cooperation between the industrialized nations on questions of assistance to the Third World, so that European aid would not be granted for motives of national interest or mercantilist expansion, but as part of a coordinated free-market and anticommunist struggle. The other element designed to consolidate the transatlantic partnership was the opening of another GATT round of tariff reductions, concentrated on both manufactures and agricultural goods, where the United States feared European protectionism.[87]

In sum, American reshaping of the international economy rested on three pillars. First, the USA encouraged modernization through the stimulus of private enter-prise in the Third World and the reform of international aid institutions in order to block the expansion of socialist planned economies and state-run industries. Sec-ond, it supported renewed collaboration with western Europe to prevent those nations from shirking their responsibilities in the global war on communism by walling themselves off with preferential trade relationships in certain parts of the globe. Third, after the demise of quantitative trade restrictions among the EEC countries, Washington launched a new trade round between Europe and the United States that was supposed to benefit American exports to the Old Continent.

UNIONIZING THE THIRD WORLD: THE G77 AND THE ORIGINS OF UNCTAD

Kennedy's efforts to reshape the international economy, however, like those we have just described to institute a new foreign aid policy for developing nations, did not account for the growing radicalization of the Third World, even outside Latin America. Many in these areas had begun to view the end of direct military rule over the former colonies as insufficient, and were slowly becoming convinced of the legitimacy of a battle to achieve the same standards of living enjoyed by the indus-trialized nations: High levels of technological development, cultural and social advancement, and rising life expectancy. From the political and military struggle for independence, the fight against economic "neocolonialism" was born. The order of the day among those newly independent nations, seeking to escape the tutelage of the developed world, was "trade not aid": Growth in trade with the industrialized

---

[86] G. Selser, *Alianza para el Progreso. La Mal Nacida* (Buenos Aires: Ediciones Iguazú, 1964).
[87] F.L. Block, *The Origins of International Economic Disorder: A Study of United States Interna-tional Monetary Policy from World War II to the Present* (Berkeley: University of California Press, 1977), p. 172.

economies, accompanied by changes to the rules of international commerce and increased prices for raw materials, was thus linked to their desire to break out of the vicious cycle of dependence hidden beneath the benevolent face of foreign aid.[88]

At the forefront of these radicals was the Egypt of Nasser, who had come away from the Suez crisis with enormous prestige throughout the Arab world.[89] His announcement, broadcast by radio across Europe on July 23, 1956, that the Suez Canal had been nationalized and that it would be Egyptian technicians, and not foreigners, who thenceforth would guarantee the regular passage of ships through the strait, was memorable for the insolent jubilance of his laughter. The son of a postman—the first symbol of the efficient modern state—Nasser thought he could play the superpowers off against one another in the search for financial and technical support, establishing a trend imitated by other Middle Eastern leaders.[90] He believed that only economic planning along socialist lines, married to a confederation of Arab socialist republics, could secure the share of world markets, returns on investment, and a minimum of "living space" to give his leadership adequate breathing room.[91] But following closely behind the Egyptian president were several leaders from an Africa suddenly alive with new political ideas, many of whom were beginning to believe that direct rule by the former colonial powers was slowly giving way to another, more insidious form of domination based on international capital's control of the levers of the world economy and big businesses engaged in the extraction of raw materials. One of the African leaders who fulminated most vigorously against neocolonialism was Ghana's Kwame Nkrumah. Certain elements of his thought were shared and indeed discussed with Western specialists on development, from Arthur Lewis to Mary Kaldor, who argued for massive industrial investment to break the cycle of dependence on the agricultural economy.[92] Tony Killick underlined the importance of the choices confronting African leaders:

> One may sometimes wonder if the Western Powers fully understand the dilemma facing political leaders in the emergent lands. They have gained independence for their peoples. The hazards and the excitements of the struggle lie behind. Ahead lies the workaday world in which people must live and eat and hope and prosper. Independence of itself does not change this world. It simply creates the right political atmosphere for a real effort of national regeneration.[93]

---

[88] This book interprets the fight of the Third World to change the rules of international trade, and obtain greater influence in the Bretton Woods institutions, as a struggle that cannot be explained fully in terms of the pressures of the Cold War. An alternative interpretation views the developing countries as the puppets of international communism, which masked its expansionist designs in the guise of peaceful competition, nuclear disarmament, freedom from unequal trade relations, and close ties with the Third World. See B. Crozier, *The Struggle for the Third World: A Background Book* (London: The Bodley Head, 1966).

[89] D. Hopwood, Egypt, *Politics and Society 1945–1984* (London: Allen & Unwin, 1985), pp. 43–4.

[90] M. Trentin, *Engineers of Modern Development. East German Experts in Ba'athist Syria: 1965–1972* (Padua: Cluep, 2010).

[91] R. Schulze, *A Modern History of the Islamic World* (New York: New York University Press, 2002), pp. 151–3.

[92] P. Nugent, *Africa since Independendence* (New York: Palgrave, 2004), p. 170.

[93] Killick, *Development economics*, p. 49.

Nkrumah's essay *Neo-Colonialism: The Last Stage of Imperialism*—the title para-
phrases Lenin in 1917—described economic dependence as part of a precise
political strategy by the ex-colonial powers based on "breaking up former large
united colonial territories into a number of small non-viable States which are
incapable of independent development and must rely upon the former imperial
power for defence and even internal security."[94] Nkrumah was critical of the
creation of African states dependent on their ex-colonial masters, though he saw
de Gaulle's France as a potentially useful obstacle to the creation of a larger and
united Western system of exploitation. He was one of the principal supporters of
the idea of an African federation of states, which had its moment in the spotlight
in 1963 with the creation of the Organization of African Unity—a body that, it
must be noted, ultimately failed to fulfill Nkrumah's ambition to eliminate colonial states altogether.[95] The Ghanaian leader considered economic neocolonialism a system based on the collapse of commodity prices, loans at high interest, a
multilateral aid system that emphasized potential return on investment, and the
trade and maritime transport monopolies enjoyed by the wealthiest nations. In
his view, the "free" trade unions of the industrialized world were another instrument of neocolonialism, above all those affiliated with the British Labour Party,
since their demands imposed constant price increases for Western manufactures
while insisting on the protection of industrialized nations' domestic markets.
A General Electric commercial of the period that invited viewers to invest in the
company's shares offered a concrete image of the "predatory" reality that Nkrumah described:

> A General Electric advertisement carried in the March/April 1962 issue of *Modern
> Government* informs us that "from the heart of Africa to the hearths of the world's steel
> mills comes ore for stronger steel rails". With this steel from Africa, General Electric
> supplies transportation for bringing out another valuable mineral for its own use and
> that of other great imperialist exploiters.... But is it for Africa's needs? Not at all. The
> site, which is "being developed by the French concern, Compagnie Minière de
> l'Ogooue, is located on the upper reach of the Ogooue River in the Gabon Republic.
> After the ore is mined it will first be carried 50 miles by cableway. Then it will be
> transferred to ore cars and hauled 300 miles by diesel-electric locomotives to the port
> of Point Noire for shipment to the world's steel mills." For "the world" read the United
> States first and France second.[96]

---

[94] K. Nkrumah, *Neo-Colonialism: The Last Stage of Imperialism* (London: Thomas Nelson & Sons, 1965), p. xiii.

[95] On the failure of the OAU, see M. Michel, "Les réactions francophones et anglophones face aux premiers regroupements africains," in C.R. Ageron and M. Michel, eds, *L'ère des décolonisations* (Paris: Editions Karthala, 1995), pp. 280–95.

Until 1963 pressures for a regional solution to the problem of African underdevelopment seemed much greater than those which would push for privileged relationships between Europe and Africa. But circumstances would change quickly. See G. Migani, "La Communauté économique européene et la Commission économique pour l'Afrique de l'ONU: la difficile convergence de deux projets de développement pour le continent africain (1958–1963)," (2007) 13 *Journal of European Integration History*, pp. 133–46.

[96] Nkrumah, *Neo-Colonialism*, p. 14.

Such criticisms, which emphasized the obstructionism of the industrialized states, were also spread by the Marxist analyses of the American publication *Monthly Review*, directed by Paul Baran and Paul Sweezy. In these circles, formally independent from international communism, it was not uncommon to hear the use of the term "imperialism" with growing frequency in reference to the policies of the industrialized nations toward the Third World. Their ideas had a degree of influence over Third World leaders, like Guyana's Cheddi Jagan who, while declaring himself a social democrat, admitted in conversation with a skeptical Kennedy that he was an assiduous reader of the *Review*.[97]

The ex-colonial states sought to rebuild a viable identity and to construct concrete symbols of their independence not just economically but culturally. This was particularly true of the Senegalese leader Leopold Senghor, who developed the concept of *négritude* and sought a path to African socialism that did not adhere strictly to the writings of Marx, but was autonomous, collectivist, and not necessarily hostile to Europe. Such was also the position of Frantz Fanon, the physician from Martinique turned combatant in the Algerian war of liberation, who conceived of the search for identity—in contrast to Senghor—as a process of rejecting Western culture. In *The Wretched of the Earth*, first published in 1961 and soon to become the manifesto of "Thirdworldism" even in western Europe, Fanon passionately asserted the need to fight for the redistribution of resources in favor of colonized peoples:

> The fundamental duel which seemed to be that between colonialism and anticolonialism, and indeed between capitalism and socialism, is already losing some of its importance. What counts today, the question which is looming on the horizon, is the need for a redistribution of wealth...
>
> In the same way we may say that the imperialist states would make a great mistake and commit an unspeakable injustice if they contented themselves with withdrawing from our soil the military cohorts, and the administrative and managerial services whose function it was to discover the wealth of the country, to extract it and to send it off to the mother countries. We are not blinded by the moral reparation of national independence; nor are we fed by it. The wealth of the imperial countries is our wealth too... From all these continents [Latin America, China, and Africa], under whose eyes Europe today raises up her tower of opulence, there has flowed out for centuries toward that same Europe diamonds and oil, silk and cotton, wood and exotic products. Europe is literally the creation of the Third World.[98]

To understand the seemingly intractable economic obstacles facing the newly independent Asian, African, and Latin American states, the observations formulated in the 1970s by Paul Bairoch are still useful.[99] He was among the first to take note of these nations' growth in gross domestic product, and the development of certain important social indicators like rates of education, in the two decades from 1950

---

[97] Packenham, *Liberal America*, p. 78. For a good synthesis of the principal theories in this area, see T. Kemp, *Theories of Imperialism* (London: Dobson, 1967).

[98] F. Fanon, *The Wretched of the Earth* (New York: Grove Press, 1963), pp. 98–102.

[99] P. Bairoch, *Rivoluzione industriale e sottosviluppo* (Turin: Einaudi, 1967), pp. 216–17.

to 1970. At the same time, Bairoch argued that the absence of certain factors present in the European nations of the First and Second Industrial Revolutions of the nineteenth century actually militated against growth in the poor countries, and trapped them in a vicious circle that caused them to sink even further into relative underdevelopment:

1. the fact that manufacturing processes had become much more complex, making it much more difficult to introduce or copy industrial production techniques in places still dominated by artisanal modes of production;

2. the decrease in transportation costs that made it possible to do the previously unthinkable, that is to maintain manufacturing plants far from the producer nations of raw materials; and

3. the demographic explosion of the Southern nations, which could not sustain levels of agricultural production sufficient to feed their people, notwithstanding the productive revolution in farming techniques.

Already by the beginning of the 1960s, the most perceptive economic historians were emphasizing how simple imitation of the model followed by the industrialized countries—the idea put forward by the Rostowians—would not raise the poor countries out of their poverty, because they would simply fall prey to sabotage or outright corruption by established elites.[100]

Although rarely mentioned by historians, the creation in 1960 of the Organization of Petroleum Exporting Countries (OPEC), the first and most crucial organization among producers of raw materials, should also be viewed as a vital element of the Third World's new activism and of the increasingly global reach of some of its ideas. Far from being an Arab gathering, it included Iran and extended its global reach to the nationalist and interventionist governments of Indonesia and Venezuela. The gentleman's agreement leading to the creation of OPEC was reached in 1959 at the margins of the First Arab Petroleum Congress in Cairo, with a handshake between the Venezuelan Oil Minister Pérez Alfonzo and the Saudi Director of Petroleum and Mineral Affairs Abdullah al-Tariki (soon to become that nation's first Oil Minister). Venezuelan diplomats had been trying since at least the 1950s to blunt competition with cheaper Middle Eastern oil by reaching some form of effective agreement on oil production and prices, but were initially quite skeptical that the proposed organization would prove a success. As the Venezuelan ambassador commented regarding his meeting with the Saudi Prince Faisal, "it seems that the main producer in the Arab world does not share our concepts and that, considering its position, it could very well soon become a terrible competitor."[101] Eventually, the fateful decision by the oil companies in 1959 to decrease the posted price for oil (the reference price on which the taxation and income of oil-producing countries was

---

[100] W. Kula, *The Problems and Methods of Economic History*, 2nd edn (Burlington, VT: Ashgate, 2001), p. 435.

[101] Archivo Histórico Ministerio del Poder Popular para Relaciones Exteriores (AHMPPRE), Arabia Saudita, Situación Política, 1960, Embajador Antonio Araujo, "Entrevista con el Príncipe Heredero Faisal, en Arabia Saudita," Cairo, March 31, 1960.

determined), created the favorable climate for OPEC to be formally constituted in 1960 in Baghdad, at a meeting that went completely unnoticed by the foreign press and major leaders at the time.[102]

The ongoing cultural ferment in the Third World formed a more tangible part of the background to the July 1962 Cairo Conference on Problems of Economic Development, following up on decisions made the year before at the Belgrade meeting of the non-aligned countries. Some thirty-six nations representing the three major regions of the global South participated at the conference, which witnessed a tightening of bonds between the Afro-Asian founders of the Non-Aligned Movement, the most radical African leaders who advocated a harder line in the struggle against neo-colonialism, and the Latin American nations most experienced at criticizing the role of international economic institutions while working with them.[103] With the Cairo Declaration, approved with the active support of Raúl Prebisch—invited as a representative of the United Nations—the developing countries presented a resolution in support of a new UN conference on "all vital questions relating to international trade, primary commodity trade, [and] economic relations between developing and developed countries." In the course of discussions a common viewpoint had clearly emerged: Trade was considered the primary motor of development, and the privileged economic relationships among the developed countries, or between them and the poorer nations, an unjust instrument of pressure or discrimination. It did not take long for French diplomats, who had requested that their African allies refrain from participating at Cairo, to foresee a situation in which the European Economic Community could find itself the target of heavy fire from these "rebels":

> The Cairo Declaration contains a number of criticisms directed at "regional economic groups," which, it is known, means above all the European Economic Community. The hostile attitude of the Cairo meeting to the Common Market was otherwise so marked that France was compelled to advise the AASM nations [the Association of the African States and Madagascar] not to participate at the conference, with the result that the majority of the associated nations refused to send representation.[104]

The path to this new forum, which would become the United Nations Conference for Trade and Development (UNCTAD), was outlined on August 1, 1962 in a resolution of the UN Economic and Social Council, and subsequently confirmed on December 8 by the General Assembly. All the EEC nations with the exception of the Netherlands voted against the convocation of the conference.[105] Several

---

[102] J.C. Boué, "OPEC at (More Than) Fifty: The Long Road to Baghdad, and Beyond," (2010) 83 *Oxford Energy Forum.*

[103] UNCTAD, *The History of UNCTAD 1964–1984* (Geneva: United Nations, 1985).

[104] Historical Archives of the European Union (HAEU), Conseil des Ministères (CM) 2/1964, 830, "Répresentation permanente de la France, Note," December 4, 1962.

[105] Archives du Ministère des Affaires Etrangères Françaises (AMAEF), Nations Unies et Organisations Internationales (NUOI), Direction des Affaires Economiques et Financières, "Projet de Conférence Commerciale Mondiale," September 24, 1962: "What is certain is that, beyond the occasion that this conference will provide to place a large number of nations against the Common Market, the risk is that it will also put up for discussion the development of GATT, if it is true that, as claimed by the USSR, the conference will demand the creation of a global trade organization."

factors contributed to the success of the Third World initiative.[106] First there was the general disenchantment with the functioning of the UN Economic and Social Council (ECOSOC). Second was the general inattention paid to the development requirements by the World Bank and the IMF, and the complete lack of an international organization to deal with commodities and foreign investment. In addition, as we have noted, since the death of Stalin the Soviet Union had begun to treat the United Nations as a forum for global propaganda; after having opposed the Havana Charter in 1948 it gradually changed course, eventually supporting the idea of the creation of a World Trade Organization. This was seen as a way of breaking the Western monopoly over international economic institutions and at the same time of weakening the EEC, which had in the meantime become one of the primary targets of Soviet attacks. Finally, and most significantly, after the admission of seventeen new nations—all from Africa—the vote of the General Assembly in favor of the conference was a foregone conclusion. There could be nothing to do but accept it.

The next step was to create a preparatory committee for Geneva—quickly dubbed by the international press the "GATTicide Committee"—which would meet three times to agree upon conference details. The European Community used these meetings, as we shall see in the next chapter, as a forum to defend itself from the inevitable pressure which the conference would produce, ensuring that the conference would not take place before 1964, and thus that Geneva would not interfere with the finalization and ratification of the Yaoundé Convention treaty with the AASM.

The preparatory committee was the place where, for the first time, the economic solidarity of the developing nations took concrete organizational form. This nascent solidarity was in many ways unexpected, even in the experienced and somewhat jaded eyes of the diplomats in the British Foreign Office:

> The main impression left one of slowly gathering momentum and of greater co-ordination between less-developed countries. The movement is still uncertain and stumbling but it is better in control than during the first session and it seems to have caught some of the more developed countries slightly off balance, and induced them to modify the main idea with which they came to the conference.
>
> Inevitably the European Economic Community was the main target for criticism because its policies have tended to accentuate processes which are apparent in the trade of all developed countries with those at a lesser degree of development.[107]

At the second meeting of the preparatory committee, the developing countries presented a joint declaration on anticipated voting procedures, later submitted to the General Assembly with the signatures of seventy-five nations.

Two additional signatories were added at the end of the Geneva Conference, making a total of seventy-seven: Thus was born the Group of 77 (G77), a name

[106] R.N Gardner and M.F. Millikan, *The Global Parntership: International Agencies and Economic Development* (New York: Praeger, 1968), p. 99.
[107] National Archives (NA), Foreign Office (FO) 371/172276, Telegram, "Preparatory Committee for the United Nations Conference for Trade and Development," July 3, 1963.

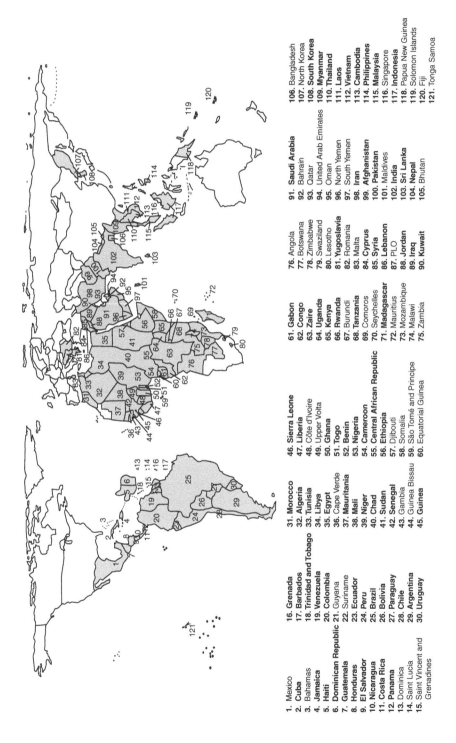

Figure 1.2. The G77 from its Origins to 1976. The countries in bold are founding members.

1. Mexico
2. Cuba
3. Bahamas
4. Jamaica
5. Haiti
6. **Dominican Republic**
7. **Guatemala**
8. **Honduras**
9. **El Salvador**
10. **Nicaragua**
11. **Costa Rica**
12. **Panama**
13. Dominica
14. Saint Lucia
15. Saint Vincent and Grenadines
16. **Grenada**
17. **Barbados**
18. **Trinidad and Tobago**
19. **Venezuela**
20. **Colombia**
21. Guyana
22. Suriname
23. **Ecuador**
24. **Peru**
25. **Brazil**
26. **Bolivia**
27. **Paraguay**
28. **Chile**
29. **Argentina**
30. **Uruguay**
31. **Morocco**
32. **Algeria**
33. **Tunisia**
34. **Libya**
35. **Egypt**
36. Cape Verde
37. **Mauritania**
38. **Mali**
39. **Niger**
40. **Chad**
41. **Sudan**
42. **Senegal**
43. Gambia
44. Guinea Bissau
45. **Guinea**
46. **Sierra Leone**
47. **Liberia**
48. **Côte d'Ivoire**
49. **Upper Volta**
50. **Ghana**
51. **Togo**
52. **Benin**
53. **Nigeria**
54. **Cameroon**
55. **Central African Republic**
56. **Ethiopia**
57. **Djibouti**
58. **Somalia**
59. **São Tomé and Príncipe**
60. **Equatorial Guinea**
61. **Gabon**
62. **Congo**
63. **Zaire**
64. **Uganda**
65. **Kenya**
66. **Rwanda**
67. **Burundi**
68. **Tanzania**
69. Comoros
70. Seychelles
71. **Madagascar**
72. **Mauritius**
73. **Mozambique**
74. **Malawi**
75. **Zambia**
76. Angola
77. Botswana
78. Zimbabwe
79. Swaziland
80. Lesotho
81. **Yugoslavia**
82. Romania
83. Malta
84. **Cyprus**
85. **Syria**
86. **Lebanon**
87. PLO
88. **Jordan**
89. **Iraq**
90. **Kuwait**
91. **Saudi Arabia**
92. Bahrain
93. Qatar
94. United Arab Emirates
95. Oman
96. North Yemen
97. South Yemen
98. **Iran**
99. **Afghanistan**
100. **Pakistan**
101. Maldives
102. **India**
103. **Sri Lanka**
104. **Nepal**
105. Bhutan
106. Bangladesh
107. North Korea
108. **South Korea**
109. **Myanmar**
110. **Thailand**
111. Laos
112. Vietnam
113. Cambodia
114. **Philippines**
115. **Malaysia**
116. Singapore
117. **Indonesia**
118. Papua New Guinea
119. Solomon Islands
120. Fiji
121. Tonga Samoa

that would stick, though in the future the number of associated countries would grow steadily.[108]

The G77 that began to coalesce in 1963 would become a major actor in international economic negotiations until at least the end of the 1970s, something akin to a trade union of Third World governments. Already at its birth the group was divided between radicals—nations like Indonesia and Cuba, which regarded the Conference as the first step in a global class conflict against the wealthy nations—and pragmatists like India, which sought to use Geneva more concretely as a new forum for international cooperation to work toward more short-term goals. It is not easy to evaluate which of the G77 countries were best positioned to play a front-line role in the negotiations; the relative size of the nations and the international prestige accorded to individual leaders, like Nasser or Nehru, were certainly important. But the practical preparations of the delegations and the charisma of individual diplomats were equally significant, as in the case of the Brazilian Silveira, as well as Lall from India, Stanovnik from Yugoslavia, Santa Cruz of Chile, and Mahmood of Pakistan.[109]

No similar degree of cooperation was evident on the western front, which had also begun preparations for the conference at the end of 1963 within the OECD. Here the atmosphere was poisoned by tension, in particular that between the pro-Atlantic powers and de Gaulle's France, which in January 1963 had officially rejected the British application to join the EEC.[110] The Kennedy administration, having pushed hard for British inclusion in the Community, regarded the newborn Franco-German axis as little more than a front for domestic political self-preservation, which would prevent Europe from assuming its international and Atlantic responsibilities.[111] In addition to the divisions within the Community, the OECD negotiations also revealed diametrically opposed visions for the future of global trade: While France supported price controls for basic commodities in order to defend the Common Agricultural Policy (CAP), Great Britain appeared to want to embark on a crusade for the complete liberalization of world commerce.[112] The only point of genuine consensus to emerge among the Western powers was the need to avoid the prospect of the Conference leading to the creation of a World Trade Organization that would jeopardize the primacy and role of GATT.

In 1963 London presented a seven-point plan to reform GATT that would have partially met the demands of the less developed countries (LDCs), agreeing to some liberalization of the industrialized world's markets. The plan was deemed completely inadequate by the Belgian trade minister, Brasseur, in light of the more

---

[108] K.P. Sauvant, *The Group of 77* (London: Oceana Publications, 1981).

[109] For an analysis of the G77 as well as an understanding of its internal dynamics, see B. Gosovic, *UNCTAD: Conflict and Compromise: The Third World's Quest for an Equitable World Economic Order through the United Nations* (Leiden: A.W. Sijthoff, 1972).

[110] P. Winand, *Eisenhower, Kennedy, and the United States of Europe* (London: Macmillan, 1993).

[111] A French editorial also argued that the formation of the Franco-German axis raised the risk that Europe would close itself off from international engagements: "Europe fermée, Europe ouverte?," *Le Monde*, January 24, 1963.

[112] HAEU, High Authority of the ECSC (CEAB) 05, 1196/1, Note du Secrétariat Ocde, "Conférence des Nations Unies sur le Commerce et le Développement," June 27, 1963.

radical requests then coming out of the developing world: The abolition of all existing trade preferences; greater access to the markets of the developed world for producers of raw materials and unfinished goods; abolition of agricultural protection; higher prices for basic commodities; abolition of quantitative restrictions, quotas, and inverse preferences; regional privileges for the developing nations, in contravention of GATT rules; safeguards on profits for exports; and price stabilization for raw materials.[113]

One issue on which the Western nations found themselves in full agreement was that Prebisch should not be allowed to assume the role of Secretary-General of UNCTAD. Prebisch had tried, using all the means at his disposal, to undermine GATT and remove it from its position of primacy in the oversight of international trade.[114] This time, their opposition would be in vain.

To understand the terms of the debate at the Geneva Conference it is necessary to examine the Prebisch Report, distributed before the opening of the final phase of negotiations.[115] The final document was radical in its premise, yet apparently moderate in its conclusions; so moderate, in fact, that some scholars would later attack Prebisch and his followers for having recommended only minor concessions on trade, while understating the need for radical changes in the internal dynamics of the Southern countries.[116] But the report was based on the sweeping premise that the economic geography of the nineteenth century, based on profound inequalities in international trade, should be officially recognized as a thing of the past:

> The great depression precipitated the break-down of this old order, already undermined by the political impact of the First World War. In view of all this and of the consequences of the Second World War, it is out of the question to think of restoring the old order now. In the not too distant days of Havana it might have been possible to harbour illusions of doing this, but the subsequent course of events has finally dispelled these illusions once and for all... Today it is imperative to build a new order with a view for solving the serious problems of trade and development that beset the world.

These trade imbalances were the product of the same historic circumstances that had made Great Britain the first industrialized nation. Prebisch limited himself to examining the goals defined by the Decade of Development—the program approved by the UN in 1960—which had as its objective the achievement of 5 percent annual growth rates in the poorer countries. He noted, however, that this goal was wholly inadequate because, given the considerable growth in population in the Third World, a 5 percent annual increase in GDP would actually amount to

[113] HAEU, OECD 148, Council, "Statement by Mr. Brasseur, Belgian Minister for External Trade and Technical Assistance, on the relations with countries in process of development," Paris, November 20, 1963.

[114] HAEU, CM2–1964, Note, "Résultats de la première session du Comité préparatoire de la Conférence des Nations unies pour le commerce et le développement," February 7, 1963.

[115] R. Prebisch, "Towards a New Trade Policy for Development. Report by the Secretary General of UNCTAD 1964," in P. Braillard and M.R. Dyalili, eds, *The Third World and International Relations* (London: Frances Pinter, 1986), pp. 175–6.

[116] G.P. Calchi Novati, *Decolonizzazione e Terzo Mondo* (Rome and Bari: Laterza, 1979), p. 138.

a net impoverishment of the South's inhabitants. Furthermore, according to the calculations of UNCTAD economists, a growth rate limited to 5 percent would also imply a rise in imports, with the result that by the end of the decade the Southern countries would find themselves left with some $20 million in debt. To avoid this trade gap measures needed to be taken in order to place more resources at the disposal of Southern governments. This could take essentially three forms: First, increasing profits derived from a growth in manufactures exported to the industrialized world; second, raising the amount of direct aid afforded the poorer countries; third, increasing the number and value of the basic commodities exported from the South to the industrialized world. These measures were not mutually exclusive, according to Prebisch, but rather were complementary.

With respect to the growth in exported manufactures and unfinished goods, the principal charge leveled at the GATT was of having given birth to a system of free trade tailored to the needs of the developed world. As the English economist Sidney Dell, one of Prebisch's primary collaborators, noted of the Kennedy Round: "Particularly striking in this connection is the provision in the United States Trade Expansion Act of 1962 whereby tariffs may be eliminated on items in which the United States and Common Market countries together supply 80 percent of the world's trade."[117] Regarding commodities, the Prebisch Report posed a number of unresolved questions: The system of taxation leveled on products from the Southern countries, like those of the tropics, created the paradox that the Italian government, for example, could benefit from tax levies to earn more from the import of a given product than it offered in aid.[118] The prices of raw materials were for the most part out of the hands of the producing nations, which possessed only 6 percent of the world's mercantile fleet, and were regulated principally by the financial centers of New York or London.

The first UNCTAD conference took place in Geneva, not by coincidence in the same city which hosted the GATT headquarters, from March 23 until June 15, 1964. It was the largest meeting on trade issues and development ever organized to that date. During the course of discussions the Western nations betrayed notable divisions among themselves while the Soviet Union displayed a measure of prudence by paying greater attention to the international political balance of power, denying China opportunities to radicalize their conflict, rather than exploiting the opportunity to attack the capitalist system.[119] At the end of more than two months of confused negotiations, no agreement had been reached on the vast majority of questions.

---

[117] S. Dell, *Trade Blocs and Common Markets* (London: Constable, 1967), p. 152.

[118] Calchi Novati, *Decolonizzazione*, p. 138.

[119] NA, FO 371/178077, "Preliminary Report, United Nations Conference for Trade and Development," July 1, 1964: "The attitude of the Americans has been the most disappointing part of the conference. The French idea for organization of the raw materials market has surprisingly made a few converts, while Francophone Africa has aligned itself with the 75 developing countries. The Belgians have hewed close to the French line, and the Germans and Dutch, even though in open disagreement with the French and Belgians, have let themselves be dragged along. The Canadian delegation was too small to play a role, while the Australians made a noteworthy impression with a sizable delegation. The Soviet bloc was not unanimous, and was almost completely absent in the negotiations during the last few months."

Recommendations were approved by majority vote but without binding clauses, exactly as the Western governments had wished.

All the same, significant new trends emerged. On an institutional level it was unanimously decided to create a series of new bodies within the UN: The Conference itself, which would continue to meet every three years, beginning in 1966; a Trade and Development Commission composed of fifty-six members (including eighteen Western states, six socialist countries, nine Latin American and twenty-two Afro-Asian nations); and an UNCTAD Secretary-General (Prebisch himself would be subsequently confirmed in the post). In addition, three working groups would be created: One on commodities (nonagricultural products), one on manufactured goods, and one on the so-called "invisibles" (direct aid, investment, loans, etc.).[120]

While no binding decisions were taken, the conference helped clarify a number of debates that would later have a profound impact in a different international context. In the commodities field, it was agreed to undertake a study of the organization of the market and excise taxes assigned to petroleum products—a demonstration, contrary to British assertions, of the traction of French ideas. With respect to manufactures, India won adherents to its appeal for preferential treatment of the developing countries' finished goods. This came as quite a shock to the Americans, who were not disposed to give in on the issue, particularly because such preferences implied a radical redesign of GATT rules, rigorously based on the concept of reciprocity. As regards aid, an issue accorded rather peripheral status, it was decided that this should amount to a total of 1 percent of GDP from the developed nations, and that it would be calculated on the basis of both private foreign direct investment and public aid.

In his speech before UNCTAD as the head of the Cuban delegation, Ernesto "Che" Guevara had warned that:

[i]f, on the other hand, the groups of underdeveloped countries, lured by the siren song of the interests of the developed powers who profit from their backwardness, compete futilely among themselves for crumbs from the tables of the world's mighty, and break the unity of numerically superior forces; or if they are not capable of insisting on clear agreements, without escape clauses open to capricious misinterpretations; or if they rest content with agreements that can simply be violated at will by the powerful, then our efforts will have been to no avail and the lengthy deliberations at this conference will result in nothing more than innocuous documents and files for the international bureaucracy to guard zealously: Tons of printed paper and kilometers of magnetic tape recording the opinions expressed by the participants. And the world will stay as it is...

The International Monetary Fund is the watchdog of the dollar in the capitalist camp; the International Bank for Reconstruction and Development is the instrument for the penetration of US capital into the underdeveloped world; and the Inter-American Development Bank performs the same sorry function in Latin America. All these organizations are governed by rules and principles that are represented as safeguards of fairness and reciprocity in international economic relations. In reality,

---

[120] HAEU, CEAB 05/2017, Note, "Fin de la Conférence de l'ONU sur le Commerce et le Développement," June 17, 1964.

however, they are merely fetishes behind which hide the most subtle instruments for the perpetuation of backwardness and exploitation. The International Monetary Fund, which is supposed to watch over the stability of exchange rates and the liberalization of international payments, merely denies the underdeveloped countries even the slightest measures of defense against competition and penetration by foreign monopolies.[121]

While it lacked this revolutionary tenor, the Joint Declaration of the G77 at the end of the Conference demonstrated that on economic issues the South, as long as it acted in unison, could represent a force to be reckoned with. The declaration stated:

> The developing countries regard their own unity as the outstanding feature of this conference. This unity has sprung out of the fact that facing the basic problems of development they have a common interest in a new policy for international trade and development.

International observers were impressed by the fact that Arab and sub-Saharan countries like Egypt and Ghana, without historically strong foundations or common ties, were able to unify in their fight against the "white man" and demonstrated their willingness to cooperate in future battles against poverty and for industrialization.[122] The Belgian Ambassador Forthomme, who had been charged in the OECD with coordinating the position of the industrialized nations, could not help but express his concern for the future of the international economy:

> The great danger is that, if a constructive dialogue is not opened with the 77, they might undertake restrictive trade policies with the result of closing entire regions off from one another, which would have very serious consequent effects on both the developed and developing countries... They are seeking compensation not only for the deterioration of their exchange rates but also for the impact of competition from synthetic products; and the line of compensation has almost reached so far as to request compensation to address different standards of living. Considering this situation the Western countries will run the risk that the 77 might impose their solution unilaterally, combining this with a tendency toward national or regional autarky.[123]

Growing anxieties within the industrialized states regarding the emergence of a unified front of Southern nations softened the stance of even the most hard-line Western liberals, and made possible the first reforms of the Bretton Woods economic institutions. In 1965, one year after the conclusion of the first UNCTAD, Part IV of GATT was adopted, recognizing the vast differences in standards of living between the developed and developing worlds, taking into account the importance of adequate incomes for Third World exporters, and encouraging nonreciprocal trade agreements between countries with different standards of living. In 1963 the IMF had created a new type of loan to protect commercial trade balances, and in 1966 it conceded the opening of this Compensatory Financing Facility to the emerging nations, though the conditions offered were no more advantageous for

---

[121] Che Guevara, *Che Guevara Reader*, 2nd edn (New York: Ocean Press, 2003), pp. 308–12.
[122] P. Worsley, *The Third World* (London: Weidenfeld, 1964), p. 333.
[123] HAEU, OECD 151, Trade Committee, "Summary Record of the 9th Meeting held at the Chateau de la Muette, Paris, September 18, 1964."

them than for the industrialized countries, contingent as these loans were upon strict "cooperation" with the Fund.[124]

The birth of a trade union of Third World countries meant not only the creation of a new economic institution within the UN, but also parallel and temporary weakening of more radical, conflicting, political impulses with respect to the industrialized world, which pre-dated the emergence of the independence movements.

In 1965, with the failure of the second Bandung Conference, the Afro-Asian movement was finally and permanently defeated. In the Afro-Asian Economic Summit of 1965, Che Guevara had urged the creation of new, autonomous instruments for common dialogue and action among colonized peoples, sparing no one from criticism, not even the Soviet Union:

> How can it be "mutually beneficial" to sell at world market prices the raw materials that cost the underdeveloped countries immeasurable sweat and suffering, and to buy at world market prices the machinery produced in today's big automated factories?
>
> If we establish that kind of relation between the two groups of nations, we must agree that the socialist countries are, in a certain way, accomplices of imperialist exploitation.[125]

Guevara's entire strategy, of a revolutionary conflagration spreading among the peoples of three continents, was revived with his speech at the 1966 Tri-Continental Solidarity Conference in Cuba—best known for its call to "create two, three, many Vietnams"—but it never took off, undermined in the short term by the logic of détente between the USA and the USSR, which put a brake on Third World radicalism. Guevara's speech, delivered *in absentia* while he was preparing his Bolivian campaign, was based on his notion that the peoples of the developing world possessed an unlimited capacity for indignation, action, and ultimately for battle:

> We must definitely keep in mind that imperialism is a world system, the final stage of capitalism, and that it must be beaten in a great worldwide confrontation. The strategic objective of that struggle must be the destruction of imperialism.
>
> The contribution that falls to us, the exploited and backward of the world, is to eliminate the foundations sustaining imperialism: Our oppressed nations, from which capital, raw materials and cheap labor (both workers and technicians) are extracted, and to which new capital (tools of domination), arms and all kinds of goods are exported, sinking us into absolute dependence.[126]

But in the span of a few short years, one after another, an entire generation of Third World independence leaders would lose their power or their life, or both, substantially weakening the effort to create an autonomous, politically militant bloc in international affairs. Nehru died in 1964; Sukarno, the Algerian leader Ben Bella, and Nkrumah were overthrown by military coups between 1964 and 1965, after having relied too heavily on their own personal charisma and too little on

---

[124] J. Adda and M.C. Smouts, *La France face au Sud* (Paris: Karthala, 1989), p. 118.
[125] Guevara, *Che Guevara Reader*, p. 341.
[126] Che Guevara, *Global Justice: Liberation and Socialism* (New York: Ocean Press, 2002), p. 58.

mechanisms of mass political participation. Che Guevara himself would of course be killed in 1967 in Bolivia, while he attempted to put into practice his strategy of revolutionary *foquismo* (guerrilla *focos*, or "fires") elaborated at the Tri-Continental Conference. The *coup de grâce* to the idea of African autonomy was delivered with the severe lesson imparted to Egypt by Israel in the Six Days' War, a conflict the larger significance of which we shall return to later.[127] In short, in the aftermath of the first UNCTAD the most revolutionary impulses among the Third World leadership seem to have largely exhausted themselves. At the same time the consolidation of power by new national elites, whether civil or military, appeared to be proceeding faster than the implementation of internal social reforms or mechanisms of popular participation.

In the long run, the several projects of regional integration founded in the heady years of the early 1960s, and subsequently heralded at Geneva as the strategic solution to the problems of underdevelopment in the UNCTAD Final Declaration, failed to take root. It has been estimated that by the middle of the 1960s there were at least fifty countries that were taking part, in one way or another, in regional integration initiatives, the most notable of which was probably the Latin America Free Trade Association (LAFTA). Between 1964 and 1968 all these projects faced substantial crises.[128] Among the reasons for the failure of these efforts at regional integration in the Third World were the excessive emphasis placed by the developing nations on the defense of industrialization; the fact that in Asia two of the great powers, India and China, were largely focused on national development schemes; the strong ties binding Latin America to the United States; the fact that none of the major Western powers favored the regionalization of development aid, as had happened, for example, in the case of western Europe during the years of the Marshall Plan.[129]

That said, while in 1960—when pressure from the newly elected Kennedy administration had resulted in the creation of the DAC and reform of the World Bank—the Western world seemed to be comfortable with the idea that the efficient planning of aid would be sufficient to solve the problems of the Third World and to bring it closer into line with an economy based on free markets, the birth of the G77 forced the industrialized countries to come to grips with the need to partially reassess and reform the structures underlying trade and the international economy.

---

[127] Westad, *The Global Cold War*, p. 107.

[128] In the formulation of projects for regional integration in Africa, like that put forward by Nkrumah at the Pan-African Conference held at Addis Ababa in 1963 ("we are already at the point where it is necessary to unite if we want to avoid being picked off one by one, like the situation in Latin America"), Europe was invoked as the primary power against which it was necessary to unite. In the Latin American case, the proposed treaty advanced by Raúl Prebisch in 1965 instead cited the EEC as a positive example. On the relationship between African regional integration and the EEC see G. Montani, *Il Terzo mondo e l'unità europea* (Napoli: Guida Editori, 1979); M. Noelke, *Europe–Third World Interdependence: Facts and Figures* (Brussels: Commission of the European Communities, 1979). On Latin American efforts to create a common market on the model of the European Community see S. Dell, *A Latin American Common Market?* (Oxford: Oxford University Press, 1966).

[129] M.S. Wionczek, ed., *Economic Cooperation in Latin America, Africa, and Asia* (Cambridge, MA: MIT Press, 1969).

2

The Myopia of the European Community

If not a founding father of the European Economic Community, the Belgian Fernand Dehousse was certainly one of its most distinguished senators. An illustrious jurist and member of both the Council of Ministers and the Parliamentary Assembly of the ECSC, he had hoped that Europeans' colonial experience would not be so easily or carelessly discarded:

> Allow me to express all the sympathy that I personally feel for the struggle of a France that fights to avoid a conflict between East and West, which would also be fatal to the European Community, with all that it represents, as well as for all mankind.
>
> It is in Algeria today that French and European claims toward universality are being put to the test. A French abandonment of Algeria would signify the retreat of Europe into itself.[1]

Born from the twin traumas of a world war and the progressive crumbling of its nations' various imperial projects, the EEC—which would be included within the European Communities (EC) with the Merger Treaty signed in 1965—lacked any ambition to promote the cause of world civilization. It proved to be a rather more bland, pragmatic entity, mainly aimed at establishing a European Common Market and defending European agriculture. Retrenchment within national borders prevailed over grander strategic visions, while advocates of pro- or neo-Atlanticism—Atlanticism combined with aspirations to enhance national greatness and develop special links with newly independent countries—had their way on the most pressing international issues of the day. We shall see that once the idea of *Eurafrique* had been definitively shelved,[2] the French managed to overcome the outright opposition of the other Member States to an association between the EEC and the former French colonies in Africa only by threatening to sacrifice the entire integration project if no agreement was reached.

Once the colonial state was no more, so went the notion of "colonial development" and with it, all of the European empires' considerable, if misconceived, efforts to build colonial economies or integrate and educate their colonial subjects. Frederick Cooper has brilliantly summarized the situation of these newly independent governments with regard to international aid: "Independence turned entitlement into

---

[1] F. Dehousse, *L'Europe et le Monde. Recueil d'études, de rapports et de discours 1945–1960* (Paris: Librairie Générale de Droit et de Jurisprudence, 1960), p. 524.

[2] The idea of *Paneuropa*, including Europe, Africa, and regions of the Middle East was present in the German geopolitical thought of Karl Haushofer. This new aggregation should have been able to oppose itself to *Panamerica*, *Panrussia*, and *Panpacifica*. E. Deschamps, "L'Afrique belge et le projet de Communauté politique européenne (1952–1954)," in E. Remacle and P. Winand, *America, Europe, Africa. L'Amérique, l'Europe, l'Afrique 1945–1973* (Brussels: PIE Peter Lang, 2009), p. 310.

supplication."[3] As developing nations in Asia and Africa became independent, they mainly came to be seen in western Europe as useful providers of labor and raw materials, potential outlets for surplus manufactures, junior partners to be preserved from the spread of international communism.

THE PASSING OF IMPERIAL ILLUSIONS

In his memoirs, Jean Monnet recalled how Louis Armand—one of the "three wise men" charged, after the failure of the European Defence Community in 1954, with relaunching a common European initiative through a joint atomic energy project—provocatively proposed the erection of a statue honoring Nasser as "the federator of Europe."[4] Having dealt a severe blow to the imperial dreams of France and the United Kingdom in 1956, the Egyptian leader had also cleared the path for a new French commitment to Europe.

But the signing of the Treaties of Rome in 1957—which formally established the European Economic Community—cannot be considered the conscious decision of national leaders to place their hopes in Europe as a political actor or even in the idea of Europe as their primary theater of economic activity. The Beyen plan, which formed the basis for the Common Market, was based strongly on Atlantic inspirations, centered on the need to reduce tariff barriers first among the Six, and later between the Six and the United States. While Euratom, as initially proposed by the "wise men," never seriously managed to develop plans for an independent European energy program, the creation of a Common Market greatly helped oil multinationals—of which only Shell was partially based in one of the EEC's six founding members—to dominate western Europe's energy market in the passage from coal to oil.[5] In fact European federalists had viscerally opposed the EEC treaty because it did not provide enough space for a supranational dimension.[6] The 1960s were years of substantial economic growth in Europe, a period of great vitality for its nation states, which invested in infrastructure improvements, communications, and manufacturing, pumping fresh blood into national economies and placing citizens in contact with each other, often for the first time, by means of new technologies such as the television.[7] Behind European economic cooperation there was profound and deeply rooted reciprocal distrust.[8] As late as the early 1960s surveys showed that, in

---

[3] Frederick Cooper, "Writing the History of Development," (2010) 8(1) *Journal of Modern European History*, p. 15.

[4] J. Monnet, *Mémoires*, trans. Richard Mayne (London: Collins, 1978), p. 422.

[5] T. Mitchell, *Carbon Democracy. Political Power in the Age of Oil.* New York: Verso, 2011, p. 108.

[6] The Treaty of Rome was an important contribution to the construction of European economic regionalism, and constituted without a doubt a political decision. But the consequences of this act would be felt only at the end of the 1960s. On the nature of the Common Market and the theoretical issues it raised see (2003) 14 *Memoria e ricerca* (December 2003). On the political debate within the European left after the birth of the EEC see S. Cruciani, *L'Europa delle sinistre. La nascita del Mercato comune europeo attraverso i casi francese e italiano (1955–1957)* (Rome: Carocci, 2007).

[7] C.S. Maier, "Secolo corto o epoca lunga? L'unità storica dell'età industriale e le trasformazioni della territorialità," in C. Pavone (ed.), *'900: I tempi della storia* (Rome: Donzelli, 1997), p. 51.

[8] D.J. Puchala, "Western European Attitudes on International Problems, 1952–1961," (1964) 1 *Yale Research Memoranda in Political Science*, pp. 266–79.

the event of war, only 25 percent of the French would trust the British, 20 percent the Germans, and 14 percent the Italians; for their part, only 21 percent of Germans held any faith in the French, 19 percent in the Italians, and 17 percent in the English. The Italians were, if possible, even more skeptical of their European neighbors over the Alps, influenced perhaps by the treatment of Italian emigrants in Northern Europe.[9] Pieter Lagrou has argued that it was only after 1965, with the celebrations of the twentieth anniversary of the end of the Second World War, that an era characterized by the recrudescence of jingoistic patriotism and the construction of official myths and heroes could be considered over, allowing space for the diffusion of more dispassionate national histories.[10]

Among the six members of the European Community in 1957, only tiny Luxembourg—and the Federal Republic of Germany, albeit for very different reasons—had no formal colonial relations or special ties with one or another of the countries in the developing world. France, Belgium, the Netherlands, and to certain extent even Italy, were still colonial powers when the Rome Treaty was signed and managed to include their colonial possessions, such as French Africa and all other French Overseas *départements* and territories, the Belgian Congo and Rwanda, Dutch New Guinea, and Italian Somalia, as associated to the EEC.[11] The French even sent three African representatives from their colonies to the Parliamentary Assembly of the EEC, allegedly in an effort to "make it clearly be understood to the representatives of the five signatories of the treaties on the Common Market and Euratom, the importance that France attributes to the defence of the interests of the African people."[12]

Martin Shipway has defined the policies of the old European *metropoles* up to the end of the 1950s as a "late colonial shift," characterized by the attempt to relaunch their imperial projects through economic rationalization programs and efforts to improve the political organization of the colonial states.[13] In 1946 the French had launched their *Fonds d'Investissement en Développement Economique et Social* (Fund for Economic and Social Development) to revive their colonies' economies, and even as late as 1958 the government set up a FFR2 billion plan to relaunch the Algerian economy. The British boasted that the sterling area continued to represent between 36 and 40 percent of world trade up to the end of the 1950s, and constituted a fundamental source of foreign currency. Belgium, in 1949, launched a Ten-Year Plan aiming at reinforcing Congo's infrastructure and creating a native middle class that would remain politically reliable and form a backbone of

---

[9] On the "selling" of Italian emigrants by the Italian government in the 1950s and their working conditions in northern Europe, see M. Colucci, *Lavoro in movimento. L'emigrazione italiana in Europa 1945–57* (Rome: Donzelli, 2008).

[10] P. Lagrou, *The Legacy of Nazi Occupation. Patriotic Memory and National Recovery in Western Europe, 1945–1965* (Cambridge: Cambridge University Press, 2000), p. 15.

[11] Part IV of the EEC Treaty provided for the association with "*pays et territoires d'outre-mer*": <http://eur-lex.europa.eu/fr/treaties/dat/11957E/tif/TRAITES_1957_CEE_1_XM_0114_x555x.pdf>.

[12] AMAEF, Cabinet du minister Couve de Murville, Carton 331, lettre de Emile Roche au Président Charles de Gaulle, 15/0771958.

[13] Shipway, *Decolonization and its Impact*, p. 51.

potential consumers. The East Indies accounted for 14 percent of the Netherlands' GDP after the war, and represented a vital source of oil and and other raw materials to be processed at home—a source over which they would refuse to relinquish control until the end of the 1950s. Once their colonial states had crumbled, European states abandoned their serious efforts at development, but by no means did they cease attempting to profit from their ties with their former colonies.[14]

De Gaulle, who returned to power one year after the signing of the Treaties of Rome in 1958, nurtured an ambitious plan to create a French Community that would include all the Francophone territories of Africa. France's natural sphere of influence, he believed, extended from continental Europe across Africa and the Middle East: A notion that prompted the French government to revive the idea of a *Eurafrique*, potentially linking the two continents through common institutions.[15] Although the idea was already dead by 1960, when the African nations of the French Community opted for independence, de Gaulle fought until the bitter end to retain control of Algeria.[16] For the French government 1962, with the formal declaration of Algeria's independence, represented not only the end of its colonial ambitions but also the defeat of the Fouchet Plan, its project for European political unity based on a federation of the six major states, which would have counterbalanced the Community's existing institutions.[17] At the end of that year, France thus sought a new grand idea that would bring it a global role equal to de Gaulle's ambitions.[18] In his traditional end-of-year speech, de Gaulle reminded the nation that "aid must be given to peoples in need for their modern development and, above all, for the spirit of cooperation with those nations of Africa, Asia, and Latin America which ask for assistance from France."[19] He considered the European Community, through its ties with the Association of the African States and Madagascar (AASM), formalized in the 1963 Yaoundé Convention imposed by France on its partners,[20] as an instrument for the maintenance of France's privileged

---

[14] Nicholas J. White, "Reconstructing Europe through Rejuvenating Empire: The British, French, and Dutch Experiences Compared," in Mazower, Reinisch, and Feldman (eds), *Post-War Reconstruction in Western Europe*, pp. 211–36. On Belgium in particular, see J.P. Peemans, "Imperial Hangovers: Belgium—The Economics of Decolonization," (1980) 15 *Journal of Contemporary History*, pp. 257–86.

[15] R. Girault, "La France entre l'Europe et l'Afrique," in E. Serra (ed.), *La relance européenne et les traités de Rome (Actes du colloque de Rome, 25–28 mars 1987)* (Milan: Giuffré, 1989), pp. 351–78; G. Bossuat and M.T. Bitsch (eds), *L'Europe unie et l'Afrique. De l'idée d'Eurafrique à la Convention de Lomé I* (Brussels: Bruylant, 2005).

[16] In his memoirs de Gaulle wrote that he understood full well by 1960 the need for Algerian "self-determination," which was not exactly the same thing as "independence": See A. Horne, *A Savage War of Peace: Algeria, 1954–1962* (New York: New York Review of Books, 2006), pp. 343–4.

[17] G.H. Soutou, *L'alliance incertaine. Les rapports politico-stratégiques franco-allemands 1954–1996* (Paris: Fayard, 1996), pp. 176–229.

[18] M. Vaïsse, *La grandeur: politique étrangère du général de Gaulle 1958–1969* (Paris: Fayard, 1998), p. 453. According to Vaïsse the new French policy was guided by the division of the communist world between the Soviet Union and China, the dialogue between the nuclear superpowers, and the emergence of the Third World after decolonization.

[19] Institut du Droit de la Paix et du Développement, Institut Charles de Gaulle, *De Gaulle et le Tiers Monde* (Paris: Editions Pedone, 1983), p. 247.

[20] G. Migani, *La France et l'Afrique sub-saharianne, 1957–1963. Histoire d'une décolonisation entre idéaux eurafricains et politique de puissance* (Brussels: PIE Peter Lang, 2008).

role with the Francophone nations at the lowest possible cost. The new association was symbolically signed in Cameroon, thus avoiding the eurocentrism of Rome in 1957, and included a development fund and common institutions. In the long run this institutional link between the EEC and some former colonies did bear some fruits in terms of cooperation. But in the short run Yaoundé was managed by French administrators with a colonial background—the Commissioner for Development up the 1980s would be French-backed and controlled by a German Director-General—and, according to the definition of Jacques Ferrandi, the all-powerfull French Commissioner, the distribution of funds was quite subject to political pressures: "Justement: Aucune procédure. La procédure n'était pas fixée."[21]

De Gaulle was convinced at the same time that, with his plans for a *Eurafrique* definitively sunk, France should also play its global role as partner to the non-aligned countries.[22] This policy was based largely on solemn speeches and grandiose gestures, on the rupture with NATO—more symbolic than substantive, it succeeded only in forcing the alliance to move its headquarters from Paris to Brussels, while France remained a member of the Atlantic Pact—and on the idea of Europe as a "Third Force." At the same time, France held onto its special economic and cultural relationships with its former colonies. The Francophone nations remained tied to the French franc, and were inundated by a sea of French teachers in order to preserve their common cultural bonds, a mission given by de Gaulle to Minister of Culture André Malraux.[23] Some have claimed that de Gaulle's openness to the global South was little more than a "marriage of convenience";[24] others have spoken of an "empire of words." For Paris, at any rate, the end of its colonial empire had not signified the weakening of its politics of national prestige, in favor of common European cooperation with the developing world.

Nowhere was the relinquishing of colonial ties a completely painless process, not even for Belgium, a country that—as home to the European institutions and even-

---

[21] See <http://www.eui.eu/HAEU/OralHistory/pdf/INT711.pdf>.
For an analysis of French aid in the 1960s, see J. Meimon, "L'invention de l'aide française au développement: Discours, instruments et pratiques d'une dynamique hégémonique," in (2007) 21 *Questions de recherche*, September 2007, pp. 15–16. On DG VIII, see V. Dimier, "L'institutionnalisation de la Commission Européenne (DG Développement): Du rôle des leaders dans la construction d'une administration multinationale, 1958–1975," in (2003) 34(3) *Etudes Internationales (Canada)*, pp. 401–28. On EC development policy, see G. Laschi, "La nascita e lo sviluppo delle relazioni esterne della Comunità dalle colonie alla cooperazione allo sviluppo," in G. Laschi and M. Telò, *Europa potenza civile o entità in declino? Contributi ad una nuova stagione multidisciplinare di studi europei* (Bologna: il Mulino, 2007), pp. 51–81.
Some figures give an idea of how European cooperation policy was essentially designed to prolong French colonial ambitions: "Of the $580 million of the European fund, $511 [million] are distributed to states which have 'special relations' with France, against $30 [million] for the former territories of Belgium and $35 [million] for New Guinea... The detachment of the DGVIII from French interests was, however, far from a reality up until the end of the 1970s." F. Turpin, "Alle origini della politica europea di cooperazione allo sviluppo: la Francia e la politica di associazione Europa-Africa (1957–1975)," in (2007) 6 *Ventunesimo Secolo* (October 2007), p. 137.

[22] Only in 1966 did development aid and cooperation begin to be directed by the Quai d'Orsay. G. Bossuat, "French Development Aid and Cooperation under de Gaulle," in (2003) 4 *Contemporary European History*, pp. 431–56.
[23] J. Chipman, *French Power in Africa* (Oxford: Blackwell, 1989), p. 197.
[24] Vaïsse, *La grandeur*, p. 453.

tually to NATO—Nkrumah considered little more than a beachhead for American capital and multinationals. A 1947 memo on social policy circulated by the Belgian Union Minière in Congo well encapsulated the sense of entitlement and of a "civilizing" mission of Belgian economic concerns in the region after the war:

> The colonizer must never lose sight of the fact that the Negroes have the souls of children, souls which mould themselves to the methods of the educator; they watch, listen, feel, and imitate. The European must, in all circumstances, show himself a chief without weakness, good-willed without familiarity, active in method and especially just in the punishment of misbehavior.[25]

Even for the socialist leader Paul Henry Spaak, the Congo was the jewel in Belgium's crown, a profitable and prestigious resource that, among other perks, allowed the nation to enjoy greater influence within the Atlantic military alliance. A group of Congolese students visiting Brussels in 1956 were left perplexed by this typically colonial cast of mind, such conservatism in one of the most prestigious leaders of European socialism, not to mention one of the most influential promoters and founding fathers of European integration.[26] In 1960–61 Belgium underwent some of the most violent social upheavals in its history as the socialists began a period of electoral dominance, yet none of this turmoil made any significant impact on the nation's stance toward its colonies. Spaak boasted of having defended the French government before the UN in 1960, describing the Algerian question as a domestic matter, to be handled according to the French constitution of 1946, and criticizing the mistaken beliefs of those who would bargain with the new Arab Hitler, General Nasser.[27] Only the final withdrawal from the Congo in 1964 freed Belgium from the contradictions of its colonial policy, which had received scarce support from its Community partners, forcing the country to face the difficult task of rebuilding a national identity threatened from within by the claims of its diverse linguistic groups.

After the defeat at Suez, even the conservative British government was forced to recalibrate its imperial aims.[28] London viewed its application to join the European Community as an instrument to bind the Six more tightly to its Atlantic partners, but the French refusal to admit the United Kingdom, followed by the victory of Harold Wilson's Labour Party in 1964, breathed new life into the concept of the British Commonwealth. In this vision, Great Britain was conceived as the hub at the center of ever-widening concentric circles of global relations, the cultural and economic special relationship with the United States given pride of place alongside the Commonwealth.[29] In the course of a parliamentary debate in 1961, Wilson

---

[25] D. Litvin, *Empires of Profit. Commerce, Conquest and Corporate Responsibility* (New York: Texere, 2003) p. 160.

[26] R. Coolsaet, *Histoire de la politique étrangère belge* (Brussels: Vie Ouvrière, 1988), p. 172.

[27] P.H. Spaak, *Combats Inachevés. De l'Indépendance à l'Alliance* (Paris: Fayard, 1969).

[28] John Darwin describes the painful process of departing from "overseas interests" that had a very large constuency even though "enthusiasm for imperial rule was confined to a limited section of the upper class." J. Darwin, *The Empire Project. The Rise and Fall of the British World System 1830–1970* (Cambridge: Cambridge University Press, 2009), p.15.

[29] P. Ziegler, *Wilson. The Authorised Life* (London: Weidenfeld & Nicolson, 1993), p. 219.

had made it clear that "we are not entitled to sell our friends and kinsmen down the river for a problematical and marginal advantage in selling washing machines in Dusseldorf."[30] Wilson was firmly entrenched in the intellectual lineage of the first postwar Labour government of Clement Attlee, which had hoped to export the benefits of the British welfare state to the Commonwealth nations—a notion as far-sighted in theory as it was untenable in practice, given the ever-diminishing foreign currency reserves of the United Kingdom.[31] Upon election, Wilson was quick to assert that the borders of Great Britain reached as far as the Himalayas, hurriedly created an Office of Overseas Development—which was supposed to coordinate its aid efforts—and was involved in the inauguration of the Institute for Development Studies at the University of Sussex, which became one of the first and most advanced centers in Europe for the study of the problems of underdevelopment. Even Raúl Prebisch was invited to collaborate.[32]

Even Italy, the most underdeveloped of the EEC countries and a defeated military power that had been forced to renounce control over Libya and Eritrea, managed to return to one of its former colonial possessions in the Horn of Africa. In 1950, Rome obtained a trusteeship over Somalia which allowed it to guide that country's transition to independent government, which Somalia eventually achieved in 1960. During that time, Italy made efforts at colonial development by opening elementary schools for a population some 90 percent of which was illiterate—classes were taught rigorously in Italian—and in 1958 Rome offered a hundred scholarships and planned an investment of US$2 million to help the Somali economy.[33]

While renouncing colonies could coincide with a greater commitment to harvesting the fruits of economic collaboration among European states, the idea of political and cultural integration was still insufficiently developed to replace imperial imagery. The imperial past either was celebrated up to the end of the 1950s or it simply seemed to give way to the "politics of forgetting," whereby the fundamental economic role of the colonies in building the great European cities and industries was overlooked, while the violence of occupation was simply removed.[34]

The epic stories of glorious colonial campaigns still constituted one of the primary foundations in the development of French and English students' historical consciousness. A 1949 French text on "imperial expansion," for example—comparing French Prime Minister Jules Ferry, Belgian King Leopold II, Italian Prime Minister Francesco Crispi, the British statesman Austen Chamberlain, and US President Theodore Roosevelt—opened with a tribute "to the force of will, to the tenacity, to

---

[30] H. Young, *This Blessed Plot: Britain and Europe from Churchill to Blair* (London: Papermac, 1998), p. 157.

[31] F.S. Northedge, *Descent from Power: British Foreign Policy, 1945–1973* (London: Allen & Unwin, 1974), p. 220.

[32] A. Thorpe, *A History of the British Labour Party* (London: Palgrave, 2001), p. 156.

[33] A. Morone, *L'ultima colonia. Come l'Italia è tornata in Africa 1950–1960* (Bari: Laterza, 2011).

[34] A. Hochschild, *King Leopold's Ghost* (New York: Houghton Mifflin, 1908), pp. 296–306.

the civic courage of the statesmen that had the *sens de la grandeur*."[35] The newly independent states were typically seen as inadequate to the task of managing the transition to a society based on industrial labor, and ungrateful to the civilization that had spent so much in means and manpower so that they could escape barbarism. The passing of imperial illusions was accompanied by a retreat behind national borders, and a consequent cynicism regarding Third World nations' ambitions for autonomy. This cynicism was not necessarily overt racism, a notion widely discredited by the memory of Nazi racial policy, but a peculiar blend of benevolent paternalism and a growing consciousness of living through a productive revolution that had left the world's periphery increasingly far from modernity. The retreat from empires also meant the progressive restriction of access to the *metropole* for citizens of the former colonies. Often they were suddenly transformed from potential nationals—that is, persons endowed with rights—to mere manpower, hired through short-term contracts with foreign governments that did not have much concern for the living conditions of such workers (in France, for example, migrants largely still lived in *bidonvilles*). According to one of the few comparative studies of postwar immigration policy in western Europe, the British approach, for example, could be called "an attempt to remove rights of citizenship too generously extended during the colonial period."[36] Europeans who came back after the failed imperial wars, meanwhile, even though their numbers were by no means small (at least 250,000 Dutch came back to Europe from the East Indies alone), were absorbed with relative ease: Until the late 1960s their voices and their painful memories of war and often of torture were very rarely given any space in the press or in academic debate.[37]

In the United Kingdom policy toward citizens of the Commonwealth was nominally anything but racist: Residents from as far away as the Caribbean and Pakistan had the right to British citizenship. Their contribution as laborers was considered vital in the service sector, in domestic employment, and in the hospitals as in public transportation and all the new functions and services generated by the tremendous expansion of the role of the state. V.S. Naipaul, a native of Trinidad who moved to England for university study, described the welcome experienced by the first young immigrants of the 1950s in the bohemian salons of London:

> The immigrants, from the Caribbean, and then the white colonies of Africa, and then Asia, had just arrived. They were still new and exotic; and there were English people—both high and low, with a taste of social adventure, a wish from time to time to break out of England, and people with colonial connections who wished in London to invert the social codes in the colonies—... who were ready to seek the more stylish

---

[35] C.A Julien, J. Brohat, G.Bourgin, M.Crouzet, and P.Renouvin, *Les politiques d'expansion imperialiste. J. Ferry, Leopold II, F. Crispi, J. Chamberlain, Th. Roosevelt* (Paris: PUF, 1949).

[36] G. Freeman, *Immigrant labor and racial conflict in industrial society: The French and British experience: 1945–1975* (Princeton, NJ: Princeton University Press, 1979) p. 38. See also A. Geddes, *Immigration and European Integration. Beyond Fortress Europe* (Manchester: Manchester University Press, 2008).

[37] H.L. Wesseling, "La décolonisation et la mère-patrie: Mentalités et mémoire collective," in C.R. Ageron and M. Michel (eds), *L'ère des décolonisations* (Paris: Editions Karthala, 1995).

and approachable of the new arrivals. They met in Notting Hill, neutral territory, in dimly lit furnished flats in certain socially mixed squares...; and they were gay and bright together. But few of the immigrants had proper jobs, or secure houses to go back to.[38]

The Labour program of 1958 described the Commonwealth as the best means of achieving racial understanding.[39] This does not mean, of course, that there was not widespread skepticism regarding the ability of the ex-colonies to develop, or that some in certain circles harbored deeply rooted racial convictions just below the surface. In one of his African travel stories from 1963, the Italian author Alberto Moravia described a lunch among the English travelers in a grand hotel in Mombasa, Kenya. There in the ex-colonies, he wrote, specimens of *homo Victori-anus* remained perfectly preserved, in both their physical bearing and their native dress, not to mention in their dinner-table chatter, overheard by the author:

> The summary of it is this: The Africans will prove themselves incapable of carrying on the administrative, economic and social machine created by the Europeans in Africa. Once the whites have departed, everything will go to pieces. And this, not so much because the Africans are lacking in certain qualifications that can be acquired with time, as because they are essentially incapable of doing certain things, in other words because they are racially inferior.[40]

In a televised interview Hugh Trevor-Roper, the famous Oxford historian, demonstrated his intellectual honesty: "Perhaps in the future, there will be some African history to teach. But, at present there is none: there is only the history of the Europeans in Africa. The rest is darkness, and darkness is not the subject of history."[41] In August 1958, a week of skirmishes between local Teddy boys and Caribbean immigrants suddenly disrupted the quiet of the residential London neighborhood of Notting Hill. Notwithstanding the fact that it was the Teddy boys that instigated the incidents, for which the majority of the 120 persons arrested were white, the incident raised eyebrows and suspicions throughout the UK; a Gallup poll in 1961 found that some 67 percent of those interviewed supported tighter controls to check the flow of immigrants from the Commonwealth. The next year, the Conservative government introduced a voucher system that restricted entrance to those who could provide proof of employment, thereby abolishing the automatic welcome previously reserved for the citizens of the ex-colonies.[42] The minutes of a debate in a mid-sized urban section meeting of the Labour Party capture the evolution of citizens' thinking on immigration, from the idealistic view of a Great Britain as beacon of civilization and integration, to the more modest effort to manage racial conflict within the country and thereby defend existing levels of social progress:

[38] V.S. Naipaul, *Half a Life* (New York: Vintage, 2002), pp. 68–9.
[39] C. Knowles, *Race, Discourse and Labourism* (London: Routledge, 1992), p. 95.
[40] A. Moravia, *Which Tribe Do You Belong To?*, trans. Angus Davidson (New York: Farrar, Straus, and Giroux, 1974), p. 50.
[41] J.H. Mittelman, *Out from Underdevelopment. Prospects for the Third World* (New York: St. Martin's Press, 1988), p. 31.
[42] A. Porter and A.J. Stockwell, *British Imperial Policy on Decolonization 1938–1964*, vol. 2 (London: Macmillan, 1989), p. 77.

A member said we might just as well give the whole damn country to the Blacks as they would get it in the end anyway. Before long we would have a Black king on the throne and then it would be God help us! The poor old white man might just as well emigrate and leave the place to them....

He said that this Black menace had ruined our towns and forced the whites out of them. The best thing we could do would be to send the whole damn lot back to where they came from!

Mr Storrow said he was not aware that Ian Smith [Prime Minister of the white government of Rhodesia] was present but apparently he was.

Mr Whittle said they must learn to reject some of their ways. Some of them would gladly do without education for their children and street lighting, etc. if it saved them paying Rates and Taxes. We were gradually winning the battle but it was a long fight....

Mr. Bell said he didn't see why we should accept their ways as it was our country.

Mr. Blair said they worked well alongside us. But he believed in the old saying of when in Rome do as Rome does.

Dr. Tombs thanked everyone for an interesting discussion.[43]

In France such attachment to the colonies—which, it will be recalled, formed a vital base for the armed Resistance against the Nazis—suffused the entire nation. The colonies were considered a part of the country, vital to national prestige, the economy, and the national culture. In his 1944 series of lectures on European history at the Collège de France, Lucien Febvre had predicted that the problem facing Europe after the war would be deeply entwined with that of the former colonies, so that it would be impossible to provide distinct solutions to each that would not affect both Europeans and colonial citizens:

Before the war it was estimated that France contained some 40 million persons, but a census counted some 100 million French citizens in total, dispersed throughout the various parts of its colonial empire. If France enters into a European federation, should it leave out all these members of its family? What about Algeria, for example, which is composed of three French *départements*, with senators, deputies, and ministers— among them ministers of great historic stature, like [Eugène] Etienne, and [Gaston] Thomson? What about Martinique? What about Guadalupe? What about India? What about Senegal? In short, what about all the rest? And if you admit all the rest, you admit the entire world, bit by bit, into this European federation.[44]

In 1949, 81 percent of the French thought that France should possess an empire, and 62 percent were convinced that Paris had done a good job with its colonies. This consensus might have motivated high levels of investment in the colonies but, with time and the ever-larger military commitment to the Algerian war, the percentage in favor went into steady decline.[45] That said, in 1956 the Socialist Prime Minister Guy Mollet proudly declared before Parliament that:

[43] S. Fielding, *The Labour Party. Socialism and Society since 1951* (Manchester: Manchester University Press, 1997), p. 47. The debate took place on October 12, 1967.
[44] L. Febvre, *L'Europe: Genèse d'une civilisation* (Paris: Perrin, 1999), p. 305.
[45] C.R. Ageron, *La décolonisation française* (Paris: Armand Colin, 1991), p. 109.

[b]ecause it contains 8 million unassimilated Muslims, Algeria is not a French province like any other, Artois or Normandy for example. At the same time, because it contains 1 million Frenchmen who run everything, neither can it be a Muslim nation state. We reject absolutely this idea of an Algerian nation state that bears no relation to any historic or ethnic reality.[46]

A year later, following the disastrous defeat at Suez, François Mitterrand could still write that "without Algeria there will be no French history in the twenty-first century."[47] In 1959, *Esprit* magazine published an interview with a soldier ordered to execute members of the Algerian resistance after they had been tortured. The French soldier allowed that it wasn't "a very easy job," but believed nevertheless that he was combating criminals and communists: "after a while I didn't think about it too much, but the first one was hard."[48] The defeat in Algeria and its consequences—the return of the *pieds noirs* and the debates over the methods used by French soldiers in their war on terror, the strife provoked in France by the conflict, and the discussions on the ever-higher costs of colonial policies—were all factors which favored retreat within national borders. Todd Shepard, in a seminal study published in 2006, has gone so far as to argue that in 1960 the identification of French citizenship with the *Hexagone* and continental Europe could only take place after Algerians had been definitively labeled as Africans with no right to French citizenship in 1962.[49] A period of national forgetting ensued, in which questions of responsibility for colonialism were strenuously avoided in the name of progress and modernity, but such memories would return to trouble the tranquil face of French identity like a "ghost that would not pass."[50]

Having lost the war, Italy was forced to surrender its colonies; its only remaining overseas commitment was the temporary administration of Somalia. Anticolonialism was thus a choice adopted out of convenience rather than a strategy born of conviction. In 1960 the Africanist Carlo Giglio wrote in the weekly newsmagazine *Epoca* a glowing analysis of both the British Commonwealth and the *Union Française* as civilized instruments to prevent racial segregation. He believed Italy's colonial experience, in particular that accumulated after the First World War, to have been an experiment which had the natives' best interests at heart.[51] Until the beginning of the 1970s Italian historiography on Africa continued to praise the

[46] Cited in Cruciani, *L'Europa delle sinistre*, p. 96.
[47] Chipman, *French Power in Africa*, p. 28.
[48] P. Leuliette, "Aventures d'un parachutiste," in *Esprit*, April 1959, p. 65.
[49] T. Shepard, *The Invention of Decolonization. The Algerian War and the Remaking of France* (Ithaca, NY: Cornell University Press, 2006); although the same kind of approach had been taken as early as the 1970s in many of the works of Henri Wesseling on the Netherlands.
[50] For a book that extensively documents the traumas of decolonization see M. Thomas (ed.), *European Decolonization* (Aldershot: Ashgate, 2007); J.L. Miège and C. DuBois, *L'Europe retrouvé. Les migrations de la décolonisation* (Paris: l'Hamattan, 1995).
[51] B. Bagnato, "Alcune considerazioni sull'anticolonialismo italiano," in E. Di Nolfo, R.H. Rainero, and B. Vigezzi (eds), *L'Italia e la politica di potenza in Europa (1950–60)* (Milan: Marzorati, 1992), pp. 289–317. See B. Bagnato, *L'Europa e il mondo. Origini, sviluppo e crisi dell'imperialismo coloniale* (Milan: Le Monnier, 2006).

country's colonial past, so much so that the authoritative reference remained that written by Raffaele Cascia under the Fascist regime.[52] Even in 1967 when, with the exception of Portugal, all the European nations had given up control of their colonies, a historian and public intellectual like Arturo Carlo Jemolo could argue, in a debate with the Communist philosopher Nicola Abbagnano, that not all civilizations were equal, and that Western civilization was undoubtedly superior.[53]

The Dutch historian Henri Wesseling has written:

> Every Dutch student learned, beginning in elementary school, that nature had been tight-fisted with raw materials on his home soil. Every Dutchman who wasn't barricaded inside his home was forced to realize that his country was cold and damp, and densely populated. New Guinea, on the other hand, seemed to have everything the Low Countries lacked: Sun, space and raw materials.[54]

In Holland before the loss of Indonesia, a popular saying warned that "if the Indies are lost, the Low Countries are fucked". History would demonstrate otherwise. But whatever the popular frustration at the loss of the colonies, it could be transformed only very slowly—if indeed it ever has been—into enthusiasm for Europe.

The complexity of western Europeans' attitudes, torn between hostility toward the Africans, the desire for peace and tranquility, and disinterest in colonial matters, was visible in the reactions to the last-ditch intervention of Belgian paratroopers in the Congo, at Stanleyville in November 1964, to rescue white citizens under siege from armed rebels tied to Lumumba. It would be the final act of this small federal state as a great global power. The immediate reactions of Belgian citizens from various regions and social classes were captured by a journalist for *La Libre Belgique*:

> *A town clerk*: I followed it only from a distance but in general I'm "in favor." It was necessary to do something to save our citizens from the hands of those savages.
>
> *A pharmacist*: It's not good to intervene in a foreign country, but we did right to save the lives of our citizens. Let's hope that the Congo can develop itself with the help of Belgian assistance.
>
> *A professor at the Conservatoire*: A fever kept me from reading the papers and listening to the radio the last few days. However I believe the responsibility falls on all those who in forty-three years of colonization did nothing to train one single black official or engineer. And yet there have been many priests and bishops of color.
>
> *A prelate*: I'm in favor of the intervention as long as our soldiers return to Belgium once the mission to save human lives is over.[55]

---

[52] M. Lenci, "Dalla storia coloniale alla storia d'Africa," in A. Giovagnoli and G. Del Zanna (eds), *Il Mondo visto dall'Italia* (Milan: Guerini e Associati, 2004), pp. 109–10.

[53] A.C. Jemolo, "Le civiltà non sono tutte uguali: Occidente e Terzo Mondo," in *La Stampa*, July 23, 1967.
S. Romano, "Il Continente Africano fra petrolio e sapone," in *Il Corriere della Sera*, December 5, 2007.

[54] H.L. Wesseling, "Les Pays-Bas et la decolonization: Politique extérieure et forces profondes," in *Opinion publique et politique extérieure, III 1945–1981 Actes du colloque de Rome* (17–20 February 1982) (Rome: Ecole Française de Rome, 1985), p. 225.

[55] *La Libre Belgique*, November 25, 1964.

The two most important western European political networks, those of the Christian Democratic parties and of the Socialists, both made overtures to the Third World in the course of the 1960s, for rather different reasons. But their attitudes remained markedly cold toward the requests made by the countries of the developing world in the global forum of international organizations.

The Nouvelles Equipes Internationales (NEI) were created in 1947 as an instrument of cooperation between European Catholic and Christian Democratic parties. According to Charles Rutten, one of the leaders of the Dutch Catholic Party who participated at its founding congress, the name "had no meaning" and derived simply from the need to avoid any religious references, rejected by the French in the name of the *laïcité* of the state.[56] Throughout the 1950s, above all because of the influence of the French, Belgian, and Dutch Catholic parties, the organization concentrated its attentions on the dangers presented by the Cold War and the threat of international communism. In this context the NEI supported European integration—and even the possible creation of an integrated European military force—as a defensive instrument against communism.[57] Any reference to questions of decolonization was diligently avoided. In 1960, however, during the course of an NEI meeting in Paris on the relationship between the Christian Democrats and the Third World, Paolo Emilio Taviani, one of the founders of the Italian *Democrazia cristiana* (DC), recalled that:

> [t]hanks to colonization, the majority of African populations without culture, without tradition and without any history became "peoples," and they learned what the concepts "society" and "state" mean…We may not forget that the existence of modern states like Ghana, Cameroon, Togo and Somalia would not have been possible if those territories had never been colonized by the British, the French or the Italians.[58]

In 1961, the international Christian Democratic movement made an overture to the Third World, and especially to Latin America, with an international conference held in Santiago, Chile. The occasion marked their first effort to mine this potentially rich vein of propaganda and influence, but in the event the needs and desires of the peoples themselves were largely ignored. The Non-Aligned Movement was warned that neutrality toward international communism was unacceptable, and that any neutral position was in fact immoral: An early sign of difficulty in the effort to find common ground between European and non-European peoples. In 1965 the NEI assumed the new name European Union of Christian Democrats (EUCD).[59] In 1966, at its Fifth Congress, the split between the European and Latin American contingents became official, when a EUCD majority refused to

---

[56] Available online at: <http://www.ena.lu/integralite_interview_charles_rutten_haye_29_novembre_2006_duree_20820-012500519.html>.

[57] P. Chenaux, "Les democrats-chrétiens au niveau de l'Union Europèenne," in E. Lamberts (ed.), *Christian Democracy in the European Union 1945–1995* (Leuven: Leuven University Press, 1997), pp. 449–59; S. Delureanu, *Les Nouvelles Equipes Internationales. Per la rifondazione dell'Europa (1947–1965)* (Soveria Mannelli: Rubbettino, 2006).

[58] P. Van Kemseke, *Towards an Era of Development: The Globalisation of Socialism and Christian Democracy, 1945–1965* (Leuven: Leuven University Press, 2006), p. 262.

[59] W. Kaiser, *Christian Democracy and the Origins of European Union* (Cambridge: Cambridge University Press, 2007).

approve a resolution of its Latin American partners calling for an effort to stabilize commodities prices with an international agreement. The Italian Christian Democrats, more open to the ideas of Third World leadership, distanced themselves from the positions of their German counterparts in the Christlich Demokratisches Union (CDU).[60] But despite such growing internal tensions, the Atlantic Alliance, the market economy, and the anticommunist struggle remained the basis for the international outlook of European Christian Democrats until the mid-1960s.

The story was only slightly different for the other great European political family, the socialists. The Socialist International was reborn in Frankfurt in 1951, and its headquarters based in London, underscoring the importance of the British Labour Party in its reorganization. Europeans formed the vast majority of its member parties, and financial backing for the organization was drawn exclusively from European party sources.[61] Socialist doctrine on international relations—many parties had officially distanced themselves from Marxism at the end of the 1950s in favor of a free-market reformism, in order to position themselves as electorally legitimate alternatives—still drew upon the thought of the prewar Austrian theorist Otto Bauer, for whom progress down the road to socialism could only be achieved where the leap forward to industrial capitalism had already been completed. The newly independent nations, with their primarily agricultural economies, were not considered fertile terrain for socialist propaganda in the short term, until they had experienced a measure of economic development to match their political independence.[62] Even as late as 1960, at their meeting in Haifa, Israel, the International did not assume a clear anticolonial position. The presence of the French socialists, who defended their government's actions in Algeria, put a halt to any direct relationship with the alliance of the non-aligned and indirectly responded to the question raised by Ho Chi Minh in his memoirs: "What I wanted to know—and this precisely was debated in the meetings—was: which International sides with the peoples of the colonial countries?"[63] One substantial difference that separated the Socialist International from the European Christian Democrats, however, lay in the fact that the former did not consider the European Community as a forum in which to consider development issues. This reticence cannot be explained solely in terms of the influence of the British Labour Party, because of their conviction that the ties between the Community and the African states were nothing more than an extension of the colonial experience. Rather, European socialists placed greater faith in the possibilities for action through multilateral economic institutions. In 1961 the Socialist International organized a conference on development held in Baden-Baden: Fourteen European experts were assembled alongside fifteen

---

[60] R. Papini, *L'Internazionale DC. La cooperazione tra i partiti democratici cristiani dal 1925 al 1985* (Milan: Franco Angeli, 1986), p. 291.

[61] G. Devin, *L'Internationale socialiste. Histoire et sociologie du socialisme international* (Paris: Presse de la FNSP, 1993).

[62] J. Braunthal, *History of the International 1943–1968* (London: Victor Gollancz, 1980).

[63] Ho Chi Minh, "The Path Which Led Me to Leninism," in *Selected Works of Ho Chi Minh*, vol. 4 (Beijing: Foreign Languages Publishing House, n.d).

Asian and fifteen African counterparts, while Latin America remained absent out of respect for the preponderant role played in their hemisphere by the United States. The conference opened with remarks by the Dutch economist Jan Tinbergen, who would become one of the primary European interlocutors in debates on the Third World underdevelopment. It was the first step in a process that would lead in 1962 to the Oslo Declaration, with which the Socialist International presented a new look to the nations of the South. European socialists, heavily criticized at Baden, that would finally distance themselves from colonialism. They acquiesced fully, however, to the American approach based on "modernization" theory, according to which the developing countries themselves should be held fully responsible for achieving growth, by rapidly adopting democratic systems of government to make themselves more attractive to foreign investment. Tinbergen, alone, proposed a system to stabilize profits from commodities exports. Otherwise, the primary goals of Oslo remained to prioritize gains in productivity and eliminate trade barriers between Western nations; the redistribution of wealth to the South was accorded secondary status, relegated to increasing the availability of international aid.

For their part, western European communist parties, while beginning to contemplate a multipolar international communism by the early 1960s, had not yet distanced themselves sufficiently from the internationalist and anti-imperialist policy of the Soviet Union, so much of which was concentrated on shielding the USSR from the attacks of Beijing.[64]

The passing of imperial illusions had taught the Europeans a painful lesson on the need to distance themselves from colonialism of a military type, and opened the eyes of European politicians and organizations to the issues of the Third World. But the ideas circulated by the leadership of the developing countries regarding the need for structural changes to the international economy found no takers in European ministries. For individual citizens in western Europe the imperial illusion was replaced with another mirage, based on optimism and hopes for a constant rise in living standards, without consideration of the consequences for whatever happened to exist outside of national and European borders.

THE WONDER OF MODERNITY: IN DEFENSE OF THE COMMON MARKET

European nations, destroyed by years of war, were revived through economic reconstruction, sustaining their high rates of growth throughout the 1960s thanks both to the moderate wage policies of their trade unions, abundant public and private investment, cheap oil and shrinking defense budgets. Western European leaders were consistently able to raise domestic tax rates without provoking visible signs of public protest because citizens were full of hope for their own future and

[64] M. Bracke, *Which socialism, whose détente? European Communists and the 1968 Czechoslovak Crisis* (Budapest: Central University Press, 2010).

had faith in the positive role of the central government.[65] Europeans could even continue to believe they lived at the center of world culture; after all, the "old continent," attracting three-quarters of the world's travelers, remained the most sought-after destination in global tourism.[66]

Growth in trade during the first half of the 1960s, first among the European nations, and then between Europe and the other industrialized economies, was a tangible and exciting phenomenon not quantifiable simply in terms of statistics or the profits of exporting businesses. Modernity and mass consumption arrived in western Europe later than in the USA, but by the beginning of the 1960s, even citizens of relatively backward nations like Italy were endowed with the purchasing power to buy new domestic technologies such as washing machines.[67] Refrigerators, televisions, automobiles, radios, tires, and other consumer goods entered more visibly into daily life, their brand names becoming synonymous with quality in many countries. In 1966 the Federal Republic of Germany surpassed the United States in world commercial rankings in manufactures, a signal of western Europe's rebounding commercial strength.[68] The most cited Western economists revealed themselves to be incorrigible optimists, turning on its head the common conception of their discipline as the "dismal science." Financial resources, once limited in number and inadequate in distribution, seemed ever more abundant and ready for allocation in new investments. Roy Harrod's economics textbook, in its 1969 edition, asserted with an impudence characteristic of the spirit of the decade that "full employment should be considered a structural feature of the British economy." Friedrich Hayek's liberal theories, which described the power of the state to regulate the economy as the "road to serfdom," were seen instead as vaguely irrational exaggerations. Collaboration between the public and private sectors and a modest amount of investment planning were considered the key ingredients in a miraculous growth formula. The state and the market would move, as they should, hand in hand.[69] The agricultural sector shrank in significance before industry, and the fields emptied further as the rural population was increasingly displaced toward the cities. Social inequalities and architectural travesties aside, Western Europe and its cities were quickly overwhelmed by cement and traffic jams, buses and streetcars, and all the other trappings of modernity. This fascination with progress, and especially with technology, was inescapable for even the most skeptical and discerning intellectuals. The Dutch director Joris Ivens, in his documentary *L'Italia non è un Paese povero* (1960), commissioned by the Italian Ente Nazionale Idrocarburi (ENI) run by Enrico Mattei, depicted an

[65] Progressive taxation rates reached up to 70 percent of yearly earnings, and by 1970 general government taxes ranged between 20 and 30 percent of Gross Domestic Product. See I. Berend, *An Economic History of Twentieth-Century Europe* (Cambridge: Cambridge University Press, 2006), p. 227.

[66] A. Williams and G. Shaw, *Tourism and Economic Development. European Experience* (Chichester: John Wiley & Sons, 1998), p. 107.

[67] M. Nolan, "Consuming America, Producing Gender," in R.L. Moore and M. Vaudagna (eds), *The American Century in Europe* (Ithaca, NY: Cornell University Press, 2003), pp. 243–61.

[68] M. Walker, *The Cold War: A History* (New York: Henry Holt and Company, 1995), p. 213.

[69] S. Padgett and W.E. Paterson, *A History of Social Democracy in Postwar Europe* (London: Longman, 1991), pp. 153–4.

enormous sulfide plant, along with other miracles of modern engineering, inter-spersed with spaceships and science fiction backdrops through the eyes of a dreaming child. Andrew Schonfield, in one of the most important and often-cited economics texts of the 1960s, echoed this optimistic wonder at the industrialized economies' seeming invulnerability:

> Since the collapse of the Korean War boom the industrial countries have generally enjoyed the benefit of falling prices for the primary produce which they import and the rising prices for industrial goods which they export. They would, of course, have been ruined by this situation long ago, if they had depended for the prosperity of their export trade on the buying powers of the primary producers. Because industrial coun-tries have learned how to replace some primary products with synthetics and to reduce their requirements of others by means of improved techniques both in manufactures and in agriculture, they have become less dependent on other channels; and they have seized it. The result of this increase in the volume of manufactured goods exchanged among the advanced countries is that the share of manufactures in world trade, in rela-tion to foodstuffs and raw materials, has risen dramatically.[70]

The Third World had become a global actor. It had started to organize itself to defend its own interests and to create international bodies to further cooperation but, paradoxically, its greater political significance seemed to carry diminishing economic weight: The share of exports coming from developing countries had shrunk from 26 percent of the world total in 1953 to 19 percent in 1970. The principal problem facing western European economists and ambitious political leaders like de Gaulle was not so much how to devise measures to deal with the demands of the G77, but how to stabilize the international monetary system, making it less dependent on the dollar and more responsive to the needs of the wealthiest European nations. Guido Carli, head of the Banca d'Italia, recalled how already by the beginning of the 1960s debates had sprung up in the heart of the IMF on the need to increase international liquidity:

> On the other hand, those countries that are still largely monocultural, after having undertaken more or less demanding development schemes to raise their respective income levels, exploiting to that end the substantial financial contributions of the World Bank, now find themselves facing a foreign debt burden that appears to be maturing rather quickly and that cannot continue to accumulate without pernicious consequences. In addition, these same countries are witnessing a perceptible deteriora-tion of their exchange rates with respect to the industrialized countries... the impor-tant fact to emerge in the course of our discussions is their clear awareness of the interdependence of such problems...[71]

The Europeans, however, had refused to acknowledge the requests of those in the Third World to create and make available new reserve currencies.

---

[70] A. Schonfield, *Modern Capitalism: The Changing Balance of Public and Private Power* (Oxford: Oxford University Press, 1965), p. 23.
[71] Archivio Storico della Banca d'Italia (ASBI), direttorio Carli, cart. 62, fasc. 1, fasc. 10, "Appunto di Carli per Tremelloni," Rome, September 27, 1962.

Regarding commodities and agricultural products, developments within the European Community nations had raised new dangers, particularly for countries like those in Latin America that since the Second World War had placed their faith in exports to European markets. The CAP, at least on paper, came into force in 1962 and protected European farmers from foreign competition by guaranteeing elevated internal prices and exports of overproduction.[72] In the autobiography of the Frenchman Edgar Pisani, the first European Agricultural Commissioner from 1961–6, the author does not reflect even once upon the effect of the CAP on the less developed countries.[73] But raw materials, whether agricultural or mineral, were even further threatened by a new type of Western industrial model of production, which never ceased to invent and produce substitutes for traditional natural resources.

Industrial development of new synthetic materials had ingrained itself so deeply in the postwar world that its echoes were felt even in the art world. Take the case of the Italian Alberto Burri, who moved from the use of natural materials like cloth, tar, and sawdust in the 1950s to experiments with plastics, acrylics, and "cellotex" insulation in the following decade. Gino Marotta also began to work with Plexiglass, establishing a relationship of mutual curiosity with industries that would go on to help popularize the use of materials derived from petroleum. At the beginning of the 1960s, the Italian Montecatini (later Montedison) began to invest in synthetics, for which it saw a bright future, even financing a journal called *Plastics and Elastomers*. In its first issue, the esteemed Italian chemist and Nobel laureate Giulio Natta wrote in an editorial that until recently there had been few types of synthetic rubber, all inadequate to replace natural products, but warned that:

> [i]t could be that the situation will change in the future as a result of the new rubbers synthesized in the last few years after the discovery of polymerization.
>
> There remains a substantial profit margin for synthetic rubbers, such that their production will not depend primarily on reasons of political, economic, financial, or military necessity, as was the case at the dawn of that industry. Rather, they will be based on solid economic principles that are valid even in a completely free market. It is those principles that will justify the rise of synthetic rubber factories in many places throughout Europe.[74]

A cursory glance at the issues in the journal's first year demonstrates how new plastics and other similar synthetics being substituted for traditional materials were making a profound impact on daily life. Synthetic materials were increasingly used for the interior and exterior surfaces of homes, automobiles, or wherever rubber, glass, and metals were used. Among the unlimited number of applications for the new synthetics were automotive repair, road signs and signals, belts and garments, tires, tables, chairs, food packaging, shipping, sails, tubing, disposable utensils, bicycle helmets, toys, toilet seats, life preservers, and waste baskets. A minor

---

[72] M.T. Bitsch, *Histoire de la construction européenne de 1945 a nos jours* (Paris: Ed. Complexe, 2004); A.C. Knudsen, "Creating the Common Agricultural Policy. Story of Cereal Prices," in W. Loth (ed.), *Crises and Compromises: The European Project 1963–1969* (Baden-Baden: Nomos Verlag, 2001), pp. 131–56.

[73] E. Pisani, *Un vieil homme et la terre* (Paris: Seuil, 2004).

[74] G. Natta, "Nuovi sviluppi della chimica macromolecolare nel campo degli elastomeri," in (1963) 1 *Materie plastiche ed elastomeri*, pp. 1–10.

revolution that made the fortunes of more than a few European businessmen also promoted a popular euphoria for the modern, and in so doing overwhelmed waste management systems, producing an explosion of nonrecyclable waste. At the same time, it freed the expansion of European economies—or so it seemed—from the constraints imposed by the import of commodities from the Third World.

Popular enthusiasm for the modern was also generously supported by organized labor. The European working classes appeared to be in the midst of a great transformation, from fiery supporters of class conflict to a new category of consumers, whose needs were increasingly being met (or created) by advertising that had previously targeted the housewife as homemaker.[75] Union leaders, who vigorously supported the creation of a social welfare state, were not necessarily interested in nor sensitive to events happening outside their national borders. This phenomenon was recognized early on by the Swedish economist Gunnar Myrdal, who noted that the creation of the welfare state had produced such a strong confluence of fundamentally conservative interests that it constituted an almost insurmountable barrier against the types of reform that might take into account the interests of the Third World:

> The welfare state is nationalistic, indeed very much more so than a *laissez faire* type of State would be. Thus tremendous forces of vested interests, often spread out among broad layers of the citizens, are so created that they can be mobilized to abstain from policies for underdeveloped countries. In this case, it is wrong to put the blame on the "capitalists," as is often done by some ignorant radicals. On this point the people are the reactionaries.[76]

Galbraith, focusing on the United States, took this observation a step further, arguing that organized labor could no longer effectively oppose the government's foreign policy: The Cold War had brought with it massive investments in technology that had strengthened the national economy, and with it salary and employment levels.[77] The "free" European trade unions, like those in the USA, were little interested in the debates under way at the UN, in the demands of UNCTAD, or in the accusations of neocolonialism leveled against the Europeans. The International Confederation of Free Trade Unions (ICFTU), which until the end of the 1960s was dominated by the leaders of the Anglo-Saxon unions, paid little heed to these matters except to reiterate calls for a rise in the living standards of the industrialized nations, as a means of freeing more money to aid the underdeveloped. If anything, the free European unions began to concentrate their attention on European integration, as a means of incorporating migrant laborers and encouraging investment in social policy throughout the continent in order to sharpen the Common Market's competitive edge.[78] Even the French Confédération Generale

---

[75] A. Sangiovanni, *Tute blu: La parabola operaia nell'Italia repubblicana* (Rome: Donzelli, 2006).

[76] G. Myrdal, *The Challenge of World Poverty. A World Anti-Poverty Program Outline* (New York: Pantheon Books, 1970), p. 299.

[77] J.K. Galbraith, *The New Industrial State* (Princeton, NJ: Princeton University Press, 1967), p. 408.

[78] A. Ciampani, *La Cisl tra integrazione europea e mondializzazione. Profilo storico del "sindacato nuovo" nelle relazioni internazionali: Dalla Conferenza di Londra al Trattato di Amsterdam* (Rome: Edizioni Lavoro, 2000).

du Travail (CGT) and the Italian Confederazione Generale Italiana del Lavoro (CGIL), both members of the Soviet-backed World Federation of Trade Unions (WFTU), which had previously attempted to block the Common Market and shown an interest in the creation of a Third World trade union, began to move closer to the Community by the end of the decade, after that body had demonstrated such extraordinary growth in production, and to consider it a credible forum in which to confront the business world.[79]

Initially it was the Soviets who attacked the creation of the EC as a device for the self-preservation of its capitalist member nations. It was no coincidence that their attacks intensified between 1961 and 1962, amid the heightened tensions of the Cold War and the construction of the Berlin Wall, symbol of the division of Europe. In this context the Western efforts at integration represented by the EC signaled a disturbing trend in international politics for Soviet leaders, and especially for eastern European communists.

At the beginning of the 1960s the Soviet government began a concerted effort with each individual member state of the Community to determine the treatment that would be reserved for Soviet and eastern European products in the light of the construction of the Common Market. Threats of retaliation were carefully calibrated to each specific bilateral relationship, with the express goal of dividing the Six and creating fissures at the precise moment when Kennedy was proposing a new transatlantic partnership. The country that experienced the strongest pressure was France, in the effort to detach it from the ongoing integration process. This was the diagnosis given by a panel of experts to the Council of Ministers:

> The USSR portrays itself as the spokesman of the People's Democracies, which, as exporters of industrial and agricultural products (while the USSR primarily exports commodities), feel particularly threatened by the creation of the Common Market.[80]

The Soviets launched similar attacks through their initiatives to strengthen their relationship with the countries of the Third World. In the official letter of September 17, 1962 with which the Soviet Foreign Minister Andrei Gromyko asked the United Nations to call for an immediate conference on international trade reform—which would ultimately become UNCTAD—Moscow's strongest words were reserved for the European Community, defined as a "closed group" primarily responsible for the discriminatory terms of global commerce.[81] In a March 1963 interview with a Brazilian daily, Khrushchev expounded the well-known theory that suggested the industrialized Western nations were imperialist powers which needed "appendages" to supply them with raw materials.[82] He added that, accord-

---

[79] I. Del Biondo, *L'Europa possibile. La Cgt e la Cgil di fronte al processo di integrazione europea* (Rome: Ediesse, 2007).

[80] HAEU, CM 2–1962, 1078, "Aide-Mémoire, Problèmes posés par le projet de declaration soviet-ique concernant la cooperation économique internationale présenté dans la cadre de l'ONU (Résumé des échanges des vues intervenes en cette matière au sein du Groupe de travail de relations extérieures)," February 21, 1962.

[81] HAEU, CM 2–1962, 1078, lettera a Émile Noël con allegato, September 22, 1962.

[82] HAEU, CEAB 05/1996/1, "Extrait de l'interview accordée par M. Kroutchev a la *Hultima Hora* de Rio de Janeiro, March 29 and 30, 1963."

ing to the most careful economic statistics, the Latin American countries lost roughly US$1.5 million annually because of the difference in the price of manufactures and raw materials, and upped the ante by claiming that in the the previous decade Western aid to Latin America had failed to equal the amount lost to the decline in the prices of raw materials. The USSR sought in this way to shift attention from what was likely its primary goal in reopening talks on international trade: Re-stimulating the flow of goods between eastern and western Europe.

For their part the nations of Latin America, among the strongest supporters of the Geneva Conference albeit far from falling under the spell of international communism, also sided openly against European integration. In the Altagracia Charter,[83] signed at the conclusion of a coordinating meeting of Latin American nations in preparation for the first UNCTAD, the trade agreements between the EC and the African states came under heavy criticism, with the charter calling for their abolition or, in any case, some form of compensation for the alteration of international exchange.[84]

The newly independent nations were beginning to take an interest in the global economy, and the Community had immediately been put in the dock. And it was not only the Soviets, or the G77 nations, that attacked the EC for its role in the international economy.

The primary role assumed by the European Commission was thus to defend integration. Accordingly, it attempted to gather together all the charges leveled at the EC, and to deploy all its persuasive diplomatic tools and counterarguments in response. One inventory of such criticisms listed some forty-three possible offenses, along with their respective defenses. The accusations ranged widely: That the Community constituted nothing more than the economic arm of NATO; that it was dominated by the church and the Catholic parties; that it widened regional disparities potentially generated by the Common Market; and that the CAP would impoverish small farmers to the advantage of large agribusiness.[85] In the negotiations leading up to the first UNCTAD it had been decided that only four policy areas should be subjected to the joint coordination and decision of the Six. It was not a coincidence that all four were areas the Six sought to defend: The CAP, the Common Market, the Yaoundé Convention, and the association agreements with Greece and Turkey.[86]

At the GATT ministerial meeting of May 1963 the British government—whose admission to the EC had been rejected by France only shortly before—presented a ten-point Action Programme which called for the liberalization of world trade across all sectors. This program greatly resembled a similar document already

[83] NA, FO 371/178085, British Embassy, Santiago, April 24, 1964.

[84] HAEU, CM 2–1964, 841, Commission, "Memorandum élaboré au vue de la Conférence des Nations Unies sur le Commerce et Développement," March 23, 1964.

[85] HAEU, CM 2–1962, 122, Note, "Critiques à l'égard de la Communauté dans le cadre des Nations Unies," November 8, 1961.

[86] HAEU, CM 2–1964, 845, Note, "Procédures suivant lesquelles les points de vue de la Communauté et des Etats members seront exprimés lors de la Conférence Mondiale de l'ONU sur le Commerce et le Développement," February 19, 1964.

presented by the developing countries to GATT, of which India had been the primary signatory.[87] The British strategy was to bypass UNCTAD and use GATT to
address several of the problems advanced by the Global South:

> We think that the Action Programme is important not only with respect to the Rus-
> sians, but also as a demonstration of the practical work that GATT is doing to help
> the Less Developed Countries. We think we should not be forced to adopt a less liberal
> stance simply because the EEC is not with us. We place our faith in the fact that the
> most liberal elements in the EEC will be aided by the continual pressures on the EEC
> to assume a more liberal attitude.[88]

In the event, the Six succeeded in finding the cohesion necessary to oppose an
Anglo-American policy that, in the name of solidarity with the developing world,
threatened the Common Agricultural Policy and thus risked endangering one of
the very pillars of integration.[89] The European Commission, so often described as
an institutional monolith, was and remains today a collegial body subject to various pressures. In fact, while the remarks of Jean Rey, Commissioner for External
Relations, reflected an effort to find potential points of accommodation with the
requests emerging from the Third World, the German president Walter Hallstein
demonstrated the impact of a culture—widely shared among the leadership of a
postwar Germany strongly opposed to Nazi centralization—that viewed the free
market as a strategic tool for development and the reduction of poverty. In a 1965
speech Hallstein, dismissing every inconvenient argument in favor of trade preferences and the organization of raw materials markets, outlined a plan of action in
complete harmony with American designs:

> The European Economic Community wants to take this opportunity [GATT negotia-
> tions] to promote the productivity and expansion of the economy, to raise the living
> standards of the poorer countries, as well as of the Six, and to bring about a better
> distribution of labor in the world economy by liberating the natural forces of free
> competition.[90]

Edward Heath, who represented the British government at UNCTAD I, recalled
without any undue modesty how the common culture of Oxford men—which
linked the British and Algerian delegations—was decisive in enabling a compromise
with the countries of the South. The British role at Geneva would be to create
sufficient consensus to promote significant tariff reductions in GATT.[91] In 1964,
as we have already mentioned, the Labour Party had returned to power after

[87] NA, Foreign and Commonwealth Office (FCO) 371/172271, "Brief, United Nations Conference for Trade and Development: Second Meeting of the Preparatory Committee, May–June 1963."
[88] NA, FCO 371/178076, "Brief for visit of Sir Patrick Reilly and Mr Golt to Washington, UN
Conference for Trade and Development."
[89] NA, FCO 371/172274, Memorandum, "Preliminary Considerations on items listed in the provisional agenda of the conference," May 24, 1963.
[90] Address by Professor Dr. Walter Hallstein, President of the Commission of the European Economic Community, given at the British Institute of International and Comparative Law, London,
March 25, 1965, 3574/X/65–E. [s.l.]: Commission of the European Economic Community, 1965.
[91] E. Heath, *The Course of My Life. My Autobiography* (London: Hodder & Stoughton, 1988),
p. 604.

fourteen years in opposition. If in domestic policy Labour distinguished itself with important innovations on the terrain of democracy and civil liberties, in foreign policy its new course betrayed a stubbornly optimistic analysis of the room for maneuver open to the UK. Its opposition to efforts to organize commodities markets, an idea put forward by the French and given lukewarm support by the other countries of the Community, derived from its very different conception of its past relationships with former colonies. Great Britain had not conceived of its colonial sphere of influence as an economic bloc divided into producers of manufactured goods and raw materials, and in this sense was heavily critical of Yaoundé: "The new convention represents the acceptance on the part of France's partners in the EEC of the principles and practices of French colonial economic policy."[92] The British also accused the French of having influenced their partners in the Common Market by threatening to block the course of integration. It was believed that by attacking the association policy of the Community in an international gathering it would be possible to modify it for the future:

> If Part IV of the Treaty of Rome did not exist, it would have been much more difficult for France to bury the GATT Action Programme in 1963…If it doesn't concern us to see the Six support French ideas rather than our own, if we don't dislike it that the Six accept special responsibilities towards Africa, that's all well and good. But if we don't like to lose, and we have our own ideas that we want to prevail, then we certainly might adopt a less ineffectual strategy.[93]

One of London's primary concerns was to avoid concessions on the increase of funds for development aid. The government feared being constrained to allocate resources desperately needed for domestic use.

Countervailing pressures did exist, particularly within British public opinion, which favored cooperation with the South. It should suffice to recall how in 1953 Wilson himself had given to the press a book on the war on poverty, in which he had posited that some 3 percent of British GDP should be earmarked for such a battle.[94] But times had changed, the resuscitation of the empire had failed, and London sought to avoid all discussion of development aid and the form this should take.[95] In this respect there were also notable differences not only with the French, who had no difficulty accepting an aid target of 1 percent of GDP—particularly since it had already surpassed that mark by 1964—but with other Community nations like the Netherlands that placed a heavy priority on aid as a motor for development.

While trade among the states of the Community grew both inside the Common Market and with third parties, Great Britain continued to wrestle with balance of

[92] NA, FO 172282, "Memorandum, Association of African Territories."

[93] NA, FO 371/178077, "Brief on the EEC and Developing Countries for the UN Trade Conference."

[94] H. Wilson, *The War on World Poverty* (London: Gollancz, 1953).

[95] NA, FO 371/172268, Cabinet, GATT Policy Committee, "United Nations Conference for Trade and Development," January 1963.

payments problems. In 1964 it was forced to introduce a special 15 percent surtax on all imports, and in 1967 to make the humiliating decision to devalue the pound by 14.3 percent—which also implied, of course, a consequent decline in the value of British development aid.[96] If Community imports from the developing countries grew in the course of the 1960s, in England such imports dropped from 37 to 24 percent from the beginning to the end of the decade. Accompanying the British loss of economic weight was the symbolic military retreat from its bases east of Suez,[97] a decision taken in 1967 by Wilson, who thereby bid Britain's imperial role in the Middle East a formal farewell.[98]

France's first reaction to the preparations for UNCTAD was defensive: The government feared that the conference might reopen debates over the CAP and the Yaoundé Convention, which had been depicted as a neocolonial imposition. Discussions on preferences for manufactured goods left Paris cold, and the widespread thinking throughout the Quai d'Orsay was that they would privilege only four or five relatively developed countries: India, Brazil, Egypt, and Pakistan (*sic*) chief among them.[99] The French government was at the front of the line in opposing the conference, and actually chided their Dutch colleagues for their weakness.[100] France found itself in the position of having to respond to the threat posed by the ten-point program announced by the British Prime Minister Macmillan in the GATT negotiations, which, according to the analysis of French diplomats, was receiving broad support:

> The elimination of these "obstacles" would seem to be the primary concern on the commercial plane of the underdeveloped countries not associated with the EEC. There seems to be no doubt about the fact that their delegates have been for the most part seduced by liberal doctrine, the influence of which is beginning to assume all the features of intoxication.[101]

It was at the GATT ministerial conference of 1963, and later again at the second reunion of the UNCTAD preparatory commission, that the French government elaborated its economic strategy for the Third World, aimed at countering the spread of this "liberal intoxication," which would go by the name "organization of markets." In essence, the French strategy recycled a principle and a plan that Paris had long put into practice in its colonies.[102] The fundamental idea was that to increase incomes in the commodity-producing nations it was not enough simply to

[96] G. Mammarella, *Storia d'Europa dal 1945 ad oggi* (Bari: Laterza, 1995), p. 325.

[97] J. Tomlinson, "The Commonwealth, the Balance of Payments and the Politics of International Poverty: British Aid Policy 1958–1971," in (2003) 4 *Contemporary European History*, p. 415.

[98] R. von Albertini, *La decolonizzazione: Il dibattito sull'amministrazione e l'avvenire delle colonie tra il 1919 e il 1960* (Turin: Società editrice internazionale, 1971), p. xiii.

[99] AMAEF, NUOI, Carton 998, "Question de la convocation d'une Conférence internationale chargée d'examiner les problèmes du commerce," 1962.

[100] AMAEF, NOUI, Carton 998, Note, "Instructions pour la delegation française au Comité preparatoire de la CNUCED," January 1963.

[101] AMAEF, NOUI, Carton 998, "Deuxième session du Comité préparatoire de la Conférence mondiale pour le commerce et le développement (Géneve May 22–June 28, 1963)," July 10, 1963.

[102] By 1962 a serious debate had begun in journals close to diplomatic and governmental circles regarding the possible creation of international stabilization funds for raw materials: See G. Ardant,

open to them the markets of the industrialized countries. The French position was developed further in an important memorandum of February 1964. It recognized that there were significant imbalances in world trade that adversely affected the prices of primary resources.[103] For tropical industries, exclusively the domain of the South, it was vital to determine an appropriate price, below which there would have to be intervention by transferring resources directly to the producer nations (the principle behind the CAP). As for developing countries' requests to increase exports of their own manufactures, the French proposal was to follow the lead of the European Community which, to avoid the loss of international liquidity, had chosen regional integration and the reciprocal rise of exports. That is, the poor nations would have to intensify trade among themselves rather than count solely on imports from industrialized countries.

The American ambassador in Paris came away impressed not only by the appeal of the French proposals, but also by their internal contradictions: "when the LDCs declare themselves in favor of the organization of markets, at the same time they demand the abolition of customs barriers."[104] The organization of markets clearly had its limits. Primary among them was that it potentially affected all commodities except the agricultural products of which France was a primary producer and which were defended in Europe by the CAP. It was justly noted that "the usual tactic of the French consists of pointing out those elements of French policy which agree with the demands of the Third World (aid, the organization of markets) while hiding behind the EEC on more controversial matters (protectionism)."[105] Notwithstanding his much-discussed trip to Latin America in 1964, when he spoke Castilian Spanish and incited the crowds with the phrase "marchamos mano en la mano," de Gaulle's Thirdworldism did not envisage the new nations playing a meaningful role as a real interlocutor with the traditional great powers.

THE ALGIERS CHARTER

We have already seen how the years 1966 and 1967 were full of dark omens for the developing countries. In 1965 Sukarno's regime in Indonesia, which had sponsored the Bandung Conference and contributed to the birth of the Non-Aligned Movement, was overthrown and replaced with a "pro-Western" military dictatorship. In 1966 Nkrumah died, and with him the primary—and increasingly the only—supporter of African unity and autonomy. We have already mentioned the death of Che Guevara in Bolivia in 1967, during his effort to export the Cuban

"La réforme des échanges internationaux par la création d'un fonds de stabilization des matières premières," in (1962) 9–10 *Tiers Monde*, pp. 115–41.

[103] HAEU, CEAB 05, 2016, "Aide-mémoire du gouvernement français sur certaines questions a l'ordre du jour de la Conférence des nations unies sur le commerce et le développement," February 14, 1964.

[104] National Archives and Records Administration (NARA), Central Policy Files (CPF), FT3, Box 962, Paris Embassy, "UNCTAD—French Reaction," July 8, 1964.

[105] Adda and Smouts, *La France face au Sud*, p. 123.

revolution to South America. The American intervention in Vietnam, which expanded massively after the Gulf of Tonkin incident in 1964, also grew in intensity, as did feelings of revulsion for US foreign policy and the South Vietnamese government. But, at least until the North Vietnamese Tet Offensive of 1968, the most vitriolic criticism of American military action came primarily from the Soviet bloc of states, while in the West such critics remained at the margins of society. With the notable exception of de Gaulle, busy breathing life into his "empire of words," most European governments prudently avoided openly contradicting the propaganda emanating from Washington, which portrayed its Marines valiantly defending the cause of the free world in Southeast Asia. Even the Socialist International, divided between the British, Dutch, and Danish on one side, and the more critical Italians and Swedes on the other, "barred any consideration" of the issue at its 1966 Stockholm Congress.[106]

The impression of Western technological and tactical superiority was particularly striking following the shocking swiftness of the Israeli victory in the Six Days' War. The Israeli offensive began on June 5, 1967 with an incursion against Egyptian air bases, and within less than a week the Israeli army had occupied several strategic positions within Egypt's allies Jordan and Syria. The Israeli Defense Force also occupied the holy city of Jerusalem. The Israeli *Blitzkrieg* demonstrated the military strength of a Western army in the open field, but at the same time it created the conditions for the radicalization of the Palestinian nationalist movement, which could now claim to be fighting for the liberation of the "occupied territories." On this occasion the European powers once more sided against Nasser, who the press continued to depict as the "Egyptian Hitler," assisted in this portrait by his calls for the annihilation of Israel which Egyptian radio had broadcast shortly before the onset of hostilities. In France, strange bedfellows like Mitterrand and Giscard d'Estaing, or Sartre and Raymond Aron, found themselves side by side signing petitions and disseminating appeals in favor of Israel.[107] But even here, as Tony Judt noted—and as we shall see in the next chapter—the contradictions implicit in such views would soon make themselves apparent:

> The Old European Left had always thought of Israel, with its long-established Labor leaders, its disproportionately large public sector, and its communitarian experience, as "one of us." In the rapidly shifting political and ideological currents of the late 1960s and early 1970s, however, Israel was something of an anomaly. The New Left, from Berlin to Berkeley, was concerned less with exploited workers and more with the victims of colonialism and racism.[108]

[106] G. Devin, "L'Internationale Socialiste face à la guerre du Vietnam," in C. Goscha and M. Vaïsse (eds), *La guerre du Vietnam et l'Europe (1963–1973)* (Brussels: Bruylant, 2003), pp. 215–22.

[107] H. Laurens, "1967: A War of Miscalculation and Misjudgment," trans. Krystyna Horko, in *Le Monde Diplomatique*, English edition (June 2007). Available online at <http://mondediplo.com/2007/06/09warofmiscalculation>.

[108] T. Judt, *Reappraisals. Reflections on the Forgotten Twentieth Century* (London: Vintage Books, 2008), p. 280.

Nasser, a leader of the Non-Aligned Movement who had enjoyed great prestige from his victory at Suez, emerged discredited as a regional interlocutor in the Arab world, although he remained popular with his countrymen. With him the vision of a secular, socialist pan-Arabism appeared in decline. The Arab countries found themselves rudderless; the oil blockade of Arab oil producers had failed its purpose, while at the fourth summit of the League of Arab States held in Khartoum the moderate line captained by Saudi Arabia, fundamentally opposed to any rise in oil prices, emerged triumphant.[109]

The 1950s and 1960s had been important decades for industrial development in Latin America. Between 1945 and 1973, Mexico's productive capacity quadrupled, that of Brazil grew eight times. The largest Latin American countries, from Brazil to Chile, Argentina to Venezuela, had undergone extraordinary socioeconomic structural changes: Between 61 and 81 percent of their inhabitants now lived in urban areas, while the industrial sector had grown to employ between 30 and 42 percent of their workforces. But this development had come at the price of a vigilant protection of national industry from foreign competition, a dwindling presence on world export markets, a neglect of the agricultural sector, and a tolerance for high levels of social inequality.[110] Overall, with the exception of countries like South Korea or Taiwan, which had concentrated on developing an economy based primarily on exports, the economic outlook for the developing world appeared no more rosy than its political situation. In a 1967 study, an MIT economist noted with exaggerated emphasis the structural weakness of the South's economies: The industrial world could do without its commodities and, given time, could even learn to replicate the taste of coffee; new oil deposits were being discovered, for example those in the North Sea, that would make the West less dependent on its oil reserves; the industrialized countries were already self-sufficient in food production, and agreements on sugar cane between Cuba and the USSR were not replicable for other goods; in short, the only countries of the South that held any hopes for development were its largest nations, like India, and its largest oil producers, like Algeria. Overall, the American economist concluded, "the South is becoming irrelevant for the economies of the industrialized nations."[111] This interpretation would prove incorrect, and failed to take into consideration just how much the growth in industrialized countries still owed to imports of raw materials and commodities. But the comments were nevertheless indicative of a widespread sentiment among international economic experts.

What was really occurring was the onset of differentiation within the developing world. In almost all the countries of the South, democratic experiments were giving way to authoritarian temptations, whether these were motivated by social

---

[109] E. Rogan, *The Arabs. A History* (New York: Basic Books, 2009), pp. 363–4.

[110] Frieden, *Global Capitalism*, p. 308; L. Zanatta, *Storia dell'America Latina contemporanea* (Bari: Laterza, 2010), pp. 144–90.

[111] Miguel Wionczek (ed.), *Economic Cooperation in Latin America, Africa, and Asia* (Cambridge, MA: MIT Press, 1969), p. 3.

progressivism or, more likely, conservatism. Some nations with close ties to the US, like Brazil and South Korea, placed their hopes on investment in export-leading industries. Others continued to invest in the development of domestic markets. Whatever their goals, such industrialization also produced dramatic social tensions, income inequalities, and the haphazard creation of mega-cities that were unable to offer jobs and services to all their citizens, with greater or lesser capacity to attract aid and private investment.[112]

The charismatic and organizational void left by the absence of the historical leaders of the Non-Aligned Movement could not be filled by Soviet support. Although it conducted an active foreign policy in the areas of technical and military assistance, the USSR had decided to focus its influence on a select few strategic nations, rather than give blanket support to the South. At the meeting of Central Committee that deposed Khrushchev in October 1964, the ousted premier was criticized for having squandered Soviet resources on foreign aid, which committed it to some 6,000 projects around the world at an exorbitant cost to the economy.[113] In January 1967, the Soviet Foreign Minister Andrei Gromyko stated openly that conflict with the capitalist world was not inevitable, and that it was necessary to concentrate Moscow's scant resources on the most progressive and promising nations for international communism, states like Algeria, Egypt, Guinea, and the Congo.[114] Khrushchev's optimistic crusade against the Western world, conducted with some support within the United Nations, was followed by a lower-profile attitude under the new General Secretary of the Soviet Communist Party, Leonid Brezhnev. Consolidating his leadership at a moment of heightened tensions within the communist world, during the conflict between the Soviet Union and China, Brezhnev returned Moscow to the path of realism and its more traditional course of power politics: Negotiations with the United States, and trade relationships with western Europe (such as the 1966 accord with the Italian automobile maker Fiat). In conversation with Prebisch, the Soviet Minister for Foreign Trade pledged Moscow's support for the cause of Third World unity. They agreed upon the need to combat the European Community's regional trade preferences, but otherwise Moscow was completely indifferent to the G77's principal demands for commodities agreements and preferences for manufactures, reiterating that the underdeveloped nations should invest primarily in heavy industry—an area where the USSR could lend real technical assistance.[115] Soviet leadership believed that the main contribution the South could make to the cause of world peace and prosperity was to support the reopening of trade between eastern and western Europe, in order to provide the Soviet Union with greater liquidity to import goods from the G77 countries.

---

[112] For a good synthesis of the economic evolution of the developing world see B. Droz and A. Rowley, *Storia del XX Secolo. Sviluppo e independenza (1950–1973)* (Florence: Sansoni, 1989).

[113] Andrew, *The World Was Going Our Way*, p. 7.

[114] A. Dobrynin, *In Confidence. Moscow's Ambassador to America's Six Cold War Presidents 1962–1986* (New York: Random House, 1995), p. 642.

[115] United Nations Office in Geneva (UNOG), UNCTAD, ARR 40/2344B8, "Record of Dr Prebisch's conversation with the Minister for Foreign Trade of the USSR Mr N.S. Patolichev, Moscow, July 27, 1967."

Equally worrisome for the South at the second UNCTAD—held at New Delhi in 1968—was the revelation of the delicate economic state of the two great post–Second World War Western powers, the United States and the United Kingdom. British balance-of-payments problems and the consequent weakness of the pound have already been discussed. Even more important was the crisis facing the American dollar. The financing of the Vietnam War, the constant shrinking of the country's positive trade balance, as well as the continuous leaking of capital for investments had left the dollar dependent upon the support of the other Western nations. America's increasingly negative balance of payments was especially hard on the developing countries, as it made any generous trade or development aid concessions by Washington extremely unlikely. Already by the beginning of 1965 criticisms were being voiced in Europe, and especially in France, of the manner in which the dollar was being used to finance Washington's political and military hegemony—what is known in economic jargon as the "power of seignorage."[116] Midway through the 1960s, however, the monetary battle was above all a battle to harness the power of western Europe, which in fact succeeded in winning veto power over all-important decisions of the IMF.[117] The proposal had already been made to institute a new reserve currency to flank the troubled dollar, so-called Special Drawing Rights (SDRs), to be disbursed in relation to an improvement in development aid, which had been in steady decline and increasingly tied to imports from the donor nation. To all such efforts the members of the European Community erected a unified wall of opposition.[118]

On June 30, 1967 the GATT negotiations known as the Kennedy Round came to a close. This was the site of an important demonstration of strength by the European Community, represented in the trade negotiations by the European Commission. Intense debate continues to this day between economists and historians over which of the two sides of the Atlantic proved the more able negotiator.[119]

---

[116] Robert Triffin cites the arguments made by General de Gaulle at a February 1965 press conference:

> Why should the two richest countries of the world be allowed to monopolize the benefits of international-reserve creation for the financing of their own deficits? Why should the Bank of France be expected to participate—by its purchases of dollars—in the financing of United States policies in which France has no voice and with which she might be in fundamental disagreement? Are not the United States deficits ascribable, at least in part, to the flurry of United States private investments abroad (substituting United States for French ownership), to United States assistance to Chiang Kai-shek, to the escalation of the war in Southeast Asia, and so on?

R. Triffin, *Our International Monetary System: Yesterday, Today, and Tomorrow* (New York: Random House, 1968), p. 108. For a fine summary of the main points of the dollar crisis and the end of the Bretton Woods system see B. Eichengreen, *Globalizing Capital: A History of the International Monetary System* (Princeton, NJ: Princeton University Press, 1996), pp. 125–36.

[117] T. Ferguson, *The Third World and the Decision Making in the International Monetary Fund* (London: Pinter Publishers, 1988), p. 137.

[118] D. Caviglia and G. Garavini, "Generosi ma non troppo. La Cee, i Paesi in via di sviluppo e i negoziati sulla riforma del Sistema monetario internazionale (1958–1976)," in E. Calandri (ed.), *Il primato sfuggente. L'Europa e l'intervento per lo sviluppo (1957–2007)* (Milan: Franco Angeli, 2009), pp. 53–89.

[119] T. Cohn, *Governing Global Trade. International Institutions in Conflict and Convergence* (Burlington, VT: Ashgate, 2002); L. Coppolaro, "US Payments Problems and the Kennedy Round of GATT Negotiations 1961–1967," in D.M. Andrews (ed.), *Orderly Change: International Monetary Relations Since Bretton Woods* (Ithaca, NY: Cornell University Press, 2008), pp. 120–38.

Whatever the answer, two things are certain. The first is that the Community succeeded in remaining united during one of its first international tests, defending the CAP, and that it maintained this cohesion at a particularly delicate time for the fate of integration. The second is that the clear losers of the Kennedy Round were the developing countries, which pressed in vain for a decision on trade preferences for their manufactures, or at least for the abolition of import barriers to tropical goods. The European Agricultural Commissioner, Sicco Mansholt, alone underscored the limits and risks of purely commercial agreements that ignored more complex questions related to development.[120]

Considering the political and economic weakness of the developing world, it was by no means a given that the Asian, African, and Latin American countries would succeed in elaborating a common line before the second UNCTAD. Criticism of the G77 was not in short supply, particularly from other UN bodies like the Food and Agriculture Organization (FAO) in which the industrialized countries had greater weight, and which were competent to address the relevant issues. The FAO's directors did not hide their skepticism at G77 attacks on the CAP or the Group's hopes of using the forum to reach accords that would entail a rise in commodities prices.[121]

Different strategies were emerging behind the South's united front. The African nations, which were almost exclusively exporters of raw materials, had little interest in preferences for manufactures, and asked above all for the deployment of any type of aid to help them industrialize. Those nations with ties to the Community, which already maintained privileged relationships with the Six, requested adequate compensation in exchange for their acceptance of the extension of a system of preferences for all the countries of the South.[122] The Asian nations, led by India, spent their energies trying to obtain as wide a system of preferences as possible, and to this end were willing to act as go-between for the most radical delegations. The Indian ambassador in 1964 had even let it be understood by the American government that, should the GATT regulations be relaxed, India was prepared to negotiate in that forum and relegate UNCTAD to secondary importance.[123] The Latin American states, meanwhile, were interested in both the question of commodities and that of trade preferences. For Prebisch, in particular, the primary goal was to avoid the consolidation of large regional economic blocs that would handcuff Latin America to the United States, Africa to the European Community, and Southeast Asia to Japan.[124] Such an outcome would have entailed the disintegration

---

[120] UNOG, UNCTAD, ARR 40/2344B7, H. Mathias to Dr Raúl Prebisch, "Important differences of view between Mr Rey and Mr Mansholt regarding the results of the Kennedy Round and future action that might be taken," Geneva, July 18, 1967.

[121] Food and Agriculture Organization Archives (FAO), 12 ESC, UN 29/1, D'Amico, "UNCTAD paper on the development of an International Commodity Policy," September 21, 1967.

[122] NARA, CPF, FT3, Box 958, Report of the US Delegation of the Fourth Session of the UNCTAD Conference, September 23, 1966.

[123] NARA, CPF, FT3, Box 961, Memcon, UNCTAD (Indian Ambassador and Under-Secretary Ball in New Delhi), August 22, 1964.

[124] HAEU, CM 2–1965, Conseil, Note d'Information, "Examen des problèmes concernant la prochaine reunion du Comité special des preferences de l' UNCTAD," May 4, 1965. The European Commission representative expressed skepticism at multilateral preferences, and indicated that "to resolve the problem for the three developing continents, each of the industrialized blocs (US, EEC, Japan) could create a network of preferences along a North–South axis on the basis of the demands presented by each of the three continents (Africa, Latin America, Asia)."

of the South's united front, and for Latin America would have meant the inevitable return beneath the yoke of subordination to the dictates of Washington.

Notwithstanding these significant differences, the states of the South continued to reinforce the institutional mechanisms for their continued cooperation. In 1965 the Council for Trade and Development, UNCTAD's largest internal body, met for the first time, and within it the thirty-one states of the developing world set up a coordinating committee.[125] In 1966 the Asian, African, and Latin American regional economic committees of the UN agreed to organize a joint conference at ministerial level for the following year, to reconcile their differences in light of the approaching UNCTAD meeting at New Delhi.

This conference was to take place in Algiers and was designed to map out the final guidelines for the G77;[126] it would also demonstrate the pattern of negotiations that would characterize the South's preparations: Meeting before UNCTAD in regional assemblies, and then in a joint assembly at ministerial level, the highest echelon of the G77, where a strategic document would be drafted for presentation to the industrialized countries.

The Algiers ministerial conference was held from October 10–25, 1967 in an atmosphere of extreme tension. Though Cuba had been denied admission by the veto of the other Latin American states, in the hopes of dampening any anti-imperial rhetoric, such polemics erupted instead against the delegation from South Vietnam. The fundamental principle around which Prebisch had shaped UNCTAD was that negotiations and debates should concentrate only on international economic structures, and not on the domestic politics of individual Third World member states. But the war in Vietnam had begun to cause radicals to dig in their heels against Washington and its allies. Vociferous American protests could not prevent the South Vietnamese delegation from first being forced to abandon their residential quarters, under the pretext of threats to their safety, and finally to leave Algiers altogether.[127]

It was the Algerian president Hourari Boumedienne who sought to repair the damage. He had come to power in 1965, after a military coup overthrew the first leader of an independent Algeria, Ahmed Ben Bella.[128] In contrast to his predecessor, Boumedienne was not a politician capable of exciting the masses; he lacked the rousing charisma of the stump speaker. His military coup had been received with indifference by the leaders of the developing nations, in particular those of the African and Arab world who had come to admire Ben Bella as a symbol of resistance to the French. He was considered more of a technocrat or a military man than a pure politician, without the close ties his predecessor had enjoyed with the USSR.

---

[125] Sauvant, *The Group of 77*, pp. 27–59.

[126] NA, FO 371/19006, Note, "Preparation for the Second Session of the Conference," September 23, 1966.

[127] NARA, CPF, FT3, Box 957, Director of Intelligence and Research to the Secretary, "The Pre-UNCTAD Meeting," October 13, 1967.

[128] G.P. Calchi Novati, *Storia dell'Algeria indipendente: Dalla guerra di liberazione al fondamentismo islamico* (Milan: Bompiani, 1998); B. Stora, *Histoire de la guerre d'Algérie* (Paris: La Découverte, 2004).

His critics in the Arab world, however, overlooked the fact that, in contrast with many other Algerian leaders, including Ben Bella, Boumedienne had not been educated in French schools, and had instead completed his university studies in Cairo. The Egyptian defeat in the Six Days' War had brought out his latent Arab nationalism, and indeed it was from the humiliation of the Arab armies that he drew the inspiration to immerse himself in politics and become one of the most authoritative and radical heads of the Arab world.[129]

Boumedienne opened the Algiers conference with a violent attack on both the West and the Soviet Union, criticizing the politics of peaceful coexistence between the two superpowers for justifying the subjection of the rest of the world.[130] On the specific issue of the next UNCTAD, in contrast to the African and Latin American delegations he argued against relying on the healing powers of commodity price stabilization. An eventual rise in commodity prices would in fact play into the hands of the West, since ownership of the industries responsible for extraction and transformation of such raw materials was entirely in their hands. The real aim of the South's struggle should be to reappropriate the wealth of its land and develop industries capable of transforming raw materials on the spot. If price stabilization talks were necessary, he continued, they should include in the final document a signal to open discussions on petroleum prices. In 1967 there did not seem to be any consensus in favor of such a radical program implying "internal" structural modifications, with the exception of China, which at any rate was not welcomed as a member of the Group of 77.

Instead, the item on which the representatives of the Third World could find agreement was the Algiers Charter, the final document of the G77 ministerial conference.[131] In essence, the document outlined a compromise between the Latin American position, which demanded the abolition of special preferences, and that of the African delegates, who requested adequate compensation in exchange for an eventual abolition of their special preferences with the EC. Its evaluation of the state of the global economy drew largely on the Prebisch Report of 1964, and if anything even emphasized that report's pessimism with the reminder that three years had passed since the first UNCTAD without clear signs of a narrowing of the gap between North and South. While the global annual income level of the average citizen had risen by US$60 in that time, in the developing world wages had actually fallen by US$2. Purchasing power of exports from the developing world was declining at a rate of approximately US$2.5 billion a year, and only half of this decline was being compensated for by public aid from the developed nations.

---

[129] On the Algerian international discourse, see J.J. Byrne, "Our Own Special Brand of Socialism: Algeria and the Contest of Modernities in the 1960s," in (2009) 33(9) *Diplomatic History*, pp. 427–47.

[130] AMAEF, NOUI, Carton 10000, Ambassade de France en Algérie, "Conférence des 77 à Alger," October 30, 1967: "Colonel Boumedienne's speech, which contrasted the wealthy North with the poor South, mainly irritated the ambassadors from eastern Europe. Their disappointment was even greater at the end of the conference, given that all the members of the G77 accepted his proposed plan." Boumedienne, according to French diplomats, had spoken against "peaceful coexistence" at the expense of the South, and advanced "*ultragauchiste*" ideas.

[131] Charte d'Alger, Adoptée par la Reunion ministérielle du Groupe des 77, October 24, 1967.

Added to all this was the crushing weight of debt, which had grown from US$10 billion in 1955 to US$40 billion in 1966. In terms of potential solutions, the G77 proposed progressively eliminating barriers on raw materials and studying various price stabilization mechanisms. At the same time—backed by the AASM—it was proposed to undertake a study of the possible consequences of an eventual abolition of preferences on certain goods in order to mitigate any potential negative effects. General preferences on manufactures were requested but, again with African backing, it was declared that the most underdeveloped states would receive special consideration. The other important request was to fix development aid at 1 percent of the industrialized states' GDP.

The Charter was presented to the most important Western nations by a special "goodwill mission" designed to alert leaders to the concerns of the G77. The name given to the mission was not an accident: To obtain satisfaction for their demands the developing nations would need a great deal of goodwill on the part of the developed world.

Negotiations among the Western nations were proceeding at the same time within the OECD, rather than in the commission on preferences established by UNCTAD. The United States softened its violently hostile stance against any debate that might threaten the "most favored nation" clause and agreed in 1965 to an OECD study on trade preferences. In an important speech at Punta del Este in April 1967, President Lyndon Johnson declared that America was prepared to discuss generalized preferences.[132] This was a bold American overture before the close of the Kennedy Round, perhaps intended to make the outcome of GATT a pill less bitter to swallow for the countries of the South. The primary motivation of the Democratic administration, however, was fear of the fact that, after its eventual enlargement by the admission of Great Britain, the European Community would become the largest trading power in the world, requiring some form of opposition to its tendency to grant progressively preferential agreements in the Mediterranean and Africa.[133]

On November 30 and December 1 of that year an OECD ministerial conference was held to discuss the question of preferences in the light of the decisions reached by the G77 at Algiers. Johnson had received the green light from the United States Congress to move forward on the issue of preferences, on condition that such mechanisms were opened to all the countries of the South and accompanied by the elimination of inverse preferences by all that held such special preferential systems—which meant the Community.[134] In the OECD meeting the

[132] For a much-discussed book of 1967, dealing specifically with the question of trade preferences for developing countries, see H. Johnson, *Economic Policies Toward Less Developed Countries* (Washington, DC: Brookings Institution, 1967).

[133] Foreign Relations of the United States (FRUS), 1964–1968, Vol. VIII, Memorandum from Secretary of State Rusk to President Johnson, "A New Trade Policy for the United States," Washington, February 11, 1967.

[134] NARA, CPF, FT3, Box 598, Action Memo from Anthony Solomon to The Secretary, "US position on Tariff Preferences for Developing Countries," November 24, 1967.

Western states reached a general agreement on two points: First, the system of preferences would include all the developing countries; second, to protect the AASM countries tied to the Community, special treatment would be reserved for the "less developed," that is for the African states.

The issue most heavily debated before the New Delhi conference was, by far, that of trade preferences.[135] This was a potentially delicate question for the Community, which did not want to concede much in the area of processed agricultural products and which was threatened with the future abolition of inverse preferences. The issue was even more pressing, however, for the Soviet Union: Moscow could not afford to give up anything. The Soviet economy was a planned one, in which the quota of manufactured imports depended exclusively on state decisions, which made it very difficult to adjust to requests for greater imports from the developing countries, given that it had to give precedence to exports from eastern Europe.[136]

A COMMON MARKET WITHOUT A COMMON IDENTITY

The process of European integration as it appeared in the 1960s seemed a primarily commercial project that promoted growth in the productive capacities of six European states—Belgium, France, Italy, Luxembourg, the Netherlands, and the Federal Republic of Germany—binding their economies closer together.[137] Yet, as we have seen, European economic cooperation was also based on a profound and deeply rooted reciprocal distrust.[138] An apparent paradox, described by Joseph Weiler, was created in which the constitutional foundations of economic integration among the Six were steadily reinforced—backed by the decisions of the European Court of Justice in Luxembourg, which favored the free circulation of goods within the Common Market—while national politicians sought to defend their freedom of maneuver by questioning the legitimacy of the stateless bureaucracy in Brussels. The fewer the opportunities that existed to exit the legal web of integration, the more national leaders raised their voice to undermine it.[139] The EC, the institutions of which had assumed greater power and control over certain areas of

---

[135] NA, Bureau of Trade (BT) 241/1868, Paper by Commonwealth Office, "The Question of Preferences," January 1968.

[136] NARA, CPF, FT3, Box 960, Strategy Paper, UNCTAD Trade and Development Board, April 5–23, 1965: "The Soviets will find themselves even more in the same situation as us and the other developed states. They will find the same ingratitude for their aid. And they are even more vulnerable to these attacks than we are when it comes to imports of those goods and commodities that the developing states are capable of exporting."

[137] On the commercial nature of the Common Market, which, until at least 1963, was dominated by high-level pacts and considerations of national political prestige over notions of supranational governance, see A.S. Milward, *The Rise and Fall of a National Strategy, 1945–1963* (London: HMSO, 2002).

[138] Puchala, "Western European Attitudes on International Problems," pp. 266–79.

[139] J.H.H. Weiler, *The Constitution of Europe. "Do the New Clothes Have an Emperor?" and Other Essays on European Integration* (Cambridge: Cambridge University Press, 1999), pp. 10–16.

economic life, thus entered a static phase in terms of political cooperation, as demonstrated by the "empty chair" crisis of 1965, only resolved the following year with the decision by the Six to make all important decisions dependent on unanimous voting.[140] This situation could not but be reflected in the coherence of western European governments' actions in the international arena.

In 1967 Great Britain could no longer claim, as it had at UNCTAD I, to be a credible or reliable partner to the developing countries. It had been forced to make a second application for admission to the European Community, and received another flat refusal by the French. It had been the victim of a grave liquidity crisis, which prevented it from making any type of charitable contribution to Third World nations. The devaluation of sterling that same year had signified not only an admission of the weakness of its economy, with its negative trade balance, but also a net decline in the worth of British development aid. In a speech of March 1967 Edward Heath neatly stated the new British attitude: The United Kingdom had lost its position in the Third World, and the Commonwealth had been transformed from a valuable network of allies into evidence of British inadequacy. The United Kingdom could no longer continue to oppose agreements on raw materials indefinitely, but would have to content itself with pressuring France to accept a wider extension of trade preferences. Its primary objective thus became avoiding the possibility that the East–West standoff might give way to a new conflict based on the economic gap between North and South, and using its remaining influence to persuade its friends in the European Community to this end.[141]

If economic conditions did not permit Great Britain to play its usual role, and if the war in Vietnam was generating both internal tensions within the United States and international hostility toward its foreign policy, the European Community was also incapable of becoming the primary partner of the Third World states. In contrast with GATT, where the European Commission represented the Six, in UNCTAD Member States shared no such joint representation. Confronted with the emergence of the developing world, the Community revealed itself for what it was: Efficient as an instrument of European economic cooperation, but scarcely credible as a political actor. Every effort to construct a model of integration based on more stringent mechanisms of political or cultural cooperation had been rejected from within. France had been opposed to the creation of a Community budget, to the point of threatening to withdraw from Brussels. European social policy remained purely ancillary, inconsistent with respect to the creation of a free market area devoid of any redistributive character.[142] The proposed creation of a

---

[140] For an explanation of the "empty chair" crisis as an example of this conflict, which constituted an essential element of the model of European integration assumed during the 1960s, see N.P. Ludlow, *The European Community and the Crisis of the 1960s: Negotiating the Gaullist Challenge* (London: Routledge, 2006).

[141] E. Heath, *Old World, New Horizons. Britain, Europe, and the Atlantic Alliance* (Cambridge, MA: Harvard University Press, 1970), p. 66.

[142] L. Mechi, "Le questioni sociali nel processo d'integrazione europea," in *La cittadinanza che cambia. Radici nazionale e prospettiva europea* Annali della Fondazione Giuseppe Di Vittorio (Rome: Ediesse, 2005), pp. 241–58.

European University at Fiesole (near Florence), which would throw a veil of culture over a predominantly economic body, had not gotten anywhere.[143]

The politics of national prestige remained extremely important, as did the ambitions of its Member States to compete against each other for dominant positions in Third World markets. Aid distributed by European states remained primarily of a bilateral nature, and tended to be "linked" to—or directly financed by—exports. While US government aid steadily declined in the years from 1965–70, the importance of aid from large European states like France and Germany steadily grew, as to an even greater degree did the contributions of emerging donors like Canada, Denmark, Sweden, and Holland, all of which placed more emphasis on multilateral assistance.[144] The President of the World Bank, George Woods, pushed hard for a greater contribution to multilateral aid from the European powers, especially Germany. The German government, however, barricaded itself behind its special relationship with France, reiterating the importance that both countries placed on bilateral aid and thus on national politics of cooperation.[145]

The Dutch Foreign Minister Joseph Luns, who headed the Netherlands Foreign Ministry for almost two decades from 1952 to 1971, held the bar of transatlantic foreign policy firmly in favor of Western economic institutions, above all GATT.[146] One of the most salient characteristics of the Dutch economy was its heavy reliance on the import of raw materials to feed important refined goods industries. Through its multinationals—first among them Royal Dutch Shell, the most international of the oil multinationals since it had no oil at home—the Netherlands made considerable foreign investment in the developing world. In the course of the 1950s, one of the Dutch reactions to the end of colonialism had been to institute a program of multilateral development aid. The economist Tinbergen, Nobel Prize winner in 1956, had developed for the Dutch Labor party a plan which called for aid to the South amounting to 1 percent of GDP in addition to its multilateral aid commitments, as well as a project of international trade reform. Dutch aid grew steadily throughout the 1960s. At the same time, however, bilateral aid also increased—as did conditioned aid, which amounted to 90 percent of the total by the end of the 1960s—in addition to foreign direct investment. Dutch relations with the developing nations seemed to move simultaneously in two directions: That of cooperation and aid, which pushed for acceptance of the South's requests for a partial modification of international commercial and financial mechanisms; and that of trade and investment, which pushed for guarantees on foreign investment and promoted the progressive liberalization of world trade. An advertisement

---

[143] S. Paoli, "La politica comunitaria in materia di istruzione nel corso degli anni Sessanta," in L. Leonardi and A. Varsori (eds), *Lo spazio sociale europeo. Atti del convegno internazionale di studi, Fiesole 10–11 ottobre 2003* (Florence: Firenze University Press, 2005).

[144] J. White, *The Politics of Foreign Aid* (London: The Bodley Head, 1974), p. 228.

[145] World Bank Group Archives (WBGA), Records of George Woods, Travel Files, Box 1, Steckham, Mr. Woods' visit to Bonn, January 1968.

[146] E.H. Arens, "Multilateral Institutional-Building and National Interest: Dutch Development Policy in the 1960s," in (2003) 12(4) *Contemporary European History*, pp. 457–72.

by the Anglo-Dutch concern Unilever, aimed at attracting future management candidates, revealed the strong economic interests concealed by an open-minded stance toward the South's demands:

AVIS UNILEVERENSIS (MANAGERIALIS):

Plumage: highly variegated; habits: too numerous to list; habitat: the world; distinctive characteristics: a high flyer. The birds who run Unilever come in many shapes and sizes. For a marketing man, for example, a spell in a sales team in Yorkshire may lead to experience in an advertising agency in London. Later, from London our man may go to Brazil—or Pakistan, or Australia, or to one of many such overseas stations. The Parent Board of Unilever itself and the Management of our 400 companies are peopled by men like this. So, if you are a bird that likes a varied habitat, above all, if you're feathered for flight into the higher realms, Unilever's atmosphere may be congenial to you.[147]

In 1962 the Netherlands had been the only European country to abstain from voting in the General Assembly on the convocation of the first UNCTAD. In the course of the negotiations which preceded the Geneva conference the Dutch government never ceased to push its European partners to assume a more open position toward the developing world, following a line which seemed to renounce any defense of the Community so long as the G77 did not put up for discussion the basis of free trade or some form of automatic global income redistribution. The Netherlands aimed to play the role of mediator between the haves and the have nots.[148]

The Federal Republic of Germany took a tougher line, subordinating its aid policy to both the financing of exports for its ever-efficient industrial base and the application of the "Hallstein Doctrine," which dictated the breaking of relations with any nation which recognized the Communist German Democratic Republic to the East. The application of the Hallstein Doctrine, which led the Federal Republic to cut off diplomatic relations with Egypt and Tanzania, was subject to steadily harsher criticism. But so long as the government was led by the Christian Democrats of Konrad Adenauer, no German leader demonstrated the desire or the political strength to alter its fundamental tenets. As Adenauer remarked, "I don't feel conscious of any moral guilt toward a colored person, I didn't give him the color."[149] At the end of the 1960s, some 80 percent of German aid consisted of bilateral assistance.[150]

Italy lived through some of the contradictions characteristic of the North–South divide. The consistently productive economy of its industrialized north, though weighed down by serious social and educational inequalities, coexisted with a

---

[147] E.P. Thompson, K. Alexander, S. Hall, R. Samuel, and P. Worsley, *Out of Apathy* (London: Stevens, 1960), pp. 45–6.

[148] J. Voorhoeve, *Peace, Profits and Principles. A Study of Dutch Development Policy* (The Hague: Nijhoff, 1979).

[149] W.G. Gray, *Germany's Cold War. The Global Campaign to Isolate East Germany, 1949–1969* (Chapel Hill: The University of North Carolina Press, 2003), p. 120.

[150] S. Lorenzini, *Due Germanie in Africa. La cooperazione allo sviluppo e la competizione per i mercati di materie prime e tecnologia* (Florence: Polistampa, 2003); H.L. Schmidt, "Spinti in prima linea: La politica di cooperazione allo sviluppo della Repubblica federale tedesca (1958–1971)," in L. Tosi and L. Tosone (eds), *Gli aiuti allo sviluppo nelle relazioni internazionali del secondo dopoguerra* (Padua: Cedam, 2006), pp. 111–64.

preindustrial southern *mezzogiorno* that received serial infusions of capital but somehow failed to jump-start the virtuous cycle of growth. At the end of the 1950s a segment of the Christian Democratic leadership had pushed for Italy to establish new relationships with Latin America and the countries of the Mediterranean. This "neo-Atlanticism," which found one of its primary supporters in Prime Minister Amintore Fanfani, represented an effort to play the role of bridge to the Third World without giving up Italy's transatlantic loyalties, indeed while continuing to offer indispensable service to Washington.[151] Rome also worked to promote the birth of a politics of European cooperation that could help it fully exploit its limited financial resources. However, both its idea of wider political cooperation and its Latin American initiative, though supported by Germany and Holland for the opportunity to expand European regional ties beyond Africa, found stiff opposition from French interests. The Italian government committed itself instead—in a decision not without risk for a country in its financial position—to participate in the donor's group within the OECD.[152] Important sectors or large state-run industries, like Enrico Mattei's ENI, had already established agreements that would anticipate the demands subsequently put forward by the developing nations in the coming years. ENI had built five or six refineries and twenty-three distribution networks in Africa under particularly favorable conditions for the producer nations (at least by contemporary standards). The refineries were of mixed ownership, as were the distribution companies. ENI had also invested in technical cooperation, for instance through the Scuola Superiore di Idrocarburi, created to develop managerial talent from the producing nations. Mattei, however, died in 1962 in a plane crash under mysterious circumstances, and his most ambitious plans, like a project to open a university in Florence for students from the Third World—many of which might have created frictions with the United States—were quickly scuttled.[153]

One of the most important developments of the 1960s, the weight of which would be felt well beyond Italian borders, was the Catholic Church's changing attitude toward the Third World. In order to compete with communist influence throughout the decolonized world and within international organizations like the UN, the Vatican was progressively forced to give meaningful support to the Third World cause. In 1963, only a year after the Cuban Missile Crisis had shown the risks of potential nuclear war, Pope John XXIII proclaimed in the encyclical *Pacem in Terris* that war could no longer be considered an instrument of justice, since it could now possibly result in the total destruction of mankind. His successor, Paul VI, not only speeded up the process of adapting to the new society of mass consumption in the industrialized countries but took another notable step forward in the Church's global positioning, increasing from 61 to 109 the number of papal nunciatures and establishing apostolic delegations throughout the world. In

---

[151] A. Brogi, *L'Italia e l'egemonia Americana nel Mediterraneo* (Florence: La Nuova Italia, 1996).

[152] E. Calandri, "Italy's' Foreign Aid Policy 1959–1969," in (2003) 12(4) *Contemporary European History*, pp. 509–25.

[153] M. Colitti, *Energia e sviluppo in Italia: la vicenda di Enrico Mattei* (Bari: De Donato, 1979); B. Bagnato, *Mattei in Morocco* (Florence: Edizioni Polistampa, 2004).

the 1967 encyclical *Populorum Progressio*—which the Italian neo-Fascist Movimento sociale italiano derisively called "*Avanti populorum*" (after the first lines of the Communist anthem "Bandiera Rossa")—the Pope put forth the idea that the only way to work for peace consisted of incentivizing economic development of the poorer nations. The Church also responded positively to initiatives on price stabilization for commodities and the need to fight against racism.[154] The encyclical, the first to be entirely dedicated to economic issues, also referenced UNCTAD: "With all our heart we encourage the organizations which have taken up this call for collaboration for development, and wish that they be granted greater authority."[155]

This interest in the themes of development and reform of international commerce was limited, however, to individual figures in Italian politics, and was certainly far from the collective consciousness of a people in thrall to an economic boom and an unhindered rat race of new consumer pleasures, captured in Dino Risi's 1962 film *Il Sorpasso*. The Italian Mario Pedini, Christian Democratic representative in the European Parliament, was charged with presenting the parliamentary report on UNCTAD in Geneva as well as that of New Delhi in 1968. In both cases Pedini's report expressed disappointment that the European Community did not have a common representation and that its member states held different positions on important issues. Pedini had been a Europeanist since his university days, when he completed his thesis on Erasmus of Rotterdam, and in his district his friends knew him as "the European" [*Pedini l'Europeo*]. The Italian Socialist Mario Zagari, Under-Secretary in the Foreign Ministry, also threw himself into the discussions of both UNCTAD meetings, with the result that the Italian government announced in 1965 the creation of an Inter-Ministerial Committee on UNCTAD, making explicit reference to their experience with the question of the Italian *mezzogiorno* to demonstrate their credentials to address general issues of underdevelopment.[156] The following year Italy, in discussions with its European partners, confirmed its support for a system of trade preferences, and above all a more active role in the area of technical cooperation with the Third World, in particular

---

[154] L. Tosi, "La cooperazione allo sviluppo della *Pacem in Terris* alla *Populorum Progressio*," in A. Giovagnoli (ed.), *Pacem in Terris* (Milan: Guerini e Associati, 2003), pp. 147–67.

[155] FRUS, 1964–1968, vol. XXIV, n. 287, Memorandum from John Reilly of the Vice President's Staff to Vice President Humphrey, "Pope's Encyclical *The Development of Peoples*," April 14, 1967:

> The encyclical provoked a stronger reaction both here and in Europe than most encyclicals do. The reason is clear: [its] language is blunt and direct...Because it condemned the evils of unrestrained capitalism and insisted that private property and profit must be subordinated to a higher common good, it was criticized by the *Wall Street Journal* as "warmed-over Marxism"...The status of the underdeveloped countries is regarded as similar to the proletariat in European nations a century ago. The Pope makes it unequivocally clear that not only individuals have a moral obligation but nations as well. Humanitarian aid is not enough, but rather "it is a question, rather, of building a world for [*where?*] every man, no matter what his race, religion or nationality, can live a fully given life..." But, if the prescriptions suggested in this encyclical are ever to be followed, it will take a long-term massive shift in public opinion before any legislative body will approve a program implementing what the encyclical proposes.

A "long-term massive shift in public opinion": Prophetic words, in a sense, if one considers what would take place the following year.

[156] HAEU, BAC 2/1967, n. 24, Note, "Conseil UNCTAD," April 26, 1965.

through the furnishing and training of experts.[157] In general, the government's attention seemed directed primarily toward areas for cooperation that would not require extensive state spending. In November 1967, prompted by questions raised by Italian Communist deputies in parliament regarding the fate of the Algiers Charter, the government reiterated the position it had taken in New Delhi.[158] Zagari declared a strategy for development: Tighter collaboration between eastern and western Europe; adjustment of each country's contribution in line with per capita income; commitment to establish a program on several levels, including diversification of production in the developing states, stabilization of commodities markets, loans on favorable terms, and the application of a general system of trade preferences; transmission of aid through multilateral channels (the World Bank and US AID); regional integration of the developing states; and the widening of debate on the technological gap beyond the US–Europe axis to include the less industrialized areas of the world.

The reply of Renato Sandri in the name of the Italian Communists is interesting because, while engaging a colleague well versed in Third World issues, he revealed an understanding of a new dimension in the North–South conflict that would emerge more clearly only after 1968. Sandri noted the insufficiency of the Italian government's efforts, for instance with respect to state aid, and added that the government's proposals appeared quite generic, because:

> [w]e need to begin taking the bull by the horns: To admit, for example, that the development of Latin America is impossible as long as 75 percent of the commodities it produces are absorbed by the United States. So long as the United States of America supports nefarious regimes, how can you put into practice what is merely a wish... We believe that Italy has the potential—through its own experiences, through the prestige it enjoys in the countries of the "Third World," dare I say through the presence of great forces upholding internationalist or ecumenical ideals—to approach the conference at New Delhi as a testing ground for a national and European platform founded on principles defending the independence of those nations.

Sandri's comments reveal a readiness to debate with the majority the question of cooperation, but also an attentiveness to issues of nationalization and the internal social structures of the developing nations, issues with consequences (potentially, politically explosive ones) still hidden beneath the surface of the international debate on development.[159] Until the end of the 1960s Italy would have one of the worst records of all the donor states. Its occasionally quite advanced public proclamations were married to rather traditional mercantilist practices.[160] A large part of

---

[157] HAEU, BAC 2/1967, n. 8, Note, "Conclusions de la reunion du Groupe des Relations Extérieures," April 1, 1966.

[158] Camera dei Deputati, IV Legislatura, "Discussioni," sitting of November 15, 1967.

[159] Up to the end of the 1960s the Italian Communists would be embarrassed by the contradictions of their opposition to the Cuban idea of international revolution, the internal autoritarian evolution of many Third World countries that seemed to question the role of a potentially "progressive" Non-Aligned Movement, and the need to defend the international role of the Soviet Union in the transition to Socialism. M. Galeazzi, *Il Pci e il Movimento dei non allineati, 1955–1975* (Milan: Franco Angeli, 2011).

[160] E. Calandri, "L'Italia e l'assistenza allo sviluppo dal neoatlantismo alla Conferenza di Cancun del 1981," in F. Romero and A. Varsori (eds), *Nazione, interdipendenza, integrazione. Le relazioni internazionali dell'Italia (1917–1989)*, vol. 1 (Rome: Carocci, 2005), pp. 253–71.

the Italian political class continued to see the United States as their primary reference point in foreign policy, despite some hostility toward specific initiatives and in particular to the Vietnam War.[161]

The driving organizational force of the second UNCTAD was the Indian delegation. The president of the UNCTAD Commission on Preferences was Indian (T. Swaminathan), as was one of the most outspoken minsters of the G77 (K.B. Lall). Indian authority and moderation were well received by Western diplomats, and especially by Washington.[162] In Lall's view, the devaluation of the British pound and America's growing trade balance problems allowed the South to hold few illusions about the possibilities of exploiting generous aid packages. The developing countries would have to make strides with their exports if they were to achieve notable increases in their standards of living.[163] This might also explain why France, which held a very dim view of preferences while calling for increased aid, was among the favorite targets of the occasionally spiteful polemic barbs of Indian diplomats. Aid, for the Indians, was nothing more than an expedient solution that only scraped the surface of the poor nations' deeper structural issues, and that confined them to a lasting subaltern role.

Indian foreign policy hinged on the position of the Soviet Union. The USSR was deeply hostile to China, which called upon it to man the ramparts against imperialism according to the theory of "people's war": The revolutionary masses of the South, who represented the "fields" of the world, were supposed to form a "worker–peasant" alliance to wage an incessant war against the exploitation of the capitalist world's "cities."[164] Indira Gandhi, elected President in 1967, sought to strengthen India's position among the non-aligned states and accepted vast sums of Soviet technical aid, without at the same time refusing American shipments, which in 1965–6 brought daily containers of grain to Bombay.[165] In 1967 the Indian government was forced for the first time to alter its economic plan to reduce the amount of state funds dedicated to industry and development.[166] This was compounded by a particularly dry farming season, making the market for industrial goods in particular need of stimulus from exports. New Delhi's need to obtain tangible results from UNCTAD on the question of preferences was thus particularly acute. Chester Bowles, the American Ambassador to India, reminded Washington of the need to pay close attention to the subcontinent in order to avoid running the risk of seeing it "drawn into the Soviet bloc within a few years."[167]

---

[161] A. Varsori, *L'Italia nelle relazioni internazionali dal 1943 al 1992* (Bari: Laterza, 1998), p. 165.
[162] NARA, CPF, FT3, Box 960, Embassy in New Delhi, "Consultations with GOI on UNCTAD Matters," January 12, 1965.
[163] AMAEF, NOUI, Carton 1001, Ambassade de France en Inde, New Delhi, April 4, 1968.
[164] The theory of the cities and the fields was officially announced by Lin Biao in an article in the *People's Daily* on September 3, 1965: "Let us examine the entire world: if North America and Western Europe can be called the cities of the world, then Asia, Africa, and Latin America represent its rural areas." See P. Richer, *Cina e Terzo Mondo* (Milan: Mazzetta, 1972), p. 83.
[165] Y. Malik and D. Vaspeyi, *India: the Years of Indira Gandhi* (New Delhi: E.J. Brill, 1988).
[166] F. Frankel, *India's Political Economy, 1947–1977* (Princeton, NJ: Princeton University Press, 1978), p. 295.
[167] WBGA, Records of Robert S. McNamara, General Correspondence, Chester Bowles, Letter to Robert S. McNamara, April 30, 1968.

The European Community had long debated the issues to be discussed at UNCTAD II.[168] They had agreed to accept preferences in principle, but there remained substantial internal differences both over the right formula to put them into practice and over eventual exceptions, as well as on the proposal to abolish inverse preferences with the African states. Within OECD it had been agreed that each industrialized nation should choose its own list of manufactured and unfinished goods to which it would apply preferences. But within the Community there was no such agreement. France sought to exclude from preferences both textiles and refined agricultural produce, a particularly restrictive position. Holland, in contrast, fought for the inclusion of refined agricultural goods and in the long term to replace the Yaoundé association with a new global system of preferences with the entire South. The majority of the delegates, however, agreed to avoid putting up for discussion the renewal of the Yaoundé Convention, scheduled to expire in 1969. With regard to commodities, the idea of a general fund to stabilize prices— an idea which would predominate in North–South negotiations during the mid-1970s—was eliminated without discussion.

In the course of negotiations the French delegation, sensing the hostility toward their most defensive positions, requested and obtained the right to change the agreed position on questions on which they perceived they had greater room for maneuver: The aid target of 1 percent of GDP, as well as the clause establishing a fixed share reserved for state aid.[169] The delicate nature of the French position stemmed from the need not to risk rupturing their partnership with the African states that, in fact, had stated in the Algiers Charter their support for a generalized system of preferences, if only because they believed the Six (as well as the other Western powers) would reject it.[170] France could not have accepted any alteration of the CAP, not even in exchange for a system of preferences for raw materials, because this would have implied revising its special relationship with Africa.

Great Britain arrived at the New Delhi conference without serious expectations or room for maneuver. British diplomats—less far-sighted than Heath—believed that four years before at Geneva the risk of a Soviet-led revolt against GATT had already been avoided, and that in the future North–South relations would be less tense. UNCTAD II would not generate any grave new dangers, and at any rate London, as we have already seen, did not possess the economic resources to play a vital role.[171]

[168] AMAEF, NOUI, Carton 1000, Communauté Européennes, Le Conseil, "Preparation de la deuxième session de la Conference des nations unies sur le commerce et la développement," Brussels, January 4, 1968.

[169] AMAEF, NOUI, Carton 1001, Telegram, Burin des Roziers, January 3, 1968. The message states that France is isolated among its European partners and that UNCTAD could be an opportunity to make its voice heard on the international level.

[170] AMAEF, NOI, Carton 1001, Ambassade de France en Inde, Maurice Viaud, New Delhi, March 14, 1968.

[171] NA, FO 371/190067, Inter-departmental group on the United Nations Conference for Trade and Development, "Preliminary Report on the Second UNCTAD Conference," April 1, 1968; NA, FO 371/190067, Draft paper "UNCTAD: Preparations for the Second Conference at the Board of Trade," November 8, 1967: "It was not possible to take a more advanced position as in 1964, the important thing was to stay in line with the other western nations."

Italy, whose delegation was led by Zagari, adopted a line similar to that of the French, with two important differences. First, the developing countries were considered strategic markets for European Community exports; second, Italy attributed great importance to cooperation for the training of local technical experts and the easy financing of production sites.[172]

The Germans, under the influence of their new socialist Foreign Minister Willy Brandt, demonstrated a more progressive line than in the past, declaring their willingness to increase by 60 percent their contribution to the IDA program of the World Bank, to extend the system of preferences toward products not competing with German goods, and to abolish internal tariffs on tropical goods. They remained resolutely opposed, however, to more detailed price controls on raw materials. Bonn reminded France of the importance of the size of the Dutch delegation—twenty-two members, including six parliamentary deputies, as well as union and industry representatives—which showed the weight the Dutch placed on their relations with the South.[173]

The EC, which could participate in UNCTAD only as an observer, found internal agreement on the need to defend and promote its role in the expansion of global commerce. Speaking on behalf of the Six, the French Minister Michel Debré noted that the Community's exports had grown from US$15.911 billion in 1958 to US$29.112 billion in 1966,[174] a growth rate of 84.8 percent; European imports, meanwhile, had grown from US$16 billion to US$30 billion, an increase of 90.2 percent. Imports were thus growing faster than exports, and the Community maintained a passive trade balance with third-party nations. What's more, the Community's imports amounted to some 24.5 percent of the developing nations' exports, representing their largest trading partner. It was thus impossible, he argued, to call the Community short-sighted or selfish. Though not completely uncritical, many of the AASM countries also came to the Community's defense in talks with the other countries of the South.[175]

The second UNCTAD conference thus took place in a political climate much less hostile to the EC than the Geneva conference, at which both the memories and the embers of the wars of decolonization had still burned brightly. The only signs of tension flared up on the arrival of the South African delegation at the hotels where they made their headquarters: Graffiti artists had altered the signs

---

[172] AMAEF, NUOI, Carton 1001, "Consultations franco-italiens de la CNUCED," November 1967–January 1968.

[173] AMAEF, NUOI, Carton 1001, L'Ambassadeur de France prés la République Fédérale d'Allemagne, "Avant la Conférence des nations unies pour le Commerce et la Développement, Bad Godesberg," January 18, 1968.

[174] Michel Debré, on the occasion of the second session of UNCTAD, New Delhi, February 1968.

[175] NA, BT 241/1902, Déclaration de Jazairy, représentant de l'Algérie à la cinquième Commission, March 4, 1968. According to the Algerian representative, criticism of the Community was vague and imprecise because it should not have addressed preferential relationships but, first, the CAP, which protected European agriculture even from its trade partners; and second, the unsatisfactory results of negotiations with GATT, which had not helped Algeria, which saw its exports of manufactures to the Community decline from some US$250 million in 1961 to US$160 million in 1966, while Yugoslavia, Hong Kong, and India had seen their exports rise.

warning "no dogs allowed" to add "no representatives of apartheid"; Indians in fact constituted a significant ethnic minority in South Africa. The negotiations were intense, and in the final weeks of discussion took place less in plenary assembly than in the inner sanctum of Prebisch's hotel, where he assembled the key delegates under the name of the "Everest Group" to untangle the toughest knots holding up the negotiations.[176] At the last moment an accord was reached, but by the universal judgment of the press as well as the delegates from the South, the agreements were a disappointing and unsatisfactory compromise.

No definitive agreement could be reached on the international prices of sugar or cocoa, which had been one of the primary objectives seemingly within reach. It was established that the Western countries should plan to allocate 1 percent of GDP for development aid, and all countries accepted in principle a general system of preferences. But the devil is in the details, and none of the recommendations produced by the conference had binding effect. Furthermore, while the acceptance of generalized preferences marked a minor revolution compared to the "liberalism" of the "most favored nation" clause, no agreement had been reached on which products would be included under such a system, and no date had been fixed to put such a system into effect. In substance, then, there was no guarantee that concrete measures would be taken on any of the items presented by the South. On the contrary, the evolution of the international economy left the impression that certain key countries were walling themselves off, and that total aid would diminish in the future.

The perception of UNCTAD's slowing momentum was so strong that even Raúl Prebisch himself believed the scant progress achieved did not justify him remaining at the head of the organization, and he resigned as Secretary-General not long after the conference's conclusion. In an interview shortly thereafter, he even acknowledged the wisdom of Che Guevara's logic from the 1961 Latin American meeting at Punta del Este, at which the revolutionary leader had presented to Prebisch his treatise on guerrilla warfare with the dedication "a means for economic development."

In the European Parliament report on the results of the conference, Pedini admitted that:

> the UNCTAD conference of New Delhi closed with a negative balance sheet. Even if the failure predicted on the eve of its concluding session was avoided, the results are mostly inferior to what had been hoped and appear ever more modest and disappointing.[177]

One might say that one of the defining characteristics of the second encounter between North and South had been a certain Western solidarity, which had al-

---

[176] NARA, CPF, FT3, Box 959, Report of the US Delegation to the UNCTAD Conference, March 29, 1968. The Everest Group was composed of the Presidents of the three regional subgroups (Chile, Ivory Coast, the Philippines), the President of the group of Socialist nations, and the leaders of the French, English, German, and US delegations.

[177] European Parliament, Speech of On. Pedini, "Risultati della seconda sessione della conferenza delle Nazioni Unite sul commercio e lo sviluppo," July 1, 1968.

lowed it to avoid engaging the questions of preferences and prices for raw materials.[178] At the same time, within the European Community the commitment to defending the relationship with the African nations remained strong, at the expense of more advanced positions with respect to the general needs of the South. The EC countries focused their efforts on national initiatives, hoping to guarantee themselves vital living space and control over their own economies. The external image of the Community remained that of the Kennedy Round and the liberalization of trade between wealthy nations, and its internal logic that of an instrument designed to ensure the advantages of the already prosperous economies of the industrialized world, without an independent policy toward the Third World other than one of perpetuating colonial ties with selected group of countries of Francophone Africa.

[178] NARA, CPF, FT3, Box 959, Telegram for Greenwald from Solomon, "Target date for Preferences," March 21, 1968: "Better to air dirty laundry in OECD than to repeat our differences in public." NARA, CPF, FT3, Box 958, US Mission to the European Communities, "European Community Image Polished at UNCTAD II," February 9, 1968. While Debré asserted that from around 1960 the Community's exports had grown less than its imports, on the other side the vast majority of imports between 1960 and 1966 were composed of rising petroleum imports. The United States could have used strong counterarguments to oppose Debré's point, but chose not to do so. At the same time, the Europeans avoided making any reference to Vietnam, which was also among the primary concerns of the countries gathered in India.

3

1968: Empires and Shopping Malls

On April 2, 1968, Gudrun Ensslin and Andreas Baader—future leaders of the terrorist group better known as the Rote Armee Fraktion—placed incendiary devices at two department stores in Frankfurt, the beating heart of German finance and capital of the country's liberal bourgeoisie, as well as an intellectual center for critics of the consumer society. It was late at night, and the two bombs produced extensive damage but no injuries. Only one day before Rudi Dutschke, the charismatic leader of the German "New Left," had been the victim of an attack by a right-wing extremist goaded into action by the histrionics of the conservative press, led by the Springer editorial group. Tensions in the country were slowly rising to a boil, particularly in Berlin, on the border between the two worlds of Soviet Communism and democratic, capitalist Europe. One month after the attack on Dutschke the French Mai '68 would explode, transmitting the energy of European youth movements across the globe, along with televised images of the chaos on the streets of Paris, giving birth to the most important social and political protest movement in western Europe since the end of the Second World War.[1]

Signs of discontent were everywhere in European societies during the 1960s, but they had been too vague to be perceived clearly. The explosion was both sudden and unforeseen. Captured shortly after the bombing, Ensslin released the following statement:

> The people in our country and in America and in every West European country, they have to eat like animals, in order not to think about what we have to do for example with Vietnam . . . Wonderful, I too like the cars, I too like all the things one can buy in department stores. But when one is compelled to buy them, in order to remain unconscious, then the price is too high.[2]

The year 1968 is still considered to represent a watershed event in European culture and customs. Eric Hobsbawm writes:

> What has really transformed the western world is the *cultural* revolution of the 1960s. The year 1968 may prove to be less of a turning-point in twentieth-century history

---

[1] Daniel Cohn-Bendit has repeatedly stressed that 1968 was a "revolt" and not a "revolution," in which cultural concerns prevailed over political matters: see D. Cohn-Bendit, *Forget 68* (Paris: Editions de l'Aube, 2008).

[2] U.G. Poiger, "Imperialism and Consumption: Two Tropes in West German Radicalism," in A. Schildt and D. Siefried (eds), *Between Marx and Coca-Cola. Youth Cultures in Changing European Societies 1960–1980* (Oxford: Berghahn Books, 2006), p. 112.

than 1965, which has no political significance whatsoever, but was the year in which the French clothing industry for the first time produced more women's trousers than skirts, and when numbers training for the Roman Catholic priesthood began visibly to collapse.[3]

There is a growing literature portraying 1968 in western Europe as the embodiment of, rather than a rebellion against, a new consumer society: While there may have been credible protest movements calling for democracy and freedom of speech in communist Europe, particularly in places like Poland and Czechoslovakia, the other half of the continent witnessed little more than irresponsibile, hedonistic revolts.[4] Some scholars have sought to emphasize the ephemeral or meteoric quality of the French *Mai*, those two months of violent street demonstrations from May 3 to June 30 that shone a spotlight on a generation, but ultimately failed to leave any lasting trace on the institutions of the French Republic.[5] Other historians have attempted to broaden its temporal dimension, focusing on the participatory spirit of 1968 as a feature characteristic of a wider range of cultural and working class protests in the two decades from 1956 to 1976.[6] In recent years even diplomatic historians have jumped on the bandwagon, depicting 1968 as a global phenomenon—perhaps the first truly global political event—which had an impact not only on social relations within individual states but also on the chessboard of international relations itself. Jeremi Suri has described the global revolution as a critical factor that reinforced the convergence of American and Soviet interests in quelling such revolts, and that helped create and promote that season of diplomatic *rapprochement* that went by the name of détente.[7]

Whatever interpretive lens is used, the global 1968 marked a shift in western Europe. What interests us here is not just that it was a protest against a model of development based on the steady accumulation of wealth and focused on rampant productivity growth, entirely indifferent to the effects of such growth on either the environment or on those areas of the Global South left behind by the industrialized world. Also crucially important is that these protest movements waged a cultural and political battle against the discredited notions of European nationalism and the entrenched logic of power underlying the Cold War.

Thanks in part to the rapid diffusion of information across truly global means of communication, the symbols, slogans, and gestures most popular among European youth came from the rebels and heroes of independence movements in the developing world, in particular those in Vietnam who took on the vastly superior

---

[3] E. Hobsbawm, *Interesting Times: A Twentieth Century Life* (New York: Random House, 2002), p. 261.

[4] Judt, *Postwar*, pp. 407–12

[5] J.F. Sirinelli, *Mai 68. L'événement Janus* (Paris: Fayard, 2008).

[6] G.R. Horn, *The Spirit of '68. Rebellion in Western Europe and North America 1956–1976* (Oxford: Oxford University Press, 2007).

[7] J. Suri, *Power and Protest: Global Revolution and the Rise of Détente* (Cambridge, MA: Harvard University Press, 2003). Immanuel Wallerstein has argued that the primary result of the global 1968 was to allow the Third World to free itself from the choice between Wilson and Lenin: see I. Wallerstein, *L'histoire continue* (Paris: Editions de l'Aube, 1999).

military and technological power of the United States.[8] The stereotypical poster on the walls of university dormitories throughout the West portrayed an enormous, heavily equipped *yanqui* soldier held prisoner by a small and seemingly harmless Vietnamese peasant. The image of Third World innocence was exploited by militants to instigate an uprising and evoke comparisons with inequalities within the industrialized countries themselves. This "Thirdworldism," far from being confined to a few thousand young students or dedicated radicals, was to become for more than a decade the lens through which the majority of Europeans—students, labor and Catholic movements, and the bulk of militants of mass political parties, each with their own distinct accent or perspective—understood the crisis of nationalism, the emancipation of the Third World, and the waning influence of the Cold War.

THE LIMITS OF AMERICANIZATION

Throughout the 1960s the United States had maintained a strict hegemony over western Europe. Its supremacy was based on a whole complex of factors, of which its heavy military presence to defend the continent against a possible Soviet invasion was only the most visible element.[9] With the notable exception of de Gaulle's France, engaged in its quixotic pursuit of a politics of *grandeur*, other western European states, led by the Federal Republic of Germany, had not backed away from supporting the American war in Vietnam, continuing to purchase overvalued dollars and pledging not to convert them into gold. Also, European labor relations had partly been shaped by American financing and diplomatic pressures to favor those trade unions that proved to be more amenable to the free market economy— and more willing to contain the influence of communist labor organizations. The costs of European energy requirements, meanwhile, were kept low by the influence of Anglo-American petroleum companies, in exchange for the increasing subordination of western European policy in the Middle East.

To all this was added the weight of heavy investment from American banks and multinational enterprises, which encouraged processes of product standardization and the diffusion of consumption patterns similar to those prevalent in the United States. While in 1956 the value of American private investment in western Europe equaled US\$4.14 billion, in 1970 the total value had reached US\$24.52 billion. American businesses that had watched their profit margins on standardized

---

[8] This work rejects the notion that the European student movements and leftist intellectuals were somehow the tools of international communism, or were duped by Soviet propaganda into singing its praises, a thesis supported most prominently by scholars like Robert Service, who otherwise rightly highlights these movements' deliberate blindness toward the oppressive or otherwise illiberal elements in many of the countries subscribing to Communism or "real socialism." See: R. Service, *Comrades! A History of World Communism* (Cambridge, MA: Harvard University Press, 2007), pp. 366–79.

[9] Charles Maier has called American hegemony in western Europe an "empire of production," others "empire by invitation." See C.S. Maier, *Among Empires: American Ascendancy and its Predecessors* (Cambridge, MA: Harvard University Press, 2006).

products like soap or toothpaste shrink in North American markets, creating growing concerns about competition from European companies (with their lower labor costs), began to take an interest in the great potential on offer from a growing European market.[10] By 1970, eleven of the fifteen largest French perfume brands— those icons of Parisian style—had been acquired by American businesses.[11]

Economic collaboration inside what was not infrequently called the "Atlantic Community" appeared to be producing an ever-closer union. This bond was consolidated not only by significant levels of investment, but also increasingly through the formation of transatlantic pressure groups, composed of an educated and "enlightened" elite driven by hopes of promoting the progressive ideals of liberalism and international cooperation. The Fulbright program, an initiative that involved American and European university students, was a smashing success.[12] The Bilderberg Group, established in 1954 (and named after the site of its first meeting at the Hotel Bilderberg in Holland), had been set up by those, like the President of Unilever and the Dutch Prince Bernhard, who were concerned about a potential rise in anti-Americanism and nationalistic retrenchment after the failure of the European Defence Community.[13] In a secretive and rather optimistic 1966 meeting—participants in which included the Italian president of FIAT Giovanni Agnelli, the liberal French philosopher Raymond Aron, and the Dutch socialist economist Jan Tinbergen, as well as members of the Swedish Wallenberg dynasty, the President of the World Bank George Woods, and the German Chancellor Ludwig Erhard, alongside his Socialist opponent Helmut Schmidt—members stressed the need for coordinated action by the Atlantic countries towards the Third World. Such unity would be even more urgent in light of the crisis of Soviet Communism following its split with China, and the consequent opportunity to promote an international expansion of the market economy. Great things were expected of European social democrats who, it was believed, would be more receptive than the conservative Catholic and Christian parties to progressive Bilderberg ideas.[14] The Ford Foundation also engaged in efforts to promote liberalism among primarily intellectual circles. The Foundation sponsored and financed the publications and meetings of "end of ideology and class conflict" theorists, and advocated broadening access to consumer goods in order to defend democracy. Galbraith capably summarized the content of this progressive liberal vision: "Consumer wants can have bizarre, frivolous, or even immoral origins, and an admirable case can still be made for a society that seeks to satisfy them. But the case cannot stand if it is the process of satisfying wants that creates the wants."[15] William McNeill's *The Rise of the West*, first published in 1963, can be considered the intel-

---

[10] P.S. Jha, *The Twilight of the Nation State: Globalization, Chaos, and War* (Ann Arbor, MI: Pluto Press, 2006), p. 90.

[11] De Grazia, *Irresistible Empire*, p. 369.

[12] R. Pells, *Not Like Us. How Europeans Have Loved, Hated and Transformed American Culture since World War II* (New York: Basic Books, 1997), pp. 205–63.

[13] H. Wilford, "CIA Plot, Socialist Conspiracy or New World Order?," in (2003) 3 *Diplomacy and Statecraft*, pp. 70–82.

[14] WBGA, Records of the President George Woods, Travel Files, Box 1, "Bilderberg Meetings," March 1966.

[15] J.K. Galbraith, *The Affluent Society* (London: Hamish Hamilton, 1958), p. 120.

lectual background for this idea of a common Western civilization, the gravity of
which may have shifted during the twentieth century from one shore of the Atlantic
to the other, but which retained its unmatched ability to influence and interact with
other global civilizations.[16] Pressures from American cultural foundations for the
creation of classes in the history of Western civilization within European universities,
however, never found complete acceptance in European academic curricula in the
1960s, and were rejected shortly thereafter.

Such was the faith of Washington policymakers in the successful Americanization of the European political and economic elite and in the replacement of their
old conservative, religious, or colonial convictions, that in 1961 the Foreign Leaders Program began to redistribute its funds toward the Third World, considering its
task in western Europe to be complete: By this point (1964), "[there was] a growing recognition that for a European to be considered fully and properly educated
he should have gained substantial knowledge about the United States through
either travel or study or both."[17]

In a study financed by the Ford Foundation and published in 1968, the American economist Richard Cooper—who would become one of the principal architects of international economic policy under President Jimmy Carter—observed
that, while there might be certain differences in foreign policy concerning relations
with eastern Europe, the Atlantic economies were largely interdependent and their
economic policies inextricably linked. The only item left to resolve was the question of the dollar, on which an agreement could be reached in select, high-level
circles and without the unnecessary involvement of the developing countries. To
support this contention Cooper noted that in 1966 some 128 million visitors had
traveled across the Atlantic, that there were an estimated 1 million Americans in
Europe—its military presence included—as well as more than a million Greeks,
Italians, Turks, and Spanish in the Federal Republic of Germany, and that more
than 1 million Canadians currently worked or studied in the United States. American businesses were opening some 500 new branches in Europe every year. Goods
flowed between countries without major problems, and via satellite one could even
watch or listen to the President's speeches live from the White House.[18]

On the other hand, if the weight of the American economy was playing an increasingly preponderant role in western Europe, the ostentatious protests of General de Gaulle were not the only voice contesting American ideological and political
predominance over the continent. While the structure of political parties, interplay
of social actors, and role of the state in the economy were never truly identical on
both sides of the Atlantic,[19] minorities on the fringes of their intellectual and

[16] William H. McNeill, *The Rise of the West: A History of the Human Community* (Chicago: University of Chicago Press, 1963).

[17] G. Scott-Smith, *Networks of Empire. The US State Department's Foreign Leader Program in the
Netherlands, France and Britain* (Brussels: Peter Lang, 2008), p. 43.

[18] R.N. Cooper, *The Economics of Interdependence: Economic Policy in the Atlantic Community* (New
York: Council on Foreign Relations/McGraw Hill, 1968).

[19] M. Nolan, *The Transatlantic Century. Europe and Amercia, 1890–2010*. Cambridge: Cambridge
University Press, 2012.

political worlds had begun to develop strong critiques of the capitalist economy even outside the orthodoxy of west European communist parties. Their thinking was deeply engaged with Marxism, but they had elaborated new formulas that could take into account the recent history of capitalism—often described as "neocapitalism"—the authoritarian machinery of the consumer society, and the emergence of the Third World. A prime example was furnished by Sartre's unorthodox reflections in his preface to *The Wretched of the Earth*, which helped make Fanon's book the bible of "neocolonial" discourse. While the French Communist Party avoided declaring outright opposition to the Algerian War, believing French workers unresponsive to antinationalist propaganda, writers like Albert Camus— soon to become obligatory reading for every European teenager—condemned the hypocrisy of Western travelers when confronted by the poverty of the underdeveloped world. After a visit to a *favela* in Rio de Janiero he wrote: "In reality, [I am] haunted in the glorious light of Rio by the idea of the harm we do to others from the moment we look at them."[20] Such perspectives called into question Europeans' consciousness of what it meant to be Western, and the sense of superiority that went along with it. In Great Britain, intellectuals like E.P. Thompson evoked a vision, as improbable as it was provocative, of England at the vanguard of international neutrality, yearning hopefully for a time when its people "would have to learn Gujarati and Chinese, as well as French and German, and to read classic Chinese literature as well as Dostoyevsky." Similarly, Thompson and his colleagues underscored how the hyperproductive system of global capitalism, be it managed by the state or the private sector, was only *apparently* invulnerable:

> Colliery engine-winders can halt the pits: bus or tube drivers can disorganize the metropolis: a few score electricians can cut off power supplies to a whole industrial region…
>
> So that the apparent immobility of "the Establishment" conceals points of extreme sensitivity; and, equally, the bureaucratization of public life (most noticeable in the Labour Movement) is as much a product of apathy as a cause.[21]

In northern Italy, with its deeply entrenched manufacturing culture, the intellectuals and activists who gathered in Turin around the journal *Quaderni Rossi* examined how the industrial economy, including even those concerns run by the state, crushed labor in both body and spirit. They focused on the need to humanize factory conditions by raising workers' consciousness, participation, and agency. A similar sense of oppression, couched in an artistic sensibility more given to broader reflections on the general crisis of civilization, permeated the thought and writings of the Italian poet and filmmaker Pier Paolo Pasolini. In his famous article on the "disappearance of the fireflies," Pasolini described a society in the vise-like grip of

---

[20] A. Camus, *American Journals*, trans. Hugh Levick (New York: Paragon, 1987), p. 114.

[21] Thompson *et al.*, *Out of Apathy*, p. 7. On the effects on of the "revolt against the West" on British international relations theory see I. Hall, "The Revolt against the West," (2011) 33(1) *International History Review*.

a consumerist "neofascism" that systematically destroyed established values in order to replace them with the anonymous technological power of modernity. He had been struck by the religious symbolism of an ad campaign for a brand of jeans—"you shall have no other jeans before me"—as an example of how even the most revered Catholic cultural values were now up for sale in the name of commercial success. He placed the advent of this change around the middle of the 1960s when, as a result of either urbanization, environmental pollution, or both, the fireflies had disappeared from the Italian countryside. His conclusion: "I, as multinational as I may be, would give the whole of Montedison for one firefly" ("*Io, ancorché multinazionale, darei l'intera Montedison per una lucciola*").[22]

But it was probably in Germany that the critique of the modern capitalist society reached its most thorough and sophisticated level, as well as its greatest potential for international export. From the pockets of the heavy parkas that had become the uniform of the most fashionable university students, paperback books began to sprout bearing the seemingly ubiquitous name of Herbert Marcuse. In *The One-Dimensional Man*, first published in the United States in 1964, Marcuse condemned the era of the citizen consumer weighed down by the extraordinary commercial choices at his disposal, yet deprived of the ability to decide truly important social or political issues. In response, Marcuse called for a "great refusal" of such a technocratic society, with a sympathetic eye toward the events taking place beyond Western horizons. The Italian sociologist Luciano Gallino, who taught in the United States at Stanford University before returning to the University of Turin, recalled how in the years leading up to 1968 "there was not a single student who had not read the book, or who hadn't in some way come into contact with its ideas through conversations with their companions"; an observation supporting Marcuse's point that the most dangerous aspect of industrial societies was precisely that they give the illusion of living in complete freedom.[23]

In 1964 the Venice Biennale awarded its *Grand Prix* to an American artist, Robert Rauschenberg, rewarding his informal Pop Art over the more traditional entries of his European colleagues. At the same time, in quite a different way, American toilet paper and toothpaste had become household items from Amsterdam to Palermo. But none of this was sufficient to produce a definitive homogenization of European and American societies: Consumer goods, models of industrialization, films and cultural events were still perceived and adapted through eminently national lenses. As Samuel Huntington has aptly summarized in his best-known work, the spread of consumption patterns is not enough to change value systems or political structures: "The essence of Western civilization is the Magna Carta, not the Magna Mac. The fact that non-Westerners may bite into the latter has no implications for their accepting the former."[24]

---

[22] P.P. Pasolini, *Scritti Corsari* (Milan: Garzanti, 2006), pp. 128–34. Until the 1970s Montedison was one of the world's largest chemical industries.

[23] L. Gallino, "Introduzione," in H. Marcuse, *L'uomo a una dimensione* (Turin: Einaudi, 1999), p. IX.

[24] Huntington, *The Clash of Civilizations*, p. 58.

Perhaps rather than talk of "Americanization," the phenomenon that most profoundly influenced European and American societies in the course of the 1960s
was the emergence of a powerful combination of shrinking distances, increasing
ease of communication, and spreading consumer goods and popular culture. In
short, everything that, after the decline of the coordinated resistance of the Third
World and, above all, after the end of the experiment with "real Socialism" in the
Soviet Union, has become commonly defined as "globalization."

The Sixties were the decade of television and of the introduction of satellite
transmission. The first transatlantic telephone cable had been laid as late as 1956.
In 1954 the Eurovision network was launched; though it did not air coordinated
international programming until 1968, it represented an initial effort to place European citizens in direct contact with one another. In the wealthier nations, increasing vacation time and disposable income inaugurated the era of mass tourism:
While in 1950 there were roughly 25 million international travelers, in the following decades their numbers rapidly expanded, reaching some 400 million by the
mid-1980s.[25] Tourism was a thriving industry that offered several opportunities for
standardized services. European entrepreneurs quickly understood its potential,
creating the Club Med chain of resorts, for example, whose golden age spanned the
period from the late 1950s until the mid-1970s.

And what an explosion of innovation both spurred and sped up the circulation
of goods and capital! On April 26, 1956, the *Ideal-X* became the first ship to
unload a container at the port of Newark, in New Jersey; the first crane built specifically to move such containers entered into service in 1959 at the port of Oak-
land in Alameda, California. These ship-to-shore cranes were capable of performing
the work of longshoremen at some forty times the speed, and standardized containers, with their uniform box dimensions, could be loaded and unloaded onto
trucks, trains, and ships. In combination, they were responsible for establishing
thriving new port cities, creating widespread unemployment among longshoremen in the old maritime centers, forcing many small manufacturing industries to
go global and others to disappear entirely. "The Box" was the propulsive agent of a
new phase of industrial production, as well as a key component of the complicated
logistical planning behind the US military intervention in Vietnam. With contain-
erization, which expanded massively after 1965 with the construction of the first
specialized container ships,[26] industries were able to place parts of their production
chain far from their manufacturing headquarters with much greater ease. The year
1962, meanwhile, marked the opening of the first Wal-Mart store: The introduction of a chain that would revolutionize large-scale distribution systems through its
obsessive drive to obliterate competition from smaller business by lowering its
prices. Although the tendency toward the megastore would find stiff resistance in

---

[25] C. Ponting, *A Green History of the World: The Environment and the Collapse of Great Civilizations*
(New York: Penguin, 1991), p. 322.

[26] M. Levinson, *The Box: How the Shipping Container Made the World Smaller and the World Economy Bigger* (Princeton, NJ: Princeton University Press, 2006).

Europe, where the tradition of local markets and specialty retailers was more deeply rooted, consumers throughout the West enjoyed new spending opportunities during this period through the creation of plastic money: The credit card, that now-ubiquitous multiplier of consumers' spending power.

While in 1950 multinational businesses comprised only 17 percent of the sales of manufactured goods, in 1967 they had managed to achieve 42 percent, and in 1974 they represented 62 percent of total trade in manufactures. In 1950, annual sales by multinationals in the free market countries represented 8 percent of world production, by 1967 they had reached 17 percent. Various factors promoted the growth of multinationals: Among them the reduction in transportation costs, which allowed such corporations to shift production wherever labor costs were lowest, and the desire to produce directly in those countries, such as Brazil or Mexico, where manufactures were protected by import tariffs. While in the 1950s multinationals were mostly created in the United States, in the 1960s they began to emerge in western Europe: In West Germany they grew from 61 to 560 between 1950 and 1970, in France from 69 to 524 during the same period.[27]

At the end of the 1960s the world seemed destined to become ever smaller. Improved means of transportation had made it easier to move both goods and people. New technologies like the satellite began to connect the globe, leading the most visionary analysts to forecast a radical redefinition of man's very concepts of time and space.[28] For the first time, technology offered the opportunity to watch the world unfold, moment by moment, on a global scale. "The Whole Earth," photo number 22,272 from Apollo 17, showed the planet in microscopic detail— united by nature, rather than divided by political borders.[29]

THIRDWORLDISM AND SOCIAL REBELLION

Thirdworldism was a political and cultural trend that struck western Europe with particular intensity in part because of the stark contrast it presented with the dominant culture of the colonial and postcolonial era. Only from the end of 1960s, and very slowly, did it become possible to question nationalism and colonialism in the movies and on television, as well as in school textbooks.

Spread primarily by the raucous social activism of the movements associated with 1968, thirdworldism soon became a widespread sensibility among European citizens and political leaders, before slowly fading and transforming itself by the early 1980s. Its popularity was also due in part to the activities of new publishers, such as François Maspero in France and Giangiacomo Feltrinelli in Italy; the latter visited Cuba on more than one occasion to meet Castro and learn guerrilla ideology firsthand, and printed hundreds of thousands of copies of Che Guevara's

---

[27] R. Vernon, *Storm over the Multinationals. The Real Issues* (New York: Macmillan, 1977).
[28] M. McLuhan and Q. Fiore, *The Medium is the Message* (New York: Bantam, 1967).
[29] A. Mattelart, *Histoire de l'utopie planétaire: De la cité prophétique à la société globale* (Paris: La Découverte, 2000), pp. 313–14.

diaries before dying in 1972 in a dubious attempt to sabotage Italy's electricity grid.[30] In this sense thirdworldism was a response to the cardinal events of European history in the second half of the twentieth century: The loss of Europe's centrality and primacy in international affairs, and its diminishing cultural weight; the search for some small margin of autonomy to counter the increasing belligerence with which the United States pursued its political and economic goals; and the first signs of social and environmental vulnerability in the Western model of development, with the consequent efforts to devise alternative solutions not necessarily based on the Soviet model.

Yet it was opposition to the Vietnam War that acted as a catalyst to activate the latent energies of the student movements in the United States, well before their European counterparts. This process was aided by the new means of communication that made the conflict in Southeast Asia the first war to be televised live.

American students began to understand that it was impossible to avoid engaging with the consequences of a war that, while fought in a far-off, foreign land, constituted the dark side of their own more privileged lives. College students in California went about chanting "Western Civilization has got to go." This core curriculum course no longer corresponded to what thay wanted to learn. Many indeed sought refuge from what they saw as a world full of such violence, in socioeconomic relations no less than in diplomatic and military affairs, taking flight on voyages of self-discovery through the use of newly synthesized drugs and winding up in self-isolating communities like those of the "hippies." The desire to engage the world proved even stronger, however, embodied by the urge to "get involved." One example of such generational restlessness was recorded in an epistolary exchange between the celebrated diplomat and professor George Kennan and a number of American university students.[31] Published in *The New York Times Magazine* on January 21, 1968 under the title "Rebels Without a Program," Kennan's article—he was at that time a professor at Princeton and the most famous contemporary American diplomat for his analyses of the Soviet Union—suggested that university students involved in the antiwar protest movement should instead focus on their own studies and emulate the "monastic character of the medieval university":

> [I]t is the ideal of the association of the process of learning with a certain remoteness from the contemporary scene—a certain detachment and seclusion, a certain voluntary withdrawal and renunciation of participation of contemporary life in the interests of the achievement of a better perspective on that life when the period of withdrawal is over.
>
> ...The fact of the matter is that the state of being *enragé* is simply incompatible with fruitful study. It implies a degree of existing emotional and intellectual commitment which leaves little room for open-minded curiosity.[32]

---

[30] J. Hege, "Editori di sinistra e lotta armata in Italia (1966–1979)," in M. Lazar and M.A. Matard-Bonucci (eds), *Il libro degli anni di piombo. Storia e memoria del terrorismo* (Milan: Rizzoli, 2010).

[31] G. Kennan, *Democracy and the Student Left* (Boston: Little, Brown and Co., 1968).

[32] Ibid., pp. 3, 7.

His suggestion provoked intense debate and he unexpectedly received numerous replies from young students, the majority of which, while demonstrating respect for Kennan's stature, nevertheless radically disagreed with Kennan's concept of the monastic ideal. One freshman from Harvard wrote:

> We are unique in the history of this country...At graduation we face the certainty of some kind of death, moral if not physical, and we must hence do all our living, endure all our agony and ecstasy in four short years. We dwell with the horrible feeling of being a pawn caught in someone else's chess game. Is it any wonder that we are disenchanted with the society that could give rise to this situation?[33]

Another student was even more blunt, arguing that it was impossible to avoid contemplating the ills of the contemporary world "with universities becoming increasingly service stations for military and corporate interests."[34]

The high-water mark of public protest in the United States probably occurred in 1967. In July of that year the Rust Belt city of Detroit—capital of the American automobile industry—exploded in fiery race riots in which forty-three people were killed. In October, 100,000 antiwar demonstrators marched on the Pentagon outside Washington, DC, shouting "Johnson withdraw from Vietnam, like your father should have from your mom." The protests quickly degenerated into disorder and arrests. After such violent episodes, the student and antiwar movements, like that for African-American civil rights, continued to fight forcefully and would indeed find a prominent role in American culture in the 1970s, but in progressively deeper political isolation.

The situation in Europe was different. 1968 was "only the beginning" of a process of wide radicalization in European society and politics. It could possibly be argued that the 1970s were for western Europe what the 1960s were for the United States.

Jacques Chaban-Delmas, who would be named French Prime Minister after the fall of de Gaulle, evoked the atmosphere on the eve of the French *Mai*:

> How peaceful it was here! The United States could not stop licking the moral wounds that the Vietnam War was inflicting on its youth, and its race problem was explosive. Great Britain, in a depression, was struggling to survive on the ruins of its past glories. Belgium was divided in two and was enduring the worst period of its history.[35]

And yet nothing seemed to be happening in France, in comparison with other European nations and the United States. An editorial of March 15 in *Le Monde* stated: "That which characterizes French society today is boredom."[36] Michel Jobert, who would become Foreign Minister under new President Georges Pompidou, recalled the same impression: "Under the General we were all content...Few

---

[33] Ibid., p. 28.
[34] Ibid., p. 42.
[35] J. Chaban-Delmas, *Mémoires pour demain* (Paris: Flammarion, 1997), p. 394.
[36] P. Viansson-Ponté, "Editorial," in *Le Monde*, March 15, 1968.

people had expected anything. But what was there to expect? That we would in all probability move from the nineteenth century into the twentieth?"[37]

In the second half of March a group of student radicals set fire to the local offices of American Express. A few days later students had occupied the Université Paris X at Nanterre. On May 3, 1968 students from the Sorbonne in Paris gathered in the main quad to protest against the closure of the university at Nanterre, but also to express their disgust at a fire which torched a local student association building: A fire set by an extreme right-wing group called, by force of circumstance, *Occident*.[38] The incident provoked violent demonstrations, which made front page news in press and television reports and is often considered the spark which ignited *Mai '68*. Even though the French *Mai* exploded well after 1966, when Flemish students at Louvain in Belgium had protested violently against Francophone cultural colonialism,[39] and months after Italian students had occupied their own universities, it was in Paris that the student movement created a paroxysm of such violence as to raise legitimate fears of a revolution, ultimately contributing to de Gaulle's final exit from the national stage.

Streets, universities, and public spaces were being occupied by a new generation that had not witnessed the horrors of the Second World War, but that found itself facing unprecedented challenges from a competitive society that appeared stuck in the outdated moral and social codes of the era preceding the world conflict. The Poignant Report of 1959 had underlined how Europe was lagging behind both the United States and the Soviet Union in terms of equal access to higher education, and even Jean Monnet himself had understood clearly how the student movement was driven by a sense of indignant frustration with a blocked society and against a nation state apparently incapable of offering fresh solutions.[40] But their protests were not born simply out of the need for reforms to improve access to a world of high salaries. European students expanded in number throughout the 1960s, so that they represented a consistently visible and vocal segment of the youth population. The majority of them also believed that the course of decolonization had not yet been completed, not while there existed, in the Third World as well as within the developed nations themselves, social hierarchies, racism, authoritarian power structures, and exploitation of workers—all elements that they held to be antithetical to authentic participatory democracy.[41] As the Italian academic Peppino Ortoleva observed:

It is not possible to comprehend fully the sympathy of the [student] movement for the Third World, including all the mythologizing which it produced, without seeing it as the product of a single need: The urgent desire for a moral clarity that one could identify oneself with completely.[42]

---

[37] M. Jobert, *Ni dieu, ni diable: Conversations avec Jean-Louis Remilleux* (Paris: Albin Michel, 1993), p. 119.

[38] M. Teodori, *Le nuove sinistre in Europa: 1956–1976* (Bologna: Il Mulino, 1976), p. 365.

[39] Horn, *The Spirit of '68*, p. 69.

[40] Monnet, *Mémoires*, pp. 489–90.

[41] At Paris X at Nanterre, where the French student movement had been born, the enrolled student body grew from 2,000 in 1963–4 to 15,000 in 1967–8.

[42] P. Ortoleva, *I movimenti del '68 in Europa e in America* (Rome: Editori Riuniti, 1998), p. 53.

The Vietnam War, which was understood not as the latest manifestation of a traditional war for political and territorial domination, but as the noble struggle of peasants against an economic and military superpower, thus assumed the symbolic weight of a conflict by the weak and exploited against the tyranny of the captains of industry in Western societies.[43]

In Germany, this antiauthoritarian struggle and mobilization against the war in Vietnam went hand in hand. In a 1966 resolution, the Sozialistischer Deutscher Studentenbund (SDS),[44] the most prestigious German youth organization, defined the war in Vietnam as:

1. a war of national and social liberation;
2. a potential model for other conflicts in semi-colonial agricultural areas of Asia, Africa, and Latin America;
3. a threat to the vital interests of the citizens of the United States and its allies;
4. the potential spark for a much wider conflict.[45]

Rudi Dutschke, the charismatic leader of the SDS, would later say that the continual mobilization against the American intervention in Vietnam throughout 1965–6 had fostered in German students an antiauthoritarian bent that would be subsequently reinforced in their dealings with the university bureaucracy.[46] It is worth citing two extended passages of a letter from Hans Magnus Enzensberger to the president of Wesleyan University, with which the then-famous German writer and journalist announced his resignation from his American academic post and intention to teach instead in Latin America. Enzensberger's comments fully capture the complexity of the European left's disillusionment with the United States, rendered more difficult by its refusal to countenance alternatives from discredited European nationalisms:

> The fact is that most Americans have no idea of what they and their country look like to the outside world. I have seen the glance that follows them: tourists in the streets of Mexico, soldiers on leave in Far Eastern cities, businessmen in Italy or Sweden. The same glance is cast on your embassies, your destroyers, your billboards all over the world. It is a terrible look, because it makes no distinctions and no allowances. I will tell you why I recognize this look. It is because I am a German. It is because I have felt it on myself...

[43] The Italian Communist Rossana Rossanda wrote: "Just as for us our political birth and adolescence were the Spanish Civil War, against Fascism, for the youth of today who occupy the universities they are the Vietnam War, against imperialism." See R. Rossanda, *L'anno degli studenti* (Bari: De Donato, 1968), p. 40.

[44] The SDS was the student organization of the German Social-Democratic Party, but it was expelled from the party after the Bad Godesberg congress for its excessively radical positions.

[45] Teodori, *Le nuove sinistre in Europa*, p. 173.

[46] U. Bergmann (ed.), *La ribellione degli studenti* (Milan: Feltrinelli, 1968), p. 199; L. Cortese, *Il Movimento studentesco, Storia e documenti 1968–1973* (Milan: Bompiani, 1973), p. 180:

> The objectives of the student movement and the struggles of the Third World were identified with one another, leading to the conclusion that the enemy was one and the same, even if its faces looked different. As a consequence, according to Dutschke, the war itself must also be the same. "It is evident," he argued, "that without a profound change in the international system, especially the struggles of the forces of national liberation in the Third World, it will be extremely difficult for us to create, on our own, a revolutionary situation."

But surely Mr Johnson is overstating his case when he implies that the American people are but a single, solid corporate giant fighting for its loot. There is more to admire in America than meets Mr Johnson's eye. I find little in Europe that could compare with the fight put up by people in SNCC, SDS, and in Resist. And I may add that I resent the air of moral superiority which many Europeans nowadays affect with respect to the United States. They seem to regard it as a personal merit that their own empires have been shattered. This, of course, is hypocritical nonsense.[47]

In Italy, students in both Marxist and Catholic circles pushed for greater attention to be paid to the human and social dimensions of the country's *miracolo economico*, while also fighting against capitalist imperialism in the Third World. From university halls their protests spread rapidly, and unexpectedly, to the workplace.[48] In Genoa longshoremen welcomed an American container ship with the banner: "*Genova rossa* ('Red Genoa') welcomes your ships with the same rage with which the Vietnamese welcome your soldiers."[49] The Italian student movement was polycentric, unlike its French and German counterparts, with multiple hotspots from Turin in the north to Cosenza in the south, each with particular concerns which prevented any one individual figure from being invested with the power to act as its spokesman. The manifesto of the student protesters in the small Abruzzese town of Chieti, for example, demonstrates how the polemic tone of the movement reached far outside the country's major urban centers:

The reasoning behind the deaths of those Mexican students killed, wounded, or arrested is the same reasoning behind those 400,000 Vietnamese exterminated by napalm. It is the reasoning behind the deaths of Che Guevara and of Camilo Torres, and the reasoning behind the widespread hunger, illness, misery, and destitution throughout Asia, Africa and the Middle East. The blood of those Mexican students is the same as that of the Chilean miners, of the Bolivian *indios*, of the Vietcong. It is the same as the blood of the French, American and Italian students scientifically eliminated in the hopes of silencing their demands for liberty, equality, democracy, the blood of the workers that are crushed beneath the weight of the machine in their factories, or of the workers in the fields forgotten by technological development.[50]

Much further to the north, Scandinavian youth were among the most passionately interested in the problems of the developing world. Swedish politics was founded on a consensual model that required every important decision to be filtered through a long process of popular consultation and participation. Education reform had

---

[47] H.M. Enzensberger, "On Leaving America," in (1968) 10(4) *The New York Review of Books*, February 20, 1968.

[48] The first issue of the journal *Terzo Mondo* came out in Italy in 1968; among its collaborators were a number of exponents of the Catholic left. Its first editorial comment stated:

In the last few years, even in Italy, enormous interest has grown in the problems of the Third World: From economic and social issues to political struggles, from traditional cultures to radical proposals for social and cultural renewal...in short, the Third World as engagement, and not as escape.

[49] S. Tarrow, *Democracy and Disorder. Protest and Politics in Italy, 1965–1975* (Oxford: Clarendon Press, 1989), p. 75.

[50] S. Paoli, "La geografia mentale del Sessantotto italiano 1967–1969," in (2007) 22 *Annali della Fondazione Ugo La Malfa* 73, pp. 85–6.

already been accomplished, following this pattern, by the social democratic government.[51] The eruption of violent student protests against the administration of Olof Palme thus appeared all the more surprising, as did the creation of a widespread pro-Vietcong movement, which by 1972 had attracted roughly 10,000 members.[52] Even so, the less conflictual nature of Swedish society perhaps allowed its students to approach the problems of the Third World from a more pragmatic, rather than ideological, perspective. The United Nations Information Center for western Europe, based in Copenhagen, referred to one of the many "thirdworldist" initiatives of Swedish youth in the following manner:

> An initiative of a different type with respect to the recent demonstrations of student unrest took place over the weekend in Stockholm, where 30 students, who had traveled from the university town of Lund, staged a sit-in and hunger strike in front of Parliament the day before discussions on the proposed budget, to protest against the measures regarding development aid, which they considered inadequate and wished to suspend. The peaceful demonstration was promoted by a group of 250 Lund students known as the U Group (Group for the Developing Countries), which also took the initiative to begin a public discussion on the question of aid with the goal of "raising ministers' consciousness."[53]

Notwithstanding Labour's many concessions on the plane of civil liberties during the 1960s, British universities were not immune to protests by student organizations opposed to their government's foreign policy. The 1967 May Day Manifesto, the fundamental theoretical contribution of the British New Left, stated:

> So far as Britain is concerned, we can only speculate that the full liquidation of Empire never in fact took place. In economic terms, it is clear that where colonial governors took off, the new international companies and financial interests took over...
>
> Of course, the help must be given. But just as the Labour movement developed as a better alternative than charity for ending poverty and inequality, so, in the problems of the poor nations, we need a different perspective, and we must begin by understanding the political and economic structures of the world we are trying to change. We are not linked to the Third World by "aid without strings", Oxfam, and Freedom From Hunger alone; but by gold, by oil, by rubber, by uranium, by copper; by aircraft carrier, by expeditionary forces, by Polaris [missile].[54]

Overcoming the insularity of the British movement with respect to their continental counterparts, and developing ties with other organizations both on the other side of the Channel and in the developing world, were the aims of the contributors to *The Black Dwarf*. The newspaper, founded in 1968 by a group including the

---

[51] F.D. Scott, *Sweden. The Nation's History* (Minneapolis: University of Minnesota Press, 1977), p. 536.

[52] T. Etzemuller, "A Struggle for Radical Change? Swedish Students in the 1960s," in Schildt and Siegfried (eds), *Between Marx and Coca-Cola*, pp. 239–61.

[53] UNOG, UNCTAD, Arr 40 2344B41, UN Copenhagen Information Centre, "Swedish Students demand Greater Support for Developing Countries," May 31, 1968.

[54] S. Hall, R. Williams, and E.P. Thompson, *New Left. May Day Manifesto* (London, 1967).

Pakistani intellectual Tariq Ali, celebrated its first anniversary with an editorial congratulating itself on its achievements:

> This is the spirit of the age. That spirit inspires *Black Dwarf.* It is the spirit of socialist world revolution, to call things by their name. *The Black Dwarf* has tried not without success to throw a bridge between the somewhat insular and traditionalist moods of the British students and radical intellectuals on the one hand, and the temper of "Che", of the Vietnamese, of the French May on the other hand. It did an excellent and necessary job in that field.[55]

The explosion of the student and New Left movements, however, should not obscure the influence of the Catholic world in drawing attention to events in the developing countries, and as a protagonist in its own right—albeit primarily among its progressive minority factions—in national liberation struggles, particularly in Latin America. Many of the progressive priests and bishops in Latin America had studied in Europe, with a preference for the Catholic University of Louvain in Belgium, and kept contact with the Vatican.[56] We have already noted the significance of two papal encyclicals of John XXIII and Paul VI. The latter, in the *Populorum progressio* of 1967, had even outlined practical measures believed necessary to win the war on poverty in the underdeveloped world. In part of the Catholic world, critique of the contradictions of industrial development, which had left at the margins entire regions and social groups, went hand in hand with sympathy for liberation movements and the rejection of the logic of the Cold War. Such was the case of the Italian Don Lorenzo Milani, parish priest of the provincial Tuscan village of Barbiana, who saw firsthand how the few kilometers that separated this small town from the city of Florence were enough to cut it off from the rest of the world. He thought that in times like those of the Vietnam War unquestioned obedience to the state could no longer be considered a Catholic virtue, and in response to those who accused him of justifying a criminal offense, for his advice from the pulpit to avoid conscription, he argued: "If you claim the right to divide the world into Italians and foreigners, then I tell you that I have no country, as you understand it, and I uphold my right to divide the world into the disenfranchised and oppressed on the one side, and the privileged and the oppressors on the other. The former are my countrymen, and the latter my foreigners."[57] At the same time, in Latin America fringes of the Catholic world were organizing in support of revolutionary struggles. In 1966, Camilo Torres actually fought at the side of Colombian revolutionaries, while the Brazilian Archbishop Hélder Cámara prayed for a social revolution against large landowners, keeping close contact with the *Sindaco* (Mayor) of Florence, the Christian Democrat Giorgio La Pira. Though not

---

[55] E. Mandel, "Editorial," in *Black Dwarf,* June 1, 1969. Available online at <http://www.ernest-mandel.org/en/works/txt/1969/black_dwarf.htm>.

[56] In 1968 the Catholic University of Louvain would help to establish in Santiago the Centro de Estudio de la Realidad Nacional within the Catholic University of Chile that would become one of the main think tanks for Salvador Allende's Socialist administration.

[57] Available online at <http://www.liberliber.it/mediateca/libri/m/milani/l_obbedienza_non_e_piu_una_virtu/html/index.htm>.

endorsed as official doctrine by the Catholic Church, such "liberation theology" began to take shape by the beginning of the 1970s around the idea that armed struggle was a necessary means "to force governments give food to the naked."[58] Evidence of just how deeply this sympathy for the liberation movements had penetrated certain sectors of the Catholic Church was provided by a flyer to publicize a "wake for the oppressed peoples and Vietnam" held on Christmas Eve 1967 in the parish of San Ferdinando in Milan:

> The existence of vast zones of guerrilla warfare in Venezuela, Colombia, Bolivia, Peru, Guatemala, the struggle waged by blacks in America against the white government, the guerrilla war that the people of Angola and Mozambique are fighting against Portugal, the agitation of the Spanish people, the war that the people of Vietnam have been waging for more than twenty years now, all seem to mark the beginning of a now irreversible process.[59]

Characteristic of the movements throughout Europe and the United States that together defined the "New Left" was a rejection of concepts of national interest and *Realpolitik* in favor of causes believed common to all mankind, a resistance to the authoritarian temptation in politics, and an openness to non-Western ideas for political, economic, and social reform. Several factors help explain why these movements enjoyed greater political leverage in western Europe than in the United States, despite the fact that it was in America that they first came to prominence.

First, student protesters throughout western Europe succeeded in uniting themselves, or at least in finding common ground, with the claims put forward by the organized labor movement or with the working class more generally. Students and workers were often divided by opposing views on the means and ends of protest, or by reciprocal distrust of each other's motives. The fact remains, however, that the two movements reinforced each other, breathing life into a season of labor triumphs and rising living standards for workers that lasted throughout the first half of the 1970s. In all the countries of western Europe a resurgence of trade union activism resulted in improvements in salary levels and vacation time, working conditions, and even educational opportunities (in Italy the "150 hours" of paid leave for auto and metal workers to pursue nonvocational schooling).[60] Ten million French people took part in strikes or demonstrations in 1968, while in Italy the metalworkers entered into popular consciousness as a protagonist in the economic life of the country through their part in the so-called "Hot Autumn" of 1969. In September of that same year West Germany was rocked by a wave of coordinated strikes.[61] In Italy, the connection between the students' and workers'

---

[58] M. De Giuseppe, "Quei ponti sospesi (attraverso l'oceano). Giorgio La Pira e le voci dell'America latina," in (2004) 236 *Italia Contemporanea*, pp. 385–408.

[59] D. Saresella, "La vocazione terzomondista del mondo cattolico degli anni Sessanta e il giudizio sulla politica internazionale statunitense," in P. Craveri and G. Quagliariello (eds), *L'antiamericanismo in Italia e in Europa nel secondo Dopoguerra* (Rubbettino: Soveria Mannelli, 2004), p. 299.

[60] D. Albers, W. Goldschmidt, and P. Oehlke, *Lotte sociali in Europa 1968–1974* (Rome: Editori Riuniti, 1976).

[61] F. Petrini, "Il '68 e la crisi dell'età dell'oro," in (2007) 12 *Annali della Fondazione Ugo La Malfa*, pp. 47–73.

movements was explicitly underlined by the use of the term *biennio rosso* ("red biennium") in reference to 1968–9. In the words of the Italian Communist head of the CGIL Bruno Trentin, one of the metalworkers' leaders at the time, the joint action of the students and workers was based on the following assumptions:

> In those years a consciousness rapidly developed, if still somewhat vague, that the construction of "rational" and all-powerful bureaucracies in various sectors of society, rather than liberating the productive and creative capacities of human labor—as the prophets of modernization theory had predicted—constituted an ever-greater obstacle not only to the expansion of freedoms and civil rights, but to development and the creativity of human labor itself.[62]

Better working conditions in industrial Europe were not considered antithetical to improvements in the quality of life and greater economic independence of the Third World. That this was so was a result of more than just a temporary alliance of the student and labor movements. The new themes raised by 1968—including thirdworldism—touched a deep chord in the Social Democratic parties as well as certain segments of the conservatives and Catholics, because of both a generational overhaul of their political classes and a comprehensive rethinking of their international strategies. The first example of this inversion of existing trends was the sudden change in attitudes toward the Vietnam War on the part of the major European mass parties, most of which moved in only a few months from tacit acceptance to outright opposition.

Another difference between western Europe and the USA lay in the fact that many leaders of the American protest movements demonstrated against Washington's foreign policy primarily because it revealed the harm that the "dirty war" was doing to the United States' global image, or because it exposed the seedy underbelly of American society. As the American writer Norman Mailer wrote in *The Armies of the Night*, "[p]art of the real damage of Vietnam takes place in America where civil rights have deteriorated into city riots, and an extraordinary number of the best and most talented students in America are exploring the frontiers of nihilism and drugs."[63] Even Eldridge Cleaver, one of the founders of the Black Panthers who subsequently took refuge in Algiers in 1972 for his violent opposition to the American political system, wrote: "I feel that I am a citizen of the American dream and that the revolutionary struggle of which I am a part is a struggle against the American nightmare."[64]

European thirdworldism, in contrast, was informed not by the desire to bring the foreign policy of nation states back to a hypothetical state of purity from a mythical past—a notion only possible if one completely distorted the grim history of civil and colonial wars fought by European nations—but rather by the idea of

---

[62] B. Trentin, *Autunno caldo. Il secondo biennio rosso 1968–1969* (Rome: Editori Riuniti, 1999), p. 16.

[63] N. Mailer, *The Armies of the Night* (New York: Penguin, 1994), p. 183.

[64] C. Zanchettin, "Il Black Panthers Party. La rivoluzione internazionalista negli Stati Uniti," in (1972) 15 *Terzo Mondo*, p. 82.

moving beyond the nation state and its power politics in the international arena. This sentiment pushed some of the more radical extremists to identify themselves with the foreign policy of other nations, like that of China or Cuba. An ocean definitively separated the "generation of 1914," those young nationalists who yearned for a war of purification and unquestioningly volunteered to serve in the First World War, from their counterparts in 1968. For sufficient proof one need look no further than at the leaders of the youth movement: Daniel Cohn-Bendit, one of the faces of the French student movement, was bilingual and possessed a German passport, while Rudi Dutschke, who came from East Germany, married an American woman and had a son named Che. Accused in the media of a lacking both patriotism and a sense of the state, student leaders replied that, just as economic productivity had been achieved by transcending national borders, they too claimed the "right to organize on at least a European level."[65] The students and youths who took part in May 1968, but also segments of the working classes, were animated by a deep indifference to both social and political barriers.[66] The end of the 1960s had witnessed a massive increase in youth tourism within Europe. By the mid-1970s three-quarters of youth in Germany, two-thirds in France, and more than one-half in Britain had visited a foreign country, usually within Europe; after 1965, Czech and Slovak youth also began to find a way to tour Austria and Germany, while Yugoslavia had become a tourist attraction for people all over Europe.[67] The obsolescence of the nation state as the primary repository of loyalty was also invoked by a number of advocates for local or regional autonomy, from Basques and Catalans in Spain to Northern Ireland, whose leaders did not fail to pick up the banner—and often the paramilitary tactics—of the revolutionaries of the Third World liberation movements.

Though the student movements made frequent references to Europe, they only very rarely mentioned the institutions of the European Community. The Europe of the young was not based on the institutions in Brussels so much as it was centered on the notion of a new and poorly defined ideal of European civilization, freed from the weight of its colonial heritage and the pursuit of power politics. This united Europe was seen as a model of cooperation among peoples, or as the precursor to an often-evoked "Third Way" between East and West.[68] In 1970, in a meeting of youth groups organized by the European Commission (which carefully excluded its most radical fringe), the dominant topic of discussion was the future role of the European Community:

> The Community offers an organization of appropriate scale to create a new society based on the fulfillment of real needs and on the responsible participation of its citizens

---

[65] Centro di Informazioni universitarie (ed.), *Documenti della rivolta studentesca francese* (Bari: Laterza, 1969), p. 47.

[66] N. Young, *An Infantile Disorder? The Crisis and Decline of the New Left* (London: Routledge & Kegan Paul, 1977), p. 163.

[67] Nolan, *The Transatlantic Century*, p. 275.

[68] A. Fontaine, *La guerre civile froide* (Paris: Fayard, 1969), p. 167.

and its workers. But it is vital to develop a new model of civilization and to spread the bases for a real democracy.[69]

The potential offered by European integration, of a sociocultural space or identity wider and different by its very nature from the nation state, was entirely missing from the American political context. In Europe a sense of the damage that could be provoked by unrestrained nationalism was certainly more diffuse and nurtured by horrific memories of dramatic events not experienced on the other side of the Atlantic.

While it also contributed to the birth of terrorist groups and efforts to import "guerilla warfare," the most significant development to emerge from the era of European protests and passion for thirdworldism was a palpable leftward shift in the entire political, economic, and cultural spectrum of the continent. The same could not be said of the United States, where such critics and advocates for change were not—and indeed did not want to be—similarly absorbed into the political mainstream. The assassination of Robert Kennedy, like that of Martin Luther King, left the political field wide open for more radical movements, like the Black Panthers, which lacked the opportunities or the organizational capacity to reach wider strata of the population. In his 1968 electoral campaign, Robert Kennedy had outlined a new plan of economic cooperation with the Third World, and a new societal ideal focused less on Gross National Product than on the collective interests of the American people:

> Too much and for too long, we seemed to have surrendered personal excellence and community values in the mere accumulation of material things. Our Gross National Product, now, is over $800 billion a year, but that Gross National Product—if we judge the United States of America by that—that Gross National Product counts air pollution and cigarette advertising, and ambulances to clear our highways of carnage. It counts special locks for our doors and the jails for the people who break them...Yet the Gross National Product does not allow for the health of our children, the quality of their education or the joy of their play. It does not include the beauty of our poetry or the strength of our marriages...It measures neither our wit nor our courage, neither our wisdom nor our learning, neither our compassion nor our devotion to our country, it measures everything in short, except that which makes life worthwhile. And it can tell us everything about America except why we are proud that we are Americans.[70]

The untimely death of the young Democratic Senator made it much more difficult to see how the twin crises of the American dollar and of American identity could be resolved in cooperation with the other nations of the world, in particular with its European allies.

---

[69] HAEU, BAC 79/182, Secrétariat européen de liaison des Organizations de jeunesse, Communiqué, "Les organizations de jeunesse se concertent en Italie et en France," Brussels, April 20, 1970.
[70] Remarks of Robert F. Kennedy at the University of Kansas, March 18, 1968. Available online at <http://www.jfklibrary.org/Historical+Resources/Archives/Reference+Desk/Speeches/RFK/RFK-Speech68Mar18UKansas.htm>.

LOSING ONE'S RELIGION

European nations had sent men abroad since the sixteenth century, a sign of territorial conquest and colonization, scientific exploration, and the entrepreneurial spirit of their merchants. The era of great popular migrations followed later, reaching particular intensity in the second half of the nineteenth century, when large masses of people resettled in Latin America and the United States, as well as in the white British colonies.[71] European emigration subsequently began a slow decline, fading from an annual outflow of roughly 2.6 percent of the total population of the continent between 1870 and 1914, to 0.8 percent during the 1950s. That figure finally reached zero in the 1960s, and in the 1970s Europe began for the first time to accept a net influx of immigrants, equal to 0.5 percent of the continental population.[72] In essence, in the short span of roughly twenty years between 1950 and 1970, western Europe went from being a major exporter of its nationals to being one of the primary destinations for immigrants from around the world. While in 1950 migratory patterns resulted in a net balance of 3 million people leaving the continent, by 1960 that figure had declined to only 400,000, and by 1970 the balance was strongly in favor of net immigration into western European nations.[73] During the same period the total number of foreigners—both European and other (these terms are explained below)—grew from roughly 4 million to 11 million.[74]

In the first half of this period the dominant trend was one of intra-European migration, and in particular the citizens of Mediterranean Europe—the Italians, the Portuguese, the Greeks, but also the Yugoslavs—were moving to the more industrialized countries of Northern Europe. After having absorbed the traumatic repatriation of German peoples from the East, the Federal Republic of Germany became, along with France, the largest European importer of foreign labor. The German government introduced legislation regulating its *Gastarbeiter* ("guest workers"), signing international accords to regulate the flow of foreign workers from Italy in 1955, from Greece and Spain in 1960, from Turkey in 1961, and from Portugal in 1964.[75] This type of immigration "on demand," highly dependent on seasonal labor needs, was considered nonpermanent and was indeed encouraged by the governments of the most industrially advanced European nations in their desperate need to augment their labor forces, preferably by increasing the number of nonunionized workers. The ceremony held in Cologne in 1964 to herald the arrival of the millionth migrant worker—"with an official welcome and the gift of a motorcycle," according to news reports—in all likelihood coincided with the peak of this intra-European migration.[76] These migrants did not possess

[71] Between 1821 and 1915 more than 46 million people left their home country, the majority of whom settled in the Americas. See P. O'Brian, "L'Europa e il Terzo Mondo," in *Storia d'Europa*, vol. V (Turin: Einaudi, 1996), p. 1308.

[72] Jha, *The Twilight of the Nation State*, p. 75.

[73] J. Foreman-Peck, "L'Europa conquista il mondo," in *Storia d'Europa*, vol. V, p. 1421.

[74] K. Bade, *Migration in European History* (Basingstoke: Palgrave, 2003), pp. 217–18.

[75] F. Romero, *Emigrazione e integrazione europea 1945–1973* (Milan: Edizioni Lavoro, 1991).

[76] Mazower, *Dark Continent*, p. 325.

the same rights as local workers, were paid lower salaries, and were expected to return to their native countries if the economy turned down or, in any event, once they had accumulated enough savings to open their own family business in their homeland. European immigrants, in short, were treated like second-class citizens.[77] These *spaghettis*, as the Italians were called in France, may have had strange habits and debatable taste in dress and manners, but at least they were white and Christian, and they shared a certain common history rooted in the horrific experience of the two world wars. Among the reasons for the decline of this intra-European emigration were the economic boom in certain regions like the Italian north, which began to attract workers from the *mezzogiorno*, and the completion of the European Common Market in 1968, which disincentivized demand for labor from other Community nations by granting all its workers the same rights as accorded to domestic labor.

In the course of the 1960s extra-European immigration began to replace migration within the Community. The influx of peoples from Asia, Africa, and the Caribbean largely reflected past colonial ties. Such population movements also coincided with the explosion of birth rates and increases in life expectancy in Third World countries, improvements due to advances in the medical field and in agricultural productivity.[78] It was these processes that caused Pakistanis, Indians, and Afro-Caribbean peoples to settle in Great Britain, and Algerians, Senegalese, and other Francophone Africans primarily in France. In Germany, it was Turkish immigration that predominated; in Holland, the inhabitants of the former Dutch East Indies. The result of all this immigration was that by the end of the 1960s there were more than 3.2 million foreign residents—both European and other—in France (totaling some 6.4 percent of the population), 3 million foreigners in West Germany (4.8 percent), 2.6 million in Great Britain (5 percent), and 1 million in Switzerland (16 percent).[79] In Germany alone the number of foreign laborers in the workforce grew from 0.4 percent in 1954 to 10 percent in 1971.[80] The majority of these immigrants were not European. A *Financial Times* special report of 1973 noted that 35 percent of German *Gastarbeiter* toiled in the metalworking industry, concentrated primarily in the large metropolitan areas. In Stuttgart, for instance, one worker out of every four was a foreigner, a trend which left a visible

[77] M. Colucci, *Lavoro in movimento. L'Emigrazione italiana in Europa 1945–57* (Rome: Donzelli, 2008).

[78] M. Livi Bacci, *La populazione nella storia d'Europa* (Bari: Laterza, 1998), p. 235;P. Bairoch, *Storia economica e sociale del mondo. Vittorie e insuccessi dal XVI secolo ad oggi* (Turin: Einaudi, 1999), p. 1042.

[79] Foreign residents by country at the end of the 1960s: In the Federal Republic of Germany, Italians (575,000), Yugoslavs (515,000), Turks (470,000), and Greeks (350,000); in France, Algerians (650,000), Spanish (617,000), Italians (615,000), Moroccans (145,000), Tunisians (90,000), and other Africans (55,000); in Great Britain, Irish and other Europeans (740,000), Caribbeans (270,000), Indians (240,000), and Pakistanis (75,000). See U. Melotti, "Migrazioni internazionali e integrazione sociale: il caso italiano e le esperienze europee," in Marcella Delle Donne and Umberto Melotti (eds), *Immigrazione in Europa* (Rome: Centro europeo di studi sociali, 1993), p. 35.

[80] A. Sutcliffe, "Cold War and Common Market: Europe, 1945–1973," in A. Sutcliffe and D.H. Aldcroft (eds), *Europe in the International Economy 1500 to 2000* (Cheltenham: Edward Elgar, 1999), p. 198.

impact on daily life in such cities: "Go to the railway stations of these cities, or Munich, on a Sunday—when the *Gastarbeiter* congregate as though at a kind of club—and it may prove difficult to find anyone who speaks much German."[81]

This new form of immigration, which contributed greatly to the growth of European economies, also structurally linked western Europe to certain regions of the developing world.[82] Non-European immigrants were willing to perform the most menial of tasks, which required little or no professional training: Jobs in manual labor and personal services—bricklayers, garbage men, janitors, porters, etc.—that Europeans had learned to consider beneath them. These immigrants were thus useful, but at the same time they raised uncomfortable questions about integration. First, such immigrants were rarely Christian; not infrequently they found their customs in open conflict with European notions of the family, most obviously in the case of Africans practicing polygamy. Second, they stood out by the color of their skin. Finally, their arrival from far-off shores appeared to be permanent, a disturbing portent for European nations that had failed to develop any systematic policy for the inclusion of such minorities and which, throughout the 1960s, tended still to deny their very existence. The nations of western Europe, having lost empires, endured waves of population transfers and the return of refugees, and witnessed the tragic destruction of European Jewry, had only just re-established a precarious ethnic homogeneity: But already issues of national identity were once more called into question!

Right at the close of the decade, the European political classes began to show signs of paying attention to the question of immigration. In April 1968, the British Conservative MP Enoch Powell delivered his "rivers of blood" speech, setting the tone for a new, racist, xenophobic political discourse. Powell claimed that by the end of the millennium there would be as many as 7 million immigrants from the Commonwealth in Great Britain, and declared his belief that in such a world all decent mothers—all white women—would be forced to leave the country. He then spoke the words by which the speech would come to be remembered: "As I look ahead, I am filled with foreboding. Like the Roman, I seem to see 'the River Tiber foaming with much blood'."[83] The voice of Powell's Cassandra was a decided minority, however, in the broader political and cultural chorus of a world in which the hopes and curiosity of the youth of 1968 sang the dominant chord; in fact, the very same youth charged the police escort assigned to the nationalist politician in order to prevent him from speaking at Oxford.[84] Until the late 1960s on average the booming economies of western Europe absorbed the mass of immigrant labor quite well, primarily because such labor was intended only to be temporary.[85]

---

[81] J. Carr, "Coping with an army of foreign workers," in *Financial Times*, October 8, 1973.

[82] C.P. Kindelberger, *Europe's Postwar Growth. The Role of Labour Supply* (Cambridge, MA: Harvard University Press, 1967).

[83] Available online at <http://www.telegraph.co.uk/comment/3643823/Enoch-Powells-Rivers-of-Blood-speech.html>.

[84] S. Heffer, *Like the Roman. The Life of Enoch Powell* (London: Weidenfeld & Nicolson, 1998), pp. 504–5.

[85] E. Comte, 'La formation du régime de migrations de l'Europe communautaire, de 1947 à 1992'. Unpublished article.

Subsequently, and only very gradually, public opinion would become aware or fearful of the opportunities and risks that accompanied the multicultural society.[86]

The Third World had moved to the center of European sociopolitical debates through the influence of the Catholic and student movements and the high public visibility of immigration. The arrival of the Third World on European shores also had a profound impact on culture and the arts in general, not just among the élite, as well as on modes of thought and the most basic of everyday customs, like dining habits. It touched entire families, for example, which by frequenting ethnic markets and restaurants widened the popularity of Turkish cuisine in Germany or Moroccan food in France. Hobsbawm has noted how the Nobel Prize for Literature—an indicator of the cultural "balance of power" which had been awarded to an American author (Sinclair Lewis) for the first time only in 1930—discovered the existence of "other" literatures beyond those of Europe and North America in the 1960s.[87] By the 1970s no Western reader with the slightest pretensions to education or refinement could claim to ignore Latin American literature. The Italian author and critic Alberto Asor Rosa, in a broad survey of his country's literature, claimed that after Italo Calvino and Pier Paolo Pasolini, Italian authors no longer measured themselves against the masters and traditions of their nation's past, but rather—in the absence of "great ideas"—against a global literature.[88] Even more paradigmatic was the case of the most famous pop group of the century: The Beatles. The four lads from Liverpool, a city symbolic of the economic crisis in England's industrial north, first captured the world's attention by playing the rhythms of rock and roll while dressed in the most classic of British attire, impeccably turned out in coats and ties, symbols of Western elegance. But toward the end of the 1960s they began to experiment with new instruments and new sounds drawn from their voyages to India, wearing the less constrictive clothing of the subcontinent.[89] The British playwright Tom Stoppard's absurdist comedy *Rosencrantz and Guildenstern Are Dead*, staged for the first time at the 1966 Edinburgh Festival Fringe, told the story of its eponymous title characters, two bit parts in Shakespeare's great tragedy *Hamlet*, epitomizing the search for new perspectives outside the safe boundaries of traditional Eurocentric culture.

Particularly evident, by the end of the 1960s, was the mounting cultural attack on nationalism as the driving force of political action. This was especially true in the Federal Republic of Germany, where intellectuals kept questioning the never fully-severed links between the country's political elite and their past militarism or overt Nazi affiliations. But this assault also incorporated new research into the colonial pasts of the European nations and into their crimes that, as we have seen,

---

[86] L. Lucassen, *The Immigrant Threat. The Integration of Old and New Migrants in Western Europe Since 1850* (Chicago: University of Illinois Press, 2005), pp. 215–18.

[87] Hobsbawm, *The Age of Extremes*, pp. 502–3.

[88] A. Asor Rosa, *Storia europea della letteratura italiana*, vol. III (Turin: Einaudi, 2009), p. 579.

[89] A. O'Hagan, "Back in the US of A," in (2004) 51(9) *The New York Review of Books*.

had not been seriously examined by historians before this; such scholarly research also underlined the potential agency of the colonized, and the fact that they had a history independent of that of their prior European masters.[90] Social scientists even began to question the idea that national identity was a matter of real importance: Nations had not existed forever, commanding allegiance from their inhabitants. In 1969, the Norwegian anthropologist Frederick Barth published a set of essays that portrayed national identity as little more than an instrument for personal advancement, with individuals shifting allegiance as they found this convenient.[91] It would appear that the decreasing identification of European youth with their nation was an element that encouraged the formation of nongovernmental organizations, motivated by the shared sense of being part of a humanity that was bound together by universal human rights to be preserved and defended across all political and geographical boundaries.

The international organizations set up to foster cooperation between the United States and western Europe were quick to recognize the potential for disenchantment with American models of modernization and search for alternatives presented by the course of events. The Ford Foundation realized it was no longer sufficient merely to finance conferences of intellectuals to influence a European society undergoing rapid change driven by movements engaging youth, women, and a revitalized working class.[92] In the eyes of McGeorge Bundy, one of the strategic architects of the American intervention in Vietnam and the new President of the Ford Foundation, the 1950s—dominated by the Cold War and characterized by a need for stability and nonideological pragmatism—were out of style. The key to understanding contemporary youth's adoration of Mao, Fidel, and Black Power lay, he thought, in the recognition of their common rejection of a culture privileging modernization. According to Bundy, youthful solidarity with labor movements had given way to solidarity with the peoples of the former colonies, and pacifism to the cult of necessary violence. This was not exactly what was really taking place: A new solidarity of the young with the working classes was forming, forged not by a sense of superiority but by a perceived common need for change. Taking stock of the new challenges presented by Europe, the Ford Foundation began to turn its attention to the problems of the Third World as part of a new strategic design to create new spaces for the diffusion of the American model. The words of an analyst of the Program for Foreign Leaders on the decline of the American myth at the end of the 1960s were unequivocal: "[Europeans] no longer see America as the goal for the future, but now fear that what we have been, they too will become."[93]

[90] J. Darwin, *After Tamerlane: The Global History of Empire since 1405* (New York: Penguin, 2008), pp. 6–14.
[91] Described in P. Heather, *Empires and Barbarians. The Fall of Rome and the Birth of Europe* (Oxford: Oxford University Press, 2010), p.15.
[92] V.R. Berghahn, *America and the Intellectual Cold Wars in Europe. Shepard Stone Between Philanthropy, Academy and Diplomacy* (Princeton, NJ: Princeton University Press, 2001).
[93] Scott-Smith, *Networks of Empire*, p. 44.

THE CLOSING CIRCLE

It has been said that the industrialized nations' perceptions of the Third World constituted a process of transference which reflected their own dissatisfaction with Western models of development. Rossana Rossanda, an Italian intellectual close to her country's New Left, described this critique of the foundations of Western industrialized society:

> It was all too easy to see the fragility of this uprising of a generation that didn't oppose itself, as we did, to "reaction" but to the entire architecture of the capitalist system: We claimed the right to education, they laid siege to the universities as the instrument of consent; we argued for the right to work, they wanted the end of wage labor; we wanted a more just distribution of resources, and they couldn't have cared less about consumerism. To them, the world appeared guilty for everything... They were the first generation to protest against progressivism.[94]

Such protests against the intellectual architecture of progressivism and modernization theory provide a key to understanding the evolution of economic thought at the end of the 1960s. Radical economic ideas were spreading, in part through Europeans' constant dialogue with economists from the developing world.[95] By the end of the decade, the concept of economic imperialism was widely accepted, alongside that of military imperialism, as an analytic paradigm for the international economy and the role played in it by the industrialized nations. Eduardo Galeano was only thirty when in 1971 he published *Open Veins of Latin America*. The book by the Uruguayan journalist, subtitled *Five Centuries of Pillage of the Continent*, was to become classic reading for world radicals by showing how the Europeans and the USA, with the support of the very same Latin American elites, were able to impoverish the continent and the majority of its inhabitants first by extracting raw materials for their own purposes, and later by also swallowing up its new-born industries:

> This book, which seeks to chronicle our despoliation and at the same time explain how the current mechanisms of plunder operate, will present in close proximity the caravelled *conquistadores* and the jet-propelled technocrats; Hernan Cortés and the Marines; the agents of the Spanish Crown and the International Monetary Fund missions; the dividends from [the] slave trade and the profits of General Motors.[96]

The French Marxist economist Pierre Jalée, in his classic monograph on the "pillage of the Third World," first published in 1965, highlighted the extraordinary wealth of the developing world in terms of raw materials: In 1962, over half the world's petroleum and copper were extracted from the Third World, 139,000 of

---

[94] R. Rossanda, *La ragazza del secolo scorso* (Turin: Einaudi, 2005), p. 357.
[95] A. Dirlik, "The Third World," in C. Fink, P. Gassert, and D. Junker (eds), *1968: The World Transformed* (Cambridge: Cambridge University Press and German Historical Institute, 1998), p. 314.
[96] Eduardo Galeano, *Open Veins of Latin America. Five Centuries of the Pillage of the Continent* (New York: Monthly Review Press, 1997), p. 8.

165,000 tons of all ethanol, 17 out of 25 million tons of all bauxite, two-thirds of all zinc, some 70 percent of all diamonds, and so forth.[97] This list served to prove the author's contention that the "proletarian nations" were just that, not because they were the victims of some hypothetical original sin, but rather because of their riches: "they have been and continue to be pillaged by the imperialist nations for their own industrial needs."[98] A third classic account, the Guyanese economist and activist Walter Rodney's 1973 bestseller *How Europe Underdeveloped Africa*, centered on the idea that there would have been no European industrialization had this not been supported by the African slave trade and raw materials. Writing in a similar vein as Galeano, Rodney insisted that that the European capitalist conception of development damaged African communitarian society.[99] The same idea was put forward by the Franco-Greek economist Arghiri Emmanuel. In his book *Unequal Exchange*, he strove to demonstrate that the industrialized world appropriated for itself the value added by Third World labor and resources, and that Western labor movements were themselves partially complicit in this exploitation by fighting to protect the higher salaries of their workers. According to Emmanuel the only way to exit this vicious circle would be a constant rising of prices for the raw materials produced by the developing world.[100] His thesis provoked countless debates. Charles Bettelheim, editor of the French series that published the book, criticized the idea of unequal exchange for considering the conflict between proletarian and wealthy nations of greater importance than that between the proletariat and the bourgeoisie. Whatever the distinctions that separated one approach from the other, the debate held with ever greater frequency among economists, even in university departments, was not over the existence of economic imperialism—by now an accepted fact—but rather over the way to prevent international economic institutions from contributing to the structural impoverishment of those countries in the process of development.

These analyses made the battle fought within UNCTAD to modify the rules of international trade seem excessively pedantic, and suggested that more direct action was necessary in the economic conflict between North and South. The objective for the countries of the South remained one of rapid, forced industrialization, as recommended by Prebisch; but the tools of economic diplomacy, intended to reform international economic institutions, were beginning to be joined by those of open conflict, aimed at a frontal assault on the economic interests of the industrialized countries themselves.

In debates over the reform of international economic structures, the controversial case of the English economist Teresa Hayter served as a cautionary tale to both sides. Hayter initially worked for the British Overseas Development Institute under the leadership of Professor John White, publishing in 1967 a book on aid

---

[97] P. Jalée, *Le pillage du tiers monde* (Paris: François Maspero, 1965).

[98] Ibid., p. 27.

[99] W. Rodney, *How Europe Underdeveloped Africa* (Dar-Es-Salam: Tanzanian Publishing House, 1973).

[100] A. Emmanuel, *L'échange inégal. Essai sur les antagonismes dans les rapports internationaux* (Paris: François Maspero, 1969).

for development that, in line with the spirit of the times, called for a substantial increase in the allocation of funds for such purposes. While preparing a new work on development aid, financed by the World Bank, she had the opportunity to interview dozens of officials in Washington, as well as bureaucrats and experts on the subject from several developing countries. When she submitted a first draft of the text, she was invited repeatedly to revise the manuscript, which was ultimately rejected by the Bank's reviewers. In her introduction to the book, subsequently released by a commercial publishing house in 1971 under the title *Aid as Imperialism*, Hayter wrote:

> The availability of "official aid" increases the likelihood that the governments of Third World countries will tolerate the continuation of massive outflows of private profits and interest on past debts. It may help to bolster up such governments by providing a few short-term solutions to their economic difficulties. It may also help to create and sustain, within Third World countries, a class which is dependent on the continued existence of aid and foreign private investment and which therefore becomes an ally of imperialism.[101]

The tone of this paragraph alone would have justified the Bank's alarm. From such isolated cases of individual scholars, all more or less well-versed in Marxist theory, the abandonment of the Rostowian paradigm of modernization and growth began to spread like wildfire to the most prestigious universities and even to international economic institutions themselves. Dudley Seers, the director of the Institute for Economic Development at the University of Sussex, a body with close ties to the British Foreign Ministry, opened the 1969 academic year with a speech critical of Gross Domestic Product as a measure of development. Simple growth in productivity, he explained, could be linked to the formation of entrenched elites who zealously guarded their privileges and were uninterested in accompanying such growth with programs for social spending or redistribution of wealth. According to Seers, the real questions to ask about development were: "What has been happening to poverty? What has been happening to unemployment? What has been happening to inequality?"[102] Even more controversial was the 1970 announcement by the head of the UN's International Labor Organization (ILO), David Morse, who provocatively claimed that GDP had been "dethroned." Morse's declaration opened the doors for international economic organizations to change their policy on development to what would come to be called the "basic needs strategy": Concentration on poverty and on primary needs like healthcare and education, rather than an obsession with productivity and growth in profits.

In 1969, the Commission on International Development, headed by the former Canadian Prime Minister Lester Pearson, presented its report to the World Bank, following up on the mandate issued to it by the Bank's President George Woods in 1967. Woods had observed with growing alarm how the quantity of development

---

[101] T. Hayter, *Aid as Imperialism* (London: Penguin, 1971), p. 9.

[102] H.W. Arndt, *Economic Development. The History of an Idea* (Chicago: University of Chicago Press, 1987), p. 91.

aid had undergone a steady decline through the years, and the Pearson report, unsurprisingly, made several familiar recommendations: A growth in aid to reach the target of 0.7 percent of public aid; a gradual passage toward more multilateral aid to reach upwards of 20 percent of total aid; the "untying" of aid and encouragement of private investment; and facilitating access by the developing nations' products to industrial countries. Even if these ideas were motivated by a reformist spirit mostly lacking in the World Bank's activities during the previous decade, they were by now judged to be insufficiently radical by both the developing countries and Western experts in the field. In a packed conference of economists, political leaders, and experts on questions of development held over the course of a week from February 15–21, 1970 at Columbia University in New York, following hours of impassioned debates conference organizers issued a statement declaring the Pearson report to be inadequate because it failed to take into consideration the decline in commodity prices and unemployment, as well as the growing influence of multinational corporations. The report had failed, in other words, to take into account the structural problems that blocked the path of Third World development: "We leave this conference with the conviction that there is nothing more unrealistic than the apparent realism of those who argue that the Pearson report is fully adequate or even overambitious in terms of the future prospects."[103]

After 1968 the World Bank, under the new presidency of former US Defense Secretary Robert McNamara, seemed to slowly adjust to this changing climate. Its officials could not help but notice how investments in productivity and growth in GDP had failed to halt the civil war in Indonesia, racial tensions and strife in Malaysia, and, even more significantly, the outbreak in 1971 of hostilities between the two nations which had been the greatest beneficiaries of the Bank's loans, India and Pakistan. McNamara began to prioritize the question of population control as a brake against the erosion of GDP per capita, and initiated a move from financing by program to financing per project, which allowed money to be better directed toward education and agriculture, a restructuring of funding that reduced investments in India and Pakistan—areas of strategic interest to the United States—to no more than 65 percent of the total.[104] In a 1973 speech in Nairobi, McNamara appeared to have officially launched this new strategy, more attentive to inequality than to growth: Aid alone, deprived of the ability to intervene to improve growth, did not provide the expected results. McNamara recalled how in Vietnam the United States had spent the stratospheric sum of $168 billion between 1962 and 1975—a figure greater than the total of all aid of any kind given by the industrialized world to the developing nations during that same period—without rendering the guerrilla war any less popular, or the government of the South any less hated.[105]

---

[103] B. Ward, *The Widening Gap. Development in the 1970s* (New York: Columbia University Press, 1987).

[104] WBGA, Office of the President, Records of Robert S. McNamara, General Correspondence, Box 1, "Memorandum on Informal Meeting with Representatives of Part I Countries Concerning IDA Lending Program," September 29, 1969.

[105] Wood, *From Marshall Plan to Debt Crisis*, p. 197.

The evolution in the World Bank's reasoning was not received with great fanfare in the developing world, where few wished to hear about population control as a tool for resolving underdevelopment. Even fewer wanted to see tighter controls over the purse strings from which such aid was distributed.

Alongside the theories emerging from the world of professional development economists, others voiced ideas critical of the damage caused by industrialization and the predatory logic of capitalism itself. These critics condemned industrial growth and modernization, not only for its exploitation of the working classes or the underdevelopment into which it confined the poorest corners of the planet, but more generally for the destructive power of the capitalist model of develop-ment on the natural environment and the resulting concerns for the quality of human life.

Intellectuals outside the established political or academic orthodoxy began having an impact on public debates, influencing, as we shall see, certain segments of the traditional left. Ivan Illich was born in Vienna, educated as a priest in Rome, worked for the integration of Puerto Ricans in New York, and ended up opening a globally renowned research center in Mexico in the 1960s from which he con-tinuously attacked the Alliance for Progress, the Peace Corps, and all the other "multinationals for the export of optimism." In an essay published for the first time in the French magazine *Esprit* in 1972, Illich criticized the very essence of indus-trialized society, responsible in his view for an irresponsible excess of productivity that reduced the potential for genuine human interaction and created an over-abundance of unnecessary goods and services. He argued for a measure of austerity, not as a moral censure to deprive people of the fruits of their labors, but to elimi-nate that excess of productivity without which there might be greater space and time to enjoy such pleasures, or perhaps even room for growth in the productivity of those less-developed areas of the world.[106] In another essay begun before the oil crisis of 1973, Illich criticized the trend to prize ever greater increases in speed and haste in society, epitomized by the dominance of the automobile, which marginal-ized other commuter means like the bicycle without necessarily improving the ease of urban transportation, and even creating new social divisions based on unequal access to such rapid means of transport: "It is urgent to clarify the reality that the language of crisis obscures: High quanta of energy degrade social relations just as inevitably as they destroy the physical milieu."[107] He further criticized the health-care industry and nationalized health services which, given ever greater sums of money, deprived individual citizens of their natural defenses against the most common of illnesses through the standardized prescription of medications applied indiscriminately throughout whole communities. A cosmopolitan intellectual, Illich himself constituted a literal representation of the global ferment of ideas that moved beyond Marxism and notions of class conflict to focus on quality-of-life concerns and the impact of human endeavors on the environment. Another essay by another such cosmopolitan intellectual, the German-born student of Keynes

---

[106] I. Illich, *Tools for Conviviality* (New York: Harper & Row, 1973).
[107] I. Illich, *Energy and Equity* (New York: Harper & Row, 1974), p. 3.

and lead economist of the British National Coal Board Ernst Friedrich Schumacher, would become one of *Time* magazine's 100 most influential books of the twentieth century. Published in 1973 with the eloquent title *Small is Beautiful: Economics as if People Mattered*, Schumacher raised awareness of the damage produced by large-scale industrialization, calling for a return to the local, a scale of activity more apt to produce improvements in the quality of life.[108] One of its four chapters was dedicated to the Third World, suggesting models of development that did not simply imitate Western models, and calling for a revolution in aid distribution. The economist Richard Easterling's paradox, published in 1974, went more or less the same way by arguing that there was no common world scale of material aspirations that could be used as a model and that "the positive correlation between income and happiness that shows up in within-country comparisons appears only weakly, if at all, in comparisons among societies in space and time."[109]

Other critics attacked the foundations of the economic systems on the basis of one of the most visible subjects of protest against the consequences of the industrial economy: Pollution. Until 1945, in fact, the already intolerable levels of pollution in the world's great urban centers were produced primarily by two sources, fossil fuels and heavy industry, in addition to rising levels of common garbage. But after 1945 the world witnessed unchecked growth in the production of synthetic materials, nonrecyclable plastics, pesticides and detergents that poisoned fields and waterways, and finally in the popularity of the automobile, with its gaseous emissions. In 1967 the shipwreck of the supertanker *Torrey Canyon* near Cornwall, which caused an environmental disaster spilling some 100,000 tons of oil off the English coast, raised concerns about the precarious instability and the dangers presented by a system that remorselessly devoured ever-increasing amounts of energy.[110] In one of the earliest bestsellers on the question of the environment, the American biologist Barry Commoner postulated that the creation of nonrecyclable waste was breaking the natural cycle of life, death, and decomposition, and that it was urgently necessary to make profound technological changes to restore a sustainable equilibrium.[111] His approach was animated by an optimism about the possibilities for a more conscious civilization, more aware of the environment's natural limits and less beholden to an uncritical adulation of modernity. In contrast, the 1972 Club of Rome report titled *The Limits to Growth*—promoted by the Italian Aurelio Peccei, a manager of the Italian car company FIAT who had established a worldwide network of intellectuals, economists and managers of different political beliefs—was written in a darkly pessimistic vein that emphasized the apparent limits of natural resources, from agriculture to energy, available on planet

---

[108] E.F. Schumacher, *Small is Beautiful: Economics as if People Mattered* (New York: Harper & Row, 1975).

[109] R.A. Easterlin, "Does Economic Growth Improve the Human Lot? Some Empirical Evidence," in P.A. David and M.W. Reder (eds), *Nations and Households in Economic Growth: Essays in Honor of Moses Abramovitz* (New York: Academic Press, 1974), p. 119.

[110] Ponting, *A Green History of the World*.

[111] B. Commoner, *The Closing Circle: Nature, Man and Technology* (New York: Knopf, 1971).

Earth.[112] This Malthusian concept of finite resources, like Commoner's environmentalism, could be exploited not only to warn the industrialized countries and invite them to adopt a more sober attitude, but also to limit Third World nations' pretensions to development.

The liberation movements of the Third World, the protest movements of the young and the working classes, and the evolving neo-Marxist intellectual currents had opened Europe's doors to a partial rethinking of economic science, and to reconsider the damage caused to the nations of the Third World, to the Earth, and to all mankind by Western models of development. Far from being confined to the USA or western Europe, this critique also indicted many of the ruling elites in the oil-producing countries, a primary example being the former Venezuelan oil minister Pérez Alfonzo, an admirer of Ivan Illich who eventually came to define crude oil as "the Devil's excrement."[113]

How to marry economic growth in the less-developed areas of the world with opportunities for greater equality within the West? How to obtain better working conditions for Western workers and simultaneously support a structural redistribution of resources toward developing countries? How to pay attention to the environment without halting the development of technological innovation where it was most needed? These were the questions and challenges which confronted those at the intellectual frontiers of economic thought in the 1970s. These themes were all interrelated and, we shall see, would provoke confrontations—albeit with different degrees of awareness and in a social climate marked by rising tensions—among political and trade union elites as well.

---

[112] D. Meadows *et al.*, *The Limits to Growth: A Report for the Club of Rome's Project on the Predicament of Mankind* (New York: Universe Books, 1972). On the history of the Club of Rome report see L. Piccioni and G. Nebbia, "I Limiti dello sviluppo in Italia. Cronache di un dibattito 1971–74", in (2011) 1 *Altro 900. I quaderni di Altronovecento*.

[113] J.P. Pérez Alfonzo, *Hundiéndonos en el excremento del Diablo* (Caracas: Editorial Lisbona 1976).

4

The Developing Countries'
"Most Favored" Partner

The winds of change unleashed by 1968 affected the European political climate, by altering parliamentary majorities and bringing new issues to the attention of party leaders. Richard Nixon aptly summarized the new political scenario to Henry Kissinger:

> The way the Europeans are talking today, European unity will not be in our interest, certainly not from a political viewpoint or from an economic viewpoint. When we used to talk about European unity, we were thinking in terms of the men who would be at the top of Europe who would be in control. Those men were people that we could get along with. Today, however, when we talk of European unity, and when we look ahead, we have to recognize the stark fact that a united Europe will be led primarily by left-leaning or socialist heads of government. I say this despite the fact that Heath is still in power. Even in Britain and France we have situations where the media and the establishment strongly pull to the left at this point, and also where the media and the establishment take an increasingly anti-US attitude.[1]

The European left had gained the moral high ground even though it had to endure the tensions provoked by challenges from both a reactionary right and a revolutionary left, as well as the periodic threats from various—and not necessarily European—terrorist movements.[2] As the head of the Italian Central Bank, Guido Carli, was himself forced to admit, "the 'hot autumn' of 1969 forced us to change our interpretative keys to monetary phenomena"; after the *biennio rosso* any effort to impose a more restrictive monetary policy would inevitably be perceived as "subversive."[3]

After the caution of the 1960s, new western European leaders—especially the British Prime Minister Edward Heath, the French President Georges Pompidou, and the German Chancellor Willy Brandt, all three of whom came to power in 1969–70—did not hesitate to support the relaunching of European unity as a means to offer an outlet for social tensions, and to respond to the numerous claims

---

[1] FRUS, Foreign Economic Policy, 1973–76, n. 31, draft memo from President Nixon to the President's Assistant for National Security Affairs (Kissinger), March 10, 1973.

[2] Tony Judt considers 1968 to be a marginal event, giving it a largely negative spin for the disproportionate influence exerted on many of its protagonists by an anachronistic view of Marxist theory and thirdworldist mythology. Pierre Chassaigne, in contrast, sees the 1970s as a *caesura*, from an international relations perspective, in which lie the origins of our "modernity": see Judt, *Postwar*, pp. 360–89; P. Chassaigne, *Les années 1970. Fin d'un monde et origine de notre modernité* (Paris: Armand Colin, 2008), pp. 50–86.

[3] G. Carli, *Cinquant'anni di vita italiana* (Bari: Laterza, 1996), p. 230.

for regional autonomy unleashed by 1968.[4] With the Hague summit of December 1969, the heads of state and government of the Six opened the door for Great Britain's entry into the European Community, began to work toward closer economic and political coordination, and even reached an agreement on a first, albeit limited, effort at cultural cooperation by giving the go-ahead to the creation of a European University—what would become the European University Institute at Fiesole, inaugurated in 1976.[5]

Thanks to the increasingly insistent pressures of a European public opinion disillusioned with a power politics based on military might and infused with a new consciousness of the vastness of the problems confronting the Third World, the priorities of European Community governments—both socialist and other—began to change in three important aspects. First came a recognition of the need to reinforce the politics of an active détente with the Soviet Union, which would allow governments to cut further military spending and open dialogue on all matters, including economics, with the East. Second was a commitment to deepen western Europe's economic and political integration, in order to reinvigorate Europe as an economic area, incentivize technological innovation, redistribute resources to more disadvantaged areas, and provide a parallel imagined community that could act as a possible alternative identity in place of discredited nationalism but also of increasingly discredited American and Soviet models. Finally, there was the search for a common ground with the developing countries, aimed at finding new commercial outlets but also at building political bridges for formerly imperial powers that seemed ready to recover some capacity for autonomous action on the international stage.

THE ATLANTIC WIDENS

While the political shift to the left carried unique implications within the cultural context of each individual nation, in all the western European countries it marked a common rise in social concerns. In Italy, for example, the creation of factory councils (*consigli di fabbrica*), and later of neighborhood and school councils, were a direct response to a popular impulse for political participation. In France, important segments of the trade unions believed in such "self-government" (*autogestion)* as a third way between the planning of real socialism and the free market economy. The editor of the newsletter of the Confédération Française Démocratique du Travail (CFDT) accorded such self-governance "the role that was once that of democracy and of socialism."[6] Throughout the Western world—or at least the OECD countries—the percentage of GDP allocated to public spending, static throughout

---

[4] On the efforts from 1969 to 1974 by the new leaders of France, Germany, and Britain to create a common European foreign policy, see D. Möckli, *European Foreign Policy during the Cold War: Heath, Brandt, Pompidou and the Dream of Political Unity* (London: IB Tauris, 2008).

[5] J.M. Palayret, "'A Great School in the Service of a Great Idea.' The Creation and Development of the European University Institute in Florence," in (1997) 1(3) *EUI Review*, pp. 1–3.

[6] P. Rosanvallon, *L'âge de l'autogestion: Ou la politique au poste de commandement* (Paris: Editions du Seuil, 1976), p. 15.

the 1950s, rose only four points to 31 percent in the 1960s, but reached 40 percent by 1980. In western Europe the state's contribution to the growth of GDP was even greater, passing 45 percent and, in the cases of Holland and Sweden, reaching nearly 60 percent.[7] The growing role of the public purse in both manufacturing and the provision of services to citizens, not to mention the apparent cultural hegemony of Marxism or its various leftist offshoots, led liberal intellectuals like Raymond Aron to speak of Europe's decline. With a desperate *cri de coeur*, he lamented western Europe's seemingly inexorable slide toward eastern European-style communism:

> Today western Europe, after twenty-five years of an economic growth without precedent, is unquestionably floundering in a crisis at once economic, political, and spiritual. This is why men of little faith turn to a future that they already consider inevitable. In 1974, during the electoral campaign, I was struck by the contrast between the number of signatures at the bottom of certain petitions in favor of François Mitterrand and Valéry Giscard d'Estaing: on the former, hundreds; on the latter, at most several dozens. It was as if the lawyers, the university professors, the writers, the actors were by a vast majority all supporters of the social-communist opposition, while everyone else, perhaps an equally numerous group, dared not expose themselves to the risk of declaring themselves openly in favor of a man held to be on the right or, at least, an opponent of the left.[8]

The golden age of social democratic parties began in 1969, with the first government led by a social democratic majority in the Federal Republic of Germany and the nomination of Willy Brandt, former Foreign Minister and mayor of Berlin, as its Chancellor. The country at the center of Europe's fragile Cold War equilibrium had finally overcome its reservations about socialism, and the foreign policy activism of the new Chancellor no longer ran the risk of being mistaken for neutrality toward the Soviet Union. In that same year Olof Palme overcame another taboo of the normally pro-Atlantic social democrats, allowing himself to be captured on television arm in arm with the Ambassador of North Vietnam, thus openly declaring his opposition to the war being conducted by the United States. While the German Social Democrats raised budget allocations for public transportation, education, and public housing, the Swedish government worked tirelessly to consolidate the myth of the Scandinavian welfare state, proposing what was unthinkable elsewhere in Europe: Loans to furnish homes for newlywed couples, or free vacations within national borders for children under 14 years of age. Beginning in 1970, it was the turn of the new Austrian Chancellor Bruno Kreisky to join the European social democratic pantheon, opening his mandate with a reduction in the duration of obligatory military service, the introduction of free textbooks in the schools, and a progressive nationalization of the economy, which ultimately placed some 20 percent of the manufacturing and financial sectors in public

---

[7] A. Glyn, *Capitalism Unleashed: Finance Globalization and Welfare* (Oxford: Oxford University Press, 2006), p. 17.

[8] R. Aron, *Plaidoyer pour l'Europe décadente* (Paris: Robert Laffont, 1977), p. 12. Aron's preface to the original French publication does not appear in its English translation.

hands. Three years later it was the Dutch Labor Party that came to power with the government of Yoop Den Uyl, one of the most controversial and best loved politicians in Dutch history, and the leader of an unusually radical coalition that viewed the reorientation of international relations in favor of the Global South as a fundamental ideological principle of its own foreign policy. In 1974 the British Labour Party returned to power in London under Harold Wilson, a hostage of its own trade unions that sought to protect employment rates and welfare state benefits.

Italy and France, two of the founding members of the European Community, remained nominally immune to this general leftward trend in western European politics. In France the Gaullists managed to retain power under Georges Pompidou, while in Italy the permanence in power of the Christian Democrats was guaranteed by a political system blocked by the presence of the most powerful Communist party in western Europe. This does not mean, however, that neither France nor Italy experienced profound changes in domestic politics and society.

In France, Pompidou named Jacques Chaban-Delmas Prime Minister in 1969. Evidently modeling himself on Kennedy, the new Prime Minister launched his "new society" program, developed with the help of Jacques Delors, an economic theorist with a trade union background. The principal aim of the "new society" project was to increase the competitiveness of the French economic system: The idea, that is, that the state needed to respond to the challenges presented by a society desiring new opportunities for consumption and by the fierce technological and commercial competition coming from abroad. But the solutions it proposed were not in fact so different from those proffered by the social democrats: Workers' participation in the management of business and improvements in working conditions, opportunities for permanent education and vocational training, improvements in public transportation, and investment in public housing.[9] In 1971, at the Epinay Congress, the French socialists chose a strategy of unity and a common program with the communists. Amid the celebrations of the delegates at Epinay François Mitterrand, newly named party secretary, warned that "those who [did] not accept this break with capitalist society cannot call themselves a member of the socialist party," then stated his intention to increase public intervention in the economy, calling for greater attention to socialist experiments around the world, above all those under way in Latin America (such as the Chile of Salvador Allende).

In Italy, amid constant threats of military *coup d'état*, technocratic revolutions, and seemingly permanent popular mobilization in the streets, important changes were taking place: New bodies like the *consigli di fabbrica* democratized labor's participation in the workplace, the empowering of regional governments promoted the decentralization of public administration, and new legislation was passed to protect civil rights, such as the law on conscientious objection. These trends did not pass unnoticed by the leadership of the ruling Christian Democratic party. By the end of 1968 party leader and former Prime Minister Aldo Moro had proclaimed that "new times" called for a shift away from his party's traditional conservatism:

---

[9] Chaban-Delmas, *Mémoires pour demain*, p. 435.

New times are upon us and are advancing as never before. The head-spinning succession of claims for rights; the feeling that distortions, injustices, gray areas, conditions of insufficient dignity and insufficient power are no longer bearable; the broadening horizon of expectations and hopes of all mankind; the vision that the rights of others, even of the most distant, should be safeguarded no less than one's own; the fact that young people, feeling that they live at a crucial stage in history, do not identify with the society they live in and which they call into question: These are all signs of great changes and of the painful labor from which a new mankind is born.[10]

At their eighth congress, held in 1971, the socialist parties of the European Community supported as the primary goal of the Community that of promoting social change, leaving economic and technical considerations on a secondary level. Turning Rostow's model on its head, European socialists argued that economic growth would follow the train of social reform, and not the other way around. As the subsequent Bonn Congress of 1973, built around the theme "For a Social Justice in Europe," declared: "without social justice for all, European integration will remain nothing but a castle in Spain."[11] Notwithstanding that Austria was not part of the Community, Kreisky predicted that the battle for European political unity would represent the third great challenge for the socialists, after having built European workers' class consciousness and helped create the welfare state.[12] For their part, European Christian Democratic parties set off down the road that would lead them in 1976 to create the European People's Party. This new party, under its first president Leon Tindemans, author of a 1975 report on European political union, would attempt to make up for the weakness of the Christian Democratic parties at the national level.[13]

But this changing political climate and relative weakening of nationalist ambitions were not the only factors driving the European Community—which in 1968 had eliminated internal tariff barriers two years earlier than anticipated—to seek a loosening of the Atlantic bonds.[14] In 1967 the French journalist Jean-Jacques Servan-Schreiber had published a book titled *Le Défi Americain* ("The American Challenge"), which was destined to become one of the most widely read European political essays of the 1960s. Its opening lines summarized the thrust of his argument:

Fifteen years from now it is quite possible that the world's third greatest industrial power, just after the United States and Russia, will not be Europe, but *American industry in*

---

[10] A point repeated at an international conference titled "Il governo delle società nel XXI secolo. Ripensando Aldo Moro," Accademia di Studi Storici Aldo Moro (Rome, November 17–20, 2008). See A. Moro, "Speech to the National Council of the Christian Democrats," November 21, 1968.

[11] Devin, *L'international socialiste*, p. 164.

[12] B. Kreisky, "Social Democracy's Third Historical Phase," in (1970) 5 *Socialist International Information*, pp. 65–7.

[13] Chenaux, "Les democrats-chrétiens au niveau de l'Union Européenne," p. 454.

[14] For a review mainly concentrating on the diplomatic transatlantic relations and emphaising the changing patterrn of these relations in the 1970s see M. Schulz and T. A. Schwartz, *The Strained Alliance. US–European Relations From Nixon to Carter*, New York, Cambridge University Press, 2010.

Europe. Already, in the ninth year of the Common Market, this European market is basically American in organization.[15]

The author noted that in 1958 American businesses had concentrated one-third of their international investment—a total of approximately US$10 million—in Europe. But the real strength of American enterprise lay not so much in their superior financial resources, he argued, but rather in the flexibility of their internal organizational models and in having pursued a genuine "Europeanization" of their foreign branches. Demonstrating his European pride, the author declared his faith in the continent's ability to resist the American challenge of the book's title, concluding that "Europe is not Algeria or Senegal." Yet Servan-Schreiber was no anti-American. On the contrary, he was a profound admirer of the United States and a diligent contributor to the Bilderberg Group. As owner and editor of the French weekly newsmagazine *L'Express*, which he had founded while still in his twenties, he was a prestigious and pugnacious exponent of that European bourgeoisie that simultaneously urged for reform while subordinating social progress to the absolute need for economic growth rates of at least 4 percent. He was, in other words, a voice of the new European industrial elite, a member of a managerial class that aimed first and foremost to reduce the role of American multinationals in Europe but also aspired to overcome European businesses' inferiority in technology and organization.[16]

The revival of European integration in December 1969 by the Hague Summit of heads of state and government of the EC was inspired not only by a need to respond to the social turbulence of 1968, but also by the desire to stimulate the European economy to create a level of prosperity that they assumed would calm such tensions.[17] The new lines of Community policy established at The Hague were: first, the widening of the EC to include Great Britain, signaling the demise of the European vision put forward by French Gaullist nationalists; second, the financial regulation of the Common Agricultural Policy, providing the Community with additional economic resources; third, the decision to pursue economic and monetary union, with the ultimate goal of achieving the complete unification of the European market.

Inasmuch as the strategy outlined at The Hague was still largely centered on stimulating the European economy, EC leaders also showed signs of a willingness to reconsider the relationship with the developing countries. The German Federal

[15] J.J. Servan-Schreiber, *The American Challenge* (New York: Atheneum, 1968), p. 3. [Italics in original]

[16] HAEU, BAC 25/1980, n. 1827, Secrétariat-Général de la Commission, "Consultations entre la Commission et l'administration américaine," Brussels, April 27–28, 1972. The issue of regulation of American multinationals in Europe was addressed in meetings between the European Commission and the American government in April 1972. On that occasion, the Commissioner for Industry Altiero Spinelli made the following requests: Assistance in the creation of "European multinationals," respect for European competition, and controls over arbitrary delocalization of manufacturing. On this subject see H. Zimmermann, "Western Europe and the American Challenge: Conflict and Cooperation in Technology and Monetary Policy, 1965–1973," in M. Trachtenberg (ed.), *Empire and Alliance* (Lanham, MD: Rowman & Littlefield, 2003), pp. 127–53.

[17] M.E. Guasconi, *L'Europa fra continuità e cambiamento: Il vertice dell'Aia e il rilancio della costruzione europea* (Florence: Edizioni Polistampa, 2004).

Republic seemed to be distancing itself from the rigidity of the Hallstein Doctrine in order to embrace a new development policy less conditioned by the imperatives of the Cold War, supported with particular vehemence by the future socialist Minister for Economic Cooperation Erhard Eppler. The new German development policy aimed to increase aid, including multilateral assistance, to the poorest nations and in strategic sectors, rather than simply finance German exports indiscriminately. In a small pamphlet printed in 1971, Eppler suggested the ultimate goal was "an ambitious effort to make life for all on Earth more bearable so that it will not become unbearable for all."[18] Albeit at the cost of some harsh exchanges with his colleague in the Ministry for Economic Affairs, Karl Schiller, Eppler succeeded in inserting in Brandt's government program a reference to the Pearson Commission report discussed in Chapter Three, much to the satisfaction of the World Bank, which believed it could count on a new ally.[19]

In March 1970, shortly after the conclusion of the Hague summit, the Italian commissioner for industrial policy Guido Colonna di Paliano presented a memorandum that outlined the contours of a future Community strategy in the manufacturing sector.[20] This very ambitious plan, conceived in view of the imminent arrangements for further European political integration and in a period of economic expansion and high levels of industrial employment, was seen as an element in a more comprehensive policy of collaboration between the trade unions and employers' organizations. It drew upon a strategy, sponsored with particular energy by the Italian government, of industrial planning on a continental scale as a means of safeguarding employment and ensuring investment in economically depressed areas.[21] The Community would join the United States at the top of the global ranks in manufacturing, while at the same time committing itself to promoting the entry of developing countries at the lower levels of the productive pyramid. Put together by a member of the Italian nobility, a diplomat who had occupied high-level offices in both the OECD and NATO, the Colonna memorandum expressed an outlook quite distinct from American economic concepts. It was full of *dirigiste* ideas, an intellectual hallmark not restricted to the European social democrats, and stated that:

> policy on the industrial development of Europe could not be conceived without due regard being paid to the need for a more harmonious distribution of the world's wealth... In addition to the special effort it is making to assist the associated European and African States, the Community must be ready to accept the progressive and orderly transfer of certain industrial activities to the developing countries.[22]

---

[18] E. Eppler, *Not Much Time for the Third World* (London: O. Wolff, 1972), p. 135.

[19] WBGA, Office of the President, Records of Robert S. McNamara, General Correspondence, Box 1, "Notes on Bank–German Relations," February 5, 1969.

[20] L. Mechi and F. Petrini, "La Comunità europea nella divisione internazionale del lavoro: Le politiche industriali, 1967–1978," in A. Varsori (ed.), *Alle origini del presente. L'Europa occidentale nella crisi degli anni Settanta* (Milan: Franco Angeli, 2007), pp. 251–85.

[21] P.L. Ballini and A. Varsori (eds), *L'Italia e l'Europa*, vol. 2 (Rubbettino: Soveria Mannelli, 2004), pp. 723–36.

[22] Commission of the European Communities, Commission Memorandum to the Council, *The Community's industrial policy*, March 18, 1970, *Bulletin of the European Communities, Supplement 4/70*. Archive of European Integration (AEI). Available online at <http://aei.pitt.edu/5598/>.

The idea of a new international division of labor, largely unheard-of in Washington, was also making headway in the various bodies of the European Commission. The Mansholt Plan of 1968, named after the Dutch Agriculture Commissioner Sicco Mansholt, was born out of the need to rein in European agricultural protectionism and at the same time incentivize the modernization and increased productivity of continental farms, thus encouraging the European agricultural market to open to the outside world.[23]

The reference to a more equitable international division of labor had penetrated western Europe to the point that it had become common currency not only in the press, but also in the deeds of labor movements. The European Confederation of Free Trade Unions, in a document of 1970—three years before the Communist Italian and French trade unions were admitted to form the European Trade Union Confederation (ETUC), in 1973—put forward a strategic action plan for development of the countries of the South.[24] The text, evidence of the unions' self-assurance fresh from their recent victories and in an age of full employment, demanded of the Community governments:

> that from today, and using in particular the resources of the European Social Fund, structural reforms and reorganization in the industrialized countries be undertaken, in such a way as to allow the creation and development of manufacturing in the developing countries, while avoiding making the workers of the industrialized countries the victims of the necessary transformations.

On the other side of the Atlantic, the obsession was with the growing American balance of payments deficit, which in 1971—for the first time since 1883—was accompanied by a parallel deficit in the balance of trade. Washington was in debt to the rest of the world, and at the same time importing greater quantities of goods than it could export. The creation in 1969 of a new reserve currency in the IMF, the Special Drawing Rights (SDRs), was not sufficient to halt the dollar hemorrhage. The issue of the dollar's convertibility into gold, long stabilized at $35 per troy ounce, and the role of America's currency as the pivot of international monetary system, were thus definitively called into question.

This serious state of affairs pushed members of Congress and the Republican administration to reinvigorate the ongoing debate over the reduction of the American military presence in Europe, and to criticize those elements of the Community's economic policy that openly conflicted with American interests. Such was the case with the CAP, which protected the European market from imports of American corn and grain, and especially with the European system of preferences for the markets of certain African nations that gave European goods an advantage

---

[23] G. Thiemeyer, "The Mansholt Plan, the Definite Financing of the Common Agricultural Policy and the Enlargement of the Community, 1969–1973," in J. van der Harst (ed.), *Beyond the Customs Union: The European Union's Quest for Deepening, Widening and Completion 1969–1975* (Brussels: Nomos Bruylant, 2007), pp. 197–223.

[24] IISH, ETUC, Box 3007, CESL, "La CE et les Pays en voie de développement," October 20, 1970.

over those produced by their American and Latin American competitors—a large number of which were US multinationals.[25] As early as 1969, Senator Jacob Javits of New York, an influential member of the Senate Foreign Relations Committee, spoke of the Common Market as an entity "that is ever more openly assuming the contours of a small and introverted protectionist bloc."[26] US labor leaders pushed insistently for protectionist measures to safeguard American manufacturing industries and employment rates, and for cuts in the foreign aid that they believed—wrongly—had contributed to a reduction of domestic employment. At the same time they called for tighter controls over the activities of multinationals, in particular over the delocalization of production.[27] Deflation to defend dollar convertibility was not really an option, in a country where Keynesian mindset was still dominant and where between 1970 and 1973 unemployment was 5.4 percent compared to 0.9 percent in Germany, 2.1 percent in France and 1.3 percent in Japan.[28]

At the outset of Nixon's first term Henry Kissinger, then National Security Advisor, wrote an important memorandum expressing his belief that, with Europe's stabilization, America's priority should be to concentrate on relations with the Soviet Union and, in an ever more fragmented and anarchic world, to deepen its dialogues with other regional powers.[29] One result of this new approach, beyond Nixon's pathbreaking trip to China in February 1972, was that one of the most significant economic decisions of the century—the abandonment of the Bretton Woods monetary system—was taken without any consultation with America's European allies, and with the deliberate intent of making them pay for its consequences in full. Within the State Department there was broad recognition of European concerns at the growing protectionism demonstrated by the United States, the anarchic behavior of American multinationals, and the exodus of short-term capital, and many in Foggy Bottom hoped to orchestrate a concerted economic initiative between Europe, the United States, and Japan. Instead, those who wished to see Washington make a unilateral decision to demonstrate its autonomy and reassert its leadership of the Western world had their way.[30] On August 15, 1971 the Republican administration announced the suspension of the dollar's convertibility into gold, and the imposition of a 10 percent surcharge on all imports not subject to established quotas. It then communicated the fait accompli to the major

---

[25] L. Coppolaro, "The United States and the EEC Enlargement (1969–1973): Reaffirming the Atlantic Framework," in van der Harst (ed.), *Beyond the Customs Union*, pp. 135–63.

[26] UNOG, UNCTAD, ARR 40, 2344, B.48, Letter, Jacob J. Javits to Perez-Guerrero, November 12, 1969.

[27] WBGA, Records of Robert S. McNamara, Memo to McNamara, "Your Conversation with George Meany," July 14, 1971.

[28] J. Stein, *Pivotal Decade. How the United States Traded Factories for Finance in the Seventies*, (New Haven, CT: Yale University Press, 2010), p. 45.

[29] FRUS, 1969–1976, vol. I, 41, Memorandum from the President's Assistant for National Security Affairs (Kissinger) to President Nixon, "Analysis of changes in international politics since World War II and their implications for US foreign policy," October 20, 1969.

[30] FRUS, 1969–1976, vol. III, 56, Paper prepared in the Department of State, "International Economic Strategy for the 1970s," Washington, DC, March 16, 1971.

European capitals with a brief telegram.[31] Following these steps the administration decided upon a dollar devaluation, approved by the Smithsonian agreement of December 17–18, 1971, which caused the value of the ample dollar reserves accumulated by the European central banks to tumble rapidly.

The unilateral American decision to alter the international monetary system contributed in no small measure to a growing distance in the relationship between the United States and western Europe, a distance that was also brought out into the open by the debate over the creation of a Generalized System of Preferences in favor of the developing countries.

The resolution on such preferences approved at New Delhi in 1968 began to be discussed as a result of the European Community's activism and America's strategy which aimed to force the Six to abandon their policy of special preferences, if not to cancel outright the inverse preferences from which the Community continued to benefit as a result of the Yaoundé Convention. The first general preference scheme laid out by the Community had been discussed in back channels at the OECD meeting of March 1969, shortly before the Hague European Summit. This was clearly the product of a series of deals between the individual Community nations, and trod cautiously around the reservations of important industries within each of the Six; it might almost be considered a cut-rate compromise. But, considering that it entailed concessions without providing corresponding benefits, the end result was still of some note, and of even greater significance if one keeps in mind the general hostility of European industries toward any reform that made it easier to import manufactured goods from the Third World.[32]

The proposal was further reduced as the deadline approached for presentation of the Community scheme, particularly as it affected processed agricultural goods,[33] a type of product on which the developing countries had hoped to receive broad concessions. Great Britain, which was still negotiating its entry into the Community, could do no more than resign itself to going along with the plans of the Six.[34]

---

[31] FRUS, 1969–1976, vol. III, 169, Telegram from the Department of State to the Embassy in Germany, August 16, 1971. On the decision-making process that led to the end of the dollar's convertibility and the strategy of the American administration see D. Basosi, *Il governo del dollaro. Interdipendenza economica e potere statunitense negli anni di Richard Nixon (1969–1973)* (Firenze: Polistampa, 2006).

[32] *Agence Europe*, February 18, 1969. In a communiqué of 18 February the Federation of Belgian Enterprises melodramatically summarized the situation: "conceding a customs exemption for the products named, as proposed by the Commission, is equivalent to putting up for discussion the very existence of certain sectors of our own industries." If it was impossible to avoid some form of preferences system, it was essential to calibrate preferences on a country-by-country and sector-by-sector basis. HAEU, EM 155, Union des Industries de la Communauté Européenne (UNICE), "Octroi Eventual de preferences tarifaires pour les produits manufactures et semi manufactures des pays en voie de développement," January 24, 1968.

[33] HAEU, EM 155, Dg1, Note à l'attention de Monsieur Martino, "Préférences tarifaires en faveur des pays en voie de développement," February 27, 1969. The system originally proposed by the Commission foresaw a concession of preferences on sixty-seven different types of processed agricultural product, for a total sum of some US$80 million (in 1967 values). The system adopted, after varied modifications, included fifty-four products, for a total value of US$19 million.

[34] NA, FCO 69/154, Speaking Note, "Generalised Preferences": "The only logical option is that of adapting our offer to the system of generalized preferences proposed by the Community, to which we will have to adapt in any case after our admission to the EEC."

Furthermore, the EC had no intention of giving up the system of inverse preferences it had established with the Association of the African States.

At the GATT ministerial meeting held on May 25, 1971, all the contracting parties, including both developing and developed countries, approved a waiver to be applied to Article 1 of the GATT statute in order to enact a system of preferences toward the developing world. Almost all the GATT representatives from the Southern countries considered the decision an historic moment: An inversion of the past tendency to base trade policy on the presumption of equality between all parties.[35] Shortly afterward, on July 1, 1971, the Community enacted its own Generalized system of preferences.[36]

Generalized preferences went some way to counterbalancing a trend that saw the relative weight of the developing countries in trade with the nations of the Community steadily decreasing after the colonial era, with the notable exception of course of oil-producing states such as Libya, Algeria, or Venezuela.[37]

It would take another three years, in contrast, for the United States to approve provisions for their own scheme of preferences, facing intense pressures in the interim from countless entreaties by the countries of the South, before the decisive push of the first oil crisis of 1973. Even then, the Trade Act, passed by Congress in 1974, carried with it a seemingly limitless series of conditions: One excluded all states that had undertaken nationalization projects without paying an indemnity to American enterprises; the Jackson–Vanik amendment excluded from trade concessions all socialist countries that failed to respect established norms regarding emigration; yet another excluded all nations that guaranteed inverse preferences to developed countries. All these clauses made the American system of preferences a very sharp-edged instrument of *soft power*, rather than a tool for the industrial development of the Global South.

SANTIAGO, CHILE: THE RADICALIZATION OF THE THIRD WORLD

With the adoption of generalized preferences a victory had been achieved on the trade in manufactures front. While it is always wise to approach economic statistics with extreme caution, particularly those for the Third World, it is safe to argue that the period from 1950 to 1975 was one of positive growth in the countries of the South. In the course of these twenty-five years the GDP of the developing countries had grown by 3.91 percent, while that of the developed nations had risen by

---

[35] NA, FCO 69/261, GATT Council, "Minutes of the Meeting Held on May 25, 1971," May 28, 1971.

[36] T. Kuroda, "Instauration du Système de preferences généralisées de la Communauté européenne, 1968–1971," in (2011/12) 34 *Bulletin de l'Insitut Pierre Renouvin*, pp. 137–48. In total, European trade preferences involved goods valued at a sum of approximately US$7 billion in 1980, seven times the value of 1971. Likewise, there was a notable growth in processed agricultural products admitted to the system of preferences: From a total of US$30 million in 1971 to some US$500 million in 1980.

[37] H. Perroy, *Europa e Terzo mondo*, p. 323.

3.2 percent.[38] Beginning in the 1970s, however, distinctions began to emerge with ever-greater clarity among the group of developing nations.[39] In Latin America, for example, while Brazil boasted tremendous if unevenly distributed growth between 1950 and 1973, Chile grew at a minuscule annual rate of 1 percent, and Argentina grew no faster than 2 percent per year. As Jeffrey Frieden has noted, such meager rates during a period in which the world economy as a whole witnessed a boom carried significant consequences. For example, in terms of per capita income, if Argentina had grown at the same rate as Brazil from 1950–73, that is at 4 percent per year, in 1973 it would have been as wealthy a nation as France; similarly, if Chile had grown at the 5 percent annual rate experienced by South Korea, by 1973 it would have equaled the Federal Republic of Germany. At the same time, nations like South Korea or Taiwan, which had managed to find a niche as exporters of cheap manufactures, could claim extraordinary success: India, which in 1950 occupied their same level, was to become three times poorer than South Korea by 1973, and four times poorer than Taiwan.

But such trade could only benefit some, while the majority of countries in the South continued to be penalized by the low raw materials prices and the accumulation of onerous international debt burdens. Furthermore, beginning in 1971 the volatility of exchange rates and declining value of the dollar made incomes on raw materials ever—more uncertain, since their prices were fixed in American currency.

While the contentious rise of Third World internationalism in the 1960s had produced apparently meager practical results, by the end of the decade the alliance among the diverse regimes in developing countries, having renounced the global social revolution advanced by leaders such as Che Guevara, appeared to have the winds of change blowing in its direction. The Tehran Conference on human rights in 1968 was to be a surprising success for the modernizing, authoritarian Shah of Iran, Mohammed Reza Pahlavi. His message—that collective rights and economic development had to be considered a more important priority than Western conceptions of individual rights—was upheld by the vast majority of the conference's participants. As Roland Burke has reflected on this under-studied topic:

> Tehran was the culmination of a shift from the Western-inflected concept of individual human rights exemplified in the 1948 Universal Declaration to a model that emphasized economic development and the collective rights of the nation. The proceedings of the conference demonstrate with remarkable clarity the altered balance of forces in the UN following decolonization and the decisive role played by the non-Western states.[40]

---

[38] As the Nobel Prize-winning economist Dani Rodrik observed, between 1960 and 1975 more than fifty countries grew at annual rates exceeding 3 percent. Rodrik also noted that—contrary to common assumptions—the economy that grew most rapidly in this period was not that of South Korea or Singapore, but that of Gabon in West Africa: see D. Rodrik, "Globalization, Social Conflict and Economic Growth," UNCTAD, 8th Raúl Prebisch Lecture, October 24, 1997.

[39] Frieden, *Global Capitalism*, pp. 354–5.

[40] R. Burke, "From Individual Rights to National Development: The First UN Conference on Human Rights, Tehran, 1968," in (2008) 19(3) *Journal of World History*, pp. 275–96.

The 1970s had opened with the United Nations' declaration, in October 1970, of the Second Development Decade.[41] Its stated objectives were even more ambitious than those announced ten years previously: "The Developing Countries should reach, in the second Decade, an average annual rate of growth of at least 6 percent of GDP and 3.5 percent of GDP per capita, in current values, against the approximately 5.1 percent and 2.5 percent respectively reached in the course of the years 1960–1968."[42] The means to reach such ambitious targets were not clearly identified, however, and included the standard, less than persuasive recommendations of the need to loosen conditions on development loans—possibly with the elimination of tied aid—and calls to stabilize commodity prices, as well as a request to increase public development aid to 0.7 percent of GDP.

Developments in three important areas of North–South relations characterized the period between the second UNCTAD at New Delhi and the third, which would be held in Santiago, Chile from April 13 to May 19, 1972. What had begun as a diplomatic conference, in which the countries of the South assumed largely reformist positions and attempted to rein in those taking a more openly aggressive stance, began to evolve into a more open confrontation over the rules of the international economy. This shift in the international climate, already perceptible in the atmosphere of the third conference of the Non-Aligned Movement in 1970 at Lusaka, Zambia, cannot be fully understood without reference to the changes born in 1968, not only in Europe but also within the Third World itself.[43]

First, the United States had become the primary target of the developing countries' criticisms. Second, there was a shift in what the G77 emphasized, from purely trade matters (for instance regarding generalized preferences) to those concerning international law—such as legislation on coastal areas, controls over multinationals, and international labor standards—or the issue of participation in the most important decisions affecting the international economy, such as the reform of the international monetary system. Third, and in parallel with the admission of Cuba to the G77, there had been a growing bond between the Non-Aligned Movement, which up to then had concerned itself primarily with political issues, and the G77, more deeply involved with economic questions. This process of politicizating the G77, however, did not go forward without revealing a small crack in the South's united front, created by the divergence of interests among certain Latin American countries, which desired radical changes in international regulation, the African states, which hoped to obtain measures in favor of the poorest of the developing nations—that is, themselves—and the Asian nations, which continued to be primarily concerned with trade agreements to make their exports more competitive.

[41] S. Banchi, "Intergovernmental confrontation in the UN framework: How many 'Europes'!," in M. Affinito, G. Migani, and C. Wenkel (eds), *Les Deux Europes/The Two Europes* (Brussels: Peter Lang, 2009).

[42] HAEU, CM–1333, Letter from J. Rey, President of the European Commission, to P. Harmel, President of the Council of the European Community, "Nota della Commissione al Consiglio sul Secondo Decennio della Nazioni Unite per lo Sviluppo," May 12, 1970.

[43] An explicit reference to the importance of 1968 can be found in the memoirs of one of the General Secretaries of UNCTAD, Rubens Ricupero: see *Beyond Conventional Wisdom in Development Policy. An Intellectual History of UNCTAD (1964–2004)* (Geneva: United Nations, 2004), p. 9.

In November 1971 the new Secretary-General of UNCTAD (and former Venezuelan oil minister) Manuel Perez-Guerrero paid a visit to Washington alongside economic advisor Sidney Dell to express the widespread disillusionment within the G77 with American unilateralism in monetary policy, and to voice their wishes to have a role in IMF debates over future reforms to Bretton Woods.[44] He further insisted on the need to conclude several commodities agreements immediately, beginning with a controversial agreement on cocoa, which had undergone a long slide in value. To these requests representatives of the Republican administration, seemingly on an entirely different wavelength, responded that for Washington the key to growth remained the improvement of the climate for private investment in the developing world, in particular in Latin America.

The Indian Trade Minister, returning in 1971 from the second G77 ministerial conference in Lima, Peru—following that at Algiers in 1967—had also expressed bitter criticisms of the United States: First, of the temporary surcharge imposed on imports; second, of the failure to introduce a generalized system of preferences; third, for having unilaterally decided a matter of such importance for the world economy as the convertibility of the dollar. In so doing, he gave an implicitly positive judgment of the actions of the EC, the countries of eastern Europe, and Japan for having put in place their own systems of preferences.[45]

If the developing world's anger seemed to be increasingly directed at the United States, this did not mean that the feeling was uniform or unanimous among all its members. At the G77 ministerial meeting in Lima a distinction had seemed to emerge between a moderate bloc and more radical countries, like the host nation Peru or Chile. The more radical front voiced deep hostility to foreign investment, the activities of multinational corporations, and both bilateral and multilateral aid. They declared their intention to organize an international conference for the reform of Bretton Woods, demanded new regulations that would allow the nationalization of strategic industries, and hoped to foster an open debate over the role of UNCTAD toward other international economic organizations. The moderates, in contrast, put forward lower-profile requests for further trade liberalization and an increase in development aid.[46]

The product of the effort to reconcile these internal tensions within the G77 nations was the Lima Charter, signed on November 7, 1971.[47] The Lima Charter placed a spotlight on the danger of the potential bankruptcy faced by developing countries, citing a debt burden projected to reach a total of US$60 billion by the end of the 1970s and argued that in order to correct this trend, the Southern countries would first have to make difficult choices regarding their own industrialization and deep internal structural reforms. One such important choice, taken before

---

[44] NARA, CPF, FT3, Box 1020, Report, "Perez-Guerrero Visit," November 19, 1971.
[45] NARA, CPF, FT3, Box 1021, Telegram Embassy New Delhi, "UNCTAD III: Recent GOI Statement on Some Issues," December 13, 1971.
[46] NARA, CPF, FT3, Box 1020, Intelligence Note, "UNCTAD III: Group of 77 surfaces differing attitudes among regional groups," November 15, 1971.
[47] HAEU, BAC 25/1980, n. 303 "Déclaration et principes du program d'action de Lima, adoptés par le Groupe des 77 à la Deuxième Réunion Ministérielle," November 7, 1971.

Lima, had been the inclusion of Cuba in the Group, a decision made by the Peruvian government against the express wishes of a number of participating countries.

The North–South debate would then carry over from the G77 conference in Lima to the third UNCTAD conference in Santiago. Earlier, in 1970, Kissinger had demonstrated in a memorandum to President Nixon the concern, he felt at the potentially dangerous repercussions of the so-called "Chilean Path to Socialism":

> The example of a successful elected Marxist government in Chile would surely have an impact on—and even precedent value for—other parts of the world, especially in Italy; the imitative spread of similar phenomena elsewhere would in turn significantly affect the world balance and our own position in it.[48]

But whatever efforts it might make, American diplomacy could not prevent Allende's Chile from hosting such a major international meeting:[49] a factor that would contribute to Washington's hostility to UNCTAD in particular, and the United Nations in general, a forum in which the United States began to find itself consistently in the minority.[50]

Allende had been elected president of Chile in 1970 and was a proponent of a socialism rooted in constitutional processes and parliamentary politics.[51] Such politics implied the acquisition, by either the state or workers' cooperatives, of a number of underperforming economic sectors: From the copper mining industry, to the great agricultural *latifundias*, to financial institutions.[52] Allende's socialist experiment drew great international attention—he had the support of the great Chilean poet Pablo Neruda and the open sympathy of Fidel Castro, among others—in large part because it represented a potential third way to industrial development in the Third World: An alternative to both the Brazilian or Iranian models, based on an authoritarian government allied with international capital, hostile to any redistributive measures, and that of Peru, similarly based on a military *junta* but in open opposition to international capital and bent on a form of wealth redistribution through state intervention.[53] The "democratic socialism" embodied by Allende showed the promise of a new paradigm for all of Latin America: A democratically elected government, attempting to free itself from the guidance of foreign financial

---

[48] Cited in A. Santoni, Il PCI e i giorni del Cile. Alle origini di un mito politico (Rome: Carocci, 2008), p. 92. Also cited in P. Kornbluh (ed.), *Nixon on Chile Intervention*, National Security Archive Electronic Briefing Book No. 110 (February 2004). Available online at <http://www.gwu.edu/~nsarchiv/NSAEBB/NSAEBB110/index.htm#doc2>.

[49] NARA, CPF, FT3, Box 1019, Department of State, "UNCTAD. Decision to hold UNCTAD III in Santiago: US Position," March 20, 1970.

[50] HAEU, BAC 25/1980, n. 303, Délégation de la Commission à Washington, "Préparation de la prochaine conference de la CNUCED par les Autorités américaines." March 13, 1971.

[51] J. Haslam, *The Nixon Administration and the Death of Allende's Chile: A Case of Assisted Suicide* (New York: W.W. Norton & Co., 2005).

[52] A. Cuevas, "Salvador Allende," in A. Cuevas (ed.), *America Latina. Uomini e idee*, vol. 2 (Rome: Edizioni Lavoro, 1995), p. 324.

[53] A. Touraine, *Vie et mort du Chili populaire: Juillet/Septembre 1973* (Paris: Editions du Seuil, 1973), p. 15.

markets and to redistribute resources more equitably among its population with the help of self-managing cooperatives.

The Chilean president immediately began by nationalizing the holdings of American multinationals that monopolized the production of copper, Chile's most vital strategic resource, but one that was some 80 percent under foreign control. The goal behind the nationalization of the mining industry was to exploit the income from the export of raw materials to finance imports of heavy machinery, in order to support the future development of Chilean industry.[54] The United States government was not unaware that American multinationals were pocketing huge profits from their investments in the strategic resources of Latin American countries; however, it justified these profits—a return on investment of up to 10 percent per year—as just remuneration for the risks incurred by foreign entrepreneurs, and argued that local governments were incapable of managing the natural resources of their own lands with the same efficiency and "know how."[55] Allende's international strategy, in cooperation with the other more radical Southern countries, was to combat this view by establishing new international standards on foreign investment that would guarantee local governments' autonomy to manage their own natural resources, allowing them to condemn and outlaw foreign intervention or political pressures regarding nationalization.

The other prongs of Allende's international economic strategy included the untying of international aid, which often created the paradox that wealthy donor nations found themselves even richer after the granting of assistance than they had been before;[56] agreements on prices for raw materials that would allow producer nations to raise their value; and consensus on the need for international cooperation to reform the international monetary system. For Allende these concepts were not the product of intellectual analysis born in opposition, but rather a practical effort to overcome the economic stranglehold that confronted a small nation of the Global South. Chile imported almost all its domestic necessities. Representatives of the Chilean government, receiving a delegation from the Italian Communist

---

[54] A. Mulas, *Allende e Berlinguer: Il Cile dell'Unidad Popular e il compromesso storico italiano* (Lecce: Manni, 2005), p. 54.

[55] NARA, CPF, FT3, Box 960, Letter from Ambassador Korry to Chilean Minister of Foreign Relations, March 26, 1969. The American Ambassador to Chile Edward Korry, contesting the validity of the figures cited by the Chilean government, argued that, while from 1960 to 1966 private investment in Latin America totaled some US$2.75 billion, the return on investment amounted to "only" some $8.39 billion.

[56] FRUS, 1969–1976, vol. IV, Letter From Acting Secretary of State Elliot Richardson to Secretary of the Treasury David M. Kennedy, June 9, 1969. The same Secretary of State Richardson, before being replaced, complained to Treasury Secretary Kennedy about the fact that the system of American aid to Latin America generated a *surplus* of US$300 million. In certain cases, like that of Colombia, the clauses attached to the loans compelled the debtor nation to conduct more than 40 percent of its trade with the United States. In other situations, like that of Chile, such clauses imposed the concession of reverse preferences on American products: "I understand we have argued vehemently that reverse preferences are bad and they should be eliminated entirely from the Common Market/African Yaoundé Convention," Richardson noted. And yet: "In order to improve our balance of payments situation and avoid the replacement of possible direct American exports by our aid shipments, we have instituted an elaborate program of negotiated 'additionality' agreements which result in a small gross gain to the balance of payments. At what cost?"

Party,[57] explained that there were only two ways that a Latin American country undertaking a program of reform could accumulate sufficient capital resources to finance its imports. The first was to obtain greater profits from the export of its own raw materials, something that would not be possible if commodity prices were to drop on the international market. The second was to obtain wider access to international credit. But on January 2, 1972 the United States had officially declared that no country that had nationalized the property of American citizens could obtain government loans. At the same time the credit granted to Chile from all the international financial agencies, from the World Bank to the Inter-American Development Bank, suffered a drastic reduction: From US$237 million to US$27 million.[58] Such events help to explain Allende's insistence on agreements to safeguard commodity prices, on new standards to regulate international loans, and on international participation over the future of the American dollar, the currency of reference for payments on virtually all raw materials.

Allende's strategy was presented in a more strident tone on December 4, 1972—after the conclusion of UNCTAD III in Santiago, to be discussed shortly—in his remarks before the General Assembly of the United Nations.[59] Allende noted that in the two years since the declaration of the Second UN Development Decade the situation facing the South had become, if anything, even worse: The industrialized countries had decreased aid from an average of 0.34 percent of GDP to 0.24 percent; the international debt of the Southern countries had grown in two years from US$70 billion to US$75 billion; and Western investment in Latin America had produced an exodus of capital between 1960 and 1970 on the order of US$9 billion. To reverse this state of affairs, Allende asked that the international economic system be changed to allow greater solidarity among the countries of the South, including in the form of regional economic accords.

---

[57] Fondazione Istituto Gramsci (FIG), Archivio Partito Comunista (APC), Fondo Esteri, Anno 1972, vol. V, "Relazione del compagno Secchia sul viaggio in Cile per il 50mo anniversario del Partito," January 17, 1972. Pietro Secchia, one of the party's *eminences grises*, had engaged in discussions with the head of the Chilean Communist Party Corvolan and with the Soviet Foreign Minister Volodia, and had come away with the following notes:

– In the course of 1971 some 1,300 *latifundias* were redistributed, and in 1972 the others are set to undergo redistribution;

– nationalization of the copper mines;

– nationalization of the carbon mines and of a large ironworks, two of the three largest cement producers, and fifty percent of the private banks;

– sixty percent of Chile's industrial production is today in the hands of the State. In certain cases this is the product of expropriation, in others the assumption of control by the government and the acquisition of shares whose price had collapsed;

– growth in salaries slightly higher than projected adjustments for the cost of living.

The problem, added the two Chilean representatives, was that Chile must import everything, from meat to raw materials, and could count neither on foreign aid, nor on a rise in the price of the goods it exported. The price of copper, which was at $0.67, had dropped to $0.45. As a result the government decided to bet everything on growth in production as well as the common struggle of commodities producers.

[58] Mulas, *Allende e Berlinguer*, p. 65.

[59] United Nations, General Assembly, Official Records, Speech by Salvador Allende, President of Chile, to the twenty-seventh session of the General Assembly of the United Nations, December 4, 1972.

Securing the meeting of UNCTAD III in Santiago had been a victory for the Chilean Ambassador Hernán Santa Cruz, an able navigator of the complicated dynamics of UN negotiations. His deft assurances notwithstanding, setting up a conference capable of hosting an organization of some 2,600 delegates, coming from 140 nations, for an entire month would be an enormous undertaking for a small country in the grip of a severe economic crisis. The most important element of the project, ordered by Allende himself, was the construction of a new conference hall, for which approximately US$9 million had been appropriated. As of January 1972, little more than two months from the conference's opening, work was still far behind schedule. At the end of the month the Chilean president went in person to the construction site and spoke directly to the 1,100 workers there, reminding them that Chile was being watched by the entire world and explaining just how urgent the success of UNCTAD was for the nation's future.[60] He asked them to volunteer to work even over the weekends in numbers greater than the 35 percent established by contract, and added that he would return unannounced to check on their progress and to see just how many laborers were volunteering to work in their free time.

The United States hardly prepared for the Santiago conference. The American delegation, which unlike their European counterparts did not include anyone of ministerial rank, was instructed to maintain "a generally forthcoming but low key approach."[61] American attentions in international economic relations were directed elsewhere, principally toward their primary goal of restoring a trade surplus through a careful manipulation of the dollar. For its part the Soviet Union, which did not boast a very positive record on development aid, did not appreciate being placed by the G77 on the same plane as the imperialist powers, and did not hold much faith in multilateral economic negotiations as a tool to help the Southern countries escape the vicious cycle of underdevelopment.[62] Among the great powers, only China expressed support for the negotiating positions of the Southern nations; the Chinese were actively courting Latin America by granting more aid than Moscow to the Allende government. At the UNCTAD in Santiago, China also positioned itself in favor of new international legislation that would expand the range of territorial waters, as requested by Peru, railing against the conduct of Western multinationals and against the trade and agricultural policies of the United States and the European Community in general.[63] But the Chinese delegation still had not realized the full import and direction of the UNCTAD negotiations, and effectively outlined a policy that tended toward autarky and self-isolation:

[60] "Showcase Lags, Allende Frets," in *Washington Post*, January 27, 1972.

[61] FRUS, 1969–1976, vol. IV, Memorandum from the Chairman of the CIEP (Samuels) to the President's Assistant for International Economic Negotiations (Flanigan), "CIEP Study Memorandum 16 UNCTAD III," March 3, 1972.

[62] NA, FCO 59/794, Draft for "trends," "Communist Economic Aid before UNCTAD III," January 20, 1972. In 1970 the Soviet Union had distributed less aid than it had in 1964: US$1 billion, down from US$1.3 billion. Soviet aid, moreover, was densely concentrated in specific areas; more than 50 percent went to two countries: Egypt and India. The rest went almost entirely to another six countries: Turkey, Syria, Iran, Afghanistan, Pakistan, and Algeria.

[63] For an interpretation of Chinese foreign policy in this regard, see Fejtö, *Chine–Urss*, p. 441.

Objectives that were not very appetizing to countries that were dependent on foreign commerce, and that possessed much smaller and more restricted domestic
markets than China's vast territorial ocean of men and materials.[64]

Even if the two superpowers were not deeply engaged in the negotiations at
Santiago, this does not mean that the conference did not produce meaningful
results. The judgment of diplomatic historians like Jean-Baptiste Duroselle has
been wholly negative, and seems to treat the Santiago conference as the final
engagement in the battle between North and South before the conflicts that
emerged over the oil question definitively ruptured the South's united front.[65] The
Santiago meeting might instead be considered as the beginning of a process of
growing combativeness in the developing world and a new, albeit brief, phase
marked by a surprising degree of internal cohesion.

The Santiago conference forced both North and South to confront new issues
that would supplant more traditional debates over trade preferences and development aid. The conference approved the creation of a commission guided by the
Mexican president Luis Echeverria, for instance, that was charged with drafting a
"Charter of the Economic Rights and Duties of States" and that, among other
things, would definitively establish the legal rights to nationalization. The participants at Santiago also reiterated their general reticence toward foreign investment
by multinationals and the industrialized world, as well as multilateral aid, and
demonstrated a tendency to widen the role of the state in the economy, even among
the non-socialist countries. Moreover, UNCTAD III determined that the countries of the South would participate in the reform of the international monetary
system, and that a "Committee for the Reform of the International Economic
Order," the Committee of Twenty—which included several developing countries—
would be the primary forum for future monetary negotiations.[66] Even if the Committee of Twenty, effectively created in July 1972, was not able to produce a
definitive reform of Bretton Woods in its two years of activity, it nevertheless contributed to a push to increase the weight of the developing countries within the
IMF, and successfully placed the issue of increasing the flow of credit toward the
developing world on the international agenda. In the same way, a resolution
approved at Santiago pledged the GATT nations to involve the G77 and the Secretary-General of UNCTAD in the multilateral negotiations scheduled to begin in
1973 and that would become known as the Tokyo Round.

[64] NARA, CPF, FT3, Box 1023, Intelligence Note, "The Communist Countries at the UNCTAD
III," June 14, 1972. The report of the American specialists noted that China had failed in its efforts to
position itself as the leader of the developing countries, and that it had not even succeeded in joining
the G77.
    [65] J.B. Duroselle and A. Kaspi, *Histoire des relations internationales de 1945 à nos jours* (Paris:
Armand Colin, 2004).
    [66] FRUS, 1969–1976, vol. III, Volker Group Paper, "Minutes of the discussion in London con-
cerning the procedures for preparing monetary reform (April 23, 1972)," Washington, May 10, 1972.
The practical procedures for the creation of the G20 were discussed within the group led by the
Under-Secretary of the US Treasury Paul Volker. The goal of the G20 was to return to a system of
"fixed but adjustable" exchange. But in June 1974, after the first oil crisis, the group was forced to
admit it was impossible to find common ground on a system of fixed exchange and concluded its
labors.

One unforeseen element to emerge from Santiago was the attention, and in some cases direct intervention, of interest groups, religious orders, student movements, and various associations in many of the issues up for debate, including on some highly technical matters—attention that gave the diplomats involved the sense of being watched by international public opinion.[67] We have already seen how the Dutch government had prepared its negotiating position in collaboration with trade unions and student groups. But even in a country with a traditionally opaque bureaucracy like Italy, long-time diplomats lamented the influence exerted by pressure groups on the inner workings of the Foreign Ministry. They demanded that the foreign service regain "that capacity and those functions which, either *de jure* or *de facto*, had been taken away from it, especially after 1968, by cooperatives, associations, parties, and unions."[68] Initiatives like the Tobin Tax (named after the noted economist), put forward in 1972 and supported by scattered intellectuals and nongovernmental organizations, were designed to levy a tax on international capital speculation. On the European level in particular, it had become clear that it would be impossible to avoid directly involving citizens in the potential risks and damage that would result from an international revolution that was inherent in the existing trade imbalances between rich and poor nations. Likewise, it was understood that it would be wiser to explicitly encourage European consumers to choose goods produced in the Third World, rather than continue to express their sympathy through sporadic, isolated gestures of charity.[69]

SICCO MANSHOLT

While the logistical planning for UNCTAD III proceeded apace, the countries of the European Community developed their negotiating positions.

Italy found itself in an unusually high-profile position during the period from the Hague Conference to the UNCTAD meeting at Santiago, which it handled with an uncommon vigor.[70] In 1970 the Christian Democrat Franco Maria Malfatti had been named President of the European Commission, joined in Brussels by another Italian in the office of Commissioner for Industry, Altiero Spinelli, a well-known proponent of European federalism. Until 1974, save for a brief interruption, the Italian Foreign Ministry was headed by the former prime minister Aldo Moro. In a meeting with Malfatti in 1970, Moro had stated his conviction that Europe needed to strengthen its relationship with Latin America, a long-held objective of Italian diplomacy that appeared to gain new traction with the enlarge-

[67] UNOG, UNCTAD, ARR 1830, b15a, Written for the World Development Movement by John Greenway and Chris Pipe in conjunction with Chris Stockwell (who represented the WDM in Santiago), "End of an Illusion. Verdict on UNCTAD III," July 1972.

[68] R. Gaja, *L'Italia nel mondo bipolare. Per una storia della politica estera italiana* (Bologna: Il Mulino, 1995), p. 25.

[69] HAEU, EM 153, Ocipe, "Rapport du colloque de Wissen, Problèmes posés par l'évolution globale du commerce entre la Cee et la Pvd."

[70] A. Varsori, *La Cenerentola di Europa. L'Italia e l'integrazione europea dal 1947 ad oggi* (Soveria Mannelli: Rubbettino, 2010).

ment of the European Community. If undertaken, however, such a strategy would have implied the creation of new frictions in relations with Washington. In a letter to Allende, the Italian Communist MP Renato Sandri explained that the ties binding Europe and the United States were loosening, as the states of western Europe began to perceive the need for greater autonomy, not least of all in the technological field.[71] Moro himself appeared convinced that the challenges created by détente, not to mention the social tensions within the EC nations, highlighted the need to reposition Europe as a "civilian power":

> This unifying action, both economic and political, of most of western Europe was born from a grand design: Replacing with fertile cooperation those suspicions and rivalries between peoples of the region—factors which had led to two world wars.
> ... Such a work can give the peoples of Europe the chance to let themselves be heard more effectively. Can such rediscovered influence be harmful to anyone? The answer is: No. It is not directed—and will never be directed—against any people, but against war, against the burden of weaponry, hunger and underdevelopment, against iniquity, against all that which can hinder free and productive contacts among all men.[72]

The Italian government was subject to multiple and often countervailing pressures in the run up to the Santiago conference. It was engaged in a war against an internal "strategy of tension" marked by sporadic acts of domestic terrorism, and preoccupied by the constant flight of capital that illustrated the Italian bourgeoisie's alarming lack of faith in the stability of its democratic institutions. Almost inevitably this led to clashes within the government, on the limits of the potential concessions Italy could make to the industrializing countries without endangering the country's own low-tech industries. The socialist Commerce Minister Mario Zagari considered the Third World the second most important competitor to Europe, just behind the United States, and criticized multinationals and neocapitalism, sparing no words in his criticism of an Italian policy of development cooperation overly focused, in his estimation, on improving trade balances.[73] During the third

---

[71] FIG, APC 1970, Esteri, Fascicolo 218, Renato Sandri al Signor Presidente della Repubblica del Cile, Santiago, November 2, 1970: "From 1955 to 1958 North American investments in the EEC countries grew by 68 percent, while the growth in American investments throughout the developing world amounted to a total of only 88 percent... The United States is concentrating on conquering European industry and finance. The branches of the American multinationals operating in Europe control 95 percent of semiconductors, 80 percent of all electronics, 40 percent of titanium oxides, [and] 30 percent of the automotive sector."

[72] Aldo Moro, Speech at the Twenty-Sixth Session of the General Assembly of the UN, New York, October 6, 1971.

[73] M. Zagari, *Superare le sfide. La risposta dell'Italia e dell'Europa alle sfide mondiali* (Milan: Rizzoli, 2006), p. 119. Regarding multinationals, Zagari writes:

> The inadequacy of the capitalist approach based on profit and private enterprise speaks for itself, in the phenomenon—as atavistic as it is alarming—of multinational corporations for whom the Third World has become either a base camp or a place of refuge. It is clear that, with this eminently modern phenomenon, neo-capitalism tends to produce anything but the promotion of the economic development and social health of the less developed countries, seeking instead to profit from their lower labor standards and overabundance of unskilled workers; with the result that it impedes any real improvement in the state of either their disadvantaged classes or their organizational structures.

UNCTAD, the question which most closely united Italy with the countries of the South was that of international monetary reform, mainly through the request for a link between the creation of Special Drawing Rights and development aid, a proposal previously advanced in 1967 by the Italian Treasury Minister Emilio Colombo.

Immediately after the conclusion of the conference in Chile, members of the Institute for Relations between Italy and Africa, Latin America, and the Middle East (IPALMO)[74]—established in 1971 to bring together trade union leaders, politicians, and scholars of different political backgrounds with an interest in development issues and UNCTAD—gathered in Rome. Its director Giampaolo Calchi Novati evaluated the Italian government's position at Santiago on international monetary reform, delivering strong criticism of its inability to offer effective opposition to the demands of more politically active Southern states like Chile or Algeria. Renato Sandri, in charge of cooperation for the PCI, supported the government's position on preferences and SDRs, but criticized its defense of European agricultural interests, indicating the priorities of an Italian Communism thoroughly in line with the predominant positions of the Scandinavian social democracies:

1. Support for the French proposal, opposed by the Federal Republic of Germany as well as the United States, to create global mechanisms to regulate raw materials;

2. Broadening of the generalized system of non-reciprocal preferences adopted by the EC, in such a way that it could tip trade balances in favor of the Third World;

3. Revision of the EC–AASM agreements from Yaoundé, created under a framework of colonial heritage and French neocolonialism;

4. Revision of the Common Agricultural Policy, which would have to center largely on reform of its structures rather than on the price controls;

5. Adoption by Europe of the socialist countries' aid concession scheme.

Among the Six, the country whose position most closely approximated an open partnership with the Southern countries was the Netherlands. Shortly after the Santiago conference a national election would result in a change in the Dutch parliamentary majority, bringing to power a new coalition of Labour and extremely progressive Christian Democrats. Yoop Den Uyl was named Prime Minister and Jan Pronk—who had long collaborated with Jan Tinbergen on questions of development—was named Minister for Development Cooperation. But even before the change in government, development issues drew heavy pressure from a wide range of public opinion, from student movements to religious groups. In January 1972 the government had organized a symposium in preparation for Santiago, calling on politicians and well-known policy experts on development. The invited repre-

---

[74] FIG, APC, Estero, Anno 1972, vol. VIII, Tavola rotonda Ipalmo, "La terza sessione dell'UNCTAD a Santiago del Cile."

sentatives of the French government would later complain that, in an atmosphere conditioned by the presence of young "socialists and radicals," a platform was approved that largely conflicted with French policy goals.[75] The final document indicated four objectives that western Europe should aim to achieve at Santiago:

1. that each member State should spend at least 0.7 percent of GDP in development aid;

2. that the creation of international liquidity—SDRs—should be tied to development assistance;

3. that the protectionist policies of the Community regarding agricultural products and its system of special preferences be amended;

4. that it should move forward on international agreements on a product-by-product basis.

These instructions were not very different from those that the current Dutch Minister for Development Cooperation Kees Boertien would support, with greater diplomatic finesse, in his remarks at the plenary assembly at Santiago. Boertien reminded the other ministers that:

> public opinion in several developed countries is gradually becoming informed about the biggest problems that the developing countries have encountered on their path to development. Political parties, churches, and student movements today all have a passionate interest in cooperation between developed countries and developing countries. This is especially true in my country.[76]

The openness of the Dutch position compared to that of the other nations of the Community led The Hague's supporters to believe that, in conjunction with the governments of Nordic socialist and other progressive nations—Sweden and Canada, in particular—they might form a new motor for international cooperation, especially within multilateral organizations like the World Bank.[77]

The French government also placed great importance on the meeting in Santiago, and decided to employ as spokesman the Finance Minister Valéry Giscard d'Estaing, one of the most distinguished voices on the French political stage. The line that he would follow did not differ much in substance from that previously maintained by de Gaulle, aimed above all at defending the interests of the Association of the African States—which required reassurance in light of the widening of the European Community—and forging a new rapport with the British Commonwealth. French diplomats had begun to reach out to the AASM at the start of the new year, in a ministerial meeting in which Giscard explained to his African colleagues France's strategy to combat the chaos of currency revaluations that

---

[75] AMAEF, NUOI, Carton 1332, Ambassade de France aux Pays-Bas, "Note sur le Symposium préparatoire à la Troisième CNUCED qui s'est tenu à La Haye les 19, 20, et 21 janvier 1972."

[76] HAEU, FMM 38, Statement by Mr. C. Boertien, Minister in charge of Development cooperation of the Kingdom of the Netherlands, "UNCTAD," May 15, 1972.

[77] WBGA, Office of the President, Records of Robert S. McNamara, General Correspondence, Box 1, Memorandum, "Meeting in McNamara's Office," November 4, 1963.

threatened to destabilize the finances of the poorest nations.[78] The French government, he explained, hoped to negotiate a devaluation of the dollar in order to return to a system of fixed exchange. The head of the French Treasury further reminded his hosts of the economic figures behind the relationship of the Community with the Association of the African States, which showed them to be running deficits in terms of goods and services while maintaining a surplus in capital transfers. Such figures clearly showed the African states' complete dependence on European aid and the marginality of their foreign trade. It should thus come as no surprise that the AASM nations had promised to fight at UNCTAD III to introduce and promote economic relief for the poorest of the developing countries.

During the Santiago conference, Giscard dutifully revived the strategy of individual commodity agreements, an instrument that promised to be able to guarantee stable profits for raw materials by freeing them from the vagaries of the market.[79] He radically opposed, however, the requests of those nations—among them certain developed nations, but above all the Latin American countries—that sought the wider opening of European markets. Broader access to European markets for agricultural produce from more temperate zones such as grain or milk, the French argued, would favor first and foremost other industrialized nations like the United States. On the other hand, even if the Community supported the import of tropical African products, such measures alone were insufficient, as the African states were among the poorest nations on earth, and especially because canceling the already low tariffs on tropical goods would not produce any increase in their consumption on the continent.

Great Britain had even less freedom of action than they had possessed at UNCTAD II in New Delhi in 1968. British diplomacy appeared to be completely subordinated to the decisions of the Community nations, which were preparing to decide on London's entry into the group. The pessimistic attitude of the analysts in the British Foreign Office left no room for novel proposals. While the relationship with the South was considered a potential card to play, either with the European Commission or with the Foreign Ministries of the Six, and could even be seen as the kernel of a future common European foreign policy, the English appeared to be well aware of their own marginal position.[80] Great Britain had tried to respond to its difficulties on the aid front—along with the United States, it was the only country not to accept the target of 0.7 percent of GDP—by announcing at the last minute in Santiago a minor effort in that area, and especially by pledging to present new proposals to improve the quality of European aid at the upcoming European summit in Paris.[81]

---

[78] AMAEF, NUOI, Carton 1332, Réunion des ministres des Finances Africains, Malgache et Français, "Compte rendu analytique de la reunion des 21 et 22 février, 1972 à Fort-Lamy."

[79] AMAEF, NUOI, Carton 1333, Nations Unies, "Note pour le Cabinet," March 16, 1972.

[80] NA, FCO 59/794, UK Delegation to the EEC, "UNCTAD III," January 17, 1972.

[81] NA, FCO 59/795, Note to the Prime Minister, "Debt Burden to Developing Countries," April 27, 1972: "We are seen, both at the international level and here at home, as brakemen, and I believe our prestige within UNCTAD and at the fall EEC summit would be markedly increased if we were to succeed in approving a higher level of public aid, without necessarily supporting the 0.7 percent target."

In its approach to the third UNCTAD, the European Community was forced to reconcile these diverse positions and the specific role of the European Commission. If it successfully managed at the last minute to take a defined position, and if the relationship with the developing countries became one of the important topics at the summit of European heads of state and government held at Paris in October 1972, this was because of the personal activism of one man: The new president of the European Commission, the Dutch socialist Sicco Mansholt, who succeeded Malfatti in April 1972 and remained in charge for only a little over seven months.

For the European Community 1970 had been full of positive signs for the decade to come. In December 1969 the Hague Summit had concluded with the historic decisions to confirm British admission and to take the first steps toward economic and monetary union. In 1970 the "transition period" came to a close with the inauguration of the Malfatti Commission, which would be empowered to represent the Community, the largest trade bloc in the world, in all international trade agreements with third party nations. The institutions in Brussels were buzzing with lively debates and new ideas, but also clouded by a certain confusion due to the obvious need to adjust its norms and structures to a new role worthy of the Community's economic strength. The period immediately following 1970 has been described by Michel Dumoulin as one of the Commission's greatest periods of intense creativity, pregnant with possibilities for innovation.[82]

Among the most obvious problems facing the European Commission was that of the Community's representation in international economic negotiations. While it was true that, under Article 113 of the Treaty of Rome, the Commission was the only body allowed to represent the Community in trade negotiations, one question remained unanswered: What was the appropriate procedure in those talks where questions of trade, other questions of Community interest, and still other questions of an exclusively national character were all discussed at the same time? Such mixed forums were many, including the United Nations FAO, the OECD, the World Bank, and UNCTAD itself. It was very quickly understood that finding a uniform solution would be impossible, and it that would be best to decide the question of the Community's representation on a case-by-case basis.[83] Thus began a battle that continues to this day, to find some form of common European representation in all international economic institutions (with the notable exception of GATT, where such representation had of course been already decided).

The same European Commission began to reorganize its own internal structures, including the slow but steady passage of responsibility for relations with the Global South from the Commissioner for External Relations to the Commissioner for Development Cooperation. Definitively completed by the negotiations at

---

[82] M. Dumoulin (ed.), *The European Commission 1958–72: History and Memories* (Brussels: European Commission, 2007), p. 197.

[83] HAEU, EM 153, Service Juridique de al Commission des Communautés Européennes, Note pour la DGI, "Relations extérieures de la Communauté Economique Européenne. Conséquences de la fin de la période de transition," December 15, 1969. The Community's Legal Services branch revealed the inefficacy of the law on matters of a political nature: "The solution that would seem to be most satisfying, in the current state of the Community's evolution, is a mixed delegation."

Lomé,[84] this process indicated French wishes (the Directorate-General for Development was by tradition a French prerogative) to retain control over relations with the developing world after enlargement, and thus to safeguard the priority the French placed on their traditional link with the AASM.

The communication presented by the Commission to the European Council in March 1972 was very cautious, because of the desire to avoid committing the Six—which group by 1973 would become the Nine—to further financial commitments, and the need to defend the CAP, but also because of the contradiction between their duty to maintain the special relationship with the African states and their desire to make overtures to the rest of the Southern countries.[85] The most important novelty in the communiqué lay in the recognition of the financial needs of the developing countries: A condition that it would not be possible to change simply with more aid. According to the calculations in the Pearson Report, developing countries would need a total of some US$28 billion in aid by 1975, a figure that would imply an increase in public development aid of some 4.4 percent for just the Community alone. The Commission acknowledged that such a prospect was entirely unrealistic, reiterating the Community's usual line of defense that it was the greatest importer of goods from the poorest countries while avoiding putting undue emphasis on the fact that the majority of such imports came from energy-producing nations. The Commission instead proposed to the Council that the Community pledge to finance a series of studies to promote the formation of regional markets throughout the South on the model of the Community itself, with the idea of fostering a virtuous circle of exports among the Southern countries themselves. But the Community also came under fierce pressure—from Continental textile industries, for example[86]—to avoid further extension of the generalized system of preferences, and from farming interests to avoid concessions to the Third World on agricultural policy.[87]

Within the European Parliament the climate was more favorable to increasing the Community's commitments toward the South. The parliamentary report on UNCTAD II presented by Pedini in 1968 had concluded by asking for an original doctrine on which the Six could agree, liberating them from their usual bartering. Four years later, in the discussions leading up to Santiago,[88] Fellarmier (speaking on behalf of the socialists) called for a quantum leap in the direction of a global

[84] HAEU, EM 158, Nota, "La necessaria salvaguardia della politica estera nei confronti dei paesi terzi in via di sviluppo": "A strong trend in favor of reinforcement of the development aid sector (DG VIII, development policy directly primarily towards Africa) is making itself felt through the addition of a 'Mediterranean policy' and a 'general multilateral policy toward the developing countries' (primarily UNCTAD and the generalized preference schemes for semi-manufactures and manufactures of the developing countries), competencies currently attributed to the DGI."

[85] Commissione europea, Comunicazione della Commissione al Consiglio, "Preparazione della 3º Conferenza delle Nazioni Unite per il commercio e lo sviluppo," March 8, 1973.

[86] HAEU, BAC 25/1980, n. 303, Comitextil, Lettre à M. J.F. Deniau, Membre de la Commission des C.E., April 14, 1972.

[87] HAEU, BAC 25/1980, n. 303, COPA, "Déclaration du Praesidium du Copa en ce qui concerne la troisième CNUCED," April 14, 1972.

[88] European Parliament, *Debates*, sitting of Tuesday March 14, 1972.

politics of development cooperation and supported the idea that the introduction of SDRs as a new reserve currency alongside the dollar should be tied to development aid. From the same socialist parliamentary group the Dutch minister Engiwarda pointed out that Sir Maxwell Stamp in 1953—the spiritual father of SDRs—Robert Triffin, and more recently the Nobel laureate Jan Tinbergen had all supported the linkage between SDRs and development aid. But there was widespread skepticism among Commission staff at the idea of international financial reform in favor of the South.

The Council of Ministers, delivering its directive regarding the Santiago conference, had expressed the cautious view that the Community could play no specific role in Chile, other than to offer generic support for an agreement on individual commodity agreements. The choice to assume more forthcoming positions would have to depend upon individual member states.[89] The official justification was that, in light of its imminent enlargement, the Community could not take any decisions that would complicate or endanger British admission.

Predictions of an uninspired Community "performance" at UNCTAD would have been realized if not for the nomination, in April 1972 and precisely in connection with the beginning of discussions in Santiago, of Sicco Mansholt as President of the European Commission. The selection of Mansholt revealed a surprising softening of the attitude of Pompidou's France toward Europe. Mansholt was in fact loathed by the Gaullists for his proposals to reform the Common Agricultural Policy, and for his overt sympathies for European federalism. As Altiero Spinelli wrote in his diary, "the choice of Mansholt is an excellent one. It is characteristic of a new wind that is beginning to blow through Paris."[90] With a personality as singular as it was authoritative, Mansholt was not known in Brussels for his diplomatic skills, and had been among the few members of the college in the Berlaymont Palace to openly criticize de Gaulle. The son of farmers in the northernmost Dutch province of Gröningen, he was well versed in socialist ideas—a rarity in the conservative and rather closed Dutch agricultural milieu. Mansholt had taken part in the Dutch resistance against the Nazis during the Second World War and lived for a period in the Dutch East Indies as the manager of a tea-producing business: A hands-on experience with agricultural labor that he would always draw upon in his political career, first at national level and subsequently in the bureaucracy in Brussels. In the postwar years he was one of the youngest members of the Dutch cabinet, serving as Agriculture Minister until 1958 before being nominated the first Agricultural Commissioner of the European Commission.[91] Mansholt did not hold strong theoretical convictions with regard to markets and agricultural production, but rather by the beginning of the 1970s he began to regard the question of development in the South as the primary issue on which to focus the

---

[89] Central Archive of the Council of the European Union (CEU), Note, "Préparation de la 3ème Session de la Conférence des Nations Unies sur le Commerce et le Développement," March 24, 1972.

[90] A. Spinelli, *Diario europeo 1970–1976* (Bologna: Il Mulino, 1991), p. 286.

[91] For a complete biography of Mansholt, see J. Van Merriënboer, *Mansholt. A Biography*. Brussels: PIE Peter Lang, 2011.

Community's efforts, and to which all other common policies should be subordinated. The evolution of his thinking certainly echoed the wider cultural shifts brought about by 1968; indeed, he often cited both Marcuse and Illich without apology as intellectual reference points. At the same time, he was the first to voice the idea, widely shared within the closed circles of the Commission itself, of the need to search for a new driving mission to animate a recently enlarged Europe.[92]

Mansholt was greatly influenced by the *Limits of Growth* report and began a personal intellectual revolution driven by the idea that a "second Marx" was needed in order to find new solutions for the crisis of capitalism. In a private letter to Malfatti, the Dutch commissioner had outlined his plan for what might today be called the "degrowth of the European economy."[93] He understood that there would not be enough natural resources to support the survival and rising living standards of a world population that within a short period of time was expected to grow from 3 to 7 billion persons. The industrialized world would have to adjust its own way of life, ceasing to venerate the false idol of GDP in favor of growth in what he called Gross National Utility. "Don't fall in love with a given rate of growth," went the oft-repeated slogan in university halls of the time. Applying the concept of Gross National Utility carried several implications: In the developed world, cutting excess consumption, financing the production of consumer durables and energy-efficient appliances, and investing heavily in education and public services—that is, "planning abundance"; in the underdeveloped world, meanwhile, it suggested widening the use of technologically modern appliances to make daily life easier and improve life expectancy—that is, "planning scarcity." The end result of this process, which would be impossible to realize without introducing a massive dose of planning into the economy, would entail a substantial redirection of net resources to the Global South.

Mansholt's letter received press coverage because it was leaked to the media as an example of the wicked machinations of the technocrats in Brussels by the French communist leader George Marchais, in his campaign against British entry to the Community. Within the very same Commission there were many, from the Commissioner for Economic Affairs Raymond Barre to the Commissioner for Industry Spinelli, who thought Mansholt's arguments were too radical. They reiterated the importance of the economic relationship among the developed countries, and placed their faith in technology as a means of solving the problems tied to the distribution of energy resources as well as those of pollution and the environment.[94] As Spinelli recorded in his diary: "Together with Barre and with Dahrendorf I helped

---

[92] HAEU, FMM 40, Commission, "Premières considerations de base relatives à un memorandum sur la politique extérieure de la Communauté," January 31, 1972. The Commission's adviser wrote that "[t]he principal struggle that animates an ever-greater number of people at the end of the twentieth century is the struggle against poverty. This is one of the few uncontested ideals of a vexing and quarrelsome cohort of youth that will take the reins of power in the next generation."

[93] European Navigator (now Centre Virtuel de la Connaissance sur l'Europe), RTL (Film), *Qui est Mansholt? Quel est son plan?*, April 8, 1972. Available online at < http://www.cvce.eu/web/ws/search/-/search?searchQuery=Qui+est+Mansholt%3F>.

[94] J. van der Harst, "Sicco Mansholt: Courage and Conviction," in Dumoulin (ed.), *The European Commission*, p. 186.

give the proper shape to that part which concerns international relations. Mansholt would have talked only of the Developing Countries. We responded that if there is a trade war between the developed countries, then everything will fall apart. In the end Mansholt conceded the point."[95] Both sides would soon be forced to rethink their positions, but in the meantime their stance showed just how deeply in 1972 faith remained rooted in the panacea of technological progress.

With a brief warning to the staff of the External Relations Directorate-General, which had put forth a more tentative position than his own, the President of the Commission arrived in Santiago for the first time in mid-April.[96] Later, after having convened representatives of the Six on the spur of the moment,[97] Mansholt decided to return to Chile on 15 May with the aim of pushing forward the stalled UNCTAD negotiations, but especially with the goal of showing the Community in a different light. If the Community had been criticized particularly for its special relationship with the AASM, and the reciprocity of tariff concessions that this entailed,[98] Mansholt proposed instead to turn the EC into the major interlocutor of the Global South.[99] His first step was to organize a series of meetings with the heads of the delegations of the Community nations and the Secretary-General of UNCTAD, as well as the representatives of the Andean Pact, the AASM, and the Association of South-East Asian Nations (ASEAN), in order to give them a forum to voice their concerns with respect to the Community. India and Brazil, in particular, feared that British entry would mean a hike in English tariffs to align them with those of the other Community Member States. They requested that in the upcoming GATT negotiations, scheduled to begin in 1973 without the participation of some fifty-nine developing countries, attention might be turned to the preferential lowering of tariffs with the Southern nations, rather than the elimination of barriers to trade among developed states. Finally, they also asked to participate in monetary talks and urged the need for concrete action on commodities. Having listened to their concerns, Mansholt, despite not having much room for maneuver, sought to stretch the Council's directive to its limits. He guaranteed that generalized preferences would be more generous in the future, and that the Community would dedicate itself to working to allow the developing countries to participate in any future trade negotiations. Furthermore, he let it be understood that if the Community was not able to deliver more at UNCTAD, this was because

[95] Spinelli, *Diario europeo*, p. 316.

[96] AMAEF, NUOI, Carton 1333, Télégramme, "CNUCED," April 17, 1972. It should be noted that Mansholt referred in his remarks more often to the resolution of the European Parliament on the conference, which he later circulated among the delegates, than to the directives of the European Council.

[97] AMAEF, NUOI, Carton 1333, Télégramme Bruxelles, "Voyage à Santiago du Chili de M. Mansholt," May 15, 1972.

[98] HAEU, BAC 25/1980, n. 298, Commission, Délégation pour l'Amérique Latine, "Préparation III CNUCED. Commentaires au sujet de thèmes traits dans une communication de la Commission au Conseil," March 9, 1972.

[99] HAEU, FMM 38, Compte rendu de la visite du Président Mansholt à Santiago du Chili et à Lima. Visite à Santiago, May 16, 17, 18 and 19, 1972, May 23, 1972; "La fogue de M. Mansholt," Journal d'Europe, May 16, 1972.

it was fully engaged in preparations for the October Paris summit: An occasion which he hoped to use to announce a global effort on behalf of the developing countries. Mansholt's report on the trip to Chile concluded with the statement that the Community was "at the center of the developing countries' hopes and fears," and that excessive attention to the African states was perceived by the Southern nations as an effort to divide them. Urgent adjustments were needed.

Participation at UNCTAD reinforced Mansholt's convictions of the need to shift the attention of the Community from its relationship with the United States to those with the South. The tensions produced by this stance were amply demonstrated in a meeting in Brussels with Peter Flanigan, President Nixon's handpicked Assistant for International Economic Affairs, shortly after Mansholt's return from Chile.[100]

Flanigan opened the meeting by stating that, with the improvement in East–West relations—referring to the Strategic Arms Limitation Treaty (SALT I) that introduced limits to the superpowers' strategic nuclear weapons arsenal—the time had come to fortify the Atlantic Pact. Mansholt replied that, to European public opinion, the primary problem was now the North–South divide rather than the Cold War, and that in this area America's attitude was deeply discouraging. Flanigan later reported that when he sought to engage the President of the Commission on the need to resolve the contentious trade negotiations that were poisoning the relationship between the Community and Washington, Mansholt replied:

> [The] EC will begin to develop commercial and industrial policies which will look to the interests of the LDCs. The problems Europe has with the US are not important. The "Eberle negotiations" earlier this year were a big mistake for Europe. It was "silly" to have spent so much time and political capital on a few million dollars' worth of trade in citrus fruit, tobacco, etc., when 20 percent of the world was starving.
>
> He assured me that he was not the least concerned with soyabeans, ("to hell with your soyabeans")...

Flanigan seemed scandalized by the affirmation that in the upcoming GATT negotiations tariff reductions between developed countries would not be considered as important as the focus on tariff reductions toward the South. Mansholt retorted by admonishing the United States for their ever-more-limited efforts in terms of aid and added that, at the Paris summit on Community relations, European leaders would concentrate on the Third World, "implying that relations with the US would be decidedly secondary."

The meeting became even more tense when Nixon's representative made it clear that Washington could not permit any increase in development aid because the United States was constrained by massive military expenditures to support its commitments around the world, including for the defense of western Europe. Mansholt acknowledged that the issue of European military spending was a real one, but replied that, as a socialist, he did not believe the Vietnam War was resolving all

---

[100] FRUS, 1969–1976, vol. III, Report by the President's Assistant for International Economic Affairs (Flanigan), "Report of visit to Western Europe May 30–June 10, 1972, Attachment 2, Conversation with EC Commission President Sicco Mansholt," Brussels, June 1, 1972.

of humanity's problems, and added fuel to the fire by accusing the American government of having cut off multilateral aid funding to Chile. Wrapping up the meeting, he restated his belief in the unavoidable need to tax the developed nations to redistribute resources to the South, and affirmed that it would be necessary to reconvert both European industrial and agricultural policy, even at the cost of swift adjustments to the Western way of life. It should come as no surprise that Mansholt did not win himself any sympathy in Washington.

REGIONALISTS AND GLOBALISTS

After the 1973 enlargement, the European Community would include some 256 million citizens, compared to 207 million in the United States and 245 million in the Soviet Union, and would reassert its prominence in global commerce, conducting some 22.6 percent of world trade.

It would emerge as an economic giant, whose decisions would inevitably have an impact on economies throughout the rest of the world. It thus faced the problem of balancing its development and cooperation policies, which up to that point had had a primarily regional focus, with a global outlook that would respond to the increasingly insistent demands of the Southern countries as well as the pressures stemming from European public opinion.

The Community of the Six had signed association agreements with Greece and Turkey in 1962 and 1964, respectively, that were supposed to lead to the two nations' eventual adhesion. Among the countries of western Europe, Spain and Austria were also negotiating similar association agreements. In 1963 the Six had also, as we have already seen, signed the Yaoundé Convention with the francophone Association of the African States. In 1969 Yaoundé II had widened the AASM to include an additional three countries in East Africa. Turning to the Mediterranean, in September 1969 association agreements were reached with Tunisia and Morocco, while negotiations were ongoing with Israel, Egypt, and Lebanon to sign memoranda of understanding that would guarantee these nations preferences for particular goods on the European market.

That was not all. In 1969 the Community had applied specific preferential duties to citrus fruits from Israel and Spain, a decision that did not fail to provoke immediate and vociferous protests from the Latin American countries.[101] With the exception of the agreements on citrus products, all of these various deals—some of which anticipated customs unification, others simply the lowering of tariff barriers—had been negotiated under GATT Article XXV, which allowed for exemptions to the "most favored nation" clause wherever the countries involved had established free

---

[101] HAEU, EM 205, Conseil, Note d'Information, "Examen dans le cadre du GATT de la demande présentée par la Communauté vivant à obtenir une derogation au titre de l'Article XXV en ce qui concerne l'application de preferences tarifaires pour les agrumes originaires de l'Espagne et d'Israël," September 19, 1969. The South American countries stated their objections to the Community's decision thus: "Our delegations have observed that the decision taken by the Community seems to contradict both the stance it has often demonstrated toward the developing countries within UNCTAD, and the declarations of good will it has repeatedly submitted to the countries of Latin America."

THE EUROPEAN COMMUNITY AND ITS AGREEMENTS WITH DEVELOPING COUNTRIES
(1957–1975)

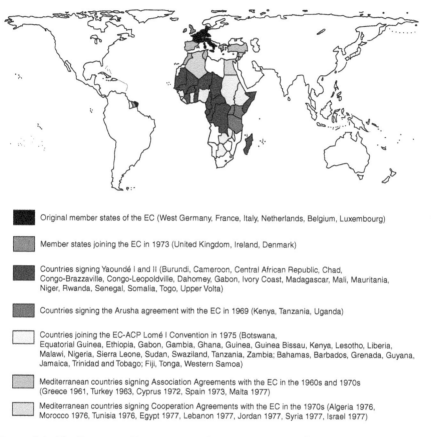

■ Original member states of the EC (West Germany, France, Italy, Netherlands, Belgium, Luxembourg)

▨ Member states joining the EC in 1973 (United Kingdom, Ireland, Denmark)

■ Countries signing Yaoundé I and II (Burundi, Cameroon, Central African Republic, Chad,
Congo-Brazzaville, Congo-Leopoldville, Dahomey, Gabon, Ivory Coast, Madagascar, Mali, Mauritania,
Niger, Rwanda, Senegal, Somalia, Togo, Upper Volta)

▨ Countries signing the Arusha agreement with the EC in 1969 (Kenya, Tanzania, Uganda)

□ Countries joining the EC-ACP Lomé I Convention in 1975 (Botswana,
Equatorial Guinea, Ethiopia, Gabon, Gambia, Ghana, Guinea, Guinea Bissau, Kenya, Lesotho, Liberia,
Malawi, Nigeria, Sierra Leone, Sudan, Swaziland, Tanzania, Zambia; Bahamas, Barbados, Grenada, Guyana,
Jamaica, Trinidad and Tobago; Fiji, Tonga, Western Samoa)

▨ Mediterranean countries signing Association Agreements with the EC in the 1960s and 1970s
(Greece 1961, Turkey 1963, Cyprus 1972, Spain 1973, Malta 1977)

▨ Mediterranean countries signing Cooperation Agreements with the EC in the 1970s (Algeria 1976,
Morocco 1976, Tunisia 1976, Egypt 1977, Lebanon 1977, Jordan 1977, Syria 1977, Israel 1977)

Figure 4.1. The European Community and its Agreements with Developing Countries (1957–1977)

trade areas or customs unions. Save for the accords with the AASM, however, none of the agreements that the Community had reached or was in the course of negotiating truly fulfilled this principle, since the proposed future free trade areas or customs unions in question had never been definitively established, nor were even scheduled to come into being according to a set timeline.

Until the end of the 1970s no action had been taken under GATT against the European Community. But the multitude of agreements that the EC was concluding throughout the Mediterranean began to raise eyebrows in the United States, among the countries of Latin America, and even in many Asian nations. From an economic point of view these countries feared discrimination against their own exports; but even stronger were the fears, already clearly outlined by Raúl Prebisch, that the world could end up being divided into large regional trade blocs: The two Americas, Euro-Africa, and Asia.

Table 4.1. Trends in World Trade

EXPORTS

Main countries in 2006 sorted on the basis of their total trade (exports + imports)

Year	World[1]	EU[2]	United States	China	Japan	Canada	Hong Kong	South Korea	Mexico	Singapore	Russia[3]	India	Switzerland[4]
					Value (Bn ECU/Euro)[?]								
1958	64.2	15.3	17.8	!	2.8	5.3	0.1	0.0	0.7	!	!	1.2	1.5
1960	78.5	19.2	20.5	!	3.9	5.8	0.7	0.0	0.8	0.2	0.1	1.3	1.9
1970	200.8	44.8	43.2	!	18.9	16.7	2.5	0.8	1.3	1.6	!	2.0	5.2
1982	1,757.7	286.0	211.1	22.3	135.8	69.2	20.5	21.0	21.4	20.5	37.5	8.4	26.5
1983	1,876.6	302.6	219.2	24.8	158.5	82.4	23.7	26.2	24.6	23.6	40.7	8.8	28.6
1984	2,256.3	350.8	268.6	31.4	206.2	110.1	34.5	35.6	30.0	29.5	51.3	10.4	32.6
1985	2,369.5	380.3	272.0	35.8	224.4	113.7	38.3	38.0	28.4	28.7	57.8	10.8	35.8
1986	1,916.0	341.9	214.6	31.8	205.8	87.2	34.7	34.1	16.1	21.9	43.7	9.2	37.9
					Share (%)								
1958	100.0	23.9	27.8	!	4.3	8.2	0.2	0.0	1.1	!	!	1.9	2.4
1960	100.0	24.5	26.1	!	5.0	7.4	0.8	0.0	1.0	0.2	0.2	1.7	2.4
1970	100.0	22.3	21.5	!	9.4	8.3	1.2	0.4	0.7	0.8	!	1.0	2.6
1982	100.0	16.3	12.0	1.3	7.7	3.9	1.2	1.2	1.2	1.2	2.1	0.5	1.5
1983	100.0	16.1	11.7	1.3	8.4	4.4	1.3	1.4	1.3	1.3	2.2	0.5	1.5
1984	100.0	15.5	11.9	1.4	9.1	4.9	1.5	1.6	1.3	1.3	2.3	0.5	1.4
1985	100.0	16.1	11.5	1.5	9.5	4.8	1.6	1.6	1.2	1.2	2.4	0.5	1.5
1986	100.0	17.8	11.2	1.7	10.7	4.6	1.8	1.8	0.8	1.1	2.3	0.5	2.0
1987	100.0	17.8	11.2	1.8	10.0	4.3	2.1	2.1	0.9	1.2	2.1	0.5	2.1

IMPORTS

Main countries in 2006 sorted on the basis of their total trade (exports + imports)

Year	World[1]	EU[2]	United States	China	Japan	Canada	Hong Kong	South Korea	Mexico	Singapore	Russia[3]	India	Switzerland[4]
Value (Bn ECU/Euro)[*]													
1958	68.6	15.7	14.5	!	2.8	5.4	0.5	0.4	1.0	!	!	1.8	1.7
1960	82.1	19.3	16.2	!	4.2	5.9	1.0	0.3	1.1	0.4	0.2	2.2	2.2
1970	210.9	45.6	42.7	!	18.8	13.8	2.9	2.0	2.1	2.5	!	2.1	6.5
1982	1,887.4	321.6	250.3	18.9	131.8	55.2	22.1	23.3	13.4	28.0	45.4	15.9	29.2
1983	1,990.0	329.6	289.4	23.5	139.1	68.1	24.9	27.7	8.2	30.7	48.6	15.5	32.7
1984	2,393.8	381.9	411.8	32.2	168.4	91.9	33.2	36.2	12.0	34.9	58.2	19.1	37.3
1985	2,518.8	399.5	450.4	54.3	166.5	98.6	35.2	37.6	17.0	33.1	70.9	21.2	40.1
1986	2,012.5	334.6	371.7	43.0	124.9	80.7	32.7	30.0	11.5	24.7	52.9	15.2	41.6
1987	1,960.7	340.1	344.3	36.9	124.4	74.4	38.1	32.9	10.9	26.8	46.7	14.5	43.6
Share (%)													
1958	100.0	22.8	21.1	!	4.2	7.9	0.8	0.5	1.5	!	!	2.6	2.5
1960	100.0	23.5	19.7	!	5.1	7.2	1.3	0.3	1.3	0.5	0.2	2.7	2.7
1970	100.0	21.6	20.2	!	8.9	6.5	1.4	0.9	1.0	1.2	!	1.0	3.1
1982	100.0	17.0	13.3	1.0	7.0	2.9	1.2	1.2	0.7	1.5	2.4	0.8	1.5
1983	100.0	16.6	14.5	1.2	7.0	3.4	1.3	1.4	0.4	1.5	2.4	0.8	1.6
1984	100.0	16.0	17.2	1.3	7.0	3.8	1.4	1.5	0.5	1.5	2.4	0.8	1.6
1985	100.0	15.9	17.9	2.2	6.6	3.9	1.4	1.5	0.7	1.3	2.8	0.8	1.6
1986	100.0	16.6	18.5	2.1	6.2	4.0	1.6	1.5	0.6	1.2	2.6	0.8	2.1
1987	100.0	17.2	17.4	1.9	6.3	3.8	1.9	1.7	0.6	1.4	2.4	0.7	2.2

* From 1958 to 1970 included, the convention is 1 ECU = 1 US$.

[1] World trade is the sum of EU (evolutive) trade with extra-EU countries and extra-EU trade with the world.

[2] Evolutive EU trade with extra-evolutive EU countries' Evolutive EU is : EU6 (1958–1972), EU9 (1973–1980), EU10 (1981–1985), EU12 (1986–1994), EU15 (1995–2003), EU25 (2004–2005), EU 27 (2006–….)

[3] Relates to the external trade of the USSR until 1991 and from 1992 to the external trade of Russia.

[4] Switzerland including Liechtenstein up to 1994.

Source: Eurostate,_External and intra-European Union trade, statistical yearbook-data 1958-2006

In a classified memo of February 1970, the European Commission took note of growing global concerns surrounding its preferential trade agreements in Africa and the Mediterranean.[102] It agreed that there could be no cause for dispute with the AASM, even in GATT, because the accords were legally watertight. The agreements with Tunisia and Morocco, meanwhile, were justified by the memorandum's authors as having been provided for by the Treaty of Rome, and the accords with the other Mediterranean nations deemed indispensable in order to avoid placing them at a competitive disadvantage with respect to those two nations. But such eminently political reasoning was not adequate to convince Europe's allies across the Atlantic, nor the other regional blocs that acted in concert within the United Nations. The memorandum also discussed whether such a policy of regional preferential agreements was in the long-term interest of the Community:

> The commercial and economic potential of the non-European countries currently associated with the EEC, or open to such association, is of relatively little importance compared with that of the American and Asian nations that could form preferential agreements with other regions of the world. In fact, less than 10 percent of the Community's foreign trade is concluded with those African and Mediterranean states that are linked to the Community through preferential agreements or those that could be in the near future. These same countries represent approximately 10 percent of the world's population and 9 percent of the GDP of the developing countries in general.

The two authors of the memorandum were French, and as such assigned the highest priority to the relationship with the African states, as well as those nations along the Mediterranean that had long been linked to France throughout the colonial period. In fact, notwithstanding their critical analysis of Europe's association policy, they were unable to formulate any alternative proposals for a comprehensive European policy toward the South. They did suggest, however, that the geographic limits of Europe's preference policy—of which they were broadly supportive—be defined once and for all: "The policy of regional cooperation constitutes a modest beginning for a Community foreign policy and, as such, is an incontestably positive development."

It did not take long before the question arose about how to attenuate the criticisms of those who criticized the EC for aiming to divide the developing world. The accusations of the Latin American countries had been briefly appeased in 1970, when it appeared that a new round of discussions between the Community and Latin America would result in the building of a new relationship based on technical and financial cooperation. But long-nourished hopes for concrete action on this front, shared by European nations like Italy, soon came to nothing.[103]

---

[102] HAEU, EM 205, Communication de M. Deniau et de M. Rocherau, Secret, "Les problèmes soulevés par les accords d'association et préférentiels conclus où envisages par la Cee," February 6, 1970.

[103] HAEU, BAC 25/1980, Parlement Européen, Rapport de M. Emile de Winter, "La Déclaration et la Résolution adoptées le 29 juillet à Buenos Aires par la commission spéciale de coordination latino-américaine," April 19, 1971. The European Parliament's report summarized the major events since the last discussions between the EC and Latin America, which had opened with an Italian memorandum in 1968. These culminated in the Buenos Aires declaration, in which the members of the UN Economic Commission for Latin America (UNECLA) made a solemn appeal to Europe, which led in January 1971 to the immediate application to the UNECLA nations of certain tariff reductions already anticipated by the Kennedy Round. The same European Parliament thought it inopportune to go beyond such limited measures, given the skepticism of many of its Member States toward the Latin American countries.

Within the European Commission voices began to circulate in support of a more global approach to the developing countries. The Commissioner for External Relations, Gaetano Martino, confirmed in a note that, with enlargement, which implied a corresponding widening of Europe's association with the African states and other nations of the British Commonwealth, there would be a greater need to balance regional activities with wider multilateral initiatives.[104] In a study by a Commission delegation the same concept was expressed, with different logic, to the international organizations in Geneva.[105] The study noted that, in light of the progressive global reductions in tariff barriers, the tool of special preferences was losing practical efficacy while continuing to generate negative reactions around the world. It was thus necessary to seek other instruments with which to conduct a European foreign policy aimed above all at technical and financial cooperation. A common policy of this type would be much more useful in the Mediterranean, because it would allow those countries to develop their own industrial base, and in so doing avoid the progressive and devastating growth of immigration in western Europe.

Debate over the creation of a proper European development and cooperation policy had been particularly intense within the Commission under Malfatti's presidency. A Commission memorandum to the European Council defended the discussions on association agreements then under way—"one can't now postpone agreements that have already been reached or which are under negotiation"—but proposed two ideas to escape from the criticism of their other trading partners:

1. go beyond mere tariff policy and "develop at the Community level some form of technical and financial cooperation as well as a policy on foreign labor";

2. "define the policy that the Community should follow as soon as possible, particularly with regard to the countries of Latin America and Asia."[106]

In 1970, discussions between government representatives on the Community's proposals demonstrated Member States' stubborn resistance to a joint policy of development cooperation.[107] They declared themselves opposed to such cooperation on technical and financial matters, and restated that the Community would have to continue to follow a trade and tariff policy that suited their individual interests, without bending to external pressures.

Only in July 1971 did the Commission put forward for the first time a specific request for the launching of a common policy on cooperation and development.[108]

---

[104] HAEU, EM 158, "La necessaria salvaguardia della politica esterna nei confronti dei paesi terzi in via di sviluppo."

[105] HAEU, EM 156, Commission, Délégation permanente auprés des organisations internationales à Genève, "Les nouvelles perspectives d'une veritable politique extérieure de la Communauté," February 6, 1970.

[106] HAEU, EM 156, Comunicazione della Commissione al Consiglio, "Politica di Associazione e regimi preferenziali della Comunità," April 4, 1970.

[107] HAEU, EM 156, Il Consiglio, Relazione del Comitato dei rappresentanti permanenti, "Comunicazione al Consiglio relativa alla politica d'associazione e di regimi preferenziali della Comunità," May 8, 1970.

[108] *Bulletin of the European Communities*, Supplement 5/71, "Commission Memorandum on a Community Policy for Development Cooperation," July 27, 1971.

The Commission noted that heavy expectations were being placed on the EC in light of its future enlargement, and declared that the Community could not respond to these expectations by simply readjusting its tariffs. It was true that its treaties left very limited space for a common policy on cooperation; nevertheless, the Community had to pursue two ambitious goals in its approach to the South. First, it must reorganize the internal economy of western Europe in such a way as to open new spaces for imports from the poorer nations. Second, it would have to dedicate itself to diversifying the domestic economies of the Southern countries. This last goal could only be accomplished by giving the Community the "additional powers that would enable it to respond to such requests for cooperation."

In debates over the Commission memorandum on July 4, 1972, the European Parliament clearly illustrated the internal division between those who sought to promote a more global role for the Community and those who believed such ambitions to be fanciful and unrealistic.[109] In a very detailed report the Dutch MP Henk Vredeling complained that the EC already possessed various means of influencing the Third World, but that these tools were not used in a coordinated fashion, and noted that the Community was increasingly becoming a reference point—both positive and negative—for the developing countries. He concluded "[a]ccording to the Commission for international economic affairs, while technical and financial aid lend themselves particularly to a regional application, the commercial aspects could instead be open to a more global approach." At the same time, Vredeling demonstrated the deep fissures present within the parliamentary commission:

> I won't hide the fact that the points of view expressed in the Commission present significant differences. A majority would view a common policy on development aid in substance as the continuation of a policy that we already employ with the Associated African States. A minority sees this differently. According to them, it is necessary in principal to base such policy on the Community's global responsibility...But this minority would have the policy of association serve as a global model. In the meantime, we mustn't treat the policy of African association as the Alpha and Omega.

In October attention shifted to the Paris summit, which the French President Pompidou had promoted in order to restore his prestige as a continental leader in view of enlargement. It was to be the first important meeting of European heads of state and government since the Hague summit in 1969, and would outline potential future scenarios for the Community of Nine. As we have already seen, Mansholt had promised that at Paris the Community would present a new face to the Global South. Expectations were equally high in important circles of the Commission bureaucracy, which viewed the summit as the potential foundation of a new approach:

> It is indispensable to present to the peoples of the Community, and particularly to its youngest generations, as well as to the entire world, the image of a Community that,

---

[109] *Official Journal of the European Communities*, n. 152/1972, European Parliament, "Report on the sitting of July 4, 1972."

after the complicated process of enlargement, will pull its weight once more and be conscious of its own responsibilities…

If what is needed is a new cycle on the model of "broadening, widening, and deepening," perhaps the following will suffice: "Solidarity, prosperity, and global responsibility."[110]

Italian Prime Minister Aldo Moro saw the Paris summit as an opportunity to reveal a new side of the Community toward its own citizens as well as toward the countries of the world. It was necessary, he believed, to explain:

[w]hat responses we intend to give to the multiplicity of problems facing post–industrial civilization, what solutions seem to us most promising to improve the quality of life, how we propose to include the vast numbers of people at society's margins in a more equitable and meaningful way, not only to enjoy the fruits of our productive processes but also the wealth of a spiritual life.

In substance: What image of a Europe of Ten do we intend to give to the young, to the workers, to the man on the street, what can we offer that is new and different, on what terms can we find "European" solutions for their problems.[111]

In the Commission's note to the Council on the third UNCTAD, a document that contained heavy traces of Mansholt's influence and was finalized shortly before the Paris summit, its authors drew a number of conclusions from their experience at Santiago for the future of relations with the South.

First, it was observed that the Six had not been able to elaborate a clear common line, given that the topics for North–South dialogue were of a nature that involved both national and community competences simultaneously. It was clearly necessary to remedy this situation as soon as possible, defining "a true Community development and cooperation policy."[112] In the commodities sector activity would have to be structured on three levels. In the case of industrial raw materials, like copper or oil, the goal was to stabilize demand and compensate producers for any eventual losses if demand should suddenly drop. In the tropical goods sector it was important to reach individual product agreements at a global level that would satisfy all producers. With respect to goods similar to or competing with European goods, like agricultural products, long-term reforms were required to favor access to European markets by modifying European support of its own agricultural sector.

The Community would have to extend the offer of preferences to all processed agricultural goods, while at the same time improving their margins. Finally, financial aid would have to be concentrated to favor the poorest among the developing countries. The note concluded:

Given that an enlarged Community can no longer limit its efforts at cooperation to the African States and its future associates on the Mediterranean basin, and must

[110] HAEU, FMM 58, E.P. Wellerstein, "Idées sur le Sommet," Brussels, October 4, 1972.

[111] Archivio Centrale dello Stato (ACS), Fondo Moro (Moro), Scritti e discorsi 1972, "Intervento al Consiglio ministeriale della Cee," May 26, 1972.

[112] CEU, CM01/1972, Commissione delle Comunità europee, "Nota della Commissione al Consiglio circa i risultati della terza sessione della Conferenza delle nazioni unite sul commercio e lo sviluppo (UNCTAD)," October 5, 1972.

progressively define a global policy with regard to all the underdeveloped continents, it will have to make use of the level of development of the interested countries, as a criterion to gauge the intensity of its efforts at cooperation.

The talk among the heads of state and government in Paris was not directed solely at international issues. In fact, particular attention was paid to following up on the objective of economic and monetary union, albeit through discussion of the social issues that this would raise, and especially the need to address the balance between the wealthy and poor regions of the continent, employment protection, and ideas for control over the anarchic activities of the multinationals. But the session dedicated to international relations was also extremely significant.[113] The only European leader to request institutional dialogue with the United States was Willy Brandt. The Federal Republic of Germany was playing defense regarding any quantification of the investment necessary for a common development policy, while Bonn's principal attention seemed to be turned to the control of internal inflation and the protection of German employment levels. All the other countries participating with the exception of Heath's Britain, which highlighted the importance of closer cooperation with Japan and private investment in the developing countries, agreed on the need to send a signal to the Third World, whether through improving conditions on aid, or widening European markets to imports. Provided that only Mansholt was prepared to indicate an exact amount for anticipated growth in imports from the developing world—from US$3 billion in 1970 to US$12 billion in 1980—almost all the Member States called for a more open trade policy and concrete measures in the area of technical cooperation. At the end of the summit, the heads of state or government, while reaffirming their commitments to the AASM and the Mediterranean, dutifully declared that:

> remembering the outcome of the UNCTAD Conference and within the scope of the development strategy adopted by the United Nations, the Community Institutions are asked to activate an overall policy of cooperation in development on a world scale.[114]

After months of intensive debate between regionalists and globalists, pushed by a public opinion highly sensitive to issues of development and critical of neocolonialism, and engaged by a combative organized labor movement certain that the future was on their side, European leaders seemed to have chosen to give the Community a global role and to act as a reference point for the developing world. Both the regionalists, who obtained reassurance concerning their African and Mediterranean commitments, and the globalists, who heralded the advent of a common policy of cooperation with the rest of the world, could claim to emerge victorious from the Paris Summit. The importance of the Community's ties with the United States appeared dramatically reduced. The Europe of the Nine would move forward with new unity and self-confidence to open discussions with eastern Europe at the Conference for Security and Cooperation in Europe (CSCE), renegotiate

---

[113] HAEU, BAC 79/1982, n. 225, "Conférence des chefs d'État ou de Gouvernement (Paris, 19–21 Octobre 1972), Troisième séance."

[114] *Bulletin of the European Communities*, "Paris Summit Declaration, October 1972," n. 10.

the agreements with the African states to include those of the British Common-wealth, open the way for a global Mediterranean policy, and side with the develop-ing countries in the upcoming GATT negotiations.[115] It was in 1972 that the French political scientist François Duchêne formulated the notion of the European Community as a "civilian power": An entity that, in a world where the threat of force was ever-less credible due to the nuclear annihilation that it would inevitably produce, would influence the rest of the world with its "normative" ability (its sup-port of supranational institutions, the resolution of conflicts though law, and the soft power of its economic weight).[116] The goal of Europe as a civilian power would be to export through diplomacy the regulatory capacity that the European institu-tions in Brussels had demonstrated in resolving the historic conflicts between nations on the continent.

Underlying this rosy view, however, there remained an element of notable ten-sion among the nations of the Community, which would become progressively stronger in the coming years. The project of economic and monetary union was, in fact, sinking in the mire of the very different economic policies implemented by the Member States of the Community to respond to the inflationary pressures and growing instability of currency fluctuations. The "monetary snake" that was sup-posed to band together the currencies of the Nine within a set limit of fluctuation against the American dollar was immediately weakened at the beginning of 1973 by the exit of the Italian lira.[117] And, adding to the tensions on the monetary front, the ambitious projects of wealth redistribution between the rich and poor regions of the Community, which were supposed to solidify regional policy, were making ominously slow progress.

[115] On the birth of Global Mediterranean Policy, see G. Migani, "Rediscovering the Mediterra-nean: first tests of coordination among the Nine", in E. Calandri, D. Caviglia, and A. Varsori (eds), *Détente in Cold War Europe. Politics and Diplomacy in the Mediterranean*. London: IB Tauris, 2012.

[116] F. Duchêne, "The European Community and the Uncertainties of Interdependence," in M. Kohnstamm and W. Hager (eds), *A Nation Writ Large? Foreign-Policy Problems before the European Community* (London: Macmillan, 1973).

[117] A. Szàzs, *The Road to European Monetary Union* (London: Macmillan, 1992).

5

The Year of Oil

On September 11, 1973, a retaliation appeared to be under way against the pretensions to economic independence of the most progressive Third World countries.[1] The new military regime that had bombed Allende out of power, with the support of segments of American capital, also delivered an unmistakable message to its fellow Latin American nations: With deliberate symbolism, it established its headquarters in the very hall built at such great expense by the Popular Unity government to host UNCTAD the year before. From this palace the military *junta* set out to overturn Allende's policy of nationalizing Chile's vital mineral resources. The World Bank signaled its tacit approval, albeit only after lively internal debate, by reopening its aid coffers to the country.[2]

Yet Pinochet's Chile, with its team of Chicago economists, proved to be quite isolated in the international arena, at least in the short term: Nationalization, reform of the Bretton Woods institutions, and redistribution of wealth toward commodity producers remained the cardinal rules of the developing nations' economic doctrine. One month after the Chilean coup, the commodity-producing nations discovered an extraordinarily powerful new tool to exert renewed pressure on the industrialized world: Oil. By unilaterally imposing a fourfold increase in oil prices before the end of 1973, both Arab and non-Arab oil producers, progressives and moderates alike, would find themselves at the spearhead of a much larger struggle to impose the *de facto* establishment of a New International Economic Order (NIEO). Oil, the quintessential raw material, appeared to hold the key, as a reinforcement or substitute for the only intermittently effective diplomatic pressures from UNCTAD, to unlocking greater redistribution of global resources and changing the organization of the international economy in favor of the Global South.[3]

Inevitably, this process entailed serious consequences for a western Europe that was heavily dependent for its energy needs on the Middle East oil fields. Intellectu-

---

[1] Lubna Qureshi underlines that in the US administration's dealing with Chile the economic model offered by Allende was possibly a more important concern than the Cold War: "Nixon's personal bogeyman was expropriation, not infiltration": L.Z. Qureshi, *Nixon, Kissinger, and Allende: US Involvement in the 1973 Coup in Chile* (Lanham, MD: Lexington Books, 2009), p. 15.

[2] The palace that was supposed to host Chile's largest cultural center was renamed, from the Gabriela Mistral (named after the Nobel Prize-winning poet) to the Diego Portales (a nineteenth-century conservative statesman), and became the seat of the military *junta*.

[3] G. Garavini, "Completing Decolonization: The 1973 'Oil Shock' and the Struggle for Economic Rights," in (2011) 33(3) *The International History Review*, pp. 473–89.

als, in particular, began to circulate ominous predictions for Europe's future. We have already noted that liberals like Aron feared the possible downward slide of a weak and frightened Europe into the socialist camp. The talk was about a possible "Finlandization" of the continent. The first edition of *The World in Depression*, Charles Kindelberger's study of the Great Depression of 1929, appeared in 1973 and was soon the subject of heated debates which, if nothing else, served to confirm widespread sensitivity to the theme of economic collapse and all its attendant dangers. Had it not been the crisis of 1929 which had helped bring Hitler and Nazism to power, and encouraged the Soviet Union's degeneration into Stalinist paranoia? Were not the contemporary episodes of terrorism that threatened the stability of the state in places like Italy and the Federal Republic of Germany signs of a pervasive discontent throughout European society ready to boil over? It was precisely this kind of pessimism among his fellow intellectuals that E.H. Carr criticized in his preface to the second edition of his classic *What is History?*:

> The revolt of the oil-producing states of the Middle East has brought a significant shift in power to the disadvantage of the western industrial nations. The "third world" has been transformed from a passive into a positive and disturbing factor in world affairs. In these conditions any expression of optimism has come to seem absurd...
>
> My conclusion is that the current wave of scepticism and despair, which looks ahead to nothing but destruction and decay, and dismisses as absurd any belief in progress or any prospect of a further advance by the human race, is a form of elitism—the product of elite social groups whose security and whose privileges have been most conspicuously eroded by the crisis, and of elite countries whose once undisputed domination over the rest of the world has been shattered.[4]

Would 1973 be remembered as the "year of Europe" and of renewed Atlantic partnership, as hoped by Kissinger; or rather as the "year of oil" and of the challenge from both oil-producing and developing countries?[5]

THE OIL WEAPON

In the course of the twentieth century, the engine of the global economy increasingly shifted from coal to oil. This development corresponded with a significant transition in western Europe, from energy independence to reliance on petroleum from North Africa and the Middle East.

The dangers stemming from the potential energy dependence of the continent had been discussed as early as 1956 in a meeting of the Action Committee for the United States of Europe, founded and run by Jean Monnet. On this occasion, the

---

[4] Carr, *What is History?*, p. xii.
[5] This was the question that historian and journalist Alfred Grosser was asking himself in the very middle of the 1970s: A. Grosser, *Les Occidentaux. Les pays d'Europe et les États-Unis depuis la guerre* (Paris: Fayard, 1978), p. 345.

After Empires

Table 5.1. Energy Use in Selected Western European Countries (1937–1985) in million tons coal equivalent—MTCE

Year	Energy use	United Kingdom	West Germany	France	Italy	Netherlands	Belgium/Luxembourg
1937	Total MTCE	202	142	82	20	15	35
	tons per capita	4.3	3	2.1	0.7	1.8	4
	% coal	74	97	89	70	87	97
	% oil	26	2	8	18	13	3
	% natural gas	–	–	–	–	–	–
	% other*	–	1	3	12	–	–
1952	Total MTCE	232	145	89	25	22	34
	tons per capita	4.6	2.9	2.1	0.6	2.1	3.8
	% coal	90	95	79	43	78	89
	% oil	10	4	18	35	22	11
	% natural gas	–	–	–	8	–	–
	% other	–	1	3	15	–	–
1957	Total MTCE	247	186	111	44	28	39
	tons per capita	4.8	3.5	2.5	0.9	2.5	4.2
	% coal	85	88	72	28	63	80
	% oil	15	11	25	48	36	20
	% natural gas	–	–	1	15	1	–
	% other	–	–	3	9	–	–
1962	Total MTCE	265	221	122	71	35	42
	tons per capita	4.9	3.6	2.6	1.4	2.6	4.4
	% coal	72	58	58	18	47	70
	% oil	28	33	33	62	51	30
	% natural gas	–	5	5	13	2	–
	% other	–	4	4	18	–	–
1967	Total MTCE	276	251	154	112	47	46

Year	Energy use	United Kingdom	West Germany	France	Italy	Netherlands	Belgium/Luxembourg
	tons per capita	5	4.2	3.1	2.1	3.7	4.7
	% coal	52	51	40	12	25	53
	% oil	39	46	50	71	58	45
	% natural gas	1	3	6	11	17	2
	% other	1	1	4	6	–	–
1972	Total MTCE	302	333	215	152	76	63
	tons per capita	5.4	5.4	4.2	2.8	5.7	7.1
	% coal	40	35	21	7	6	33
	% oil	46	52	66	75	36	52
	% natural gas	12	11	10	14	52	15
	% other	2	2	4	4	–	1
1977	Total MTCE	285	355	231	177	79	65
	tons per capita	5.1	5.8	4.4	3.1	5.7	7
	% coal	38	32	20	7	5	25
	% oil	41	50	63	70	36	50
	% natural gas	19	15	12	19	58	22
	% other	2	3	5	5	–	3
1982	total MTCE	275	370	250	195	86	68
	tons per capita	5	6	4.7	3.3	5.9	7
	% coal	35	34	22	10	6	28
	% oil	39	46	58	65	40	46
	% natural gas	23	17	14	19	52	22
	% other	3	3	6	6	1	4

Source: Peter R. Odell, *Oil and World Power*, Harmondsworth: Penguin, 1986, pp. 120–1.

group underlined the need for European cooperation on a civilian nuclear energy project:

> The energy supplies of Western Europe determine the progress or decadence of our countries...
>
> Today, Western Europe imports a fifth of the energy it uses. In ten years' time, imports will have to supply one-third of its needs. The greater part of these imports consists of Middle Eastern oil.
>
> Such dependence results in insecurity and permanent risks of conflict. Between industrial and under-developed countries it hinders the collaboration which is indispensable for freeing the disinherited masses of the world from their misery. The possibility of bringing pressure to bear on Western Europe by means of Middle Eastern oil hinders the development of peaceful relations between East and West...[6]

The world's reliance on coal for energy declined at a rate even more precipitous than that predicted by Monnet's Action Committee: Dropping from 94 percent of total global energy consumption in 1900 to 62 percent in 1950, reaching barely 28 percent by 1973. The consumption of "black gold," in contrast, grew over that same time span from 3.8 percent to 27 percent, and finally to 48 percent.[7] Western Europe was a particularly heavy consumer: Oil's share of total energy consumption rose from 20 percent in 1946–8 to 57 percent in 1971, while by 1973 Europe's energy deficit had reached some 50 percent of total consumption.[8] To explain this spiraling energy dependence Paul Bairoch notes that, until the 1950s, the transportation costs for heavy commodities were so high that the only possible solution was local consumption. The reduction of these transportation costs thus contributed, along with several other factors, to create the conditions for Europe's dependence, not only on oil but also on a wide range of commodities now available at reasonable prices.[9] Multinational oil companies were offering oil at low prices and effectively determining energy policy across the continent.

In the 1950s and 1960s, that is during the period in which Western Europe was becoming a regular importer of these commodities, we have seen how the Third World experienced notable growth in production and exports without enjoying a similar rise in profits.[10] But then, in 1970 the better part of the world's oil deposits were still extracted and distributed by the largest Western companies, which also set its price: These major conglomerates in fact controlled some 80 percent of world oil exports, and 90 percent of crude oil production in the Middle East.[11]

---

[6] Monnet, *Mémoires*, p. 421.

[7] A.A. Attiga, *Interdependence on the Oil Bridge: Risks and Opportunities* (Kuwait: Petroleum Information Committee of the Arab Gulf States, 1988), p. 10.

[8] Bairoch, *Storia economica*, pp. 1134–6.

[9] For example, while in 1950 western Europe remained self-sufficient in bauxite, by 1970 its deficit was equal to 65 percent of consumption. In the case of iron ore the deficit grew from 6 percent in 1950 to 32 percent by 1970. See Ibid., p. 1150.

[10] In 1961 the Third World produced 139,000 tons of ethane, out of a total global production of 165,000 tons; and extracted 17 million tons of the global total of 25 million tons of bauxite, and some 70 percent of the world's diamonds: See Jalée, *Le pillage du tiers monde*, p. 27.

[11] J.M. Chevalier, *Les grandes batailles de l'énergie* (Paris: Gallimard, 2004), p. 113.

Although, after the creation of OPEC in 1960, oil-producing countries had managed to raise their share in oil income by taxing the companies, the global oil market was still a consumer's market, driven by the dictates of multinational oil companies.[12]

In the span of three years, the entire global oil market would be revolutionized in favor of the oil-producing nations. Three factors contributed to this revolution around 1970: First, producers began aggressively demanding their share in the oil concessions and pressing for nationalization of their natural resources; second, there were increasing signals of oil shortage on a global scale owing in part to increasing demand from industrialized countries; and third, the Arab-Israeli confrontations were feeding Arab radicalism across the whole region. With the agreements at Tripoli and Tehran in 1971, the OPEC countries demonstrated their ability to impose unilateral hikes in the posted price of crude oil on the international oil companies. Between 1971 and 1973 the extractive industries in countries such as Algeria, Libya, and Iraq partially or fully nationalized their oil industries, soon to be followed by all the other oil-producing nations.[13]

Algeria was at the forefront of this trend toward energy nationalization, having already made preparations at the time of its independence by sending its own engineers abroad to learn modern extraction techniques.[14] Nationalization of Algeria's natural gas and petroleum resources in 1971 provoked heated protests in France: President Pompidou threatened to close the country's borders to Algerian immigrants, halt imports of Algerian wine, block any future trade agreement between Algeria and the EC, and also pressured France's European allies to cease all purchases of Algerian oil. But cooler heads soon prevailed in France, while the governments of all the Arab states slowly nationalized or obtained majority stakes in the companies that controlled petroleum extraction. The goal of the producer nations—aside from a rise in prices—appeared to be to achieve a degree of control over means, technology, and level of production that would allow them to exploit their valuable energy resources in order to plan and support further economic development and industrialization.

Once national control over oil production had been obtained, a short-term rise in the price of crude oil was next to inevitable due to the favorable conditions of the international market. And yet, although the relevant facts regarding the "oil shock" are well known, interpretations of the affair and its consequences continue to conflict.[15] On October 16, 1973, following the outbreak of the war between Egypt, Syria, and Israel, the OPEC countries announced a new posted price for crude of US$5.119 per barrel. The price increase was mainly prompted by the need to recover inflation and dollar depreciation. This adjustment was quickly followed

---

[12] On the oil-producing countries' success in raising their oil revenues in the 1960s, see B. Mommer, *Global Oil and the Nation State* (Oxford: Oxford University Press, 2002).

[13] The best account of OPEC's rise to prominence can be found in I. Skeet, *OPEC: Twenty-five years of prices and politics*. Cambridge: Cambridge University Press, 1988.

[14] A. Aissaoui, Algeria. The Political Economy of Oil and Gas (Oxford: Oxford University Press, 2001).

[15] Attiga, *Interdependence on the Oil Bridge*; D. Yergin, *The Prize: The Epic Quest for Oil, Money, and Power* (New York: Simon & Schuster, 1991).

by the political decision by Arab oil producers (OAPEC) to put pressure on Israel through planned cuts in production of 5 percent per month and an embargo targeted at specific countries, foremost among them the United States and the Netherlands. At the end of December 1973, once again all the OPEC nations set a new price for crude of US$11.65 per barrel; by the end of the year, the crude oil price had more than quadrupled. In the end, only the embargo imposed by the Arab oil producers could be considered a direct response to the war; the rise in prices was instead given a much more radical spin by the OPEC countries, among them nations like Iran, that were neither Arabic nor particularly strongly antisemitic in their foreign policy. Both Iran and Nigeria increased production to make up for the decreasing production by Arab countries.[16]

The oil shock has been considered by many, including Hobsbawm, as the end of a "golden age"—characterized in western Europe by full employment and strong rates of economic growth—and the beginning of an "age of crisis" dominated instead by inflation, unemployment, and the troubled search for post–Fordist models of production.

Many scholars have expressed surprise regarding the ease with which the Anglo-Saxon oil companies accepted the loss of all control over production and price-fixing in the span of a few short months. Equally troubling was the absence of serious plans or preparations to use force to bring the Arab states to heel, particularly in contrast with the example made of the Iranian President Mohammad Mossadegh in 1952. There are those who have seen in this moderation unequivocal signs of a cultural shift: Fossil fuels were by then considered to be a disappearing resource, and thus priority was given to the ability to dispose of these assets safely, even at the cost of unfavorable short-term conditions. There has also been a blossoming of theses in support of the idea that the rise in oil prices was the result of a deliberate American strategy to bring western Europe back in line with the Atlantic alliance by striking at its economic base, at the same time reinvigorating the banks of Wall Street and the City of London through the recycling of vast quantities of so-called petrodollars. These interpretations are based on the idea that the rise in oil prices was not unwelcome in Washington, because the USA was less dependent on imports than western Europe or Japan. It is true that the Republican administration did not spend an excessive amount of time attempting to contain the rising price of oil, and that the international oil companies benefited greatly from it. But the fact remains that a growth in oil prices had been widely predicted by almost all interested observers, given the new realities of the international oil market. All the available documentation suggests that the "oil shock" was the result of an autonomous initiative by the Arab states and the non-Arab OPEC nations, acting in concert, which should be understood in the broader context of their growing political consciousness and the radicalization of the developing world.[17]

---

[16] A very detailed account of the Arab oil embargo and its consequences can be found in Committee on Foreign Relations of the US Senate, "US Oil Companies and the Arab Oil Embargo: The International Allocation of Constricted Supplies," January 27, 1975.

[17] FCO, Documents on British Policy Overseas, Series III, vol. IV, doc. 127, Telegram to Washington, "Message from Heath to Nixon," June 15, 1973. In a letter from Heath to Nixon, (referred to in this telegram) it is perfectly clear that, even before the Yom Kippur War, the two leaders were aware of the risks facing the European economies from any potential Arab-Israeli conflict:

It must also be remembered that the years from 1972 to 1974 witnessed a spectacular rebound in the prices of many commodities other than oil. Speculation on international markets, the increase in Western demand at the peak of its cycle of economic expansion, the insistent demands for economic rights in many Third World countries, the accumulation of substantial reserves, and fears of future scarcity: Several factors combined to produce a "commodity boom." In 1973 the market price of copper grew some 115 percent and that of zinc 190 percent, while prices for phosphates, coffee, and wood also witnessed exponential growth.[18] There were strong fears that the various producers of the Third World would follow the example of OPEC, organizing themselves in cartels to drive up the prices of all such basic commodities. These fears were not entirely unfounded, when one considers that in 1974, for example, four countries alone controlled 80 percent of all copper exports, two countries controlled 70 percent of global aluminum exports, four other countries contributed more than half the rubber on world markets, while yet another four furnished 60 percent of bauxite exports.[19]

The transformation of the western European economy in the 1970s is certainly attributable to a much studied and discussed series of factors: The collapse of Bretton Woods and the return of an unstable system of flexible exchange; the labor-market rigidity imposed by the strength of the continent's trade unions; the end of a long period of mass consumption and the saturation of European markets; and the emergence of new exporting countries and strong competition from Asia and Latin America. But among these various causes of the crisis in the 1970s the oil shock should be reserved pride of place, not only for its strictly economic impact—energy costs did not represent the main component of production costs—but also for its psychological effects on the citizens and their political leaders, and for the debates it fueled over the future direction of economic policy. The oil crisis forced Europeans to confront the consequences of the interdependence of the world economy. The Third World had already penetrated western Europe through its arts and literature, through the political myths of the generation of 1968 and their rejection of the old imperialism, and most directly through the impact of widespread immigration. In 1973, it arrived on the shores of the old continent in the form of an explicit threat. Its arrival shattered the illusion that modern industrial development, with all its futuristic achievements and accoutrements, could constitute an invincible shield to protect the West from outside events. The era of "the wonder of modernity" was over, for the time being at least, and individual citizens were forced to familiarize themselves with the practical, everyday implications of the abstract concept of interdependence.

In this situation we are facing a danger with which Europe is becoming ever more aware—the risk of an energy crisis. We Westerners are becoming ever more dependent on Arab oil and ever more exposed to the consequences deriving from the movements of such large profits from oil. Every signal indicates that the situation can only become worse, and that unless we succeed in doing something with respect to Arab-Israeli tensions our industrial strength and future progress could be at risk.

[18] G.P. Casadio, "Presente e futuro delle materie prime," in (1974) 3 *Politica internazionale*, p. 36.

[19] M. Colitti, "Lo sviluppo condizionato dalla logica del profitto," in (1974) 9 *Politica internazionale*, p. 42.

Cheap gas at the pump, the "six-legged dog" of Italy's ENI or the red scallop of Royal Dutch Shell, the ubiquity of cars and motorcycles, road trips and ready replacement parts, inexpensive home heating and light at any time of day or night; no European citizen had needed to worry about the easy abundance of energy that they constantly enjoyed until the early 1970s. Within a few short months, all that changed. By October 1973 the Dutch government, despite benefiting from the ample availability of natural gas, found itself promoting basic energy-efficiency measures: Encouraging citizens to ride bicycles or take public transportation, introducing 100 km/hour speed limits for all vehicles, and endorsing the use of carpools to and from work.[20] And when the citizens of several European countries found the evening shows canceled at their local cinemas and theater halls, were suddenly prohibited from driving on Sundays, or experienced cuts to such basic public services as street lighting, it began to seem clear to many that the old days of cheap energy were a permanent thing of the past. Beginning at midnight on December 31, 1973, the Heath government in Britain declared a three-day work week, deciding to supply power to state-run businesses for only three out of every seven days. An IPALMO editorial of December 1973 reported that:

> [o]nce upon a time the Third World disturbed the peaceful security of the inhabitants of the so-called affluent societies only through their instability, through the recurrent crises which, because of the protection or interference of the great powers, threatened to compromise the general peace. In this Christmas season of 1973, although the price of gas and the lights in the storefront windows are not truly indispensable to comprehend the original meaning of this holiday, the Third World has become, in Italy, in Europe, in the countries struck by the partial oil embargo declared by the Arab states, the cause of all privation and want.[21]

Well-informed European citizens understood the oil crisis and its effects according to distinct philosophical and moral perspectives, exemplified in two letters to the *Financial Times*. One writer embraced the "environmentalist" perspective of those who hoped to exploit the hardships imposed by the Arab oil producers to promote a "green" restructuring of the economy:

> Exhorting customers to use less oil is a very unreliable way of conserving supplies. Surely it would be better to offer all those sensible people who have properly insulated their homes and factories a rebate on the installation costs or on their oil tax.[22]

Another writer, in contrast, called for a demonstration of force, such as an economic "lightning strike" against the Arab states:

> In all the commentary which has appeared in recent weeks, nothing has been said of the most daunting aspect of all which ensues from the oil restrictions imposed by the Arabs, that is to say the potential shift in the balance of power to the Russians...If

---

[20] HAEU, EN 81, Délégation néerlandaise auprés des Communautés européennes, "Situation dans le secteur du pétrole," October 31, 1973.

[21] "Questo ricco, ricco, Terzo Mondo," in (1973) 12 *Politica Internazionale*.

[22] "Letter to the Editor," in *Financial Times*, October 27, 1973.

exports to the Arab countries are stopped, within just a few months everything would grind to a halt. Is it not better to have a short sharp economic conflict rather than to be starved of energy to the point where we can no longer make an effective stand?[23]

In Italy, at the end of 1973 the government applied a series of austerity measures to reduce energy demands: A prohibition of the use of cars on weekends and holidays; early closure of public offices and state-run businesses (at 5:30 and 6:30 pm, respectively); a ban on television, theater, or film programming after 11:00 pm; and limits on the illumination of public spaces and commercial zones—street lights and shop windows were automatically dimmed after 9:00 pm.[24] It should come as no surprise that one of the first reactions to the need for more economic austerity, in places where such phenomena were most visible, came in the form of provisions to halt immigration; such measures were designed not only to protect local employment, but also to exploit the widespread fears raised by the crisis to reverse the tendency of such immigrants to establish a permanent European home for themselves and their families.[25] In West Germany, where foreign labor represented a significant part of the industrial workforce, anti-immigration measures constituted an important safety valve to channel angry public demands to protect national employment levels, without the need for government recourse to run budget deficits or commit to extra public spending.

If 1968 in Europe was marked by a certain distancing from the economic and political models offered by the United States, the oil crisis of the early 1970s shone a harsh spotlight on Europe's own preferred model for economic growth. Priority could no longer be given solely to the need to improve the conditions of European workers, nor to the gradual increase—for more or less altruistic purposes—in aid to the developing countries. There was a need to rethink the foundations of the European economy, up to that point based on a delicate balance between state intervention and private enterprise, and on high economic growth. European socialist leaders were quick to design the contours of a potential new economic outlook. In December 1973, Willy Brandt, Bruno Kreisky, and Olof Palme met at Schlangenbad in Germany to discuss the fallout of the oil crisis.[26] Brandt argued that the growing cost of oil could pave the way for a dramatic expansion of public transportation networks and encourage a new technological boom with positive effects on the environment. Kreisky, acknowledging the need for public transit based on rails rather than roads, as well as a public system of energy production and distribution, also foresaw new possibilities for the planned economy. Palme went one step further, floating the idea that socialism should cease to consider growth in GDP as a primary objective and find other strategic avenues for wealth redistribution. According to the Swedish statesman, Europe should seize this

[23] "Letter to the Editor," in *Financial Times*, November 7, 1973.
[24] G. Crainz, Il *paese mancato. Dal miracolo economico ali anni Ottanta* (Rome: Donzelli, 2003), pp. 439–40.
[25] Bade, *Migration in European History*, p. 229.
[26] G. Arfè (ed.), *Brandt, Kreisky, Palme: Quale Socialismo per l'Europa* (Cosenza: Lerici, 1976).

extraordinary opportunity to return to its roots, seeing as how both the Soviet and the American models had lost their luster.

This was but one of many contemporary debates that European social democratic leaders hoped would result in what one might call a "social democratic renaissance." And yet, somehow, not one of them thought to accuse the oil-producing nations. In a November 1975 meeting titled "Which Socialism, Which Europe?," Jacques At-tali—a prolific writer and later adviser to French President François Mitterrand—captured the issues at the heart of the matter. For Attali there were three interpretations of the ongoing crisis: The first hinged on short-term factors, such as the rise in the price of oil; the second on the saturation of the market and changes in the international economy with the arrival of new producers; the third on the struggle—of which inflation was a product—to create a society and model of development less dependent on the constant turnover of new manufactured goods, with a larger role for public services and greater responsiveness to workers' needs. "Unless profound steps are taken in the direction of socialist principles of political economy and power relations," he concluded, "the political and economic crisis in Europe is only just beginning."[27] The analysis of Stuart Holland, one of the most important theorists of the Labour left that came to power in the UK in 1974, was more pragmatic.[28] Holland argued that the reason why the application of Keynesian principles had failed to produce the desired results was because of the presence of large multinationals that could export capital and delocalize production to minimize the impact of rising tax rates. He calculated that the state should maintain control over 30 percent of turnover, 40 percent of profits, and 50 percent of employment, married to a policy focused on growth and control over imports. All of these recommendations were fully in line with the morally charged "austerity" proposals that Italian Communists began to refine in view of the possibility that the PCI might enter into government in a power-sharing agreement with the ruling Christian Democrats.[29] In an October 1976 speech on austerity, prepared by his right-hand man Antonio Tatò—which included the rather prophetic claim that "today we face a wall: either we tear it down or go home"—PCI Secretary Enrico Berlinguer argued that earlier wage increases from 1967–9 and the recent revolts in the Third World could not help but provoke a backlash in the countries of capitalist prosperity:

> Because of this, the war on waste has become a permanent part of the existence and growth of every economic system, and with it a rigorous discipline guided by principles of fairness. Even the workers' movement must adapt to the landscape of austerity, to

[27] "Quale socialismo per l'Europa," ARA, Papers presented at the conference *Quale socialismo, quale Europa*, November 1975 (Milan: Feltrinelli, 1977).

[28] P. Seyd, *The Rise & Fall of the Labour Left* (London: Macmillan Education, 1987), pp. 25–7.

[29] A. Tatò, *Caro Berlinguer. Note e appunti riservati di Antonio Tatò a Enrico Berlinguer: 1969–1984* (Turin: Einaudi, 2003), p. 48. In a note to Berlinguer, Tatò—a leader of the CGIL and later Enrico Berlinguer's private secretary—counseled the PCI leader to distinguish between a "socialist" and a "bourgeois" austerity. The latter "tends to criticize and attack the wage index (as if it were an 'inflationary' device), the Worker's Rights bill, the burdens of national labor contracts, the excesses of the trade unions in the exercise of their rights and in their defense of workers' rights to healthcare and a pension, and sees in absenteeism, low productivity, and double employment, etc., the cultural 'degeneration' of democracy and workers' rights."

new models of development and lifestyle habits, to diverse patterns of consumption and of the exercise of power, as well as solidarity with the peoples of the emerging world.[30]

If in western Europe the oil crisis seemed in the short term to have reinforced a trend toward economic planning and the entrenchment of recent progressive social policies, even in many countries of the Third World the political will to keep state control over economic indicators remained solid. The anticommunist Lee Kuan Yew, for instance, for more than forty years president of Singapore—the most advanced of the Asian Tigers—recalled in his autobiography how he refrained from touching state-run healthcare, a lesson learned from William Beveridge's Labour Party.[31]

An indirect confirmation of the impact of the oil crisis on the European political class can be seen in the dismissive words of the Italian ambassador to the United States Roberto Gaja:

> The outbreak of the first oil crisis in 1973 gave rise to a series of violent critiques of the capitalist social structure in our country. It was said that the gravity of the crisis was due to a growth model that had been followed for many decades and that had been dictated primarily by private interests, which had given rise to unacceptable amount of privilege, among the automobile industry and the builders of highways for instance. Alternative models of development were put forward, of diverse inspiration but always substantially indebted to the Soviet model.[32]

The growth in GDP of the OECD nations had reduced in real terms, from a rate of 5 percent annually throughout the 1960s to 3.5 percent from 1970–78. Over the same period growth in manufacturing reduced from 5.9 percent to 3.5 percent.[33] After having experienced a brief wave of euphoria in the first few years of the 1970s, manufacturing in western Europe fell by almost 9 percent in 1975, before beginning to recover the following year. Throughout the West unemployment had almost doubled in comparison to the period 1960–73; the same could be said for inflation, which doubled compared to the 1960s. Adding to governments' concerns were the consequences of companies' internal restructuring as a response to trade union pressures, or as part of a broader shift in employment patterns toward services, both public and private, and the tertiary sector. Right around the middle of the decade the big companies most representative of the Fordist model began large-scale diversification projects.[34] Volkswagen, for example, invested in the delocalization of its production chain to Brazil and Mexico; overall, West German foreign direct investment grew approximately five times between 1967 and 1975. Italy's Fiat likewise embarked on a program of intensive automation that would reach fruition only in the 1980s. Viewed from a different perspec-

---

[30] "Una politica di austerità ispirata a giustizia sociale per trasformare e rinnovare il Paese," conclusions of the Central Committee of the PCI, October 18–20, 1976.

[31] L.K. Yew, *From the Third World to the First: The Singapore Story: 1965–2000* (New York: Harper Collins, 2000).

[32] Gaja, *L'Italia nel mondo bipolare*, p. 25.

[33] D.H. Aldcroft, *The European Economy 1914–2000* (London: Routledge, 2001), pp. 196–203.

[34] B.J. Silver, *Forces of Labor: Workers' Movements and Globalization since 1870* (Cambridge: Cambridge University Press, 2003), p. 53.

tive, the data on the "real" economy, on anything from levels of employment to growth in production, would remain relatively good until the end of the decade—and certainly better than the figures of the 1980s. Only western Europe's interdependence with the global economy was much more clearly visible.

This was not yet the era of the "retreat" of the state from the economy, nor a moment of absolute faith in the autonomous, almost demiurgic ability of free enterprise and private finance. The long wave of 1968 was still making itself felt in the countries of the European Community. If anything the oil crisis helped push Europe's social democrats further to the left. We have seen that in 1974, Labour would take power in Great Britain once again, while the demise of authoritarian regimes in Southern Europe would open new spaces for European socialism. Starting in 1974, in fact, public spending would begin to rise throughout Europe, as politicians answered the challenge to combat the dangers of a cooling economy with increased state investment. The power of workers' movements was still such that they could prevent businesses from maintaining their profit margins by capping salaries or through recourse to mass layoffs. Socialist governments tended to encourage and promote "neocorporatist" agreements or complex revenue policies.[35] It has been estimated that in the 1970s approximately one-half of the globe's strikes occurred in western Europe, making the continent the site of the world's most active labor movements.[36]

THE NEW INTERNATIONAL ECONOMIC ORDER

It is impossible to comprehend the full meaning of the "shock" of 1973 without viewing it in the broader context of the conflict between the developed and the developing countries.

The great powers of the communist world, the Soviet Union and China, remained in the background as mere spectators—although the latter did not withhold aid nor fail to make repeated entreaties to certain countries of the South, encouraging them to develop an autonomous political economy completely independent of the industrialized West.[37] In a lengthy CIA report of 1975 regarding

[35] W. Streeck and P. Schmitter, "From National Corporatism to Transnational Pluralism: Organised Interests in the Single European Market," in E. Gabaglio and R. Hoffmann (eds), *The ETUC in the Mirror of Industrial Relations Research* (Brussels: European Trade Union Institute, 1998), p. 139.

[36] Silver, *Forces of Labor*, p. 6.

[37] NA, FCO 59/1231, Diplomatic Report, "The Soviet Union and the New International Economic Order," December 30, 1974. British diplomats eagerly speculated about possible tension between the supporters of the NIEO and the USSR, and hypothesized that the Soviets were violently hostile to the strategy of the developing countries because they recognized their inability to furnish development aid and because they viewed the NIEO as a means of reconsolidating the hold of the West. NARA, CIA archives, National Foreign Assessment Center, "The Nonaligned Movement: Dynamics and Prospects, April 1979." The Soviets' room for maneuver was also limited with respect to the Non-Aligned Movement: "It could be that Cuba will follow up on its efforts to redefine Non-Alignment as an anti-imperialist force, more strongly connected with the Soviet orbit. Cuba, however, has demonstrated a notable degree of flexibility, and it is not plausible that it will push this to the point of calling into question the unity of the Movement."

the Soviet relationship with the Third World, American intelligence analysts underlined the inability of the countries in the real socialist camp to influence international economic negotiations:

> One important aspect of Soviet economic policy toward the Third World that has not developed along with that of the United States, is its multilateral and institutional policy. The most important phenomenon of the past decade has been the way in which international economic institutions (IMF, World Bank, regional banks), multinationals (banks and "corporations"), and international organizations (OPEC, UNCTAD, GATT, FAO, conferences on commodities) have captured the attentions, energies and projects of the Third World. For the countries of the Third World whose borders are relatively stable (everyone except those in Sub-Saharan Africa, the Middle East, and Indochina), the most important issues (food, energy, development, trade, technology, health, education) are not handled bilaterally with the Superpowers but through a growing international network in which the Soviet Union is in large part either inactive or irrelevant.[38]

The fourth Conference of Heads of State and Government of the Non-Aligned Movement was held at Algiers from September 5–9, 1973, just before both the Pinochet coup and the beginning of the Arab-Israeli war. The Algerian president Houari Boumedienne hoped to use the meeting to improve the cohesion of the Movement, and at the same time to focus its activities on issues until then dealt with mostly within the UNCTAD framework: Foremost among these the redistribution of global economic resources and greater involvement of the South in the decision-making processes of the international economy.[39] For Boumedienne, "non-alignment ceased to be—if it indeed ever had been—a force based predominantly on negation (of the two blocs, of the Cold War), in order to create a positive politics aimed at affirming the rights of the emerging world."[40] Although Algeria had wanted to demonstrate a clear distance from Moscow, Castro succeeded in steering the conference away from any official declaration against the USSR by noting that the Soviets possessed neither exploitative multinationals nor direct control over Third World oil and mineral deposits.[41]

The Algerian leader was by then the entrenched leader of an authoritarian and *dirigiste* government, albeit one with considerable popular support.[42] He enjoyed growing international respect, had experienced firsthand the influence of foreign multinationals in his country, and understood the consequent need to create a national industry free from the influence of the ex-colonial powers. He was well aware of the fact that, immediately after achieving independence, Algeria's economy had contracted by 35 percent due to its reliance on French expertise and the French market, and that tens of thousands of Algerians had been left unemployed

---

[38] NARA, CIA, "The US–USSR and the Third World."
[39] NARA, CIA, National Foreign Assessment Center, "The Nonaligned Movement: Dynamics and Prospects," April 1979.
[40] Calchi Novati, *Storia dell'Algeria indipendente*, p. 201.
[41] Andrew, *The World Was Going Our Way*, pp. 90–1.
[42] M. Evans and J. Philips, *Algeria. Anger of the Dispossessed* (New Haven, CT: Yale University Press, 2007).

as a result. At the same time, while the large oil multinationals had extracted some US$4.8 billion in profits from the country's oil fields, approximately half of which swiftly left its borders, the royalties paid on these profits to the Algerian government amounted to barely US$220 million. In 1964, the government had created a national oil and gas company, Sonatrach (Société nationale pour la recherche, la production, le transport, la transformation et la commercialization des hydrocarbures), and in 1969 had joined OPEC, while in 1971 the state acquired control of 51 percent of the oil sector and the entirety of its natural gas resources, inaugurating the era of energy nationalization programs in both Arab and non-Arab countries. Through past experience, the leaders of the FLN had developed the conviction that international economic dependency could be subverted only by force, and that the bourgeoisie of the industrialized nations would never truly engage the issue of the international division of labor.[43]

The time had come to exploit the power of the oil weapon. At the beginning of 1973, Venezuela—the largest oil producer in Latin America and a pivotal country in continental politics—was seriously considering membership in the Non-Aligned Movement,[44] believing that the Movement had shifted its emphasis from neutralism to economic concerns. The Foreign Ministry's newly elaborated position was that:

> the era when the democratic governments of Venezuela were afraid of the idea of irritating the United States or conservative sectors of our own countries are over ... Right now it is important that the African and Asian countries recognize the liberating, nationalist and anti-neocolonialist content of our measures regarding oil, and that they be willing to align themselves with Venezuela in a united front of defense against the hegemonic forces that will try to deny us our right to set our own course.
>
> It is equally important that Venezuela should not be left at the margins of this historic process of the creation of new alliances and decision-making structures.[45]

In 1973, Algeria held the presidency of the Non-Aligned Movement, while an Algerian was also Secretary-General of OPEC. Manuel Perez Guerrero, the UNCTAD Secretary---General, spoke Arabic, had been Venezuelan oil minister, and was a close friend of the Venezuelan "founder of OPEC" Perez Alfonzo. At the end of the Algiers conference, the leaders of the non-aligned states had approved an Action Program for economic cooperation that touched upon their countries' most urgent problems: From the need to open up Western markets, to trade agreements on raw materials, issues of maritime commerce, and ultimately reform of the international monetary system. The Action Program, which was received with some skepticism by those nations with a more complex set of interests (such as India or Yugoslavia), presaged a combative new alliance of commodity producers

[43] M. Bennoune, *The Making of Contemporary Algeria 1830–1987* (Cambridge: Cambridge University Press Middle East Library, 1988), p. 133.

[44] In this respect, Venezuela was following the lead of Peru and the Argentina of Juan Peròn.

[45] AHMPRE, Algeria, IV Conferencia de Jefes de Estado y Gobierno de los Países no Alineados, Director de Política Internacional, "Venezuela y Los Países No Alineados," January 15, 1973.

based on the model furnished by the oil-producing nations, which could prove capable of placing tremendous pressure on the industrialized world.

Alongside this strategy of North–South economic confrontation, the Algerian president recognized the need to develop a project on a Mediterranean scale along the lines of the Helsinki Conference, then negotiating the terms of détente between eastern and western Europe. The idea was to promote some form of Mediterranean détente that would have the effect of consolidating the political and economic dialogue among the non-aligned countries along its shores, and at the same time promote talks between Europe and the Arab states. This project, which was similar to concepts floated in Italy by Prime Minister Aldo Moro, was presented during the preparatory phase of talks for the Conference on Security and Cooperation in Europe in 1972, but it found few takers.[46]

On February 7, 1974, right at the height of the oil crisis, Boumedienne used the Algerian position as president of the Non-Aligned Movement to call upon the Secretary-General of the UN to convene a special session focused exclusively on questions of trade and raw materials. He argued that, in light of the oil crisis, the issues of commodities and development should be confronted together, and that the General Assembly, as a democratic body in which all nations were represented, was the only appropriate forum for such talks. In a letter to the Secretary-General, Boumedienne expressed his conviction that the ruling class of the Western nations would be compelled in the future to resign itself to some form of compromise:

> Today, given that the working class no longer allows its rights to be trampled upon, thanks to its collective organization, and that a growing number of Third World countries have acquired the right to set the price of their own commodities, building upon the success brought about by their economic emancipation, the system of the Developed Countries is encountering serious difficulties trying to control inflation while at the same time allowing profits to follow their own course unchecked toward ever greater heights.[47]

Algeria also hoped to counteract the risk that the commodity-producing nations would become isolated from the other developing countries.

In April 1974 the UN General Assembly dutifully convened its sixth special session, the first in its history to deal exclusively with economic issues. In his opening remarks—considered one of the most celebrated speeches in the history of independent Algeria—Boumedienne accused the West of having accepted the principle of self-determination of peoples only after having grasped the reins of the world economy. The industrialized countries, he argued, had then been able to shield themselves from criticism through the granting of development aid; an effort that was even more humiliating for its small sums in comparison with the liberal amounts with which the developed countries had "aided themselves" after

---

[46] "Editorial," in (1973) 1 *Politica internazionale*.

[47] Archives Nationales d'Algérie (ANA), Lettre du Président Boumedienne au Secrétaire-Général de l'ONU.

the Second World War—the reference here is to the Marshall Plan.[48] After fierce debate and without the sanction of a formal vote, the General Assembly approved a resolution calling for the establishment of a New International Economic Order, accompanied by a Programme of Action designed to put this into practice. Among the Programme's recommendations: the creation of a Common Fund for commodities with the aim of stabilizing prices and keeping them in line with inflation; a generalized moratorium on Third World debt; the indexing of commodity prices to those of manufactures; the freer and more rapid transfer of new technologies to the developing world; and a lowering of tariff barriers in the developed countries.[49] In its Point X, the Programme also called for the acceptance of a special program in favor of the economies struck hardest by the oil crisis, an idea that was also among the primary interests of the Western countries. Both the debt moratorium and the creation of a Common Fund for commodities were designed to foster a rapid redistribution of global profits toward the South.

The measures on raw materials in particular were immediately criticized by economists, as well as by West German and American diplomats.[50] It was noted that commodities were for the most part bought and sold by the developed countries themselves, which would therefore be the primary beneficiaries of any rebound in prices. In addition, manufactured goods formed a growing segment of the developing countries' exports; while a rise in the prices of certain commodities would result merely in the greater use of synthetically produced substitutes. Last, there was one final argument against the creation of a Common Fund for commodities, and this was that oil constituted a special case: First, because the largest producers had already created their own solid, authoritative organization; second, because every Western industry was dependent upon oil as a source of energy, and a decline in oil imports—unlike any other commodity—would result in reduced growth and thus in a dangerous rise in unemployment.[51] This type of reasoning was taken to its extreme by Arthur Lewis, winner of the Nobel Prize in Economics in 1979. In *The Evolution of the International Economic Order*, first published in 1978, he postulated that the export of manufactures was becoming ever more important for the developing countries—equal to 33 percent of their total exports in 1975—and that the problem facing these countries lay primarily in the fact that extremely low salary levels had prevented them from forming sufficiently robust internal markets.[52] According to Lewis, criticisms of unequal trade were for the most part unfounded and out of date, as were requests for aid and demands for a

[48] UN, General Assembly, Sixth Special Session, Official Records, "Address by Mr Houari Boumedienne," April 10, 1974.

[49] NA, FCO 59/1231, Note, "Economic Discussions in UN Bodies: The New International Economic Order," November 25, 1974.

[50] R.L. Rothstein, *Global Bargaining: UNCTAD and the Quest for a NEIO* (Princeton, NJ: Princeton University Press, 1979), p. 40.

[51] NA, FCO 59/1231, Draft Paper, "Comparison Between the Position of the Oil Producers and that of the Producers of Other Commodities."

[52] A. Lewis, *The Evolution of the International Economic Order* (Princeton, NJ: Princeton University Press, 1978).

structural change in the global economy. The imperative issue from the perspective of the Western countries would be confined to opening their markets to the import of developing countries' manufactures, notwithstanding the difficulties that this could create in terms of domestic unemployment.

Such serious and well-grounded criticisms were not widely shared in the mid-1970s, however, and in any event partially missed the point. Commodities remained an indispensable source of income for the countries of the South. In 1973, according to the analysis of Washington's economic experts, the developing countries could count on a total of US$109 billion in exports: US$45 billion in oil and related products, US$41 billion from other commodities, and only US$23 billion in manufactured goods. More than fifty of these countries depended on three or fewer products for the near-totality of their exports.[53] Furthermore, trade in manufactures benefited only a small, if ever-more assertive, minority of emerging countries.[54] Finally, it should be remembered that the South's symbolic aims lay in moving beyond the Bretton Woods order and initiating a radical reform of Western economic institutions. Ultimately their goal was the creation of a new body, to be controlled by the developing world, which would assume a role akin to established economic institutions like the World Bank and IMF, which remained solidly in the hands of the industrialized countries.

A report of the British delegation gives a perceptive synopsis of the various positions that emerged during the course of the UN Special Session on commodities. According to the British diplomats, Algeria sought to prevent the OPEC nations from being isolated and blamed as the sole parties responsible for the economic crisis: Thus the Algerians aimed at achieving concrete measures to promote solidarity among all the nations of the South. India, and other countries that were heavily dependent on energy imports, wanted Western aid in whatever form they could get it (on one hand), but hesitated to abandon the solidarity of the G77 nations that had produced results in the past, and that they felt could produce many more in the future.[55] The communist countries were primarily interested in creating a smokescreen to disguise their own mediocre track record regarding development aid. The Western countries, meanwhile, remained passive and at cross-purposes. The United States and France had their own, largely opposing projects of how to deal with OPEC nations, while the Netherlands, and to a lesser degree Sweden,

---

[53] Gerald R. Ford Library (GFL), Office of Economic Advisers (OEA), Seidman Files, Box 312 Economic Summit Briefing Book, "Relations Between Developed and Developing Countries," June 27–8, 1976.

[54] R. Sandri, *La sfida del Terzo mondo* (Rome: Editori Riuniti, 1978), p. 235. Regarding the EC and its Generalized Scheme of Preferences adopted in favor of imports of the developing countries' manufactures, Renato Sandri notes that only a small minority of countries actually benefited from it. In 1974, ten countries had used some 72 percent of the offer (Yugoslavia, Hong Kong, Brazil, India, South Korea, Singapore, Pakistan, Mexico, and Iran). Furthermore, as the EC, along with Japan, was the only group to offer preferential duties on textiles, Sandri suggests that "in reality the GSP has heretofore made up a consistent part of preferential concessions to the production of textiles and clothing of a small number of Developing Countries."

[55] NA, FCO 59/1231, UK Mission to the UN, "Reflections on the Sixth Special Session of the UN General Assembly on Raw Materials and Development (9 April–2 May)," June 12, 1974.

showed themselves ready to meet almost any request made of them by the South with regard to the redistribution of global wealth. The English representative to the UN painted the following portrait of the contemporary state of the North–South divide:

> I believe that what we have seen in the Special Session has been the first concerted effort on the part of the developing world to demonstrate its maturity in the field of international economic theory and organization. The rise in the price of oil has brought home to the Industrialized Countries the vulnerability of their own economies and the Developing Countries have naturally tried to capitalize on this awareness.

In any event, the outcome of the Special Session was a diplomatic success for Algeria, which succeeded in reinforcing the developing countries' united front and re-iterating the message that the rise in oil prices, while damaging for the poor countries, was vital to the Arab states because in the not-too-distant future they would be left with nothing more than "a fistful of sand." Algeria managed to out-flank talks on the Common Fund with other goals that had even wider appeal, such as the free distribution of fertilizers, as well as the abolition of debt acquired prior to 1973.

The primary victims of rising oil prices, and thus OPEC's most aggrieved adversaries, should in fact have been precisely those poor countries most dependent on OPEC for their oil: The combined debt of these nations had grown from US$9.2 billion in 1973 to a whopping US$39 billion in 1975. But the internal unity of the South did not break. In part this was due to the ties, both cultural and political, that continued to bind the countries of the G77 and their leaders, despite any potential conflict, against the West. The feeling expressed during the brief encounter of an Indian delegate with a diplomatic colleague from the European Community under the auspices of UNCTAD well encapsulated the climate: "You in the West are interested only in your oil. Once you are able to buy it again at a low price, you will promptly forget about us. This is why we intend to exploit the oil crisis to force you into a general revision of the terms of exchange that will do us more justice."[56] P.N. Dhar, economic advisor to Indira Gandhi, wrote of the high hopes raised by the oil producers' success, and the undeniable prestige enjoyed, if only briefly, by the Arab states:

> The oil-producing countries suddenly acquired tremendous political clout; they became rich overnight, so rich indeed that some of them did not know what to do with their new-found wealth. This was particularly true of Saudi Arabia and the Gulf countries. Burgeoning oil revenues triggered an investment boom in West Asia, which

---

[56] HAEU, BAC 25–1980, n. 987, "Report on the First Part of the 4th Session of the Trade Council UNCTAD (August 20–September 14, 1974)." The MIT economist Jagdish Bhagwati reiterated this notion, albeit in different words: "[T]he developing countries seemed to feel that finally there was one dramatic instance of a set of primary producers in the Third World who were able to get a 'fair share' of the world incomes by their own actions rather than by the unproductive route of morally persuading the rich nations for fairer shares." J.N. Bhagwati (ed.), *The New International Economic Order: The North-South Debate* (Cambridge, MA: MIT Press, 1977), p. 6.

created vast opportunities for trade and employment… The OPEC countries led the demand for a new international economic order in the United Nations, where their group dominated the counsels of the developing countries. Media commentators talked about a new "Arab Century."[57]

But it was also money that oiled the gears of global friendship. Support for the strategy of the new international economic order was bought at a high price. According to documents of the American Treasury Department, in 1974 aid from the OPEC states to the non-oil-producing developing countries amounted to some US$7.8 billion.[58] According to French sources, in the same year the overall sum of OPEC aid reached US$16.2 billion, more than the total amount committed to the Third World by all the Western states combined.[59] Ibrahim F.I. Shihata, the director of the OPEC Fund for International Development, itself created after the Algiers OPEC Summit in 1975, declared that in 1975 the OPEC countries had provided financial assistance equal to 7.6 percent of their aggregate GDP.[60] One must be careful not overestimate the role of this OPEC money in the maintenance of the developing countries' united front, however, given that such aid was channeled primarily to specific countries, in particular the Arab states and India.[61] What also kept the South united was the trepidation of certain countries at risking their own energy supply.[62]

In 1973 a series of organizations were created by Southern nations to attempt to manage the flow and trade of several commodities: For example UNICAF, the organization of coffee producing nations like Brazil, Colombia and Cote d'Ivoire to control the price of coffee; or CIPEC (the French acronym for the Intergovernmental Council of Copper-Exporting Countries), linking the four principal copper-exporting nations (Zambia, Chile, Zaire, and Peru). An "unholy alliance" thus seemed to be materializing, with the potential to grow stronger in the future, between the OPEC states and the oil-importing developing countries.

The year 1974 was marked by radical criticism of both the Bretton Woods institutions and the mechanisms of international free trade more generally. Roughly one decade earlier, the famous Argentine writer Julio Cortázar had been on a train

---

[57] P.N. Dhar, *Indira Gandhi: The "Emergency" and Indian Democracy* (Oxford, New Delhi: Oxford University Press, 2000), p. 219.

[58] GFL, OEA, L.W. Seidman files, Box 135, Memo, "OPEC Aid Commitments to Non-Oil Exporting LDCs," September 20, 1974.

[59] Centre Historique des Archives Nationales (CHAN), 5AG3 (Fond Giscard d'Estaing), 150, Note, "Déjeuner de travail avec M. MacNamara, Président de la BIRD," April 27, 1973.

[60] I.F.I. Shihata, *The Other Face of OPEC. Financial Assistance to the Third World* (London: Longman, 1982), p. 86.

[61] OECD, *DAC Review 1979*, p. 136. Between 1976 and 1978 Egypt received 25 percent of OPEC aid, Syria and Jordan another 25 percent, and Yemen, Lebanon, and Mauritania 5 percent each, while India and Pakistan received another 11 percent.

[62] NA, FCO 59/1231, British Embassy Brasilia to Sir Donald Maitland, September 18, 1974: "The Brazilians, like India and the other Developing Countries, are hesitant to distance themselves from the rest of the G77. The Brazilian stance is in part dictated by the desire to avoid anything that might upset the African and Arab oil producers, and thus call into question the bilateral agreements that guarantee their energy supplies." See T. Skidmore, *The Politics of Military Rule in Brazil, 1964–1985* (London: Oxford University Press, 1988), pp. 178–80.

leaving Brussels when he was struck by his feelings of bitter rage, the emotional inspiration for his subsequent comic *noir* novel *Fantomas contra los vampiros multinacionales*.[63] The passage of a decade marked by growing confrontation with the United States and suspicion of "Yankee" capitalist interference in the domestic affairs of other nations saw the Latin American artist's anger transformed into international law with the Charter of the Economic Rights and Duties of States, approved by a majority of the UN General Assembly on December 12, 1974.

The drafting of the Charter had been assigned to the Mexican President Luis Echeverria by the participants at the UNCTAD conference in Santiago. Echeverria had returned from the conference deeply impressed by the atmosphere of political tension then brewing throughout Latin America, and believed that one way of defusing this potentially revolutionary dynamic—which he personally had previously experienced (and eliminated) as Interior Minister during the violently repressed student protests in Mexico City in 1968—would be the delivery of a new, international legal system capable of forming a sort of protective dyke against such outside interference.[64] The first article of the Charter, in fact, declared: "Every State has the sovereign and inalienable right to choose its economic system as well as its political, social and cultural systems in accordance with the will of its people." Among the other rights asserted in the Charter were the freedom to nationalize strategic sectors without penalty and the liberty of every state to manage its own commodities. The Western front demonstrated cohesion in a losing cause, remaining united in their hostility to such international legal dispositions.

In the 1970s multinational corporations had represented a disconcerting and striking novelty for their economic weight. In 1977 General Motors, the world's largest company by market capitalization, produced total goods and services valued at US$55 billion, a figure that—if it had attached to a state—would have made it the twentieth largest economy in the world.[65] Beyond the Charter, one of the most interesting efforts made by the global South was the enactment of a Foreign Investment Code by the nations of the Andean Pact—Bolivia, Chile (until 1976), Colombia, Ecuador, Peru, and Venezuela—to manage their relationship with the multinationals. The legislation sanctioned the creation of an administrative board to oversee the transfer of technology from the industrialized world, and required multinationals to give local actors a share of ownership.[66]

During this period, the governments of the South demonstrated their intention to create more binding, international, institutional mechanisms and to establish new regulations where the forces of the free market had previously reigned to the advantage of the stronger economies of the industrialized countries. The concerted action of the Southern countries pushed the United Nations to discuss several

---

    [63] J. Cortázar, *Fantomas contra los vampiros multinacionales* (Buenos Aires: Ediciones Destino, 1965).

    [64] NARA, CIA, "Central Intelligence Bulletin," Mexico, April 29, 1972.

    [65] W.J. Feld, *Multinational Corporations and UN Politics* (New York: Pergamon Policy Studies, 1980), p. 2.

    [66] S. Krasner, *Structural Conflict: The Third World Against Global Liberalism* (Berkeley: University of California Press, 1985), p. 181.

unresolved problems: The issues raised by the Andean Code of Conduct for Multinationals; the Law of the Sea, which was designed to expand the extent of territorial waters; maritime transport, which was monopolized by a handful of international shipping companies; management of radio frequencies and media networks; regulation of the Antarctic to protect it from partition by the wealthiest nations; and new rules for civil aviation. As Stephen Krasner has summarized, in one of the rare studies dedicated to this subject:

> Market-oriented regimes are inherently problematic because they provide unfair advantages for larger and more knowledgeable economic actors. Multinational corporations can manipulate transfer prices to evade taxation. Shipping liner conferences can freeze out competitors from the Third World. International news agencies can monopolize the flow of information and issue distorted reports about developing areas. Labor unions and firms in the North can appropriate the benefits of technological progress. Sophisticated corporations can plunder the global commons with no concern for the rights or well-being of poorer areas. International lending agencies can impose politically embarrassing, even fatal, conditions on loans.[67]

The UN also debated the question of "global public goods" as resources to be managed by international law. The Algerian jurist Mohammed Bedjaoui, for example, argued that the fight of Third World nations to obtain control over their own natural resources, up to and including through nationalization, could not be considered in violation of international law because such governments were simply trying to acquire and retain sovereignty over their own territory.[68] He therefore called for reform of international legislation to take into account the content, and not just the form, of international relations. Such multiform criticisms of the international order even called into question the way in which public information itself was governed and distributed. While some 90 percent of radio frequencies, not to mention almost all press agencies, were under Western control, the Tunisian director of UNESCO put forward the goal of a "New World Information Order" that would give more space to diverse cultures and take non-Western events and perspectives into greater account.[69]

EUROPE'S IDENTITY

On April 23, 1973, during the annual luncheon of the Associated Press in New York, US Secretary of State Henry Kissinger announced the "Year of Europe," in a speech that would include some of the most controversial remarks of his public career.[70] Kissinger's address was not a hymn singing the praises of European inte-

---

[67] Ibid., pp. 86–7.

[68] M. Bedjaoui, *Towards a New International Economic Order* (Paris: UNESCO, 1979), pp. 98–104.

[69] M. Masmoudi, "The New World Information Order," in *Le Monde*, October 26, 1978.

[70] "The Year of Europe: Address by Henry Kissinger (April 23, 1973)," in *The Department of State Bulletin*, May 14, 1973, vol. LXVIII, pp. 592–8.

gration; rather, it was a thinly veiled celebration of the United States' political *savoir faire* for its handling of the dialogue between the superpowers, and a declaration of its plans to bring America's anarchic European allies back on board by persuading them to sign a new Atlantic Charter of shared goals and ideals. Kissinger underscored the need to include Japan in the elaboration of a common Western policy, insisted on the idea of a new trade agreement to relaunch the American economy, and concluded by foreseeing growing responsibilities for the Nine at a regional level, while on the global stage the United States would remain the sole conductor of the orchestra of industrialized countries.

Rarely has an American foreign policy initiative been more poorly prepared than the "Year of Europe," in both its content and its timing. America's desire to exploit the recent entry of Great Britain into the Community by relaunching the Atlantic Alliance was too transparent. The Nixon Administration's political need to react to the signs of crisis surrounding it, with its leaders already reeling under the weight of the Watergate scandal, was too obvious. The US view of the continent was too out of touch with Europe's global responsibilities, in the eyes of a European public opinion full of hardly disguised disdain for anything related to NATO.[71]

But Kissinger's address had stung the Member States that had struggled fitfully to move closer to the goal of a European Union they had set out at the Paris Summit in 1972. The project of political union among the Nine was enmeshed in the usual tensions between a French vision based on the propulsive power of its states, and a German vision (shared by the Dutch and Italians, among others) that gave priority to the reinforcement of the Community's existing institutions. Plans for a monetary union, meanwhile, were facing grave difficulties due to the growing fluctuations in value of the European currencies. While Italy had already left the "Monetary Snake" in February 1973, France itself was also forced to abandon the Snake in 1974, following the most recent devaluation of the dollar the previous year and the ongoing impact of the oil crisis.[72] Currency instability even called into question the smooth functioning of the Common Agricultural Policy, which constituted by far the largest item in the Community budget.

At the European Summit held in Copenhagen from December 14–15, 1973, the Nine failed to devise a common policy in response to the oil crisis but did manage to demonstrate, in a declaration on European identity, their willingness to shape a vision of Europe's global role.[73] In the declaration, the Nine did not openly distance Europe from the Atlantic Alliance, but emphasized the Community's global ambitions. The very same accent on the open question of Europe's identity, to be developed through an autonomous foreign policy, signaled an obvious retort to Kissinger's paternalistic project. During the summit, a delegation of foreign ministers from the Arab states—Tunisia, the United Arab Emirates, Sudan, and Algeria, probably put together through French diplomatic pressures—was officially

---

[71] P. Winand, "Loaded Words and Disputed Meanings: The Year of Europe Speech and its Genesis from the American Perspective" in van der Harst (ed.), *Beyond the Customs Union*, pp. 297–317.

[72] Eichengreen, *Globalizing Capital*, pp. 154–5.

[73] A.E. Gfeller, "Imagining European Identity: French Elites and the American Challenge in the Pompidou–Nixon Era," in (2010) 19(2) *Contemporary European History*.

received by the Danish government; an episode that apparently helped facilitate the inclusion in the final communiqué of a declaration in support of the rights of the Palestinians (previously asserted by the Nine in a statement of November 6), as well as a call to open a dialogue with the oil producers.[74] These developments took place while, throughout the second half of 1973, Kissinger complained that "talking with the Europeans was becoming worse than negotiating with the Soviets." They constantly submitted questions on items that had already been discussed and were no longer subject to change, he continued, so that it was almost as if enlargement, rather than "elevating" Europe to the level of Great Britain, was "lowering" Great Britain to the level of Europe.[75] The Copenhagen summit had been preceded by various surveys conducted by Boumedienne and aimed at reminding the Europeans that, once peace had been reached in Vietnam, with the tensions between East and West apparently subsiding the most explosive area in world politics remained the Mediterranean, racked by the problems regarding Israel and the oil question. In an interview published in the Belgian daily *Le Soir*, the Algerian leader openly called on the Community to take a stand:

> If you look closely, we complement each other and can work together to our mutual advantage. Europe finds itself at a crossroads. It is slowly starting to assume a global role. If it accepts being the faithful ally of American imperialism it will become our adversary; if, instead, it opts for an independent role it can, with our cooperation, do great things.[76]

The Saudi Prince Abdul Aziz expressed the practical foundations of the same idea in remarks to the *Manchester Guardian* shortly after Copenhagen:

> If the winds of US policy continue to fill the sails of Israel, as they do today...the momentum of history may join ourselves and the Europeans in a unique and deep friendship....
>
> For our part we need European expertise in the field of land reclamation, industrialization, and armaments. The Europeans need our oil, our other raw materials, and our markets.[77]

Yet shortly after the summit, in which the Nine solemnly declared their intention to work toward closer unity in foreign policy, their confused reaction to the oil crisis demonstrated the obstacles lying in the path of political cooperation. The French defined the decisions taken in Copenhagen with respect to the oil question—that is, those aimed at energy efficiency—not an oil policy, which would have entailed joint European agreements on energy supply, but rather an "organization of scarcity"; they charged that the summit had defended the interests of the large oil companies in certain countries, foremost among them the Netherlands, and that this depended on the fact that not every European country was reliant on

---

[74] A. Shlaim, *The Iron Wall: Israel and the Arab World* (New York: W.W. Norton & Co., 2001).
[75] FCO, Documents on British Policies Overseas, Series III, vol. IV, Washington Telegram, "Analyses shortcomings of the 'Year of Europe'," December 3, 1973.
[76] *Le Soir*, September 27, 1973.
[77] *The Guardian*, January 9, 1974.

oil to the same degree. The Dutch Labour government, which maintained a pro-Israel stance and strongly opposed a common European overture toward the Arab countries, indeed resisted any energy policy that threatened the free market for oil, also pressured by the Anglo-Dutch Shell company and the huge refining industries of Rotterdam. The Dutch position had prompted Pompidou to grumble that "the Dutch hate France: It is the only constant of their history. They lecture us on Europe, but want it to look just like America."[78] In fact, any European oil policy based on bilateral supply agreements with the Arab states would have implied greater European autonomy from the foreign policy of the United States and a massive transfer of the Arab world's considerable oil wealth onto European shores. This was precisely the objective of the French Foreign Minister Michel Jobert, and the fears of his American counterpart Henry Kissinger.

In order to avoid the risk that Europe would develop a coordinated and autonomous energy plan, the United States had proposed a meeting of the largest energy-consuming nations to be held in Washington in February 1974. The goal was to react to the Arab oil policy by opposing it with a united Western front, and in so doing bring the oil-producing nations to heel. Along with the political desire to reconsolidate the Western alliance, the idea was born of the fears of the major oil companies at the proliferation of bilateral agreements between the oil producers and individual European countries and state oil companies, which could dry up the free market for exports and limit the opportunities to recycle petrodollars through the banks of Wall Street and the City.[79] Italy and France were not alone, in fact, in concluding bilateral agreements with the Arab states based on decades-long contracts to purchase oil in exchange for military technology and technical and financial cooperation.[80]

Eight of the nine Community countries—among them Italy, albeit with reservations[81]—had accepted the offer of a conference in Washington, the results of

---

[78] On the European reactions to the oil shock, a detailed reconstruction of the years 1973–4 can be found in D. Hellema, C. Wiebes, and T. Witte, *The Netherlands and the Oil Crisis: Business as Usual* (Amsterdam: Amsterdam University Press, 2004).

[79] Archivio Ente Nazionale Idrocarburi (ENI), Estero, Nua 979, Busta 27, GL, Stampa Estero, Riservato, "Sull'accordo Franco-Saudita," Rome, November 29, 1974. Jobert was then negotiating with Saudi Arabia an agreement to import 800 million tons of oil over twenty years.

[80] FCO, Documents on British Policy Overseas, Series III, vol. IV, Secret, Note to Prime Minister, "Oil Supplies," December 13, 1973.

[81] This was the furious reaction of Marcello Colitti, a prominent ENI executive, to the rather unprepared presentation of Italian Foreign Minister Aldo Moro in Washington:

The strategy of mediation failed, but this cannot justify an address like that given by the Italian Foreign Minister this afternoon. Moro spoke in Italian, in his cryptic style, throwing together apparently contradictory statements with those interminable circumlocutions of his, which lose all sense by the fourth word. From what you heard through the earpiece it was clear he gave the translator extraordinary difficulty; shortly thereafter the man admitted he was unable to continue, bursting out that since he couldn't understand a word he would simply remain silent. "It doesn't make sense anyway," he added, to the laughter of the entire audience. Moro droned on for another twenty minutes, for the exclusive benefit of the Italian delegation, while everyone else got up and talked among themselves. On this ridiculous note the Italian pretense to any autonomous energy policy or position toward the Third World came to a end. The untranslatable sentences of Aldo Moro buried everything we tried to construct through several years of hard work without leaving Italy anything to show for it, even forcing us to join the agency at the back of the line, the country rebuked and called upon to explain its weak if not utterly non-existent energy policy.

which would be dismissed by Jobert with the terse statement "France's friends are elsewhere." Following the meeting, the oil-consuming nations would join the International Energy Agency founded under the aegis of the OECD in November 1974. Thus the IEA did not become a new institution to confront oil producers, as Kissinger had wished, but rather a new part of an existing international institution.[82] In reality the Washington conference of foreign ministers had produced few results in terms of oil cooperation; as the Algerian oil minister Belaid Abdessalam later commented, "all this controversy has produced very little for Algeria to fear."[83] Venezuelan diplomats also remarked that, while there was no real prospect of solidarity among consumers, since the USA would never sacrifice its citizens' comfort to satisfy the needs of other consumer countries in the event of a shortage, there was a possiblity that the Energy Agency might convince new oil producers such as Norway not to join OPEC.[84] Kissinger had not persuaded his counterparts to take any decision on the emergency exchange of oil, nor to take positive steps on the alarming notion of formal cooperation between the oil-consuming nations and the developing countries. France had very different ideas, that it unveiled to both its European colleagues and the UN Secretary-General at the Community Council of Ministers meeting from January 14–15, 1974, dedicated to energy issues.[85] The French plan was to convene a global energy conference at which all nations, including the oil producers, would engage each other and discuss solutions that would ensure a stable supply at a fair price. The kernel of this French idea would in time form the basis for a new negotiating platform between North and South.

In the meantime the Euro-Arab dialogue desired by the Arab delegations at Copenhagen had taken off. It had begun to acquire foundations in the first half of 1974 with calls for cultural and immigration initiatives, as well as proposals for the creation of joint ventures employing mixed Arab and European capital. The dialogue even had its semi-official publication: The journal *Eurabia* edited in Paris from 1975 and involving intellectuals and members of parliament from western Europe and the Arab world. One weak point remained the fears of the Community's Mediterranean nations regarding a possible widening of preferential trade agreements, not to mention the Arab states' firm resistance to the inclusion of the oil question in any such discussions. But above all the dialogue stood on shaky ground because it was unable to confront the key issue of the Arab-Israeli conflict,

[82] F. Petrini, "L'arma del petrolio: Lo 'shock' petrolifero e il confronto Nord–Sud. Parte prima. L'Europa alla ricerca di un'alternativa: La Comunità tra dipendenza energetica ed egemonia statunitense," in Caviglia and Varsori (eds), *Dollari, petrolio e aiuti allo sviluppo*, pp. 79–109. See also Richard Scott, *The History of the International Energy Agency—The First Twenty Years*, vol. I: *Origins and Structures of the IEA*. Paris: OECD/IEA, 1994.

[83] ANA, Fond Abdessalam, Mission d'explication des mesures prises par les Pays arabes producteurs de petrole au landemain de la guerre du 6 octobre 1973, "Comptes-rendus des visites effectuées par MM. Abdessalam et Yameni en Europe, aux Etats Unis d'Amérique et au Japon, Commentaris sur la visite de Abdessalam aux EUA du 2 au 10 Février, 1974."

[84] AHMPRE, 1974, Interior, Petróleo (AIE), "Antecedentes, creación y perspectivas de la Agencia Internacional de energía (AIE)," Caracas, November 25, 1974.

[85] Archives Historique de la Commission Européenne (AHCE), Cabinet Cheysson, BAC 25/1980, Michel Jobert, "*Aide Mémoire*," January 1974.

and because it presupposed the two sides' complete autonomy from US foreign policy: A condition that in the mid-1970s—despite Kissinger's fears of an increasingly independent Europe—simply did not exist.[86] Indeed, it was in April 1974 that the "Gymnich formula" was adopted, according to which the United States would be consulted prior to every important meeting of European Political Cooperation, which was then handling Mediterranean issues.[87] After the trauma of the oil crisis, the Gymnich formula was erroneously heralded, even by contemporaries, as the end of "any European challenge to American hegemony."[88] Although the Europeans did not play a major role in the Arab-Israeli conflict, however, they would shortly take the initiative on questions of raw materials and the international economy.

While it is true that the process of East–West détente and the preliminary negotiations for the CSCE remained the center of attention for most European political leaders, with their goal of giving Europe a larger role in the easing of tensions between the superpowers, the Yom Kippur War and the oil crisis still seemed to have opened the eyes of the Community to new opportunities for the Mediterranean. In November 1973, at a conference of socialist party leaders, Willy Brandt—responding to the accusations of Israeli Prime Minister Golda Meir regarding Europe's pro-Arab stance—outlined this notion clearly: "Some of us, or at least those who come after us, will live to see a day in which there will be another political force in the world, and that force will be Europe."[89]

Another event that helped prompt a revision of European socialists' policy toward the Third World—strengthening the push for European independence from Washington—was the military *coup d'état* in Chile. Salvador Allende had never hidden his hostility to the Socialist International, which he believed little more than an alliance of European and North American capital,[90] but he had nevertheless received many of its leaders, such as Palme and Mitterrand, who were

[86] D. Allen, "Political Cooperation and the Euro-Arab Dialogue," in D. Allen, R. Rummel, and W. Wessels (eds), *European Political Cooperation* (London: Butterworth Scientific, 1982), p. 69. ENI, Estero, Nua 978, Busta 27, Mae, Dgae, Cee, Riservato, "Dialogo Euro-Arabo. Stato dei lavori in vista della Commissione generale euro-araba," November 29, 1974. Italian diplomats underlined the distance between the French position, "largely directed at achieving concrete results quickly," and the British position "aimed at greater preliminary detailing of the overall conditions on which to base Euro-Arab cooperation."

[87] C. Hill and K.E. Smith (eds), *European Foreign Policy. Key Documents* (London: Routledge, 2000), p. 97.

[88] D.P. Calleo, "America, Europe and the Oil Crisis: Hegemony Reaffirmed?," in J. Chace and E.C. Ravenal (eds), *Atlantis Lost: US-European Relations after the Cold War* (New York: New York University Press, 1976), p. 128.

[89] IISH, Socialist International (SI) 347, Report, "Party Leaders' Conference: London," November 11, 1973.

[90] J. Ziegler, "L'Internationale Socialiste. La reconquête de l'Amérique," in *Le Nouvel Observateur*, October 11, 1979. This was Régis Debray's note of his conversation with Allende: "Q: This explains, then, why for a long time the Chilean Socialist Party has had nothing to do with European social democracy. A: Exactly. It has nothing to say to them, not even to certain parties in Europe that call themselves socialist." See R. Debray, *Conversación con Allende* (Buenos Aires: Siglo XXI Editores, 1971), p. 145.

interested in understanding his perspective. In an emotionally charged emergency meeting of the Socialist International held in the immediate aftermath of Pinochet's coup, European socialists sought concrete means for coordinated reaction. The French suggested proposing Allende for the Nobel Prize, the Germans acting through the SPD's cultural wing (the Friedrich Ebert Stiftung) to call for the liberation of those incarcerated. The International finally decided to send an investigative committee to Chile to reconstruct the exact sequence of events.[91] The fall of Allende had seemed to eliminate any hopes that a strategy of socialist reform could succeed in Latin America through the democratic process. The future challenge for the socialists was thus made clear, and stated in no uncertain terms:

> Today it is more important than ever that the Socialist International demonstrate that, after Chile, democratic socialism is not finished; that it desires and can still play a role in this hemisphere, supporting continental emancipation and liberation movements against foreign intervention.
>
> With regard to Cuba, we have adopted too rigid a stance, an offspring of the Cold War. It is urgent that we reconsider this. Cuba is not an obstacle to the independence and freedom of Latin America. It is the political and economic interests of the United States that play the greatest role on that Continent.[92]

The Mediterranean nevertheless remained an important zone in which Europe sought to express its new identity. This was made clear in the concluding talks of the CSCE, during which many European leaders reiterated that, once the tensions of the Cold War had been eased on the continent, it would be necessary to turn their attentions southward to the Mediterranean. The words of the Austrian Chancellor Kreisky, who handled the Arab-Israeli conflict for the International and who was himself of Jewish descent, were particularly strong in this regard:

> The Mediterranean is in many respects the cradle of our civilization. The fact that the world's great religions originated there and that much of our society has come from that region imposes on us a great responsibility. Thus, even if we are fully aware of the delicacy of these issues, here we appeal to the governments of the Arab nations and to Israel to do everything they can to resolve their disputes peacefully.
>
> There must be a way to respect the rights of both Israel and Palestine. And tied to this is a question that concerns Europe in particular. A large group of industrialized nations that consider themselves belonging to the West are still dependent for their supply of oil, in some cases as much as 98 percent, on Middle Eastern imports. In fact, when we speak of oil we refer to a very particular commodity, for which we must quickly find some form of constructive cooperation between Europe and the Middle Eastern oil-producing countries. A cooperation that consists of something more than simply buying and selling. It must be a special form of cooperation that we bring into being.[93]

---

[91] IISH, SI 293, Minutes of the emergency meeting of the Socialist International, London, September 22, 1973.

[92] IISH, SI 420, Socialist Strategy Study Group, "Study Group on Socialist Strategy for the Third World," November 8, 1973.

[93] ACS, Moro, b. 122.

This impulse to a renewed investment in the Mediterranean, not only as an economic partner but also as the symbol of a more open Continental identity, was also strong in intellectual circles. One example of such cultural excavation linking past and future identities was Fernand Braudel's 1977 study of the "space and history" of the Mediterranean, a follow-up to the historian's famous work *The Mediterranean and the Mediterranean World in the Age of Phillip II*. The French historian, without denying the clash of civilizations that always populated the area, emphasized the richness of its cultural exchange and material traditions that had infused the sea in the past, and which could bring its many different shores closer together in the future:

> There is all the West on one side (the Greeks and the Latins), all the Orient on the other. The breadth of the conflict dramatizes and amplifies the shock. At Marathon the Greeks save a West threatened with subversion. Rome strikes the Orient by destroying Carthage. The Crusades all surge obstinately in the same direction. The taking of Constantinople in 1453 is Islam's impressive response. Lepanto, tardily (1571), puts in play the safety of the entire Mediterranean, overwhelmed by the Turkish fleet and the barbarian corsairs.
>
> All this is clear: once the civilizations are all on the field, how can they not clash?...
>
> Civilizations, in fact, are all too often nothing but ignorance, disdain, or hate for the other. But they are not only this. They are also sacrifice, influence, the accumulation of cultural wealth, the heredity of knowledge. If the sea has witnessed the war of these civilizations, it has also brought them a multiplicity of exchanges (technologies, ideas, popular beliefs) and the multiform spectacles that it offers us today. The Mediterranean is a mosaic of a million colors.[94]

Speaking of Braudel's work, Giuliana Gemelli has written of the search for a new European cultural universalism, posited in opposition to the American model, as a response to the continent's loss of political power. The Mediterranean, and not the Atlantic, would thus become the historical unifying center of the West, representing a sort of *Défi Latin*.[95]

THE SUCCESSES AND FAILURES OF THE COMMUNITY'S GLOBAL POLICY

In 1973, after the admission of Great Britain, the EC began the renegotiation of the Yaoundé Agreements in order to include those countries of the Commonwealth in a position "comparable" to that of the Associated African States. The inclusion of the former British colonies in the previous agreements with the AASM had been guaranteed by a provision of the UK admission treaty. Yet the negotiations proved difficult for the Community, not least because they took place amid a groundswell of growing radicalism within a South that was galvanized by the suc-

---

[94] F. Braudel (ed.), *La Méditerranée. L'Espace et l'Histoire* (Paris: Flammarion, 1985), pp. 172–3.
[95] G. Gemelli, *Fernand Braudel e l'Europa universale* (Venice: Marsilio, 1990), pp. 188–90.

cess of the oil-producing countries. Great attention was paid to perfecting the details of the accords with Francophone Africa and those African and Caribbean nations tied to Great Britain; this was due to pressure from Paris, which did not want to lose its privileged political and cultural ties, or the significant economic advantages guaranteed by the agreement, which contributed to easing French aid spending and favored its exports. French insistence on the reinforcement of European regionalism in Africa prevailed, in the end, over the increasingly pronounced doubts of countries such as Germany and the Netherlands.

The new negotiations undoubtedly signaled an improvement over the previous Yaoundé agreements, and a major step forward in the creation of a real development of a Community policy for the South.[96] A significant role was played during the negotiations by the French socialist Commissioner for Development Claude Cheysson, who was more sensitive than his predecessors to the expectations of public opinion,[97] and to the new global issues facing both sides of the North–South divide.[98] The AASM countries and those of the British Commonwealth formed a united front in talks with the Community, overcoming their mutual indifference as Anglophone and Francophone nations. As the then-Director-General of DGVIII Dieter Frisch recalls, Nigeria was to be the leader and main negotiator for African countries, "strenghened by its oil wealth and membership of OPEC."[99] Determined to obtain some concession to guarantee that the accords did not simply force the AASM to give away their existing competitive advantage over the Commonwealth newcomers, the African, Caribbean, and Pacific (ACP) group subjected the Nine to great pressure in the pursuit of their objectives, in line with the general demands of the South at that time and the need to obtain more aid than the previous agreements. This hard line brought the talks to a halt that was resolved only by a July 1974 meeting in Kingston, Jamaica. Following this meeting, the bloc of new and old associated states obtained important openings on industrial cooperation as well as guarantees on the stability of income from the

---

[96] J.M. Palayret, "Mondialisme contre régionalisme: CEE et ACP dans les negotiations de la Convention de Lomé," in A. Varsori (ed.), *Inside the European Community. Actors and Policies in European Integration 1957–1973* (Baden-Baden & Brussels: Nomos–Bruylant, 2006), pp. 369–98.

[97] Claude Cheysson joined the European Commission in 1973 and was Commissioner for Development until 1981, when he became French Foreign Minister under François Mitterrand.

[98] Comité économique et sociale européen (CES), Annexe au PV de la 128ième session plénière qui a eu lieu les 26 et 27 février, 1975, "Exposé de M. Cheysson," March 24, 1975. Cheysson believed the Lomé negotiations were a concrete means of achieving the South's ambitions regarding global raw-material agreements. Toward the end of the talks he stated:

This problem can be resolved in two ways: You can hold great ideological debates—which they certainly don't lack in the United Nations!—in which everyone defends extreme positions. Behind the Algerians, who are very gifted at rhetoric and possess a very coherent logic, the Third World together has assumed ever more aggressive and absurd positions while, at the other extreme, the Americans and a few others decide to ignore whatever recommendations come from within the United Nations or UNCTAD... If you persist down this path I believe that the world will proceed toward a series of more troubling commodities crises, with everyone trying to take advantage of their temporary positions of strength. Or, on the other hand, you can seek to move forward more modestly but pragmatically. This is what we intend to do.

[99] D. Frisch, "La politique de development de l'Union européenne. Un regard personnel sur 50 ans de coopération internationale," in (2008) 15 *Rapport ECDPM*, p. 13.

export of raw materials. Notwithstanding the hostility of the largest continental business associations,[100] European negotiators accepted the terms fixed by the future ACP countries with regard to industrial cooperation, even though the plans they had outlined were quite ambitious: The direct transfer of technology from European businesses, the training of industrial management on site, and the recognition of the need for a more equitable international division of labor. The Francophone African states also demanded that France renounce inverse preferences, joining similar pressures from both the other developing nations and the United States. A determining factor in speeding up the talks was the widespread fear throughout western Europe that supplies of basic commodities would be cut off in the event of a failure and the ensuing need for stability of supply. The final product of these negotiations would be the Lomé Convention, signed in February 1975 by the European Community and forty-six African, Caribbean, and Pacific nations, many of which ranked among the poorest nations in the world.

The fact that the Lomé Convention—termed a "convention" and not an "association" to precisely mark the distance from the previous Yaoundé terminology—opened a new era in the relationship between the developed and the developing countries was also demonstrated by the approval the Convention received from the European Community's Economic and Social Commission.[101] The European trade unions had participated in preparatory discussions, although not directly in the negotiations themselves,[102] and ultimately the ETUC gave its approval, singling out the innovative character of the protective mechanism to defend the export income of the forty-six signatory countries.[103] Even the French communist trade union, the CGT, while critical of multinationals' overbearing weight in the global economy and supportive of the struggle of the oil producers as a means to redress global economic imbalances, still admitted that in comparison with the previous agreements of association, Lomé marked "a new phase."[104] The Italian PCI distin-

---

[100] CES, UNICE, "UNICE Observations de l'UNICE sur le ACP Mémorandum ," October 29, 1974. In exchange for a commitment to industrial cooperation, European industrialists demanded: a) protection of private investment; b) free circulation of capital; c) immediate indemnification in case of nationalization. UNICE observed that the positions previously taken by the South in various international organizations did not meet these demands, and declared it was unwilling to give away technology for nothing, warning against using the pretext of transferring manufacturing to certain associated states because this carried the potential to create a serious social and economic crisis within the Community. CES, Note de l'UNICE, "Conférence général de l'Onudi à Lima," March 4,1975. European businesses underlined the importance of a favorable climate for investment, respect for legal norms, and suggested their willingness to create joint ventures rather than commit to technology transfer. They believed the responsibility for the backwardness of the South *should be attributed entirely to the Southern countries themselves.*

[101] CES, "Parere in merito alla Convenzione di Lomé," November 19, 1975.

[102] J.M. Palayret, "Il Comitato economico e socialize e le relazioni con i paesi e i territori associati e gli ACP (1958–1985)," in A. Varsori (ed.), *Il Comitato economico e sociale nella costruzione europea* (Padua: Marsilio, 2000).

[103] IISH, European Trade Union Confederation (ETUC), Box 2928, CES, Letter, "Meeting with Cheysson," April 14, 1975.

[104] IISH, ETUC, Box 2938, Cgt, "Note du départment international sur la Convention de Lomé," February 1976.

guished themselves even further from their western European communist counter-parts by voting their full support for the new agreement.[105]

Midway through the 1970s, after its first enlargement, the Community had thus concluded a diverse series of agreements—from preferential tariff agreements with associated countries hoping for future admission, via agreements on industrial and technological cooperation, to measures to protect export incomes—with a wide array of countries in northern Europe, the Mediterranean rim, and throughout Africa, the Caribbean, and the Pacific. It had in fact signed free trade agreements with the Member States of the European Free Trade Association (EFTA); association agreements with Greece, Turkey, Malta, and Cyprus; as well as the Lomé Convention with an additional forty-six nations. Between 1976 and 1977 it signed cooperation agreements with Algeria, Morocco, Tunisia, Egypt, Israel, Jordan, Lebanon, and Syria which, although falling short of the Global Mediterranean Policy outlined at the Paris Summit in 1972, still represented a major step toward closer relations with the coastal nations.[106] This impressive network of economic ties seemed to point toward the emergence of the EC as a new international actor, with its own regional economic sphere of influence.

At the same time—and all evidence suggests that this was no mere coincidence but rather a coordinated Franco-German effort, in response to pressure from Great Britain—the Community began to establish the bases for a global development and cooperation policy.[107]

One early sign of the Community's desire to develop a global approach was the concession in July 1974 of an exceptional aid package, amounting to 500 million ECU (European Currency Units), for the countries struck hardest by the rise in oil prices—the "Cheysson Fund." It was also certainly no coincidence that, barely one month after the signing of the Lomé Convention, the European Commission presented its first five-year plan (1976–80) for technical and financial assistance to

---

[105] M. Maggiorani and P. Ferrari (eds), *L'Europa da Togliatti a Berlinguer. Testimonianze e Documenti 1945–1984* (Bologna: Il Mulino, 2005), p. 130.

[106] E. Calandri, "Europa e Mediterraneo tra giustapposizione e integrazione," in M. de Leonardis (ed.), *Il Mediterraneo nella politica estera italiana dal secondo dopoguerra* (Bologna: Il Mulino, 2003), pp 47–59.

[107] AMAEF, Direction des affaires économiques et financiers, J.P. Brunet, Voyages-Visites-Rencontres, 1973–4, 60, "Entretiens franco-allemands au Sommet 26–27 novembre 1973. Politique d'aide aux pays tiers." The analysis of the French memo, drawn up in the midst of the Lomé negotiations, was as follows:

The German stance: the Germans rejected inverse preferences and had a more global approach; they opposed stabilization of incomes from exports; they were against the organization of primary commodities markets; and placed greater emphasis on the conditions on which aid was given than on the quantity of aid itself. The French stance: Defense of reciprocity with the "associable" states to give a definite legal basis to the meetings; the conclusion of agreements with the Mediterranean countries; a regional policy of export income guarantees. The French were willing, however, once their conditions had been met, to create a community system for development aid to be open to all the developing countries.

This document shows clearly how the Lomé Convention represented, in substance, a compromise in which Germany accepted European regionalism and stabilization agreements, while France resigned itself to the loss of its inverse preferences as well as the future introduction of a global community policy for cooperation and development.

developing countries not associated with the Community.[108] In 1976 the Community approved the financing for its first cooperation projects with non-associated countries—India, Bangladesh, and Indonesia—as well as the European program for cofinancing of nongovernmental organizations' projects for the Third World. Although initially extremely limited, resources for the programs with non-associated countries grew at a dizzying pace, from 20 million ECU in 1976 to approximately 138 million ECU in 1980. The approval of specific Community legislation in 1981 gave funding of these aid mechanisms a permanent institutional foundation.[109]

According to *The New York Times* a *rapprochement* between western Europe and the Third World was inevitable, for several reasons:

> The European group is much more dependent on Middle East oil than the United States. However, United Nations analysts point out that other considerations, too, dictate Western Europe's flexible attitude toward the third world. These include the lingering solidarity of the British Commonwealth, the traditional French interests in Africa, and the influence of strong Socialist parties in Western and northern Europe, which watch third-world attempts at socialism with sympathy.[110]

While at the Washington energy conference France had been isolated, even from its Community partners, this had not prevented the French government from continuing to support the strategy of dialogue with the oil producers. Both Pompidou and Jobert, mindful of the fate of de Gaulle whose government had been fatally weakened by the coordinated blows of the united student and working class movements, feared making the cuts to public services and reductions in labor standards that would have been necessary to remain competitive in international markets with the ever-higher costs of oil and basic commodities. Pompidou also believed that oil prices, which until then had worked to the Europeans' competitive advantage, could bring continental businesses to their knees in competition with their American counterparts. The Italian government was equally concerned about any further rise in the price of oil or other commodities, as they were unable and unwilling to further reduce labor costs or end wage indexation schemes.[111]

In September 1974 it was the Saudi Oil Minister Sheik Ahmed Zaki Yamani himself who proposed once again the idea of a high-level meeting between producers and consumers on a smaller scale.[112] Yamani's view, and thus that of the Saudi King Faisal, was that UNCTAD was still too chaotic and radical a forum to pro-

---

[108] "The European Community's Development Cooperation Policy 1980," in *The Courier*, September–October 1981.
[109] Council Regulation 442/81 on financial and technical aid to non-associated developing countries, February 17, 1981.
[110] "Shift in Third World Views Shown in UN Session," in *The New York Times*, September 19, 1975.
[111] ACS, Moro, Scritti e discorsi 1974, "Articolo per 'il Sole 24 Ore'," December 4, 1974.
[112] ENI, Estero, Nua 2025, Busta 2026, Ministero Affari Esteri, Dgae–Uff. VIII, "Proposta Ministro Yamani costituzione Comitato livello ministeriale per questioni energia," Rome, October 2, 1974.

vide a space for the discussion of concrete proposals. More profitable results could be achieved in a committee composed of only four producers—Algeria, Iran, Saudi Arabia, and Venezuela—and six consumers, foremost among them the European Community, alongside the United States, Japan, Brazil, India, and Zaire. Yamani worked diligently within the G77 to generate agreement to this new forum, but he had to overcome strong Algerian objections to the creation of a forum outside UN auspices that, furthermore, would include only two "progressive"—that is, anti-American—producers (Venezuela and Algeria itself).

The idea of a meeting between producers and consumers was then brought up again by Valéry Giscard d'Estaing, elected France's president after the death of Pompidou. Liberal in his ideological inclinations, but *dirigiste* in his political training (in the best tradition of the *énarques* at the renowned École Nationale d'Administration), Giscard made two important speeches in 1974 in which he surprisingly declared himself a supporter of the new international economic order. In the "Giscardian" worldview, however, the NIEO did not necessarily stand for the redistribution of resources to the South, still less the creation of a new, international legal standard based on a level playing field for strong and weak economies. More simply, it meant the creation of new decision-making structures for the heads of those states with enough international authority and power to outline new guidelines for the stabilization of the international economy on both the monetary and the energy fronts. As Giscard declared:

> Today the global economic situation includes three destabilizing factors. On one side there is global inflation and on the other the complete disorganization of the international monetary system. Finally, there is the swift rise in price of certain commodities, and in particular petroleum-based products.[113]

The Giscardian proposal of a restricted, high-level meeting was intended to create an institutional mechanism to contain the price of oil and negotiate future increases. The producing countries would thus be called upon to give up part of their sovereignty over the establishment of the price of oil. But in exchange for what?

On this question OPEC was divided into two factions. The first, represented by a radical Algeria, but also by Iran, aimed to push oil prices ever higher in order to finance the rapid industrialization and modernization of the poorest and most populous countries. The Algerian government practiced an economic policy that went under the definition of "industrializing industries": Massive investment in heavy manufacturing concerns, the operational requirements of which would in turn stimulate the growth of small and mid-sized businesses.[114] A second, more moderate school developed around the Gulf states, less densely populated and more interested in securing the investment of oil profits than in generating massive short-term earnings to reinvest on infrastructure. At their head was King Faisal's

---

[113] S. Cohen and M.C. Smouts (eds), *La politique extérieure de Valéry Giscard d'Estaing* (Paris: Presses de Science Politiques, 1985).

[114] G.D. de Bernis, "Deux stratégies pour l'industrialisation du tiers-monde. Les industries industrialisantes et les options algériennes," in (1971) *Revue du Tiers-Monde* (July–September), p. 68.

Saudi Arabia, which was acquiring growing prestige in both the West and the Arab world as a center of Islamic culture, in the process displacing Sadat's Egypt.[115] Faisal could accept a cap on oil prices in exchange for a strengthening of his country's political relationship with Europe, and seemed at least partially willing to call into question its traditional alliance with Washington, particularly after Nixon was succeeded by the more pro-Israel Gerald Ford.

The determining factor for Paris would be the unanimous support of the Nine in favor of the initiative. The Italian government led by Moro, as we have seen, tended to assume a strategy aimed at opening space for the Mediterranean in the prevailing East–West détente. While prudently taking into account the limited room for maneuver afforded by the Italian economy, and mindful of the dramatic fractiousness of its domestic politics, the Moro government appeared the most open of the Nine to French initiatives.[116] From a political perspective only Bonn, and to a lesser degree the Belgian government, supported the strategy of confrontation set out by Kissinger.

Agreement on a joint Community position for energy matters was thus very difficult. The communiqué of the Commission prepared by Energy Commissioner Simonet at the end of 1974 simply sought to mediate among various interests once more, in order to prevent national supply strategies from putting Member States in conflict with one another, and to put a halt to the protectionist tendencies on

---

[115] The decline of pan-Arab republicanism and the rise of Saudi hegemony has been traced by Reinhard Schulze:

> In 1970, more than 80 percent of the oil production in the Middle East belonged to five countries: Saudi Arabia, Iran, Libya, Kuwait and Iraq. In the same year Saudi Arabia, Kuwait and Libya earned more through their oil exports than the entire sum of Egypt's burden of debt. With this capital, the oil countries could act freely on the world market and import goods in quantities which Egypt and other countries had never experienced. The wealth produced by oil went against any development ideology which still believed in a "powerful state" and thus also undermined the attraction of Arabism, which was closely connected with utopian theories of progress.

Schulze, *A Modern History of the Islamic World*, pp. 187–8.

[116] L. Riccardi, "Sempre più con gli arabi. La politica italiana verso il Medio Oriente dopo la guerra del Kippur (1973–1976)," in (2006) 6 *Nuova Storia Contemporanea*, pp. 57–82. The Moro government appeared to be dragged against its will, however, into accepting a more pro-American position. A letter from ENI president Girotti on the meeting between Kissinger and Moro scheduled for July 1974 revealed the tension in Italian oil policy, caught between its desire for autonomy and its relationship with the USA:

> Let us not forget that Italy's energy and economic situation is so weak at the present moment that we are in no position, as I see it, to refuse Western offers of cooperation and reciprocal assistance… Now, if you agree with my judgment and if the widespread opinion is correct that the Americans have lost some of their original interest in problems of global energy cooperation, then perhaps it would not be out of place to draw Kissinger's attention to the interest that consumer nations like Italy have in pursuing the original goals of the Washington Conference [the Producer–Consumer conference].

ENI, Estero, Nua 2022, Busta 458, Girotti a Guazzaroni, July 2, 1974. But the weakness of Italy's energy position—which would have justified cooperation with international oil companies and the American government—is contested by other ENI executives like Marcello Colitti (in discussion with the author, October 12, 2006), as well as by documents of the ENI president, in which it appears that in 1974–5 Italy's privileged suppliers, like the USSR, Iraq, and Libya, could furnish exports at more advantageous prices than those of Saudi Arabia. ENI, Estero, Nua, Busta 27, Lettera del Presidente Eni Pietro Sette al ministra Affari esteri Arnaldo Forlani, December 23, 1976.

display. The only feasible options appeared to be reduction in energy consumption, investment in nuclear energy as an alternative source, and re-emphasis on coal production.[117] National energy strategies were simply too diverse and conflictual. But that did not prevent the Nine, despite lacking a clear sense of common goals, from lining up behind the French initiative as a plan to relaunch the Community politically on the international stage. The Netherlands was symbolic of the contradiction in which the Community found itself: While they opposed a European energy policy in order to defend the privileged position of their own oil companies, the Dutch were strongly in favor of the idea of a global policy to redistribute resources to the developing countries as a means to stem the tide of Third World radicalism.

The primary obstacle to Giscard's project lay instead in the White House, which, after its defeat in the United Nations with the September 1974 approval of the Charter of Economic Rights and Duties of States, had renewed its openly hostile stance toward the South.[118] The early voices of what would become the neoconservative movement were beginning to make themselves heard, calling for the reinvigoration of the free market, opposition to unconditional aid for the developing countries, and a closing of Western democratic ranks.[119] One result of their stance was Kissinger's menacing expressions at the end of 1974 regarding the need to free the industrialized countries from the stranglehold of the Arab sheiks, by force if necessary.

Preliminary French surveys of Washington had revealed the outlines of the Ford Administration's strategy regarding the oil question: Negotiating the consumers' joint position in advance; preventing the producers from obtaining structural changes in the international monetary system; relying on the inevitable decline of crude oil prices due to market forces; and emphasizing a preference for bilateral rather than multilateral talks.[120] In the Franco-American summit held in Martinique in December 1974 and dedicated principally to international monetary issues, the French President struggled to convince his American counterpart of the need for dialogue with the oil producers. In order to overcome the objections of Ford and Kissinger, Giscard agreed to reach preliminary agreements in three areas: Energy conservation, development of alternative energy sources, and financial solidarity mechanisms for the West.[121] As a result, by January 1975 the industrialized

---

[117] Ufficio per l'Italia della Commissione CEE, "Intervento del vice presidente Simonet in occasione della presentazione dei documenti di politica energetica adottati dalla Commissione," Brussels, November 27, 1974. The goals were reduction in oil dependence from 65 percent to 45 percent by 1985; procurement of 50 percent of energy needs through the nuclear sector; and maintenance of the percentage dependent on coal.

[118] H. Kissinger, *Years of Renewal* (New York: Simon & Schuster, 1999), p. 652.

[119] The neoconservative movement was still on the fringes of this uprising, it should be noted, and even counted the foreign policy realist Kissinger among its primary targets. M. Del Pero, *Libertà e impero. Gli Stati Uniti e il mondo 1776–2006* (Rome & Bari: Laterza, 2008), pp. 363–7; M. Del Pero, *Henry Kissinger e l'ascesa dei neoconservatori: Alle origini della politica estera americana* (Rome & Bari: Laterza, 2006).

[120] CHAN, 5AG3, AE 54, Note, November 1974.

[121] CHAN, 5AG3, AE 54, Note, "Martinique."

countries would create a financial network within the International Monetary Fund, in addition to the Fund's existing Oil Facility. Later, on April 9, 1975, a Financial Support Fund would be created under the auspices of the OECD.

Algeria's strategy, as expressed by the Minister of Industry Belaid Abdessalam in the course of the Extraordinary Meeting of OPEC held in Algiers in January 1975, focused instead on reacting to the attacks of Western propaganda and the media, as well as threats of American military intervention—judged to be serious—through a joint declaration of all producers. Abdessalam further declared the need to move ahead quickly with the first conference of OPEC Heads of State in order to reconfirm their ties with the other developing countries. Participation in the French initiative would be acceptable only if negotiations were to include oil, other commodities, and issues of development at the same time.[122] The Conference of OPEC Heads of State, held in Algiers from March 4–6, 1975, would be the last high-level meeting organized by Algeria, after the Conference of the Non-Aligned in 1973 and the VIth Special Session of the UN on raw materials in 1974. In his opening remarks Boumedienne sought to reiterate and emphasize the connection between the oil producers' pressures regarding the price of crude and the establishment of a new economic order.[123] The conference approved a series of ambitious documents aimed at outlining a strategy to solve the international economic crisis and preserving the role of the oil producers as the vanguard of the struggle for reform of the international economy.[124] On monetary issues, for example, the OPEC sovereigns and heads of state cited the disproportionate weight of Western states in both the IMF and the World Bank as evidence "that the policies and actions of these two institutions are calibrated for the use and consumption of the political and ideological interests of these States." The Algerian leader expressed concern regarding the West's new strategy aimed at alienating the oil producers from the other countries of the G77. The Algerian proposals instead included the complete recovery by Third World nations of their own natural resources, industrialization, aid in the form of financial transfers, renegotiation of past debt, and implementation of the UN "special program" and thus the creation of a Common Fund for commodities. French diplomats noted, however, that only seven of the twelve leaders invited were present at the opening, and that the Saudis had already rejected the idea that all financing from oil producers to the Third World should pass through a dedicated OPEC fund.[125]

At the end of March all the conditions were in place for the preparatory meeting of Giscard's proposed conference, to be held by April 1975. The approval of the

---

[122] ENI, Estero, Nua 828, Busta 11, A. Fogliano, Promemoria, "XLIII Conferenza straordinaria dell'OPEC, Algeri 24–26/1/75, Roma," March 6, 1975.

[123] ENI, Estero, Nua 828, Busta 11, Rappresentanza in Algeria, "Algeri: Conferenza dei capi di Stato dei Paesi membri dell'OPEC," Algiers, March 6, 1975.

[124] Ibid.

[125] Archives Groupe Total (TOTAL), 1 Sg/44, Télégramme, "Conference des chefs d'Etat de l'OPEC, Alger, 7 mars 1975."

Nine had been formally obtained at the EC Council of Ministers on February 10, and then seconded at the summit in Dublin (March 9–11), at which the Nine had decided that oil questions and those regarding other commodities would have to be handled separately. Kissinger's assent had arrived shortly thereafter, as had that of OPEC. The preparatory meeting was designed to give form and content to the actual conference, which would be held upon its conclusion.[126] Reporting on the latest developments to the French President, Ambassador de Guiringaud, who co-ordinated diplomatic work on the conference, could scarcely hide his satisfaction: "Eighteen months after the events of October 1973 the dialogue which everyone first deemed impossible will begin tomorrow because of French initiative." The goal of the French government remained that of freezing oil prices and reinforcing the position of Saudi Arabia within OPEC, perhaps even agreeing to the indexing of oil prices with that of manufactures. With respect to commodities in general, however, any discussion of indexing was off limits, because it would create large surpluses among producers as a result; price stabilization mechanisms for individual commodity markets could be considered instead. According to de Guiringaud, the more difficult issue would be to convince Great Britain to accept common representation for the Nine. But the problems of the preparatory meeting soon revealed themselves to be much more complex, and brought the entire project to a temporary halt. Algeria and the United States remained at a total *impasse*, with diametrically opposed objectives. Algeria feared the separation of OPEC from the other G77 nations and rejected any Western initiative that might widen this gap. On the other side of the Atlantic, in a meeting in the Oval Office at the height of the preparatory talks, Kissinger reported to Ford that "the French President has been a disaster. The Producers and the Developing Countries are transforming the meeting into a conference on commodities. I instructed to our delegation to be tough." The American President approved: "Well said. You can tell them to come home."[127]

In a report on the final outcome of the meeting, the Secretary General of the French Treasury allowed himself a few bitter reflections: "The meeting, considered one of the fundamental objectives of French diplomacy, concluded as a definite defeat."[128] The European Community had been subjected to the exhausting ritual of achieving unanimity, forcing the other participants to wait upon the Nine for hours, while they still were unprepared to negotiate on issues of energy and development at the same time. The presence of Viscount Etienne Davignon, in his role representing both the Belgian government and the International Energy Agency,

---

[126] CHAN, 5AG3, AE 54, Rapport de M. de Guiringaud à M. le Président de la République, Conference Internationale sur l'Energie et les problèmes économiques qui s'y rattachent, Paris," March 27, 1975.

[127] GFL, National Security Advisor (NSA), Country Files, Europe–Canada, Box 4, Memcon, "The Oval Office, President Ford, H.A. Kissinger, Brent Scowcroft," April 15, 1975.

[128] CHAN, 5AG3, AE 54, J.L. Lapine, Inspection Générale des Finances, "Réflexions sur la reunion préparatoire à la Conférence proposée par le Président de la République," April 23, 1975.

had further made American weight felt in all the Community's decisions. His assessment of the Nine was telling:

> Great Britain: hard line and absence of interest in the conference project;
>
> Belgium and Denmark: hard line, systematically aligned with American positions and priority accorded to coordination within the Agency (IEA);
>
> West Germany: very hard line on issues of raw materials (for doctrinal reasons) but made a visible effort to assimilate our ideas;
>
> From the perspective of the image of the Community in the Third World, the balance sheet of the meeting is rather discouraging: it appeared initially as little more than the spokesman of the industrialized countries, and was never in a position to play a role in reconciliation or mediation.

The important role played by the International Energy Agency, while pleasing to Washington, worried the Europeans: "the shameful label of instrument of opposition slapped on the Agency by Algeria worries the Europeans even more than the United States. They would rather not lose the psychological advantage the Community came away with from the Lomé Convention."

6

North–South Dialogues

In August 1975, with the conclusion in Helsinki of the Conference on Security and Cooperation in Europe, the USA formally recognized Soviet control over eastern Europe. It seemed weakened by the loss of its Presidency's prestige and the defeat in Vietnam, while Congress had rediscovered its never fully extinguished isolationist tendencies.[1] America's prestige appeared tarnished not only in western Europe, but also within the country itself. Indeed, in 1975 the Church Committee of the United States Senate began the largest inquiry ever undertaken into the dark secrets of a nation's intelligence services, bringing to light several politically embarrassing clandestine operations conducted by the CIA, from its implication in the killing of Patrice Lamumba to its covert activities against Allende, as well as its illegal investigations and cover-ups of domestic actions against America's own citizens.[2]

In addition to insisting on a policy of direct confrontation with the oil-producing countries, Kissinger's strategy—combined with increasingly strong pressure from Congress—gradually pushed Washington to withdraw its support for multilateral institutions. The Republican administration delayed payments to the World Bank and threatened to abandon the ILO and UNESCO, both accused of bias in favor of the Third World and the communist camp.[3] The director of the ILO at the time, the Frenchman Francis Blanchard, recalled the shock of even British diplomats when in November 1975 Kissinger sent him the letter announcing Washington's exit from the ILO, the oldest organization of the international system.[4]

For its part, the Soviet Union, having reduced economic aid to the developing countries, seemed to be concentrating on a new military offensive to head off any competition with Chinese communism. Their actions were so poorly planned and ultimately chaotic that they produced disastrous results for Soviet foreign policy, but this made them no less frightening at the time from the perspective of Western governments.[5] Moscow undertook fresh African offensives, in Angola and Ethiopia, that seemed to outline the contours of a new effort to achieve regional

---

[1] G.H. Soutou, *La guerre de Cinquante Ans. Les relations Est–Ouest 1943–2000* (Paris: Fayard, 2001), pp. 564–5.

[2] S. Kutler, *The Wars of Watergate: The Last Crisis of Richard Nixon* (New York: W.W. Norton and Co., 1992).

[3] C. Gwin, *US Relations with the World Bank 1945–1992* (Washington, DC: The Brookings Institution, 1993), p. 18.

[4] F. Blanchard, *L'Organisation internationale du travail. De la guerre froide à un nouvel ordre mondial* (Paris: Seuil, 2004), p. 116.

[5] J.L. Gaddis, *The Cold War. A New History* (New York: Penguin, 2005), pp. 206–8.

hegemony. At the same time they completely abandoned their support for the economic battles of the Global South, considered by Soviet leadership too costly and counterproductive, and at any rate to be subordinated to the promotion of socialist regimes within the developing countries. In a meeting between Leonid Brezhnev and Carlos Andrés Pérez, the Venezuelan President and one of the most active leaders of the South, the Soviet leader responded to pressures to raise and stabilize the price of coffee with the revealing remark: "The cheaper you sell it to us, the better."[6] The Soviet withdrawal from debates on the global economy would weigh heavily on their own future, placing them at the mercy of the outcome of a confrontation negotiated primarily between the West and the developing world.

Thus, neither the United States nor the Soviet Union seemed motivated to discuss a cooperative path out of global economic turmoil. The mantle of leadership in international economic diplomacy fell instead upon individual European leaders and the European Community of Nine. The EC had, in fact, emerged with renewed prestige from the signing of the Lomé Convention and the Helsinki Conference, where it had succeeded in including important provisions in the baskets holding protection of the right to dissent and cooperation on cultural and economic issues with eastern Europe.[7] Even more importantly, the EC and western European countries appeared to have made themselves one of the few attractive models; and demonstrated this power of attraction by influencing the democratization of Southern Europe during the crisis of autoritarian and colonial military regimes in Greece, Portugal, and Spain in the mid-1970s. In 1979 the EC took also an important step in its own effort to democratize its representative mechanisms, registering some 200 million voters in the first direct elections to the European Parliament.

In the mid-1970s, international diplomatic clashes surrounding currency instability, development aid, dept repayment, and commodities issues intensified perceptibly. These were all questions that, directly or indirectly, could fall between the cracks of the delegated competences of the EC and the European Commission.[8] France, in particular, long opposed the Commission's participation on behalf of

---

[6] AHMPRE, 1976, Interior, Visita Oficial del Señor Presidente de la Republica Carlos Andrés Pérez a Estados Unidos—Gran Bretaña—España—Portugal—Italia—Urss, "Resumen de la conversación sostenida en el Kremlin entre el señor Presidente Carlos Andrés Pérez y el Secretario General de Partido Comunista de la Unión Soviética, Señor Leónid Ilich Brezhniev," November 17, 1976.

[7] A. Romano, *From Détente in Europe to European Détente. How the West Shaped the Helsinki CSCE* (Brussels: Peter Lang, 2006).

[8] Pressure for the Community to participate in UN debates had grown steadily after the Paris Summit of 1972 and in response to the Copenhagen declaration on the identity of the Community in international relations. In 1973, the European Parliament had voted in favor of a resolution that requested granting the Community a voice in the UN. In the same year a Commission memorandum put forward four fundamental reasons in support of EC participation at the UN: 1. the enlargement to nine countries had given the EC greater political weight; 2. the Federal Republic of Germany's admission to the General Assembly meant that all the nations of the Community were now represented; 3. the Community's competences were expanding to the point at which it was difficult to foresee any international debate on economic issues in which the Community did not have a stake; 4. debates in the UN had ever-greater practical consequences on an economic level. Following these events the Community petitioned, and in the fall of 1974 was granted, the right to participate in the UN General Assembly as an observer with the right to speak.

the EC in international negotiations, arguing formally that the Commission did not represent a state and thus could not negotiate at the same table as other governments.[9] By the end of 1975 the EC and the Commission would defeat this French resistance, winning the right to participate both in the North–South dialogue negotiations launched in 1975 and, after 1977, in the summits of industrialized countries.

G5, G6, G7

With the election in 1974 of Valéry Giscard d'Estaing as French president and Helmut Schmidt as German chancellor—both former finance ministers, and members of transatlantic pressure groups—signs of an opening to re-establish closer cooperation between Europe and the United States were readily apparent.[10] Such potential for cooperation was difficult to institutionalize, however, due to the very different approaches of Europe and the United States to political economy, and especially because of the widespread fears in Bonn and Paris of the instability of the dollar. But above all, it would have been difficult to justify any stronger institutional cooperation with the United States, the main party responsible for the war in Vietnam and the principal sponsor of Pinochet in Chile, in the eyes of a European public opinion that viewed Henry Kissinger as the symbol of a diabolical and antidemocratic foreign policy.[11]

At the heart of the initiative to gather Western leaders in a forum where they could discuss major international economic issues without inhibitions or a precise diplomatic agenda, there was a fear of the potential political breakdown of the European continent. In the European Community's southern bloc, authoritarian or dictatorial regimes had collapsed one after another: In Greece and Portugal in 1974, and in Spain with the death of Franco in 1975.[12] In each of these nations the growing strength and prestige of the left, actively supported by the Socialist International, allowed progressives to step forward as potential medium-term successors to authoritarian governments.[13] In Spain popular opposition to the

[9] E. Calandri, "La CEE et les relations extérieures 1958–1960," in A. Varsori (ed.), *Inside the European Community. Actors and Policies in European Integration 1957–1972* (Baden Baden: Nomos/ Bruylant, 2005), pp. 399–432.

[10] B. Olivi and R. Santaniello, *Storia dell'integrazione europea* (Bologna: Il Mulino, 2005).

[11] Oriana Fallaci, the famous journalist and writer who would in time become an unreserved admirer of the United States, began her report on a famous 1972 interview with Kissinger with the following words: "This too famous, too important, too lucky man, whom they call Superman, Superstar, Superkraut, and who stitches together paradoxical alliances, reaches impossible agreements, keeps the world holding its breath as though the world were his students at Harvard." She concluded with these biting words: "In Stockholm they even gave him the Nobel Peace Prize. Poor Nobel. Poor Peace." O. Fallaci, *Interview with History* (New York: Liveright, 1976), pp. 17–30.

[12] The best account of the ending of dictatorships in southern Europe in the 1970s can be found in M. Del Pero, V. Gavín, F.Guirao, and A. Varsori (eds), *Democrazie. L'Europa meridionale e la fine delle dittatuer* (Florence: Le Monnier, 2010).

[13] J.M. Magone, *The Politics of Southern Europe. Integration into the European Union* (Westport, CT & London: Praeger, 2003); M. Trouvé, *L'Espagne et l'Europe. De la dictature de Franco à l'Union européenne* (Brussels: Peter Lang, 2008).

Communist party was rapidly declining: While in 1976 only 25 percent of the Spanish public declared itself in favor of the legalization of the Spanish Communist Party (PCE), one year later the percentage of those in favor of legalization had climbed to 55 percent.[14] In Portugal, at least in the eyes of Washington, there was even a very real danger that the "Carnation Revolution" would lead to a communist party taking power, with all the dramatic consequences that this would have for NATO solidarity.[15] In a demonstration of the generally favorable climate in Europe for a more regulated economy, the end of the Portuguese dictatorship had been followed by a wave of nationalizations that brought several key sectors—electricity, iron and steel, construction, and even beer—as well as the enterprises of the Melo family, which alone owned roughly 20 percent of the country's industrial capital, under state control.[16] In Greece, meanwhile, the socialist leader Papandreu was highly critical of his country's continued membership of NATO, widely discredited nationally for having backed the previous military regime. In Italy, as well, the Communists were attracting impressive levels of support that made it plausible to speculate about a potential electoral triumph over the Christian Democrats in the 1976 elections, which would lead to communist participation in a national unity government. This was an even graver danger, considering the Italian peninsula's strategic importance to NATO, and the possibly contagious effect of Italian communism on the other countries of southern Europe. In France, the general secretary of the Socialist Party, Mitterrand, had formed a united front with the Parti communiste français (PCF), and was making himself a viable candidate to succeed Giscard. The Scandinavian socialist governments, traditionally "neutral" in foreign policy and inclined toward a special relationship with the developing countries, were acquiring growing international prestige and recognition, represented by a globally authoritative figure in Olof Palme. Throughout Europe, socialist parties were proposing innovative concepts of political economy, which included a growing role for the state in the formation of national income policy and expansion of public services, that were attracting visible electoral support. Fear was in the air that the old continent's political and economic center of gravity was shifting to the East. This was the concern expressed by Kissinger, in no uncertain terms, in a 1976 letter to the new president of the Socialist International Willy Brandt:

> I have the duty to express my strong anxiety for the situation that has been created. The political nature of NATO would be destined to change if one or more of the

---

[14] S. Juliá, "Né riforma, né rottura: Solo una transizione dalla dittatura alla demcorazia," in (2010) 9 *Ventunesimo Secolo* October 2010, p. 72.

[15] Kissinger actively promoted the return of the Salazar regime out of the fear that a democratically elected leftist government would strengthen European neutralist sentiment. See M. Del Pero, "I limiti della distensione: Gli Stati Uniti e l'implosione del regime portoghese," in *Alle origini del presente*, pp. 39–67. The meeting between Kissinger and the US Ambassador in Lisbon Frank Carlucci, who believed that the democratization of Portugal did not present any danger, resulted in a heated confrontation. See B. Gomes and T. Moreira de Sá, *Carlucci Vs. Kissinger: Os EUA e a Revolução Portuguesa* (Capa Mole: Dom Quixote, 2008).

[16] R.J. Morrison, *Portugal: Revolutionary Change in an Open Economy* (Boston, MA: Auburn House, 1981), pp. 47–8.

countries of the Atlantic Alliance should form governments with communist participation, whether directly or indirectly. The emergence of the USSR as a great power on the global stage continues to be cause for concern. The role of NATO, like our unaltered military position in Europe, is indispensable and critical. My anxiety lies in the fact that these points of strength will be endangered the moment that communist parties achieve positions of influence in Western Europe.[17]

Only by reading between the lines of such fears can it be understood why the Gaullists' traditional hostility toward the creation of a transatlantic decision-making structure had been overcome. The United States would have to cooperate with the major western European powers to overcome the economic crisis, avoid any retreats behind protectionist barriers, and in so doing avert a fatal weakening of the European market economy.

First, it was necessary to relax the mounting tensions on the monetary front, both within western Europe and between Europe and the United States. Exchange rate flexibility and the constant depreciation of the dollar was destabilizing European currencies, and with them the solidity of the Common Market. By 1970 the eurodollar market had reached US$57 billion, while the total reserves of the European central banks in American dollars amounted to barely US$37 billion. Under these conditions, the ability of the central banks to withstand the activity of financial markets was seriously called into question. Speculative movements of capital could have destabilizing effects in a regime of flexible exchange rates, while the liquidity of the Anglo-American banks was growing exponentially each year with the constant recycling of petrodollars. All the European governments were tempted to limit such freedom of movement, a temptation that some were unable to resist.[18]

As we have noted, a change was under way in international economic relations, in which the United States was becoming less central to global production, while other countries were beginning to emerge as new centers of the world economy. Robert Gilpin even suggested that the emergence of these new trading nations was "already having an important impact on the international balance of economic power and the political economy, an impact that could prove to be as significant as the emergence of Western civilization as the dominant force in international economics."[19] Between 1963 and 1975 the share of total world production represented by the newly industrializing countries grew from 5.4 percent to 9 percent, while the United States saw its percentage decline from 37 percent to 35 percent.[20]

---

[17] The quote, drawn from archival material held at the National Archives, can be found in P. Popham, "How Britain plotted *coup d'état* to topple Italy's Communists," in *The Independent*, January 14, 2008.

[18] D. Reynolds, *One World Divisible: A Global History since 1945* (London: Penguin, 2000), p. 45.

[19] R. Gilpin, *The Political Economy of International Relations* (Princeton, NJ: Princeton University Press, 1987), p. 264.

[20] J.A. Hart, *The New International Economic Order* (London: Macmillan, 1983), p. 27. For a particularly interesting look at the dynamics of the international economy in the 1970s, albeit one centered primarily on questions of international finance, see R. Parboni, *Il conflitto economico mondiale* (Milan: Etas Libri, 1985).

To cite two very specific and dramatic examples, from 1970 to 1976 Korean exports grew at a rate of 31 percent per year, and those of Taiwan at 16.2 percent.[21] The overall value of all exports from the developing countries grew in the years immediately following the first oil crisis from US$24 billion in 1973 to US$44 billion in 1977.[22] During this same period the economies of the oil-producing countries also demonstrated enviable growth rates: From a high of 14.4 percent per year in the case of Saudi Arabia, to the still-respectable 5.3 percent of Venezuela.[23] The question facing the largest industrial economies was how to capitalize on this evolution to their advantage, and avoid the consolidation of an alliance between these new economies, the oil-producing nations, and the rest of the developing countries. The creation of the G7 was a direct response to the battle waged by the Global South to promote a new international economic order, and its desire to obtain greater participation in international economic institutions. Its objective was to divide the united front of the South, and at the same time integrate its most advanced economies into the Bretton Woods institutions, in particular through the International Monetary Fund.[24]

The protagonists of the decision—which could be considered as a final European response to the failed paternalism of Kissinger's "Year of Europe" initiative—were the French President and the German Chancellor. Schmidt recalled that the notion of the need for a meeting of Western leaders was formalized during the course of the Helsinki Conference, in the summer of 1975:

> On a bright summer afternoon, sitting around a garden table in Helsinki, therefore, we made plans for the first summit; so as to keep it from falling into the hands of the bureaucrats, we agreed to have all preparations made by people we could personally charge with the task.[25]

The roots of the G7 lay in the meetings that, beginning in 1973, Schmidt and Giscard held regularly in Washington with the finance ministers of the United States, Japan, and Great Britain, which were called the "Library Group." In the course of these meetings a strong friendship developed between the liberal conservative President and the socialist Chancellor, later described by the former as "a unique case in the relations among leaders of contemporary nations."[26] A sort of professional finishing school thus took shape for a Western technocratic elite, mostly those in high-level national bureaucratic and political offices, but also many from the worlds of industry and finance. This group would have growing influence in the coming decades, especially as the ties binding parties to their electorate

---

[21] B. Cumings, "The Origins of the North-Eastern Political Economy: Industrial Sectors and Political Consequences, 1900–1980," in (1984) 38 *International Organization* (Winter), pp. 1–40.

[22] C. Stoffaës, *La grande menace industrielle* (Paris: Calman-Lévy, 1977), p. 12.

[23] *World Development Report* (Washington: World Bank, 1978).

[24] GFL, NSA, Country Files Europe–Canada, Box 9, Memo from Brent Scowcroft, "Your Meeting with Luxembourg Ambassador Meisch." See W. Bello, *Deglobalization: Ideas for a New World Economy* (London: Zed Books, 2002), p. 55–6.

[25] H. Schmidt, *Men and Powers: A Political Retrospective*, trans. Ruth Hein (New York: Random House, 1989), p. 173.

[26] V. Giscard d'Estaing, *Il potere e la vita* (Milan: Sperling & Kupfer, 1993), p. 61.

began to weaken.[27] An important role in this continuing education was played by the Trilateral Commission, founded in 1973 by the American financier David Rockefeller to bring together key American, European, and Japanese business and political figures.[28] Its members included the new American President Gerald Ford, Giscard, several high-ranking members of the European Community, and influential businessmen, among them the Italian owner of FIAT Gianni Agnelli, many of whom had previously participated in meetings of the Bilderberg Group. In a 1974 report focused on the questions regarding the dialogue with the developing countries, the Trilateral Commission had put forward the argument that the Third World no longer constituted a homogenous entity: The time had come to speak of a Fourth World of the newly wealthy, composed of the OPEC nations and the newly industrialized countries.[29] This Fourth World would have to cooperate on a financial level with the countries of the Trilateral in order to finance those developing countries that remained mired in a parlous balance of payments. The fear of the Trilateral was that the predominant reaction to the oil crisis would be one of protectionism, when what was needed was the continuous expansion of international demand. Guido Carli, former head of the Banca d'Italia and then of the Italian Confindustria, and one of the most prestigious members of the Trilateral, employed an audacious historical comparison to demonstrate the need to circulate money to avoid the risk of economic decline. The objective, he argued, was to imitate the Italian city-states of the Middle Ages, in order to avoid the fate that had befallen the Muslim empires at the end of the first millennium:

> The expansion of credit in the twelfth century and the multiplication of means of payment begun by the "white" Italians freed European and international commerce from its enslavement to gold, and gave global economic development a central motor capable of sustaining itself: Precisely that which the Muslim Empires lacked.[30]

The first summit of the new group of heads of state and government (from the United States, Germany, Japan, Great Britain, France, and Italy) was held from November 15–17, 1975 in the gilded rooms of the castle at Rambouillet, not far

---

[27] Paul Volcker and Karl-Otto Pohl, for example, who represented Washington and Bonn, would both go on to head the central banks of their respective countries. One might also cite the example of Carlo Azeglio Ciampi who, after having collaborated in the preparations for the G7, became Governor of the Banca d'Italia, Finance Minister, and finally President of the Italian Republic; or Renato Ruggero who, after acting as sherpa for the G7, went on to head the World Trade Organization and then briefly the Italian foreign ministry.

[28] L. Cesari, "Que disait la Trilatérale?," in (2000) 1 *Revue d'histoire diplomatique*, p. 80:

> From its creation, the Trilateral Commission understood that the vulnerability of the exchange rate risked pushing the industrial powers to form, along with certain privileged commodities suppliers, quasi-autarchic blocs organized around a dominant currency: The United States and Latin America, Western Europe and Africa, Japan and Southeast Asia. To combat this process, the Trilateral Commission has never ceased to support the coordination of short-term macroeconomic policy among the United States, the European Community and Japan, as well as a common approach toward commodities suppliers, and in particular the oil producers.'

[29] GFL, Ford Vice-Presidential Papers, OAD, Box 62, Trilateral Task Force on Relations with Developing Countries, "A Turning Point in North–South Economic Relations," June 1974.

[30] Carli, *Cinquant'anni di vita italiana*, p. 254.

from Paris. It focused on a search for solutions to international monetary instability as well as discussions on how best to respond to the energy crisis and the radical uprising of the developing countries.[31] Italy had been invited to avoid fears, especially prevalent in Bonn and Washington, of weakening the prestige of the Christian Democratic leadership prior to its own crucial 1976 elections.

Even before the final crisis of the Bretton Woods system, France had pushed for a return to the gold standard and a limitation of the dollar's power of seignorage.[32] The need for monetary stabilization was reinforced by the constant devaluation of the "greenback" against European currencies, and in particular the deutschmark, the strongest currency in western Europe—between 1970 and 1979, the dollar lost more than 50 percent of its value against the German currency.[33] The move to flexible exchange and the continuous strengthening of the deutschmark were placing severe stress on the system of fixed prices for agricultural products set up by the CAP, and made it increasingly difficult for the French government to resist industrialists' calls for a devaluation of the franc. France and Germany ran the risk of being set on a collision course.[34] The efforts of the Committee of 20 of the IMF (which included developing coutries) to come to an agreement on a system of "fixed but flexible" international exchange rates had failed. For the Ford administration discussion of the fate of the dollar was an obligation it could happily have done without, while what truly interested Washington was a strengthening of the special relationship that bound western Europe to the United States.[35] The Ford administration demonstrated a different sensibility to that of Nixon's, which had viewed Europe as only one of several theaters for the exercise of American diplomacy. During the summit agreements were reached on several monetary issues, albeit not in the direction hoped for by the French, based on the recognition of a system of "stable but flexible" exchange; the growing weight of the developing countries in the IMF; and a redistribution of the Fund's gold reserves toward the poorest nations.[36]

---

[31] G. Garavini, "The Battle for the Participation of the European Community in the G7 (1975–1977)," in (2006) 12(1) *Journal of European Integration History*, pp. 141–59.

[32] Soutou, *L'alliance incertaine*, pp. 357–67.

[33] Block, *The Origins of the International Economic Disorder*.

[34] A. Moravcsik, *The Choice for Europe. Social Purpose and State Power from Messina to Maastricht* (Ithaca, NY: Cornell University Press, 1998), pp. 264–74; H. Simonian, *The Privileged Partnership* (Oxford: Clarendon Press, 1985), pp. 179–92.

[35] Kissinger, *Years of Renewal*, p. 692.

[36] The Rambouillet agreements took on greater focus with the meeting of the Interim Committee of the IMF on January 7–8, 1976 in Kingston, Jamaica. At this meeting several important decisions were taken: 1. a reduction in the role of gold—the elimination of a fixed price; one-sixth of the IMF gold reserve would be sold and the income from this sale distributed to the LDCs; one-sixth would be returned to members according to their share in the Fund; 2. the authorization of a floating system of currencies, with concomitant changes to the General Agreements; 3. an increase in Fund quotas— since the last growth in quotas, those that had increased their share the most had been the industrialized countries, while the last increase had most benefited the oil-producing countries. With this agreement any effort to reform Bretton Woods in the direction of a new system of fixed exchange rates based on a reserve currency other than the dollar was definitively shelved. See R. Fraser, *The World Financial System* (London: Longman, 1994), p. 114.

With one of the most bitter controversies facing the Western nations partially resolved, the six leaders turned to the fundamental issue: How to react to the various processes of global economic and political instability that called into question the efficient workings of the free market and the capitalist system. The minutes of that first summit clearly show the desire of Germany and the United States to react in a coordinated fashion to the assaults of the developing countries, to placate their antisystemic temptations, and to channel them back toward the market economy, even at the cost of acquiescing to some of their demands.[37] The British Prime Minister Harold Wilson proposed a new "Marshall Plan-type initiative" for the Third World, with the goal of allowing the poorer economies to recover their purchasing power, which would constitute "a fillip to world economic recovery from which we will all benefit." Chancellor Schmidt, however, repeated in quite a different vein: "We must find a way to break up the unholy alliance between the LDCs and OPEC." Kissinger upped the ante, stating that "this can happen, and we can achieve our results, if they [the developing countries] know that their disruptive actions could stop discussions on commodities or that they will pay a price in terms of cooperation, or military exports." Similarly, in response to Giscard—who underlined the need to increase development aid—Schmidt countered that the fundamental objective should instead be that of including the poor countries into the market economy in a stable manner: "It is more important that we educate the developing countries to understand, think, and operate in market economy terms. We should make them understand that in the long run they can't spend more than they earn." We shall see how the Rambouillet summit paved the way, or can perhaps be better seen as a parallel initiative, to the launching of the North–South dialogue, and thus did not simply represent the realunching of a Western alliance.

Another particularly delicate matter for Western leaders was the growing influence of the Italian Communist Party, and the communist movements of southern Europe in general. Even for the mostly liberal editorial pages of the United States' most prestigious newspaper, the threat of communism in Italy was among the worst dangers facing the Western economic system, as this November 1975 editorial in *The New York Times* clearly stated:

> If Communist gains in Italy and elsewhere in southern Europe are to be reversed, if Britain is to be rescued from economic disaster, if France is to avoid a Popular Front and Portugal a dictatorship of the Left or Right, the industrial democracies must take joint action to speed, recover and solve urgent problems in the fields of trade, monetary affairs, energy, food, commodities and North–South relations.[38]

One aspect of the Rambouillet summit that could have carried disturbing consequences for European integration, however, lay in the fact that—in contrast to what had occurred at every major international economic meeting up until 1975—the European Community as such had not been invited to participate. A fact rendered even more disturbing because it was in that same year, as we have seen, that

---

[37] GFL, NSA, Box 12, Memcon, "Minutes of Rambouillet Summit," December 2, 1975.
[38] *The New York Times*, November 16, 1975.

the Community had emphasized its unity in signing the Helsinki Final Act, and in the talks preceding the Lomé Convention.

One motive for the exclusion of the Community resided in the fact that Western leaders wanted frank and informal discussions among the world's foremost "deciders," shorn of their bureaucratic minders. The Community's presence would have potentially spoiled this template. But the Community's absence from this decision-making congress also threatened to weaken its unrepresented countries, given that the summit promised to deal with issues—such as trade or negotiations with the developing countries—for which the Community had significant and in some cases exclusive competence. The White House appeared to be aware of the problem, but was not willing to press for change of a decision which it believed lay with European governments themselves.[39] The Member States of the Community that were left out—the Netherlands, Belgium, Denmark, Ireland, and Luxembourg—complained individually, while the French president of the European Commission, Xavier Ortoli, spoke out about this danger only within the closed ranks of the College of Commissioners.[40] Among the European leaders participating in the G7, the only one who believed unreservedly in the medium-term goal of preserving some form of autonomous personality for western Europe in foreign policy was the Italian Prime Minister Aldo Moro. The Italian government, however, did not have the strength to force its point of view on others.[41]

The original idea of the promoters behind the Rambouillet summit was that the meeting would be a one-time affair. The exclusion of the European Community was confirmed, however, upon the convocation of a second Western summit, this time in Puerto Rico, in 1976. At the summit, held from June 27–28, an invitation was extended to Canada—a key country both in terms of its relations with the USA and also, as we will see, with the developing countries—but once more not to the Community. This time, the reaction was quicker and more effective. The Prime Minister of Luxembourg, then in office as President of the European Council, submitted a formal request to the United States to grant the Community participation, but his query received no assurances from Washington.[42] The "minor" Member States, or "Little Five," were up in arms. Even the Commission's legal service underlined the dangers deriving from the continued exclusion of the Community over time.[43] The European Parliament added its voice to the chorus of

[39] NARA, Declassified Documents Reference System (DDRS), Memo for the President, Secret, "International Economic Summit Overview," November 12, 1975.

[40] Historical Archives of the European Commission (HAEC), BAC 81/84, "Porto Rico," Com (75), Pv 362, sitting of December 3, 1975.

[41] A. Moro, *L'Italia nell'evoluzione dei rapporti internazionale* (Brescia: Ebe Moretto, 1986), p. 349.

[42] GFL, NSA Country Files, Box 9, Memcon, Sonnenfeldt and Ambassador Meisch, "Economic Summit in Puerto Rico," June 4, 1976.

[43] HAEC, BAC 81/84, Porto Rico, Service juridique de la Commission des Communautés Européennes, "Réunion au Sommet de Porto Rico," June 11, 1976: "The progress laboriously achieved on the path to recognition of the Community in all international congresses on economic affairs is still fragile, and the isolated participation of several member-states in important international meetings, without the representation of the Community, can only compromise and weaken the credibility of the Community at large."

criticism, affirming that "this initiative will endanger the very meaning of the Community's institutions."[44]

In any case, the Puerto Rico summit did not produce any important decisions on the international economy, focusing its attention instead on the delicate question of how to react to an eventual Communist victory in Italy, a matter in which the Community itself had very little say.[45] It has been said that during the two years between Rambouillet and Puerto Rico (1975–6), a series of measures contributed to a definite strengthening of the relations between leaders on both sides of the Atlantic.[46] Certainly these years were critical for the development of the "locomotive theory," strongly endorsed by the Trilateral, which prescribed an increase in growth rates and budget spending for those economies running a trade surplus—Germany and Japan—while the others, foremost among them the United States, should devote themselves to controlling their growing oil imports, which were responsible for rising oil prices and weaknes of the dollar.[47] This was a form of international Keynesianism that was aimed at overcoming the ongoing crisis by stimulating the strongest economies and, indirectly, development aid as well. One side-effect of this policy would also be to spend the way out of structural reforms in favor of the Southern countries.[48]

In 1976 Giscard paid a price for European economic stability, having to replace Prime Minister Jacques Chirac with Raymond Barre, former Vice-President of the European Commission, who promptly inaugurated a policy of economic discipline aimed at bolstering the franc and reinforcing the competitiveness of French industry.[49] An astute Italian journalist aptly described this Giscardian attempt to confront the German challenge, and to impose a new discipline on the French economic system:

---

[44] "Résolution sur la Conférence au Sommet de Puerto Rico," adopted by the Assembly at the sitting on July 9, 1976.

[45] GFL, NSA, Memcon, Box 19, Talking Paper with Giscard, Top Secret, "Specific Results of Proposed Summit Meeting," May 18, 1976:

A central focal point of a summit discussion would necessarily be the problem of Italy. It will be a prominent issue over the next several months because of the political and economic implications of what happens there, especially their significance for the future of the European Community, the Western economic system, and the Western political and security system. . . However, because a discussion of the Italian problem does not lend itself to publicity, efforts should be made to avoid portraying the summit as a meeting focusing on the Italian situation.

A. Varsori, "Puerto Rico (1976): le potenze occidentali e il problema comunista in Italia," in (2008) 16 *Ventunesimo Secolo* (June), pp. 89–121.

[46] R.L. Garthoff, *Détente and Confrontation: American-Soviet Relations from Nixon to Reagan* (Washington, DC: The Brookings Institution, 1994), p. 538.

[47] H. James, *Rambouillet, 15 novembre 1975. La globalizzazione dell'economia* (Bologna: Il Mulino, 1999), p. 172.

[48] WBGA, Office of the President, Records of Robert McNamara, General Correspondence, Box 2, Charles Percy, Committee on Foreign Relations, "Letter to President McNamara," December 16, 1976: "I believe that what should be proposed is a USA/Germany/Japan packet of fiscal and monetary measures, coupled with an expansion of monetary flows toward the Developing Countries."

[49] R. Rémond, *Notre siècle, 1913–1988* (Paris: Fayard, 1988). Giscard put containment of inflation at the heart of his program, and compared Barre to General Joffre at the Battle of the Marne.

Against the presumably triumphant left, President Giscard played his trump card in Barre. This small, round man, 53, always dressed in black, born on the island of Réunion, has been an economics professor in Paris, advisor to the Bank of France, ex-Commissioner for the Common Market, director of the Rambouillet Summit, and Foreign Commerce Minister under Giscard.[50]

One change that occurred in 1977 was that the much-feared risk of an electoral breakthrough by the Italian Communists seemed at least temporarily to have been exorcised. The PCI voted to support the "national solidarity" government—though it was barred from active participation, on the explicit request of Chancellor Schmidt and the IMF—and this ambiguous stance softened the potentially revolutionary thrust of the party. Hopes were raised, even within the circles of the Trilateral, by the new doctrine of "Eurocommunism," which appeared to imply Italian Communists' definitive break with Moscow. After their laborious transitions to democratic government, Spain and, at least symbolically, Portugal—where internal conflicts between communists and the far right had been strongest after the approval of a new democratic Consitution in 1976—put forward their candidacies for admission to the European Community. Greek negotiations for EC membership were already under way. Such developments stood to demonstrate that the Nine exercised a magnetic socioeconomic appeal and functioned as an element of political stabilization for its immediate neighbors.

Another important difference in 1977 lay in the election of two new protagonists in international politics—Jimmy Carter and Roy Jenkins—each of whom had an explicit interest in the consolidation of the European Community as an international actor. The American President had based his electoral campaign in part on the idea of a new approach to foreign policy. Together with his National Security Advisor Zbigniew Brzezinski, Carter had condemned Kissinger's policy—characterized by sudden shifts in alliances and tactics, and by privileged partnerships with single regional powers—deeming it a form of dangerous improvisation that could harm the cohesion of the West's united front. Carter aimed to climb out of the downward spiral of discredit into which the United States had fallen, not just in the eyes of the Third World. He undertook inquiries into America's image in various regions of the world and altered his administration's orientation on aid issues, working on refinancing the World Bank as well as supporting a slight increase in American public aid for development which, between 1976 and 1977, had witnessed a further decline from 0.25 percent to 0.22 percent of GDP.[51] This overture to the South was sweetened with an emphasis on global working conditions and human rights which raised many eyebrows even within the American

---

[50] A. Cavallari, *La Francia a sinistra* (Milan: Garzanti, 1977), p. 21.
[51] Jimmy Carter Library (JCL), WHCF, Co 2, Memorandum for The President from Brzezinski, "LDS Views of the US," November 17, 1977. The memorandum noted that the elites of the Third World had not the slightest sympathy for the American policy of basic human needs, which was designed to concentrate American aid contributions on food aid and family planning assistance. In the last analysis, skepticism was still widespread regarding Washington's real availability to participate in the construction of a new international economic order.

administration itself.[52] The other side of the Carter administration strategy, the reinforcement of Western cohesion, consisted of reestablishing a special relationship with western Europe as a cohesive region. Zbigniew Brzezinski had been among the founders of the Trilateral Commission.[53] Together with the Democratic president, he hoped to make the policy prescriptions of the Trilateral one of the guidelines of American foreign policy:

> We assumed office feeling strongly that US–Japanese relations had needlessly deteriorated because of the "Nixon shocks" (the unilateral measures imposed by the United States on US–Japanese trade), and that the Europeans had been pointlessly insulted by Henry Kissinger's patronizing proclamation of a "Year of Europe." In addition, both the Vietnam War and the Watergate affair had jolted confidence in American leadership.[54]

In the aftermath of Carter's inauguration, Vice-President Walter Mondale called on Brussels and Tokyo to prepare the next Western economic summit and to demonstrate the seriousness of the new US proposals for cooperation. As the Italian Bino Olivi, spokesman of the European Commission at the time, observed, "Carter wanted to speak to Europe, and the only organized structure that could speak for all of western Europe was the European Community."[55]

The other important protagonist to enter the international stage in 1977 was Roy Jenkins, the first British man to preside over the European Commission, and one of the rare Labour politicians to earn his fame as a pro-Europeanist: He had supported adhesion during the British referendum on entry into the EC. By intellectual training he held a global perspective on economic matters—he was also a fine historian of the British Empire—and was given to expound frequently, and precociously for the time, on the phenomenon of globalization. He would later say that he kept his "Europeanist flame" burning in part because, as Home Secretary, he had never had the opportunity to visit Brussels in all its bureaucratic glory. On the second stop of his inaugural "tour of capitals" through Europe Jenkins met with Giscard, with whom he began a diplomatic engagement to obtain direct participation at the G7 for the Community, a quest which through highs and lows would dominate a good part of his presidency.[56]

In this battle Jenkins was aided by the Dutch Prime Minister Den Uyl. In March 1977, in a visit to The Hague, the President of the Commission had backed the Dutch government's strict opposition to the prosecution of international encounters in which matters which affected the Community were discussed without Community participation: These included trade issues and the North–South

---

[52] JCL, NSA, Subject Files, Box 67, Memorandum from Mike Armcost to Brzezinski, "Trilateral Commission Speech," October 19, 1977.

[53] Cesari, *Que disait la Trilaterale?*, p. 84. For Brzezinski, the Trilateral's politics were in the best interests of the United States: "The multiplication of cross-border communications plays to the advantage of the United States, and at the same time that of primary producers of electronic goods and the headquarters of the largest multinational corporations."

[54] Z. Brzezinski, *Power and Principle* (London: Weidenfeld & Nicolson, 1983), p. 289.

[55] B. Olivi, *Carter e l'Italia* (Milan: Longanesi, 1978), p. 7.

[56] R. Jenkins, *European Diary: 1977–1981* (London: Collins, 1989), pp. 19–20.

Dialogue.[57] In the run-up to the European Council in Rome, scheduled for March 25–26, 1977, the French President, who feared upsetting the Gaullists in view of the upcoming national administrative elections, had revealed his opposition to Community participation at the London economic summit. He had done this by sending a detailed letter to his colleagues in which he essentially argued that there was no need for the Community's presence in a chat among friends, even if they were at the highest levels.[58] The French missive was the subject of a very harsh reply, in the form of a lengthy memorandum, from the Dutch government.[59] One of the sharpest points of the Dutch memo was that the European Community could not be considered simply as an international organization, but rather should be seen as the embryonic form of a new political community to which its Member States had delegated part of their sovereignty. With the support of the Commission, and by now also of the other Member States (with the exception of Great Britain), the Rome summit established that the Community should be invited to the next G7 summit in London, with the formula of double representation of both the Commission President Jenkins and the current President of the Council.

In a trip to Washington from April 15–17, in part to discuss the preparations for the G7, Jenkins seemed to support the cause of a greater liberalization of world trade. But he also proposed an ambitious, and ultimately unrealistic, project for a global Marshall Plan. This would generate sufficient resources for the nations of the South, he argued, for them to stimulate the Western—and especially the European—economies most dependent on foreign commerce.[60]

It is perhaps possible to consider the London G7 summit held from May 7–8 as the last that would produce some results on issues concerning the North–South confrontation. At the following summit in Bonn in 1978, the G7 plus the EC moved forward with the practical application of the "locomotive theory." The McCracken Report, presented to the OECD in 1977 with the title *Toward Full Employment and Price Stability*, understood the contemporary crisis as the product of wrong-headed public policies and "avoidable errors," and saw a solution in governments' commitment to economic expansion and full employment. This was still the position widely prevalent among all the Western governments. The effects of the 1973 oil crisis were not comparable to those of the 1930s: They did not lead,

[57] HAEU, EN, 1611, "Visit in The Hague," March 1977.
[58] HAEC, BAC 39/1986 (0114), "Lettre de Monsieur le Président de la République Française à Monsieur Roy Jenkins président de la Commission," Brussels, March 23, 1977:

> This is a conference that brings together heads of state and government exclusively, absent every other institution, for a free and informal exchange of views that cannot lead to decisions on Community matters. Nothing distinguishes these meetings from the contacts that states normally maintain with each other bilaterally, and that form the warp and woof of international relations. . . It has fallen to me, and will continue to fall to me, to attend several meetings of the Franco-African states, for example, without raising the issue of the Commission's participation.

[59] HAEC, BAC 39/1986 (0114), Europese Raad March 25/26, 1977, "Economiche Top-conferentie te Londen 7–8 mei 1977, Delname EEG aan conferentie."
[60] HAEU, EN 1586, Background papers for the President, "Visit in the United States," April 12–17, 1977.

in the short term, to the return in force of protectionism, nor to the strengthening of authoritarian rule in the government of the industrialized countries. Even the restrictive measures on non-European immigration taken by Germany in 1973 should not be misinterpreted simply as a protectionist and nationalistic device; they were also seen as a way to better integrate immigrants into German society— new regulations were in fact enacted for this purpose—and shift the focus to measures that would improve living conditions in their countries of origin.[61]

The German government announced in Bonn that it would stimulate its own economy through expansive fiscal measures equal to roughly 1 percent of GDP. The Japanese government in turn pledged to increase internal demand in order to obtain growth in GDP of more than 1.5 percent over the year before.[62] These measures, which in the German case were also aimed at obtaining the approval of the United States for the ongoing project of a European Monetary System, had effects very different to those intended. In 1979 a new dramatic oil crisis would explode, and with it a new phase in international economic relations that would signal the demise of the pretensions for a coordinated expansion of the largest world economies on the Keynesian model.

THE NORTH–SOUTH DIALOGUE IN PARIS

We have seen that in the former Portuguese colonies of Angola and Mozambique, as well as in other parts of Africa, international communism appeared to be showing signs of renewed vigor and capacity for expansion.[63] Castro's military intervention in Angola had given Cuba new prestige in the Third World, so much so that Havana was chosen in 1979 as the site of the next conference of non-aligned countries.

In 1974 and 1975 the IMF had created two new loan programs called "oil facilities," while between 1976 and 1980 the Fund made available for those struck hardest by the oil crisis US\$3.6 billion through flexible lines of credit with low conditionality.[64] The World Bank had consistently increased its own disbursements to the poorest countries, in part to satisfy such "basic needs" as irrigation, healthcare, and education, distributing a sum of US\$10 billion in 1979 alone. Overall, the World Bank's disbursements had grown sevenfold between 1970 and 1980. Counteracting the effect of the growth in Bank loans, however, was a consistent decrease in bilateral aid from the OECD countries, which had gradually diminished aid from 0.65 percent of GDP in 1965 to 0.23 percent in 1979.[65] The Bank's

---

[61] E. Comte, "La formation du régime de migrations de l'Europe communautaire," doctoral thesis presented to the Sorbonne, 2009.

[62] Available online at <http://www.g7.utoronto.ca/summit/1978bonn/communiqué.html>.

[63] P. Gliejeses, *Conflicting Missions: Havana, Washington and Africa, 1959–1976* (Chapel Hill: University of North Carolina Press, 2002).

[64] Wood, *From Marshall Plan to Debt Crisis*, p. 78.

[65] WBGA, Office of the President, Records of Robert S. MacNamara, Central Correspondence, Box 3, Memo, "The World Bank—Past, Present, and Future," August 6, 1979.

policy was bitterly criticized, by both the Scandinavian nations and the most progressive countries in the Third World, for the support it gave to regimes such as that of Pinochet in Chile, as well as for the process through which aid was conceded, which generally tended to favor the return on investment of the industrialized countries through its procurement system. Notwithstanding the efforts of the Bretton Woods institutions, however, there was still the risk of further radicalization in the Third World, of a default on international loans that would send Western financial institutions into bankruptcy, or, at the very least, of vast regions of the globe cutting themselves off from the flows of trade and international finance.

Washington's hostile stance toward any dialogue with the South had helped radicalize the united front of the developing countries, and also progressively distanced the United States from the position of the European Community countries, which were more open to dialogue with the supporters of a new economic order. Washington's worries were summed up by Egidio Ortona, Italian ambassador to the United States, in a private letter to Prime Minister Aldo Moro in 1975:

> With the creation—under Washington's "leadership"—of a certain degree of solidarity among the consumers of the Industrialized Countries, the American Administration has appeared concerned that European initiatives regarding a more advanced dialogue with the Third World (Lomé) might end up marginalizing the United States by accentuating the gap between its position and Third World ideas.[66]

Significantly, at the meeting in Helsinki where it was decided to organize a summit of the industrialized countries, Giscard, Schmidt, Ford, and Wilson had relaunched the failed project of a conference between producers and consumers. The new conference would be enlarged to include twenty-seven nations (eight developed countries and nineteen developing countries, including the OPEC nations), and its scope simultaneously widened to include issues of development, commodities, and finance, as had previously been requested by the OPEC countries, foremost among them Algeria.[67]

In the course of 1975 the American position began to show signs of greater malleability in the area of North–South relations.[68] In a long speech at the seventh Special Session of the UN in September, prepared by Kissinger and read by the American Ambassador Daniel Patrick Moynihan, the United States—while not accepting the idea of a Common Fund for commodities and indexing prices of commodities to manufactures—promoted a number of initiatives around the idea of increasing the volume of "compensatory aid" to the Third World.[69] This was a

---

[66] ACS, Moro, b. 123, Ambasciata d'Italia, Egidio Ortona, Segreto, May 22, 1975.

[67] CHAN, 5AG3, AE 54, Présidence de la République, Note pour le Président, "Conférence d'Helsinki: Déjeuner quadripartite. Questions économiques et financiers," Paris, July 29, 1975.

[68] Kissinger, *Years of Renewal*, p. 688.

[69] "Compensatory aid" was designed to compensate for a structural imbalance in international economic relations—to plug a hole in the dyke—rather than to eliminate the causes of the structural imbalance itself. For a description of the American debates on relations with the South see D.P. Moynihan, *A Dangerous Place* (Boston: Little, Brown and Co., 1978). A more dispassionate account, though still critical of the South's strategy, can be read in the minutes of the debate on the NIEO by the UN Secretary-General Kurt Waldheim. See K. Waldheim, *In the Eye of the Storm* (Bethesda, MD: Adler and Adler, 1986), pp. 112–34.

strategy that Kissinger himself had defined as "appeasement" of the South, aimed at inundating the diplomatic desks of the supporters of the NIEO with countless drafts and proposals to discuss, dampening the radicalization of the conflict, while at the same time beginning the work of re-establishing the fundamental tenets of international capitalism.[70] It is possible to view in this new American strategy the origins of a series of concrete results for the developing countries in the years 1975–6: The increase in the developing world's quota in the IMF and the use of part of European reserves for the LDCs, the tariff reductions for tropical goods in the multilateral trade negotiations of the Tokyo Round, and the conclusion of two commodity agreements on coffee and aluminum.[71]

Diplomatic pressures for the resumption of dialogue with the producers, however, were primarily coming from the direction of Europe. The assessment of Commissioner Cheysson—among the protagonists of the Lomé Convention negotiations—took up arguments similar to those made by Mansholt. To compensate for the structural deficiencies of the European economy, such as its heavy pollution and the need to protect the environment, its lack of cheap manual labor and commodities, as well as the absence of space for industrial development, the Community would have to count on the emerging countries to find new markets and ripe opportunities for investment.[72] In order to do this it was necessary to continue to negotiate preferential agreements with the emerging countries, and to plan in which sectors to increase imports from these countries. It was essential to identify the European industries in need of restructuring to favor imports and to collaborate with the unions and business associations so that such restructuring would not exclusively affect employment or the living standards of European workers. What was more, as Cheysson indicated in a report in preparation for the Dublin European Summit of March 1975:

> Politically, Europe must play an original role. With respect to its nations, it is freer from the weight of the past, larger in dimensions; it can be better placed to plan and bring to conclusion significant original actions. With respect to the other Industrialized Countries, its development and its integration favor the emergence of a multipolar world, less dangerous than a world dominated by the Superpowers, fundamental antagonists despite their efforts to promote détente. On this point the specific interests of Europe coincide with those of the LDCs, who want greater balance in international affairs.[73]

---

[70] GFL, CEA, P.W. MacAvoy Files, Box 105, P. MacAvoy, "General Orientation Paper for CIEC," December 1975. The economic adviser Paul MacAvoy thought that "the effects of our conciliatory approach have to at least slow the radicalization of the Third World, a process that could created profound changes in our economic relations and in our national security strategy."

[71] GFL, OEA, L.W. Seidman Files, Box 135, Memo, "OPEC Aid Commitments to Non-Oil Exporting LDCs," September 20, 1974.

[72] HAEC, Cabinet Cheysson, Note personnelle de M. Cheysson, "352ème réunion de la Commission Promotion du Tiers-Monde," January 29, 1975.

[73] HAEC, Cabinet Cheysson, Préparation du Conseil Européen de Dublin (March 10–11), "Le problème des relations avec les PVD," February 10, 1975.

Following the Community's modest performance at the preparatory talks for Paris, the July 1975 European Council meeting concerned itself principally with the question of how to revive the dialogue with the developing countries. A document prepared by the Italian presidency let it be clearly understood that the Community needed to rediscover the spirit of the Paris summit of 1972, when it had declared its ambition to fill the role of privileged partner to the Third World:

> The objective that the Community must pursue, in the prospect of a political purpose that it must wait to receive from the European Council, is the realization of effective progress in the direction of a more balanced and equitable structuring of international economic relations, which includes an improvement and strengthening of the position of the Developing Countries, and which responds to their expectations better than in the past.[74]

The same document stated that the Community would have to take several steps toward the G77 on the stabilization of incomes from raw materials and single product agreements, if it wished to obtain any guarantees for the steady provisioning of commodities at reasonable prices.

In certain circles, including that of the French Gaullists, the prospect of a "European-style" recovery from the international economic crisis never ceased to hold its charm. This is very clear, for example, in a memorandum by Ambassador de Guiringaud for Giscard, in which the diplomat—who would soon become Foreign Minister—viewed the relaunching of the Paris conference as an opportunity for France to leave behind its more recent provincialism and place itself at the center of the debate for cooperative management of economic globalization:

> The postwar order, founded on the collapse of economic borders, rested on agreements of American design (Bretton Woods—Atlantic Charter) and found its driving inspiration in New York, which succeeded London as the principal center for international finance... The order needed today should reconcile the right of every government to determine its own national destiny with the advantages of the free circulation of goods, of capital, of men, of ideas, of technology, in a unified economic space; it will thus be based on the formula of collective management of global economic mechanisms. In this perspective our proposal for institutional innovation fits perfectly: The creation of restricted and specialized deliberative bodies, within a larger general design that will guarantee solutions of a progressive and truly multilateral character.[75]

In May 1975 Joop Den Uyl had traveled to Washington and had opened his meeting with the US President with the reminder that the Netherlands was a "Calvinist country" that in foreign policy sought to stick to its principles, regardless of their impact on the economy.[76] In the second half of the meeting the Dutch

---

[74] ACS, Moro, Presidenza del Consiglio dei Ministri, b. 182, f. 7, Segretario generale, Nota per il presidente del Consiglio europeo, "Materie prime e cooperazione allo sviluppo," Brussels, July 15, 1975.

[75] CHAN, 5AG3, M. de Guiringaud, Rapport à M. le Président de la République, "Réunion Préparatoire à la Conférence sur la coopération économique internationale," Paris, October 20, 1975.

[76] GFL, Country Files, Europe–Canada, Box 4, Memcon, "Den Uyl, President Ford, Kissinger," May 14, 1975.

Prime Minister, backtracking slightly from such high ideals, had more prosaically reaffirmed that, if until that time their relations with the Third World had remained on an acceptable track, it was not necessarily willing to let the world explode. The Dutch economy was based on a limited public sector and its businesses were very open in relation to the rest of the world, on which they depended for the opening of overseas offices, for manual labor, and for the supply of raw materials.[77] The Netherlands had been the most important European target of the OPEC countries which, after 1973, had cut their supplies of crude oil to its impressive refineries because of the close relationship the Dutch maintained with Israel. The Netherlands could not tolerate the risk of a global economic conflict, with the rise of protectionist sentiments and the closure of borders between the world's regions. They were thus well inclined to discuss both the creation of a Commodities Fund and a generalized moratorium on Third World debt, and in this vein they fought in favor of the developing countries' proposals. In November 1975, the Dutch Minister for Development Cooperation Jan Pronk organized a public seminar, with the support of all the world's most renowned experts on development issues, to discuss the new economic order.[78] Pronk re-emphasized the centrality of the European Community as a progressive element in the United Nations system compared to countries like Japan—but also the Scandinavian countries and Canada—whose aid disbursements were after all rather limited in absolute terms. The following year, in a speech before the UN General Assembly, Pronk would also confirm the Dutch commitment to supporting a different use for development aid on the part of the World Bank, and a domestic economic policy that would take into consideration the needs of the poorest countries:

> No Developed Country has the right to judge the Developing Countries on social justice and human rights, unless they are also prepared to put these terms into practice in their own country…This implies a reconversion of industry toward a better international division of labor, more sobriety in domestic consumption, and a willingness to apply the theory of "basic human needs" to themselves.[79]

Even Italy, while lamenting the holding up of important European Community initiatives to achieve internal cohesion and solidarity among the European countries—such as the regional fund—gave its unreserved support to a dialogue with producers as a way to assure steady supplies of commodities. There was substantial agreement between the Communists and the Christian Democrats on this issue; their consensus went beyond the characteristically Catholic and Italian rhetoric of the diplomatic necessity to restart dialogue with the South. Moro and Berlinguer each expressed respect for Algerian initiatives and called for a political relationship

---

[77] D. Sassoon, *One Hundred Years of Socialism: The West European Left in the Twentieth Century* (New York: New Press, 1988), pp. 487–9.

[78] Dutch National Advisory Council for Cooperation, "The New Economic Order. Report on the seminar held at The Hague on November 11, 1975 to consider the implication of the 6th and 7th Special Session of the General Assembly of the United Nations."

[79] WBGA, Office of the President, Robert S. McNamara, Subject Files, Box 1, Jan Pronk, "Address by the Minister for Development Cooperation of the Netherlands in the General Debate of the 31st Session of the General Assembly," October 20, 1976.

between Europe and the Arab world: The former, out of a belief in a "slowing of growth";[80] the latter, out of the conviction that a "qualitative modification of growth" in the industrialized countries would allow the redistribution of vital resources to the South.[81] What Italy was lacking however, in a period of economic crisis and social unrest, was the resources—particularly in terms of aid for development, which in 1977 amounted to barely 0.1 percent of GDP—to make itself a likely candidate for European leadership in the diplomatic dialogue with the South.[82] With a new social democratic government elected in 1975, Denmark also became a vocal supporter of a structural adjustment in relations with the South; Copenhagen thus closed ranks with its Scandinavian partners, such as Sweden and Norway, which were not members of the EC but were in many ways at the forefront of the fight in favor of developing countries, and which had even voted in favor of the Charter of Economic Rights in 1974.[83]

At the Rambouillet summit Western leaders had confronted the knotty issues at the heart of the North–South dialogue in a discreet manner outside the standard official channels, in order to avoid accusations of having constituted a cabal of the wealthiest countries—a fear held particularly by the French. On this occasion they reaffirmed their decision, born at Helsinki, to convene a conference of twenty-seven nations in Paris. Fundamental differences remained over the role to be played by the International Energy Agency, which the French did not wish to see given a voice, and over commodities issues: The United States, Germany, and Japan preferred to address these by guaranteeing export earnings through improvement of compensatory IMF financing; Sweden and the Netherlands proposed the enlargement of a Lomé-type mechanism to include all the G77 countries; France pushed for the creation of single commodity agreements.[84]

Giscard's long-desired conference assumed concrete shape at an October 1975 meeting of the European Community's Council of Ministers. The event would be called the Conference for International Economic Cooperation (CIEC), and would be structured into four commissions—energy, commodities, development, and financial matters—to include the participation of nineteen developing and eight developed countries. The Western nations, for whom the numeric ratio within the CIEC would be more advantageous than within the UN, thought that they were thus giving life to a new forum to negotiate more favorable oil prices, or at least to moderate the radicalism of the oil producers. The OPEC countries

[80] A. Moro, *La democrazia incompiuta. Attori e questioni della politica italiana 1943–1978* (Rome: Editori Riuniti, 1999), p. 61.

[81] E. Berlinguer, *La political internazionale dei comunisti italiani*, Rapporto al XIV Congresso del PCI, 18 marzo 1975 (Rome: Editori Riuniti, 1976).

[82] A.R. Posner, "Italy and the Third World: Response by an Intermediate Economy," in P. Taylor and G.A. Raymond (eds), *Third World Policies of Industrialized Nations* (Westport, CT: Greenwood Press, 1982), p. 122.

[83] T. Borring Olesen, "Between Words and Deeds: Denmark and the NIEO agenda 1974–1982," in H. Pharo and M. Pohle Fraser (eds), *The Aid Rush, Aid Regimes in Northern Europe during the Cold War*, vol. I (Oslo: Unipubl, 2008), pp. 145–82.

[84] CHAN, 5AG3, AE 54, J.P. Dutet, "Réunion de Rambouillet. Conférence sur la coopération économique internationale: questions de fond concernant l'énergie, les matières premières et l'aide au développement," Paris, November 13, 1975.

would indeed be disposed to concede something on the price of crude, but only in exchange for Western commitments on the question of a Commodities Fund as well as the issue of a Third World debt moratorium.

For the European Community the great development to emerge from the CIEC would be that of common representation, a feat never before achieved in previous North–South talks. Fundamentally, the achievement of this unity was due to the efforts of France—which knew it was isolated on oil issues, and thus sought to emerge from such isolation by encouraging a common European policy in the energy sector. From the perspective of the OPEC nations, the conditions that would make the conclusion of a producers–consumers conference worthwhile— that is, those that would convince the producers to agree to a gradual lowering of prices—were summarized in overly optimistic terms by the French diplomat Henri Froment-Meurice:

> A degree of political opening in the Arab-Israeli conflict; the renunciation of divisive tactics in the Third World to separate oil producers and poor consumers; the financing of current balance of payments deficits and guarantees on earnings from exports; the return of monetary stability (I have underlined that the Franco-American agreement at Rambouillet was a good start); and guarantees on the financial surpluses of the Gulf States and Saudi Arabia.[85]

The European Council meeting held in Rome at the beginning of December gave formal approval to convene the conference. The efforts at mediation by Moro and Italian diplomats had succeeded in defeating British resistance to the joint representation of the Nine and, while there was still no consensus on the merits of the questions to be addressed, it had also put together a list of issues to confront within each of the four commissions.[86] Dutch pressures to persuade the commission on commodities to discuss explicit "indexing" schemes were turned away thanks to the unanimously negative response of all the other members of the Community. At the same time, even France had to accept the presence of the Energy Agency, if only as part of the OECD delegation. Moro reiterated several times the importance that the Nine present itself as a common bloc in the talks at the United Nations because, in front of the numerically superior voting power of the South, only a cohesive group could speak with some measure of authority: taken individually, the Community's member-states were only nine against one hundred.[87]

---

[85] CHAN, 5AG3, AE 54, H. Froment-Meurice, Note, "Entretien avec M. Perez Guerrero et M. Yeganeh," Paris, November 21, 1975.

[86] ACS, Moro, Presidenza del Consiglio dei Ministri, b. 82, f. 7, Ambasciata Britannica, Lettera a Moro, Rome, November 11, 1975. In the British letter London requested an autonomous British representative to be present at the conference, given that it would very soon become the fifth-largest oil-producing nation in the world—the USSR excluded—and was already the second-largest international financial market. The compromise that overcame British opposition to joint representation was that the Community would accept discussion of a "minimum safeguard price" for oil, an idea particularly close to British (and American) hearts as a means of defending the competitiveness of their more capital-intensive oil production.

[87] ACS, Moro, Presidenza del Consiglio dei Ministri, b. 82, f. 7, MAE, Note sul Consiglio europeo dell'1–2 dicembre 1975, "Conferenza di cooperazione economica internazionale."

The CIEC—which in the future would more frequently be referred to by the expression "North–South dialogue" or "Paris dialogue" in the international press— opened with a ministerial conference held in Paris from December 16–18, 1975. This first round of talks set up the four predetermined commissions (energy, commodities, development, finance), each guided by two co-presidents: Pierre Trudeau, the flamboyant Canadian Prime Minster who had just created a national oil company and challenged the special relationship with the USA, for the eight industrialized countries; and the Venezuelan President Pérez, who had embraced the cause of the Global South as a way to find new venues for Venezuelan business and was planning his first historic visit to Castro in Cuba, for the nineteen developing countries. It was agreed that the commissions would present the results of their labors during the course of a second ministerial conference to be held in 1976.

The opening of the CIEC was undoubtedly a major success for French diplomacy, and offered the chance for the South to exploit the oil weapon to obtain concrete results in policy areas for which it had fought long and hard for more than a decade: Reform of commodity markets, control of debt, and improvement in numbers and quality of public aid for development.

The moment of the dialogue coincided, however, with growing tensions in the confrontation between North and South. The Western countries, in part because of the strong contraction in growth registered in the course of 1975 and the consequent moderation of energy consumption, had reduced the deficits in their current account balances and transformed them into solid surpluses. The OPEC nations had received only partial satisfaction of their demands for greater decision-making power in the financial market.[88]

A specter was thus emerging, foreshadowed by Algeria's concerns, of a weakening in the foundations of the alliance between the OPEC nations and the others of the G77. The debt of the developing countries had grown from US$9 billion before the oil crisis to US$35 billion by 1976.[89]

Conspicuous quantities of capital accumulated from oil sales were, in fact, filling the coffers of Western financial institutions. In 1979, the bill for the oil purchased by the non-producer nations of the South had reached some US$39 billion, surpassing by US$9 billion the total aid the South received from both international development agencies and individual developed countries. Their debt burden with Western banks, which in 1973 totaled US$45 billion, had grown to roughly US$190 billion by 1979. The banks of Wall Street and the City followed their clients wherever they turned in search of profits greater than those they could obtain in Western economies, focusing their investments on the most "stable" and promising developing countries. For their part, countries such as Brazil, Mexico, South Korea, Argentina, or Venezuela were only too eager to accept international funding at low interest rates.[90] Without concrete measures, the ballooning of debt would erode the South's united front, forcing several

[88] Gilpin, *The Political Economy of International Relations*, p. 141.
[89] CHAN, 5AG3, AE 54, HFM, Note pour le Ministre, "Entretiens avec les représentats des PVD," Paris, October 25, 1976.
[90] B. Nossiter, *The Global Struggle for More. Third World Conflicts with Rich Nations* (New York: Harper & Row, 1987), p. 5.

countries to undergo further industrialization in order to put themselves back into the good graces of private capital markets, while others would be forced to knock on the doors of international economic institutions to beg for further financial assistance, no matter what the political and social cost. The OPEC countries would be openly accused of starving the non-oil producers. The gravity of the issues at stake was clear to the new secretary-general of UNCTAD, the Sri Lankan Gamani Corea, who had replaced Pérez-Guerrero in 1974.[91]

At UNCTAD IV in Nairobi, held in May 1976, the G77 strived above all to achieve the creation of a Common Fund for Commodities as a concrete means to redistribute resources in favor of the South. They also sought to obtain a generalized moratorium on debt which, notwithstanding the diminution of public aid from the West, was growing exponentially primarily as a result of loans from private capital markets.[92] Corea waned that the talks for the Common Fund would be "the first—and perhaps last—test to measure the validity of the entire concept of cooperation between producers and consumers in terms of commodities," and thus also to measure the practical success of the new economic order.[93] Kissinger worked hard at Nairobi to promote the American project of an International Resources Bank, but without success. The Europeans, who did not have joint representation in UNCTAD, were divided: The Dutch took more "thirdworldist" positions; the French stuck to advocating single commodity agreements; the Germans displayed an ideological resistance to any modification of the rules of the free market—determined also in part by their lack of faith in the CAP, accused of being increasingly costly and wasteful; while the Italians remained prudently in the background because of their precarious financial situation.[94]

For their part, the developing countries listed the numerous advantages that a Common Fund for commodities would create even for the industrialized countries themselves:[95] It would facilitate the creation of single commodity agreements; the consumer nations would be able to avoid accumulating large reserve stocks of commodities to guard against lean periods; it would avoid attracting speculation of private capital on commodities under inflationary conditions; and finally, the Fund would also imply a limit to the compensatory financial measures conceded by Western countries to the poorest nations, which in the end were nothing if not beggars' alms.

---

[91] G. Corea, *Taming Commodity Markets: The Integrated Program and the Common Fund of the UNCTAD* (Manchester: Manchester University Press, 1988).

[92] CHAN, 5AG3, AE 54, HFM, Note pour le Ministre, "Entretiens avec les représentants des PVD," Paris, October 25, 1976. According to Egerton Richardson, the Jamaican representative to the CIEC, the LDCs had asked that all IMF gold be restored to them, but that the industrialized countries had wanted to appropriate the majority of it for themselves: "What were those countries to do that could not obtain capital on the international market, like Brazil, in order to finance their own development or their own survival?"

[93] FAO, UN 29/20, Esc, "Comments by UNCTAD Secretary-General," July 30, 1976.

[94] G. Garavini, "L'Europa occidentale e il Nuovo Ordine economico internazionale (1974–1977)," in (2006) 6 *Ventunesimo Secolo* (March).

[95] CEU, CIEC, Document de travail du Groupe des 19, "Problèmes des marches des produits de base et expansion du commerce," March 21, 1976.

In Nairobi a commitment emerged on the part of the Western countries to study the question of the Fund and to propose practical solutions at the Paris dialogue. The Community agreed that a definite position on the issue would have to be taken before March 1977, date of the closing meeting of the CIEC. One path to a compromise solution was outlined in talks between Germany and France prior to the meeting of the European Council in December 1976. Such a compromise would have entailed an acceptance by France of an International Fund for Agricultural Development and the reconstitution of the IDA under the World Bank—reiterating Western refusal to discuss a general moratorium on debt—in exchange for German willingness to discuss a Common Fund, if only for a reduced number of commodities and without the joint consumer-producer management and participation. But this compromise was never reached.[96] In fact, a more interesting proposal for mediation was put forward by Commissioner Cheysson: His idea was to announce a special large-scale package for the countries of the South, in exchange for a guarantee that oil prices would not increase beyond a certain threshold. "This approach, in its exaggerated simplicity, has a double advantage," he argued. "It does not commit us to anything, should oil prices skyrocket; and it puts us on the side of the countries most damaged by the crisis, along the lines of India and Pakistan."[97]

Overcoming some uncertainties, the twenty-seven participants in the North–South dialogue decided to push back the closing session until the first half of 1977, waiting for the outcome of the American elections and in the hopes that the new administration would be more forthcoming than its predecessor. The chief executive of the French Finance Ministry, Pierre Dutet, made several interesting remarks on the reasons for this temporary setback to the dialogue.[98] First, he reasoned, it was impossible to ask the West for further aid transfers: That is, to aim for a new economic order drawing on additional fiscal resources. Second, within the Western grouping itself there were diametrically opposed ideas concerning the choices to be made regarding domestic political economy. Third, in an economic crisis it would be difficult to accept the imposition of sacrifices on all of the various social groups within the industrialized nations. Fourth, the West, after having made concessions at Kingston on the World Bank and the IMF, were resolutely firm on the reconstitution of the IDA and impervious to counterarguments for the Common Fund for Commodities. All the same, Dutet noted, only Europe had been able to jump-start the compromise and open the dialogue, not only thanks to its much deeper well of knowledge of the Third World, but also because the perception of crisis within the Community was much more accentuated than in the United States, owing to the centrality of foreign trade to its economy, its greater degree of energy dependence,

---

[96] CHAN, 5AG3, AE 54, Chargé de Mission, Note pour le Premier Ministre, "Conférence sur la Coopération économique internationale," November 6, 1976. At the their meeting on December 15–16, the Council of Ministers forwarded only the proposal to reconstitute the IDA and the "untying" of aid, but failed to overcome German resistance and negotiate a Common Fund.

[97] CHAN, 5AG3, AE 56, C. Cheysson, Commissaire au développement, Note, December 10, 1976.

[98] CHAN, 5AG3, AE 54, M. Dutet, Note, "De l'opportunité d'une relance européenne dans le dialogue avec le Tiers monde," December 1976.

and the tougher conditions imposed by its trade unions. If Europe did not succeed in containing the cost of commodities, and in giving a boost to international commerce, then its governments would find themselves forced to follow the dangerous strategy of salary containment and a potential full-on war with organized labor.

We have already seen how, in terms of the international economy, the strategy of the new Democratic administration of Jimmy Carter took into account certain preconceptions of the Trilateral Commission, which had placed a priority on the coordination of Western positions in their dealings with the developing countries. The French also noticed, not without concern, the heavy influence that the president of the World Bank exerted over the development of the international economic policy of the Carter administration, which contained many members in key positions with strong connections to Robert McNamara.[99] It fell to France, especially, to guide the conference to a positive end; as a result, French prestige would emerge strengthened, ever more necessary in light of the important administrative elections that would be held the following year. French experts underlined the risks of the possible failure of the dialogue:

> Of course negotiations will continue in the United Nations, but the Industrialized Countries must be aware of the political and psychological advantage that the most progressive faction of the Non-Aligned Movement will gain by defeating the conference. Supporters for some years of the theory of "collective autonomy", several leaders of this movement will be able to convince a growing number of LDCs of the validity of their ideas and the uselessness of the dialogue with the capitalist West...
>
> The CIEC is only one of the forums of the North–South dialogue but, by virtue of its originality, its defeat will not be without consequences.

European leaders were also aware of the inevitable need to support the purchasing power of the developing countries, which by now had become strategic importers of manufactured goods. Tied to this consideration were concerns for the unsustainability of the debtor status of many of these countries. In a meeting of the European Council from March 25–26, 1977, the French continued to oppose any discussion of the cancellation or generalized renegotiation of such debt, which also had the potential to create serious repercussions on a national level, where many categories of workers were deeply indebted themselves. At the same time, the English presidency put forward again Commissioner Cheysson's idea of a special action for the developing countries—also evoking, with some hyperbole, the precedent of the Marshall Plan—which would simultaneously help the indebted countries and sustain their purchasing power.[100]

---

[99] CHAN, 5AG3, AE 53, J. François-Poncet, Secrétaire-Général, Note, "Entretien avec M. Clappier," Paris, March 17, 1977: "Clappier was dumbfounded by the role played in Washington by McNamara, whose disciples seemed to hold most of the reins of power: [W. Michael] Blumenthal (Treasury Secretary); [Richard] Cooper (Under-Secretary for Economic Affairs in the State Department); [Anthony] Salomon (Under-Secretary of the Treasury for Monetary Affairs); and [Henry] Owen himself (Brookings Institution). The result is a significant growth of the World Bank's influence within the new administration."

[100] CHAN, 5AG3, AE 56, MAE, Projet d'une note commune Trésor-Affaires Etrangères, Conseil européen de Rome, March 25/26, 1977. "Dialogue Nord–Sud. Endettemente des pays en développement et transfert de resources."

In the course of the following Council of Ministers in April, the Nine finally put into place a definite strategy for the conclusion of the North–South dialogue.[101] According to its new directives, the European representative would first enumerate the numerous achievements by the countries of the South in the period from the oil crisis to 1977. This list included:

1. Reconstitution of the IDA, for a total of US$7.638 billion from 1977–80;

2. general dispositions for an increase in the capital of the World Bank;

3. the December 1975 decision of the IMF's Executive Council to free up compensatory financing (the sums drawn by exporters of basic commodities had reached US$2 billion by 1976);

4. the January 1976 increase in IMF quota-shares for the OPEC countries (while at Kingston another agreement was reached in which part of the sales of gold would be employed to finance a fund for countries with balance of payments problems);

5. the goal of a US$1 billion international fund for agricultural development, reached in 1976;

6. three agreements on basic commodities (ethane, coffee, and cocoa) put into practice in 1976; and

7. reduction of excise tax on tropical products, which would be applied by the Community beginning on January 1, 1977.

The Community's directives were completed by two important decisions that were the result of a compromise between Germany and France. First, the Community committed itself to financing a special action of some size as a form of additional aid for the poorest countries. In exchange, in an important German concession, it also agreed to undertake a study of the concrete application of a Common Fund with its own resources or, alternatively, of an income stabilization mechanism for the sales of several basic commodities—which for Schmidt held the important advantage of not entailing any alteration of their established prices.

A genuine effort at coordination on the issues of the North–South Dialogue took place at the G7 summit held in London in May 1977. At this point, even from the French perspective, concerns of a political nature clearly took precedence, and explained the need to make the CIEC a success, not simply as a new way to obtain an agreement on the price of oil and bring together a more stable new economic order, as much as a means to take ground from beneath the feet of the Soviet Union. From Giscard's perspective, every Western country should apply pressure, on the bilateral level in those parts of the world where they maintained privileged relations, and multilaterally through close coordination in international organizations—with the obvious exception of NATO, which in the

---

[101] CHAN, 5AG3, AE 56, Communautés Européennes, Le Conseil, "Directives à l'intention des représentants de la CEE (Résultats de la session du Conseil du 5 avril 1977)," Luxembourg, April 5, 1977.

Third World was viewed as a repressive instrument.[102] The poor countries' debt was, from an economic point of view, the primary Western concern. The American strategy, considering that the majority of its UNCTAD proposals would be rejected, was based on a globalization of aid around the creation of a "world development budget."[103] This included a reorientation of aid, directing it toward the poorest countries, and a specific line of credit from the IMF for "newly industrialized countries" such as Brazil and Mexico.[104] In a letter to President Carter,[105] Schmidt confirmed German refusal of a Common Fund for commodities, which would favor the United States, Australia, and Canada, and reiterated his objections to indexing and to any mechanism that implied a direct transfer of resources. Germany could accept a system based on that of Lomé, which would guarantee earnings from the export of certain commodities.[106] Both Washington and Bonn understood, however, that to oppose communist propaganda and maintain the openness of the Western system of commercial exchange, it was vital to demonstrate that only the existing international economic institutions could provide concrete solutions to the South's problems. The London summit thus closed with an encouragement in its final declaration to continue the discussion on the Common Fund, but only as a tool to regulate single product agreements, thus not fully endorsing the demands of the Southern countries.[107]

The final session of the CIEC was held shortly thereafter, from May 30–June 2, 1977. Its results were less than expected, from the perspective of both the Western nations and the developing countries.[108] Agreements were reached on:

1. the need to ensure the transition to alternative energy sources;
2. acceptance in principle to the creation of a Common Fund for Commodities, to be placed under UNCTAD management;

---

[102] CHAN, 5AG3, AE 53, Secret, "Interventions déstabilisants de l'Union Soviétique hors d'Europe." The note was prepared to brief the French President for the secret meetings of four that would be held on the margins of the London Summit.

[103] WBGA, Office of the President, Record of Robert McNamara, General Correspondence, Box 2, Henry Owen, "A World Development Budget: Issues for the Summit," March 5, 1977. The investments in non-OPEC nations totaled approximately US\$150 billion. Of these, one-quarter came from bilateral aid, one-quarter from multilateral aid, and one-half from private capital—export credits, direct investment, loans. The newly industrializing countries received three-quarters of all world investments in the LDCs, and almost all private capital.

[104] CHAN, 5AG3, AE 56, J.P. Dutet, Note pour le Président, "Conférence de Londres (7 et 8 mai 1977). Relations avec les pays en voie de développement," Paris, May 4, 1977.

[105] JCL, NSA, Brzezinski Material, Correspondence, Box 6, Letter by the Federal Chancellor, "Non-Paper on the Economic Questions of the London Summit (May 7 and 8, 1977)," Bonn, March 8, 1977.

[106] The openness of the German Chancellor to a system for stabilizing export incomes was confirmed at the end of 1978 in a summit jointly organized by Schmidt and Manley of Jamaica and including progressive—but reform-minded—countries from the North and the South: Australia, Canada, Nigeria, Norway, Venezuela. 5 AG 4, 4273, Note, "Un premier Sommet Nord–Sud: la réunion de la Jamaique (décembre 1978)," Paris, September 30, 1981.

[107] Available online at <http://www.g8.utoronto.ca/summit/1977london/communiqué.html>.

[108] CHAN, 5AG3, AE 56, Froment-Meurice, Circulaire, "Conférence ministérielle de la CCEI," Paris, June 8, 1977.

3. an increase in the volume of aid from the industrialized countries—Japan announced it would double its efforts within five years, while the American Secretary of State Cyrus Vance declared the USA would commit to a "substantial" increase;

4. a special action totaling US$1 billion; and

5. access for the developing countries to Western capital markets and investment guarantees.

The developed countries did not manage to obtain a commitment to the creation of a forum to discuss energy problems, a project which was even opposed by Saudi Arabia, the most moderate of the oil-producing countries.[109] In the analysis of the French Minister for Foreign Affairs, the reason for the breakdown of the talks could be found in the long-term interests of three groups of participants: The OPEC countries sought simply to maintain political consensus on an increase in oil prices; the poorest countries wanted to exploit the oil weapon to obtain precious advantages in terms of aid and power within international organizations; and the West wanted to divide the South. Some still believed, however, that considering the growing importance of the developing countries as importers of manufactured goods, the only solution remained the implementation of a courageous "Marshall Plan" to redistribute resources to the South and increase commodity prices. This would be a convenient solution, considering that "after Bandung a number of nations had emerged strengthened by the collapse of colonial empires. The Third World of 1955 was much more revolutionary than the Third World of today. There is still room to negotiate."[110]

Struck by the economic crisis, those theories that called for a more equitable international division of labor based on collaboration between developed and developing countries were quickly losing credibility. In essence, the end of the North–South dialogue marked a transition from the concept of a new economic order based on North–South conflict, to more benign notions of "interdependence" that implied concessions needed to be made by both sides. Proposals for redistribution of profits in favor of the poor economies, through a debt moratorium, and the Common Fund for Commodities, had been discussed and largely rejected. The international stature of the European Community was growing: It had outgrown its merely regional influence to take on some responsibilities in global politics, but it had not succeeded—or had not wanted—to push harder to obtain structural changes to the international economy. Rather, it was the United States that had succeeded in retaining a central position in the international monetary system, through the recycling of petrodollars, while the

---

[109] ENI, Estero, Nua 978, Busta 27, Lettera del Segretario di Stato per l'Energia britannico Tony Benn al Commissario Cee Guido Brunner, "Visit to Saudi Arabia 19/20 April 1977," May 3, 1977.

[110] CHAN, 5AG3, HJB 1, J. de Lipkowski, "Le dialogue Nord–Sud—échec ou Partie Remise? Pour l'instant l'impasse."

weakness of the US dollar continued to undermine the solidity of the Common Market.

With the arrival of summer 1977, the priorities of the Community nations and the European Commission itself began to lie elsewhere. The urgency of their need to play an international role began to subside, as attentions were focused inward: On the potential means to overcome the internal troubles of a European market that seemed to be stuck, given that trade with the wider world was growing faster than that inside the Community; on the search for solutions to the alarming loss of competitiveness of traditional European industries; on closing the gap between the economic policies of those countries with strong and those with weak currencies; and on preparations for enlargement to include the southern European countries, which could constitute a new stimulus for the internal market. Renato Ruggiero, an Italian diplomat who took part in the closed meeting in East Endred at which Roy Jenkins launched the Commission's new strategy—which would later lead to the birth of the European Monetary System—has furnished eyewitness testimony to the emergence of this new political climate and its changing priorities:

> I can provide a first-hand account of how the plans for the EMS were born, the first drop in the long story that ends with the common currency...I was the spokesman for the then-president of the European Commission, Roy Jenkins, and, with a few others, took part in the meeting at his home at East Endred in Wales where the strategy was decided upon. It was 5 August 1977...At East Endred we agreed that the customs union was beginning to show deep cracks: Internal trade within the Community was growing slower than that with the outside, and the competitive currency devaluations—that of Italy above all—were destroying the fabric of solidarity with the European Community. There were two positions on how to proceed. The first wanted to jump-start European industrial policy: Massive public financing of the economy. The second, strongly supported by Jenkins, aimed at reestablishing monetary cohesion. We decided that this was the right path to follow.[111]

On October 27, 1977, in a speech at the European University Institute in Fiesole, outside Florence, Roy Jenkins officially launched the new strategy of monetary union.[112] The project planned for economic expansion through priming the internal market, an increase in Brussels' budget to pump oxygen into the lungs of Europe's poorest regions, as well as a spur to speed up the passage toward European political unity. The monetary initiative desired by Jenkins, later realized by Giscard and Schmidt with the establishment of the European Monetary System (EMS) in 1979, was developed principally to fight against inflationary tendencies by placing the deutschmark at the center of the European system of exchange, creating a barrier against monetary shocks coming from outside the Community, and kickstarting the internal market, which would also favor a growth in employment. The significance of the EMS should not be overemphasized: It did not represent, as

---

[111] *Corriere della Sera*, May 5, 1998.
[112] P. Ludlow, *The Making of the European Monetary System* (London: Butterworth Scientific, 1984).

Jenkins apparently intended, the economic counterpart to the direct elections of the European Parliament, and a contribution to the deepening of European political unity. In a memorable speech behind closed doors at the Deutsche Bundesbank just before the meeting of the European Council to ratify the EMS, Schmidt deployed several arguments to persuade German bankers to approve the monetary agreement: First, that the Common Market needed a boost in exchange stability; second, that Germany's impressive economic expansion and social stability had to be protected from the envious reactions of its partners by deepening the links with the EC and NATO ("the more successful we are in the areas of foreign policy, economic policy, socioeconomic matters, and military matters," he noted, "the longer it will be until Auschwitz sinks into history"); and finally, that there was the need not to lose strategically significant countries such as Italy:

> You really only have to look at the internal political development in some Member States. I have a friend in Italy called Giulio Andreotti. I may not relate what he tells me in every time of trouble about his internal political landscape. But the mere mention of his name and the idea of internal political relations there must be enough for each of us to imagine that, if we float further apart, nobody can keep Italy in the political alliance. What that could signify in relation to Yugoslavia and the Soviet Union and to the situation in the Mediterranean, I must not depict here.[113]

If the EMS mechanism represented a notable contribution to the maintenance of the Common Market, particularly in its linkage of the Germany economy to all its weaker partners, it could also run the risk of symbolizing a return of more modest, and primarily regional, ambitions for the European Community.

WILLY BRANDT AND GLOBAL SOCIAL DEMOCRACY

The European Community was not the only western European actor or institution with the desire to design an international role for the continent through its dialogue with the non-European world. There was indeed another mainly European body with a larger membership than the EC, a much more agile institutional organization, budget, and legal framework, and similar or even more grandiose ambitions.

A stronger and wider Socialist International could have been an important forum in which to confront in a coordinated manner the economic transformation

---

[113] Margaret Thatcher Foundation (<http://www.margaretthatcher.org>), Archive, Archive (Bundesbank) "EMS: Bundesbank Council meeting with Chancellor Schmidt (assurances on operation of EMS)," November 30, 1978 [declassified 2008]. Another quotation from the same speech revealed the new-found sense of confidence of German leadership:

> When we wanted to extradite from France a lawyer—Croissant, the man was called—who lent encouragement and help to terrorists, what a revolt! When a poor old man—Kappler, he was called—escaped from an Italian military hospital with the help of his by no means young wife, and perhaps a third person helped, what a revolt in Italy, what accusations: Rebirth of Fascism. All silly stuff, all nonsense. But here manifests itself this mix of inferiority in respect of the great German success, which then reverts to the memory of crimes that were committed in the name of the German people forty years ago, more than thirty-two, thirty-one years ago, that still represents us.

in western Europe, to respond constructively to the criticism of the developing countries, and to combat the wave of authoritarian and antidemocratic movements growing across the Third World.[114] Among its members were many influential political leaders, heads of state, and of governments, from Brandt to Palme, from Leopold Senghor to the Jamaican Michael Manley. It also aimed to exert pressure on international organizations and organize the activities of its several million members and sympathizers.

The organization, whose headquarters was and still is in London, had gone through a period of acute difficulty between 1974 and 1976. In the final months of his mandate, the Austrian President Bruno Pitterman had been compelled to leave office with a grave illness. Its last congress had been held in 1972, and since then congresses had been postponed twice, first in 1974 and again in 1975. Between 1975 and 1976, socialist leaders had only had occasion to meet thanks to the initiatives of their respective parties: There were nine such meetings between socialist leaders during this time, always outside the formal machinery of the International.

At the opening of its thirteenth congress in 1976, the Socialist International was an international political organization composed of thirty-six member parties from across thirty-one nations, counting some eight million militant members and representing an electorate of tens of millions, almost all of them from within the developed world. These figures were even more significant when it is recalled that the communist movement was in the midst of a profound crisis stemming from the tensions between its two major powers in Asia, along with a dissident Eurocommunism that probably represented only the latest insidious challenge to Moscow.

In the Third World, the International retained very little prestige, because of its tight connections with the Atlantic partnership and NATO: All told, in the developing countries it could count on a little more than a million voters. Between 1973 and 1974, Kreisky undertook three missions to the Middle East representing the International, which charged him with identifying a regional strategy. By 1975 a stronger awareness of the significance of the North–South dialogue seemed to be discernible in the European socialist parties. In February, at a conference of party leaders, Brandt openly recognized the North–South dialogue's importance, while the Dutch representative affirmed that the theme of relations between developed and developing countries would have to become central to socialists' foreign policy strategy:

> We must come to terms with the difficult behavior of certain countries in the United Nations. The "majority" today is not the American bloc, but the Third World. Are we ready to accept a global transfer of power? If the answer is yes, we can open a constructive dialogue. We must support the international agencies and the dialogue with conviction, even if it had sometimes had negative origins.[115]

---

[114] On the evolution of the Socialist International before its XIII Congress see IISH, SI 264, Gianni Finocchiaro, "Una svolta dell'Internazionale socialista al XIII congresso," January 1977.

[115] IISH, SI 346, Report of Proceedings, Party Leaders' Conference: West Berlin, February 22, 1975.

At the Geneva Congress of September 22–23, 1976, Willy Brandt was elected President of the Socialist International on the strength of a program that emphasized the importance of peace and respect for human rights, and that above all underlined the need for greater economic cooperation between wealthy and poor nations. The order of the day, in a phrase coined for the occasion, was "we work for the survival of Man and of Mankind." Olof Palme's protégé, the Swede Brent Carlsson, was elected Secretary-General.

Brandt's election to the presidency was not only a demonstration of the evermore influential weight of German social democracy,[116] but also of a strong leftward tendency in international socialism, which was oriented toward countering the global crisis of capitalism with state intervention, regulatory control over private enterprise, and cooperation with the developing countries. With these aims in mind, the Congress approved a sixteen-point declaration on international economic solidarity. The declaration, jointly presented by thirty-seven parties, traced the origins of the global economic crisis to the "failure of international capitalism," provoking a rather spirited reaction from the German Chancellor Schmidt, who did not approve of his party's strategy within the International and thus distanced himself from the resolution.[117] The Chancellor instead highlighted the responsibility of governments in power—including those with socialist majorities—that allowed citizens to live beyond their means, failed to address economic policy, and underestimated the structural problems afflicting industry. For Schmidt, the crisis did not allow leaders to indulge in facile ideological solutions. A public works program to achieve full employment would simply aggravate inflation, so Schmidt instead proposed to place a priority on control of the money supply. A voice like that of the Chancellor, however, was extremely isolated in the socialist galaxy at the time, and strongly opposed even within his own German social democratic party.

The Geneva Congress was closely followed in the Western press. Attention was focused on the possible expansion of a new political movement, Eurosocialism, which had already demonstrated great potential to attract votes in Greece and Portugal, and seemed capable of similar success in Spain. In the upcoming direct elections to the European Parliament, Eurosocialism would soon show itself to be the strongest political grouping in the European Community.[118]

During the Brandt presidency, the International focused on identifying the elements of an economic strategy to escape the crisis of the 1970s. The organization could not make binding decisions for its members, but it could encourage dialogue on the most pressing issues, rather than waste time—as it often had until then—on

---

[116] IISH, SI 293, Bureau's Report, "Draft Introduction," confidential. Germany had recently increased its contributions to the organization, from £11,668 in 1975 to £12,834 in 1976. In 1976 British Labour and the German SPD paid the same amount, the PSF £3,416, the Swedes £8,162. In1977 the total contributions of the SPD took off, reaching £35,502 out of the International's total budget of £120,000.

[117] G. Braunthal, *The West German Social Democrats, 1969–1982. Profile of a Party in Power* (Boulder, CO: Westview Press, 1983).

[118] O. Todd, "Let's Not Forget Eurosocialism," in *Newsweek*, November 29, 1976.

sterile ideological debates attempting to distance itself theoretically from communism.

In September 1977, the International promoted a global conference on energy held in Marseilles. In his opening remarks, Carlsson declared that the spirit of the initiative would be to promote greater horizontal cooperation between the competent sections of socialist parties, and not simply between leaders: "Until now, not enough time has been spent on discussing the fundamental problems that the international workers' movement must face in what remains of the 1970s and in the 1980s—such as unemployment, the environment, energy, democracy, and workers' education."[119] Even though no specific solution was identified at Marseilles, the principal indication to emerge from the debates there was that any energy policy would have to go hand in hand with the fight against unemployment and for social justice. The danger, feared by the Franco-Austrian André Gorz, was that an "ecology of the rich" would simply render a certain level of consumption out of reach of the poor, because energy would become too costly.[120] Energy efficiency was, instead, a goal to be achieved out of respect for the principle of social equality, a concept which closely resembled the austerity promoted by the Italian communist Berlinguer:

> The assets that consume the most energy, such as cars, boats, houses, summer homes, private jets, are more common among persons with large incomes.
>
> Energy efficiency must thus be combined with a policy leveling incomes and fortunes. Otherwise energy efficiency will mean nothing more than the creation of a society permanently divided into classes.[121]

A second point of reflection for the Socialist International concerned multinational corporations. In a 1975 address, the Finnish socialist Paavo Lipponen—who would later become Prime Minister from 1995–2003, the height of the "Nokianomics" era—called for deeper analysis of the role of multinationals, more consistent cooperation between European countries in this sector, and a strengthening of the role of the state in the economy:

> Capitalism is now obsolete historically as the dominant form of social and economic organization. There is a growing demand for public control of the economy throughout the capitalist world, even in the United States. The famous liberal economist Galbraith himself, in his latest book, called for a "new socialism."[122]

---

[119] IISH, SI 381, Brent Carlsson, "Opening statement at Socialist International energy conference," Marseilles, September 22–23, 1977.

[120] As cited by Serge Latouche, *La Repubblica*, July 13, 2008:

> The decrease in growth and productivity, which in another system could be a positive development (fewer automobiles, less noise, more breathable air, shorter working days, etc.) will instead have completely negative effects: Polluting products will become luxury goods, inaccessible to the masses, but will remain within the reach of the privileged; inequalities will increase, the poor will become relatively poorer and the rich richer.

[121] IISH, SI 381, "Memorandum on the Socialist International Conference on Energy Policies," Marseilles, September 22–23, 1977.

[122] IISH, SI 408, Paavo Lipponen, "Social Democratic Parties and the Multilateral Corporations." IUSY Seminar on multinational corporations, Helsinki, November 21–24, 1974, February 21, 1975.

It was decided to convene a study group on multinational corporations that would meet in Rome beginning in June 1977. The group, headed by the Belgian Oscar Debunne, would prepare a draft resolution for the congress to be held in Vancouver in 1978. There were already several international organizations that were trying to construct a legislative cage to contain the anarchic growth of multinational enterprises: The ICFTU, UNCTAD, the European Council, the OECD, the European Parliament, the ILO. If the initiative of the Socialist International thus fit well within the spirit of the age, it was still particularly incisive because many of its component socialist parties were currently in power, and their cooperation could have generated concrete legislative proposals. The final report of the study group on multinationals argued that private capital should be flanked by a strong public sector and listed several measures that could help states maintain their authority: National representation on managerial boards; full access to information for governments and unions; legal protection of union membership; encouragement of industrial democracy.[123]

The third object of Brandt's initiatives and energies, which he pursued with particular intensity, was the North–South dialogue. In 1974 the Club of Rome had entrusted the Dutch socialist Jan Tinbergen with compiling a report on the necessary reforms for the international economic system. His massive study, financed by the Dutch Ministry for Development Cooperation, was completed in 1976.[124] It called for the democratization of international economic institutions, the achievement of alimentary self-sufficiency for the poorest countries, and for automatic capital transfers to the South to reach the long-targeted 0.7 percent of GDP of the developed countries. The report was warmly received by several developing countries and, even though it was largely ignored in the West, it deeply concerned Robert McNamara, for it heavily criticized the policies of the World Bank and aired the prospect of international socialist aid-planning independent of the great economic institutions based in Washington.

At the beginning of 1977 it was McNamara who proposed to Brandt that they create a high-level commission with the aim of studying measures to reduce the ever-more visible economic gap between the rich and poor countries. The idea was to create a body along the lines of the Pearson Commission, this time with less direct involvement on the part of the World Bank, that could determine the necessary volume of aid, especially for the poorest countries, and the required changes in the policies of the developing countries, as well as discuss the structural modification of the international economy.[125] Out of consideration for the fact that the Bank was criticized by both the right, which deemed it a bottomless well of wastefulness, and the left, which saw it as the accomplice of antidemocratic Third World dictatorships, it was the Dutch government that declared itself willing to finance

---

[123] IISH, SI 408, Ken Martin, British Labour Party, "Multinational Corporations. Socialist International Special Committee. Report by the Working Group."

[124] J. Tinbergen (ed.), *Reshaping the International Order* (New York: E.P. Dutton Co., 1976).

[125] WBGA, Office of the President, Robert S. McNamara, Subject Files, Box 1, "Prospects of the Brandt Commission," 1714/77.

the majority of the costs so that the Commission could present itself as an independent body in the eyes of world public opinion.[126] Brandt nevertheless had to wait until the end of the Paris conference of the CIEC to make the first convocation of his commission. And even then he then personally had to convince both Houari Boumedienne and the Secretary-General of UNCTAD that the conference was not a maneuver to avoid structural reforms, distract from the debate over the Common Fund for Commodities, or win publicity for the West's standard rhetoric calling for greater development aid and sermons on the need for population control in the poorest countries.

The constitution of the Brandt Commission was announced on September 28, 1977 and quickly raised the hopes of those frustrated by the failure of the North–South dialogue.[127] An early draft by the Swedish economist Goran Ohlin, Brandt's principal collaborator, argued the need to highlight the many differences among the various countries of the South as one of the possible outcome of their investigations, as well as to explore issues such as arms control and the environment.

At the end of 1977 and throughout 1978, the prospect of some form of collaboration between the World Bank, the European socialists under Brandt's leadership, and the Democratic administration of Jimmy Carter in the United States seemed genuinely possible.[128] Soon, however, the head of the World Bank began to worry about the slippery slope down which the Commission's debates were threatening to lead. When, in his opening remarks, Brandt spoke of a new *Sudpolitik*, McNamara realized that the German social democrat risked being perceived as too "European," and thus out of sync with the feelings of the US Congress, where the entire question of arms control and its linkage with an increase in development aid was politically explosive. The essence of Brandt's experiment, as outlined his address to the meeting of the Commission at Mont Pélerin in March 1978, appeared to be marked by a refusal to accept the concept of interdependence: "If one expects a new international order to be characterized by more justice one should not expect too much from such concepts as 'interdependence' and 'globalism' in the near future. Such concepts must not deflect attention from the fact that the sovereignty of the new states must in many cases first be given real content."[129] This new world

---

[126] WBGA, Office of the President, Records of Robert S. McNamara, Minutes 1976–1981, Box 2, "President's Council Meeting," November 18, 1977.

[127] Members of the Commission included Willy Brandt (Germany), Chairman Abdulatif Y. Al-Hamad (Kuwait), Rodrigo Botero Montoya (Colombia), Antoine Kipsa Dakoure (Upper Volta, today Burkina Faso), Eduardo Frei Montalva (Chile), Katherine Graham (United States), Edward Heath (Great Britain), Amir H. Jamal (Tanzania), Lakshmi Kant Jha (India), Khatijah Ahmad (Malaysia), Adam Malik (Indonesia), Haruki Mori (Japan), Joe Morris (Canada), Olof Palme (Sweden), Peter G. Peterson (United States), Edgar Pisani (France)—later replaced by Pierre Mendes (France), Shirdath Ramphal (Guyana), and Layachi Yaker (Algeria). *Ex officio* members included Jan Pronk (Netherlands), Goran Ohlin (Sweden), and Dragoslav Avramovic (Yugoslavia).

[128] IISH, SI 972, "Letter to Willy Brandt," April 5, 1978: "The Administration, in general, wants to cooperate with European socialists on this and on other problems. Brzezinski understands the importance of cooperation, and Robert Hunter at the White House will follow his lead."

[129] Cold War International History Project (CWIHP), permission of the Woodrow Wilson Center for Scholars, "Paper by the Chairman of the North–South Commission, Brandt, for the Meeting in Mt. Pélerin," 11 March 1978, AdsD, Nord-Sud-Kommission, 3. Berliner Ausgabe, vol.8.

order, no longer merely economic in nature, also encompassed issues of human rights, disarmament, and defense of the environment on a level parallel with economic issues:

> This requires that international public opinion and the community of nations accept the decision to achieve a balanced reduction in armaments expenditures and link it to an overproportional increase in development expenditures.
>
> The exceptionally high input of scientific and technical expertise claimed by armaments production, represents an intolerable wasting of human resources.

In practice, though without ever saying so openly, Brandt was outlining the contours of a new "global social democracy." The Vancouver Congress of the Socialist International, held from November 3–5, 1978, was completely taken up by the North–South dialogue. Carlsson presented a report for the occasion on the most significant developments of the Brandt presidency.[130] The International had broadened its contacts with the Third World. A delegation led by Olof Palme had been sent to South Africa. A second delegation, headed by the Portuguese Prime Minister Mário Soares, had traveled throughout Latin America to shed light on the need to develop regional solutions for the continent. The Marseilles energy conference had proposed the widening of economic democracy to big business, in part as an instrument to influence their decisions on energy policy. The overall balance sheet, however, remained shaded in *chiaroscuro*: So many different efforts had been undertaken, and yet the actual successes of European socialists remained primarily confined to the southern rim of Europe. The representative of the Jamaican government reminded all, in alarming terms, of the damage that would be done to cooperation with the Third World if the North–South dialogue did not soon produce any concrete results:

> When I listen to the Industrialized Countries argue that it is politically impossible to pursue economic growth because it will force rates of inflation to rise by 2 percent, or preach about the political necessity to raise protectionist barriers toward the Third World to maintain rates of unemployment below 6 percent, we must ask ourselves if they realize the terrible inequality of the situation.
>
> The concrete danger exists of an overturning of the process of internationalism that has been built in these last few years, and of the retreat of many poor nations into isolationism, or into opportunistic bilateral relations free of all principles.[131]

While major roles were played in the creation of the European Monetary System by Chancellor Schmidt and the British Labour Party member Roy Jenkins, the president of the European Commission who originally launched the initiative, in 1978 European socialism was still generally reluctant—if not openly hostile—to further deepening of European integration. There was a very strong tendency among European socialists to look for a way out of the economic crisis, from infla-

---

[130] IISH, SI 409, Socialist International Congress, "Report by Brent Carlsson," Vancouver, November 3–5, 1978.
[131] IISH, SI 409, Richard Fletcher (People's National Party, Jamaica), "North–South Relations." Speech at the Vancouver Congress, November 3, 1978.

tion to unemployment, simply through workers' participation in business, the strengthening of the cooperative movement, and less bureaucratic management of public and private enterprise, perhaps through wider employment of the system of *autogestion*. Sartre could still argue in 1977, without fear of criticism, that the European Community was an instrument of capitalism, and that the close collaboration then under way between Germany and the United States would destroy any project for a socialist Europe.[132]

Michel Rocard, probably the most charismatic French socialist leader after Mitterrand, a future prime minister and a refined writer, was part of that grassroots movement against the Common Market, because he believed further opening of markets would have impeded a serious industrial policy while favoring delocalization and the weakening of workers' solidarity. Rocard was not opposed to European integration per se, which he believed remained an ambitious international project, but hoped sincerely to see a socialist Europe: "What we call the building of Europe is in reality, yes, against nationalism, but at the same time against Europe itself in the name of free enterprise."[133]

This tendency, which called for some kind of protection against the free market, was woven even more deeply into the sinews of Labour in Britain than in France. Tony Benn, Minister for Industry in 1975, was convinced of the need for the wider use of planning, even if this should have been placed increasingly under the direct control of the trade unions rather than the state. From his most recent experience in government, Benn declared he had learned that:

> [e]x-Imperial Britain was now apparently meekly accepting the status of a colony or protectorate, whose economic policy was dictated by the International Montary Fund; whose industrial policy by the multinationals; whose foreign and defence policy was integrated with NATO and whose statutes were only legal if they did not breach the provisions of the Treaty of Rome as interpreted and administered by non-elected officials in Brussels known as the Common Market Commissioners.[134]

Even Bettino Craxi, elected Secretary-General of the Partito socialista italiano (PSI) in 1976 and destined soon to become the first socialist to lead the government of postwar Italy, had distanced himself from Italian communists by celebrating the heritage of the critics of Marx and the community-based utopian socialism of Proudhon, and remained silent on the virtues of competition and market forces.[135]

Such deeply-held hopes for a socialist Europe, to be achieved above or around Brussels and the Common Market through the success of socialist parties in their respective countries, were captured in this report by a representative of the Swedish

---

[132] Cavallari, *La Francia*, p. 63.

[133] M. Rocard, *Le marché commun contre l'Europe* (Paris: Seuil, 1973). The book's subtitle included the declaration "socialism will be European or it will cease to be" (*"le socialisme sera européen ou ne sera pas"*).

[134] T. Benn, *Arguments for Socialism* (Harmondsworth: Penguin, 1980), p. 17.

[135] A. Landolfi, *Storia del PSI. Cento anni di socialismo in Italia da Filippo Turati a Bettino Craxi* (Milan: SugarCo, 1990), p. 338.

metalworkers' union, in an analysis which again did not differ greatly that of the Italian Eurocommunists:

> An economically independent Europe could find a third way between communism and capitalism. This would require, however, the progress of the socialists through the electoral success of the left in the upcoming elections. European socialism does not mean only greater influence in the economy for organized labor, but also a greater liberty in foreign policy. For Eastern Europe an independent socialism in Western Europe would create the prerequisites for its liberation from the Soviet Union. European socialism would thus establish the foundations for a new relationship with the Developing Countries and for a New International Economic Order.[136]

François Mitterrand's electoral success in 1981 seemed capable of contributing to the establishment of a socialist Europe and at the same time advancing the North–South dialogue. Under the coordination of Lionel Jospin, before the elections the French Parti Socialiste had articulated a policy toward developing countries centered on the reform of international economic institutions and development aid.[137] Once elected, the French President named Régis Debray—a friend of Ernesto "Che" Guevara and bard of the Cuban revolution—as special assistant for Latin American affairs. The entire Socialist International was basking in the victory of the Sandinistas in Nicaragua in 1979. Mitterrand instructed his sherpa Jeannenay to ensure that the next G7 summit to be held in Ottawa, Canada would be dedicated to North–South relations. At the same time, Foreign Minister Claude Cheysson was charged with proposing a New Deal for the South at the upcoming OECD ministerial conference.[138] In view of the 1981 Ottawa G7 summit, the European Commission itself, through the French Commissioner for Development Cooperation Edgar Pisani, appealed to the Member States of the Community to side openly in favor of global negotiations with the South, which would be held in Cancun, Mexico that same year. Pisani affirmed that, for the countries of the South, Europe was their final hope, and that both they and the African states aligned with them were showing the first signs of a discouragement that could ultimately lead them to revolt against the agreements reached at Lomé.[139] To combat this trend he begged that "Europe must impose upon its partners, especially the United States, its own vision of the world."

There did not seem to be great support for the idea of an autonomous Europe as a partner to the Third World, however, neither within governments—with the exception of the socialist France of Mitterrand—nor among their electorates, which would soon opt for a more marked Atlanticism, as in the Germany of the CDU and Helmut Kohl. Certainly, there was scant interest from those social and economic forces that were beginning to experience the sting of their first defeats at

---

[136] IISH, Si 409, Jan Olsson (Swedish Metal Workers Union), "An international industrial policy," July 7, 1977.

[137] *Les Socialistes et le Tiers Monde. Elements pour une politique socialiste de relations avec le Tiers monde* (Paris: Berger Levrault, 1977).

[138] R. Dumas, *Affaires Etrangères 1981–1988* (Paris: Fayard, 2007), p. 16.

[139] E. Pisani, "Communication to the Council, North–South dialogue on the eve of the conferences of Ottawa, Cancun, Nairobi and Paris," in (1981) 69 *The Courier* (September–October).

the hands of organized industry. At the beginning of the 1980s there was a great flourishing of projects: "Marshall Plans" for the South, "New Deals" for the developing countries, even a "world employment plan." These initiatives, at once ambitious and overheated, rapidly accelerated growing frustrations with their inability to act in a concrete manner and effect real changes in the dynamics of the international economy.[140]

Brandt submitted his own report to the Secretary-General of the United Nations in 1980. The questions it raised would be discussed in detail in a dedicated international summit to be held the following year.[141] The Brandt report explored complex problems with an abundance of statistics and quantitative data. While incredibly detailed, a single unifying thread tied together its disparate analyses: The idea that between North and South there were common interests, and that reciprocal relations should be regulated through well-rounded forms of cooperation both political and economic in nature. The goal was to promote a progressive détente in global political relations, a reorganization of the military–industrial complex, and a massive flow of international aid aimed at financing not the acquisition of arms but a change in the qualitative development of poor countries to guarantee their alimentary self-sufficiency. The report put forward the proposal of a tax on international trade and the export of armaments, while it set the quantity of resources needed to be transferred to redress North–South inequality at a figure of US$50–60 billion per year. In Brandt's vision an important role awaited Europe, which would have to develop its own personality autonomous from both East and West.

Brandt's address found a warm welcome among Dutch citizens and an important foothold in the Italian Communist party. Relations between Italian communists and several European socialist leaders—among them Palme, Mitterrand, and Brandt himself—had grown closer during the 1970s.[142] It was from reading Brandt's report that Berlinguer drew several key analytical points that would help him develop the Charter of Peace and Development, which the Italian Communists would formally present at the UN Special Session at Cancun in 1981. The Charter, the fruit of lengthy discussions that began in 1979 and involved more than 100 economic specialists,[143] expressed sympathy with the Brandt report's recommendation of the need for Europe to maintain an autonomous role. The Italian Communists underlined that the new Reagan administration aimed to exacerbate the North–South conflict as part of an aggressive strategy to revive American capitalism and escape economic stagnation by stimulating military spending. Europe alone would have to continue to favor détente and push for a world regulated by norms to protect both the strong and weak alike. The Italian Communist Romano Ledda, presenting the Charter to the PCI's Central Committee, stressed that "the reversal of current international trends is therefore consonant with the general

[140] IISH, SI 409, J. Tinbergen, J.M. Den Uyl, J.P. Pronk, and W. Kok, "A New World Employment Plan," October 1980.

[141] *North–South: A Program for Survival*, The Independent Commission on International Development Issues (Cambridge, MA: MIT Press, 1980).

[142] Maggiorani and Ferrari (eds), *L'Europa da Togliatti a Berlinguer*, pp. 53–75.

[143] Author's conversation with Renato Sandri, October 2005.

interests of Europe, which coincide with the goal of a democratic and pacific evolution of international political and economic relations."[144] Fiamma Lussana summarized the Charter's proposals for Europe:

> The European Community will gain a great advantage from economic interdepend-
> ence because it depends for a large part of its energy and commodity needs on the
> global South. For Berlinguer, as for Brandt, Europe can play a positive role in the solu-
> tion to the North–South relationship in at least three ways: Overcoming the logic of
> bilateral agreements with commodity-producing nations and seeking to develop a
> common policy; undertaking a productive reorganization that is reciprocally advanta-
> geous with the Emerging Countries; promoting a development policy in depressed
> areas of the world that employs its great scientific and technological resources and
> applies them to modernization and structural reform programs.[145]

The convergence between Eurosocialism and Eurocommunism—which however
seemed to be increasingly identified solely with the PCI—in their conception of
the international economy was still highly theoretical, and blocked by the immov-
able obstacle of Italian communism's international position in the Cold War. And
in any event, it was of very short duration.[146]

For suddenly, in one of those quick turns in the course of history that make the
study of the past alternately frustrating and rewarding, precisely at the moment in
which the convergence of many leaders of the European left seemed at its peak,
European governments, their citizens, and workers found themselves forced to
cope with a second devastating oil shock and with a revolutionary change in US
monetary policy. Its aftermath revealed unequivocal signs of the decline of the
Keynesian economic paradigm and the exhaustion of the cultural wave unleashed
on the European continent by 1968, helped to revive the Cold War, and provoked
the definitive rupture of the united front of the Global South.

---

[144] R. Ledda, *L'Europa fra Nord e Sud* (Rome: Editori Riuniti, 1989), p. 339.
[145] F. Lussana, "Il confronto con le socialdemocrazie e la ricerca di un Nuovo socialismo nell'ultimo
Berlinguer," in (2004) 2 *Studi Storici* (April–June), p. 568.
[146] S. Pons, *Berlinguer e il fine del comunismo* (Turin: Einaudi, 2006).

Epilogue
Managing Globalization

In 1978, surrounded by the oppressive grey climate of a Red Brigades' prison cell and a few weeks before being found dead in the boot of a red Renault 4, the Italian Prime Minister Aldo Moro—known for his hermetic style, now only accentuated by clear-headed pessimism over his isolation—expressed his deep disillusionment with Italy's and western Europe's future possibilities for autonomy:

> Faced with multiple requests about the social and economic structures of the Europe of tomorrow, and with them of Italy, I must honestly say that what one is about to witness is the reinvigoration of the capitalist means of production on a technocratic basis, obviously tempered by modern techniques of efficiency …
>
> This way of being, of a Europe tightly bound to and conditioned by America, will not change, in general, with an alteration in the internal order of its various countries, as one sees in the equal faith given to both Labour and Conservative governments [in Britain].[1]

Just a few months later, in March 1979, the British Ambassador to Paris Sir Nicholas Henderson sent his final despatch to the Foreign Office, a document that was quickly leaked to the press and provoked heated debates in the UK.[2] Titled "Britain's Decline; Its Causes and Consequences," the despatch was full of praise for the success of France and Germany in shaping the European Community, and of equal contempt for the failures of a British foreign policy that had missed its chance to lead Europe right after the war, "when every western European Government was ready to eat out of our hand." In Henderson's analysis, for Britain to find a new sense of national purpose, it should not abandon diplomatic give-and-take on issues like the CAP, but should behave "as though we were fully and irrevocably committed to Europe." The only way to modernize British industry was in fact to adopt more of the French and German models of management and labor relations, and commit more political investment to the European integration project.

The oil shock of 1973 had only ended up reinforcing a number of tendencies already present in both western Europe and the international arena. Within western Europe governments had developed models of social democratic planning that

---

[1] A. Moro, *Ultimi scritti 16 marzo–9 maggio 1978* (Casale Monferrato: Piemme, 1998), p. 55. Aldo Moro was held prisoner for fifty-five days and wrote in this period various letters and a "memorial," the complete authenticity of which is highly contested.

[2] MTFA, "The Henderson Despatch," March 31, 1979. Available online at <http://www.margaret-thatcher.org/document/110961>.

widened the public sphere, refined forms of collaboration between labor unions and business management, made an effort to integrate migrants—while limiting their numbers—and undertaken experiments in greater direct popular participation. At the same time, the European institutions in Brussels had been significantly reinforced: Initially through the creation of the European Council in 1974, and later with the first direct elections to the European Parliament in 1979. New European policies had been introduced, from regional funds for less-developed areas in the continent, to the global development and cooperation policy, to new forms of European political cooperation raising the Community's profile in international relations. The major European political parties were weaving a tighter web of alliances at the supranational level, thus reducing the relative weight of national embassies in the conduct of intra-European affairs.

Western Europe, and the European Community in particular, had graduated from dragging its feet on international economic cooperation in the 1960s, to become its spearhead in the following decade: The 1971 approval of the Generalized System of Preferences; the ambition to play the role of "most favored" partner of the developing world at the Paris European summit in 1972; the declaration on European identity and the launching of the Euro-Arab dialogue at the Copenhagen European summit in 1973; the joint signature of the Nine on the Final Act of the CSCE, the Lomé Convention, and the simultaneous launching of the G7 of industrialized countries and North–South Dialogue in 1975.

By the beginning of the 1980s, and as a consequence of the twin oil and monetary crisis in 1979–80 that proved to have far more momentous consequences than the first in 1973,[3] the future of western European integration was all but clear. Would Aldo Moro's warnings about persistent European dependence on US-driven capitalism prove correct? Or would ambassador Henderson's remarks on the strength of the French and German economic models, as well as on the inevitable reinforcement of the European integration project, be confirmed?

THIRD WORLDS

In 1979, two years after the conclusion of the North–South dialogue in Paris, the developing countries seemed even more united and radical than at UNCTAD I in 1964. The extremism of the South was clearly displayed at the 1979 Non-Aligned conference in Havana, under the presidency of Fidel Castro. On that occasion the Third World vociferously echoed its previous accusations against an industrialized world that had refused, in its view, to grant it meaningful concessions. Similarly radical positions were expressed that same year in the course of the G77 ministerial conference at Arusha, Tanzania, the final document of which criticized the industrialized world's protectionism, denounced conditional aid, and called for global

---

[3] On the various consequences of global 1979, see Frank Bösch, "Umbrüche in die Gegenwart. Globale Ereignisse und Krisenreaktionen um 1979" in (2012) 1 *Zeithistorische Forschungen*, available at <http://www.zeithistorische-forschungen.de/site/40209215/default.aspx>.

negotiations at the UN to confront the issues surrounding debt, the Common Fund for commodities, and the reform of development aid simultaneously. Equally radical was the tone of many speakers at UNCTAD V, held in Manila in May and June 1979. Few international observers failed to notice, however, the many increasingly large fissures in the South's united front.[4] One researcher for Italy's IPALMO, which throughout the 1970s had regularly analyzed the evolution of debate over the new economic order, highlighted their contradictory priorities:

> For the oil-producing nations possessing a surplus, financial questions [are a priority]; for the LDCs that have demonstrated substantial industrial development, a new regulation of international long-term credit, facilitated access to capital markets, maximization of free trade in manufactures in the markets of the Industrialized Countries, and facilitations for transfers of technology; for the less developed, along with the urgency of a solution to their food problems, the priorities remain regulation of the commodities market, an increase in aid and the need for short-term provisions and mechanisms for immediate intervention.[5]

The speech of the Tanzanian President Julius Nyerere at the Arusha conference touched a point midway between the utopian vision and the impassioned requiem. He compared the grouping of the developing countries to "a trade union of the poor" that must remain united, for otherwise no one would give them anything other than alms. The hero of Tanzanian independence painted the portrait of a future in which the South would construct their own multinational corporations, joint shipping companies, and autonomous insurance firms that would cease to serve the interests of Western banks. First and foremost, Nyerere remarked—in his schoolteacher's tone that did not always produce the desired effects—it was necessary to reflect on the multiplicity of interests held by the peoples of the South:

> I want to reiterate that it was our nationalism that brought us together, because we must first understand ourselves in order to pursue progress. The Group of 77 does not have an ideology in common. Some of us are for a socialism that claims to be "scientific," others simply socialists, others capitalists, others theocracies, and still others fascists! And we are not necessarily all friendly with one another: Several countries are today at war with each other. Our per capita income varies from $100 to $2,000 dollars per year. Some of us have minerals, others do not; some of us have no access to the sea, while others are surrounded by enormous oceans.
>
> The immediate interests and negotiating priorities of the G77 countries are thus quite different. There is OPEC, the poorest countries, the Least Developed, the Newly Industrialized, the landlocked, and so on; some of these classifications are our own

---

[4] CHAN, 5AG3, HJB 3, Mission Permanente, "Réflexions sur la Vème CNUCED," June 18, 1979. The French representative to the United Nations noted that in 1979 the South was divided into: 1. "Genevans" and "New Yorkers"; 2. oil producers and non-producers; 3. Asians, Latin Americans, and Africans; 4. rich and poor (the efforts on behalf of the less advanced of the LDCs were beginning to concern those that were relatively better off); 5. pro-Soviets and the rest; and 6. Arabs and the rest.

[5] L. Magrini, "La V Unctad e le prospettive del dialogo Nord–Sud," in (1979) *Politica internazionale* (August–September).

     After Empires

doing, others have been created by others for their own purposes. This type of subdivision of the G77 can be useful ... But it is also very dangerous.[6]

There had always been a significant diversity of interests and diplomatic positions among the various regions of the developing world, of course, since the beginning. The tensions lurking within the developing world—not merely those of an economic nature, but also the increasingly brutal military conflicts for regional domination—exploded violently at the end of the 1970s. With the end of the era of epic wars of decolonization or crusades for economic independence, the passing of the heroic liberation generation forced the nations of the Third World to confront the fact that a common struggle was difficult to sustain in a period of economic contraction. Without social, cultural, and political structures capable of fostering cooperation and mutual understanding—without the creation of robust regional or international institutions and agreements—they found it impossible to overcome the logic of military might and economic competition.

It was in the Arab world, and in the oil-producing nations—that is, among those that with greater cohesion could have done so much more to fulfill plans for a new international economic order—that some of the decisive events occurred. Already by 1977 oil policy had begun to produce significant divergences of opinion among the oil-producing nations, as the unequivocal comments of the Iraqi President to the Venezuelan ambassador, referring to the Saudi oil strategy of reducing prices and increasing production, amply demonstrated: "They are not rational people. So what are they? They are uncultured, illiterate, erratic bedouins, a product of one of the most backwards regions in the world that apart from oil has nothing but sand."[7] At its 55th meeting in 1979, OPEC managed to ratify a US$2.4 billion increase in its Special Fund to fuel cooperation with developing countries, and agreed to convene the Second Summit of OPEC Sovereigns and Heads of State in Baghdad in 1980 to celebrate the twentieth anniversary of the creation of OPEC. But the Baghdad Summit never took place, as the oil producers erupted into internal conflict, thus undermining the possibility of further collaboration with the other developing countries.

By this time the 1978 Camp David Accords between Egypt and Israel, signed thanks to the mediation of President Jimmy Carter, had provoked the revolt of the Arab League against the leadership of Sadat, who was accused of having betrayed Palestine in exchange for the return of parts of the Sinai Peninsula.[8] Egypt, one of the founding nations of the Non-Aligned Movement, was thus forcibly isolated and treated as an untrustworthy ally of Washington. Then in 1979, the Islamic revolution in Iran that forced the Shah into exile also plunged into crisis Iran's already troubled relations with Saudi Arabia, as well as those with Iraq, another

---

[6] G. Mwakikagile, *Nyerere and Africa: The End of an Era* (Atlanta, GA: Protea Publishing, 2002).

[7] AMPPRE, Interior, Visita oficial del Señor Presidente de la Republica Carlos Andrés Pérez a: Kuwait—Arabia Saudita—Irán—Irak y Qatar, 1977, Memo, "Análisis y recomendaciones en relación al Proyecto de Comunicado Conjunto aralia-venezolano, presentado por la Embajada de Irak en Caracas."

[8] Shlaim, *The Iron Wall*.

regime with regional hegemonic ambitions.[9] The Shi'ism of Ayatollah Khomeini, the spiritual leader of the revolution, with its emphasis placed on religious identity, necessarily accented the dividing lines in the Middle East between Arabs of different beliefs—and especially the Sunni faith.[10] In Iraq that same year, Saddam Hussein expelled from the ruling Ba'ath Party those elements with socialist or pan-Arabist tendencies, who were thus amenable to unification with Syria, in order to install a nationalist regime centered ever more tightly around his cult of personality. Saddam assumed the presidency in 1980, soon entering a Pyrrhic war of attrition against Iran (aiming at, among other things, annexation of the Shatt al-Arab), which he believed had fallen prey to revolutionary chaos and would be incapable of mustering sufficient resistance.[11] In this heated climate, the death of a leader from the glorious period of Arab independence, who had been one of the voices of Arab solidarity and of the nationalization drive, assumed great symbolic importance. Indeed, the death in 1979 of the Algerian president Houari Boumedienne, who more than any other regional leader had represented the effort to modernize the Arab world through rapid industrialization, and linked this effort to broader change in the rules of the international economy to favor the Third World as a whole, provoked a spontaneous and unexpected outburst of collective mourning among the Algerian people.[12]

At the Havana summit mentioned above, the non-aligned states not only closed the cycle of Nehru, Tito, and Boumedienne, but also accentuated the divisions and conflicts between the nations of the socialist bloc: The hostility between the two communist countries of Vietnam and Cambodia in particular created a sensation.[13] When the first soldiers of the Red Army later crossed into Afghanistan on Christmas Day 1979, to provide military support to a faction of the local communist party tied to Moscow, condemnation of the invasion was unanimous in the United Nations, including even the Indian government, historically one of Moscow's strongest allies in the region. Moscow, whose star (to most international observers, especially in Africa and Latin America) had seemed to be in the ascendant for most of the 1970s, suddenly lost whatever credibility it had left as a supporter of the cause of the peoples of the Third World. The suicidal gamble of the military mission in Afghanistan had been foreseen by the Soviet Foreign Minister Gromyko in March 1979:

> All that we have done in recent years with such effort in terms of détente of international relations, arms reductions, and much more—all that would be overthrown. China, of course, will receive a nice gift. All the nonaligned countries will be against us.[14]

---

[9] E. Abrahamian, *A History of Modern Iran*. Cambridge: Cambridge University Press, 2008, pp. 155–62.

[10] F. Sabahi, *Storia dell'Iran* (Milan: Bruno Mondadori, 2006), p. 165.

[11] C. Tripp, *A History of Iraq* (Cambridge: Cambridge University Press, 2002).

[12] G. Corm, *Il Libano contemporaneo. Storia e società* (Milan: Jaca Book, 2006), pp. 166–7.

[13] C. Liauzu, *L'enjeu tiermondiste* (Paris: L'Harmattan, 1987).

[14] V. Zubok, *A Failed Empire: The Soviet Union in the Cold War from Stalin to Gorbachev* (Chapel Hill: University of North Carolina Press, 2007), p. 260.

This alteration of the international political picture would have been sufficient by itself to explain the rupture of Third World solidarity at the end of the 1970s. Reinforcing this process, however, were two additional radical changes to the global economic outlook.[15]

The first of these changes was the second oil crisis of 1979. Beginning in April of that year, and for twelve consecutive months, the price of crude kept rising until it reached US$42 per barrel, its highest level until 2006. Unlike its predecessor in 1973, this rise in oil prices was facilitated not just by deliberate decisions of the oil-producing states, but mainly by the reduction in Iranian oil production following the revolution and the later Iraqi invasion, and by the panic sown by these two events on the emerging "spot" market for oil. The overtures of OPEC solidarity with the non-producing developing countries, again unlike what occurred in 1973, went nowhere after the Iran–Iraq war and there was to be no successful offensive to exploit their temporary position of strength to force changes to the rules of the international economy. The second oil crisis simply created a tremendous aggravation of the trade imbalances of the importing countries, and at the same time produced a terrible oil glut when Saudi Arabia and other OPEC countries massively increased production at the same time as new non-OPEC oil was coming "on stream" (mainly from North Sea and Mexico).[16]

If that were not enough, precisely at the same time in 1979 the US Federal Reserve, then guided by Paul Volcker, began its epic battle to stabilize the value of the dollar after the devaluations of the 1970s and thus defeat inflation once and for all. Federal interest rates reached 20 percent through 1982—'the highest rates since the birth of Jesus Christ" as described by Chancellor Schmidt—plunging the American economy into deep crisis and recession, though at the same time funneling capital from the rest of the world toward Wall Street and into government bonds. This shift in American monetary policy represented a dramatic about-face both within the Western world, where growth and employment suffered hits, and for the countries of the Third World, which found themselves forced to pay exorbitant rates on their debt held in dollars.[17] In total, by the middle of the 1980s Third World debt amounted to the astronomical sum of US$900 billion. The possibility of remedying debt multiplication with an increase in exports was further limited by the economic stagnation of the industrialized world. According to Bernard Nossiter, the "Volcker shock" and the deflationary policy of the most important Western nations "cost third world nations… more than $140 billion in goods and services: $41 billion in extra interest, $79 billion in lower commodity prices and $21 billion in reduced export volume."[18]

The second oil crisis and the strategic decision to pursue deflation in Western monetary policy not only exacerbated the crisis of the poorest nations and in the emerging countries, but also snapped the bonds of their solidarity by widening the gap in their respective abilities to compete in a globalized economy. Beginning at the end of the 1970s, inequality between the richest and poorest nations began to

---

[15] Prashad, *The Darker Nations*, pp. 349–71.

[16] On the effects of the 1979–80 "oil shock" on the international oil market see L. Maugeri, *The Age of Oil: the Mythology, History, and Future of the World's Most Controversial Resource* (Westport: Praeger, 2006), pp. 121–33.

[17] Parboni, *Il conflitto economico mondiale*, pp. 293–300.

[18] Nossiter, *The Global Struggle for More*, p. 16.

grow ever-more obvious: The income disparity between the fifth of the world living in the wealthiest countries and the fifth living in the poorest countries of the South grew from 30:1 in 1960, to 60:1 in 1990, before reaching 74:1 in 1997.[19] A similar growth in inequality was manifest within the developing world itself. According to Manuel Castells, while between 1950 and 1973 incomes in twenty-two of the thirty-four developing countries he examined drew closer to those of the United States, from 1973 to 1992 only twelve developing countries continued to converge on the American benchmark.[20] The economic upheaval of the late 1970s created winners and losers, and certainly signaled the end of the united efforts of what to that time had been considered the Third World. At the same time such upheavals encouraged several of these countries, China foremost among them, to concentrate their efforts on international trade, to undertake modernizing reforms that would nourish their domestic markets, and finally in 1980 to join economic organizations like the International Monetary Fund and World Bank, which they had long violently opposed.[21]

The IMF historian Margaret de Vries aptly summarized the evolution of the international economy through the end of the 1970s: "Whereas the quarter century from 1945 to 1970 had been 'The Age of Growth,' the next quarter century at least as of 1979 seemed to be evolving as 'The Age of Equality.'"[22] The second oil crisis of 1979 and the emergence of changes in Western political and economic thought, symbolized by the election of British Prime Minister Margaret Thatcher in 1979 and of the Republican Ronald Reagan as President of the United States, opened a new era the consequences of which would last well into the twenty-first century. This era could well be named "The Age of Competition" or, as argued by Mark Mazower, the Real New International Economic Order based on a relaunch of the Bretton Woods institutions, the general elimination of trade and financial barriers, and the demise of the basically UN-centered economic order imagined by the Third World.[23] In the West, the evolution of the international economic system began to be described by the phrase "globalization," a term that carried the implication that the capitalist industrialized countries could no longer resist technological and financial developments that were now outside the control of any single government. The communist world, instead, continued to employ the concept of "internationalism," which allowed greater room to justify intervention in far-flung locations and the assumption of responsibility for the Third World—a burden that the Soviets were no longer capable of shouldering without aggravating the already tremendous sacrifices imposed upon the citizens of communist eastern Europe.[24]

[19] D. Harvey, *A Brief History of Neoliberalism* (Oxford: Oxford University Press, 2005), p. 19.

[20] Jha, *The Twilight of the Nation-State*, p. 149.

[21] M.C. Bergère, *Storia della Cina dal 1949 ai giorni nostri* (Bologna: Il Mulino, 2003), p. 351.

[22] M.G. de Vries, *The IMF in a Changing World 1945–85* (Washington, DC: International Monetary Fund, 1986), p. 156.

[23] On the differences between the shocks of 1973 and 1979, see J.-P. Fitoussi, Il *dibattito proibito. Moneta, Europea, Povertà* (Bologna: Il Mulino, 1997), pp. 15–17. M. Mazower, *Governing the World. The Rise and Fall of an Idea, 1815 to Present.* New York: Penguin, 2012.

[24] R. Vinen, *A History in Fragments: Europe in the Twentieth Century* (London: Abacus, 2000), pp. 469–70.

The renewed tensions of the Cold War, the sense that the world was starting to obey the laws of Shakespeare rather than those of Talleyrand—that is, responding to the staged drama of face-to-face confrontation rather than patient, back-channels, diplomatic dialogue—suggested to Robert McNamara that the World Bank, too, should take a more resolute stance. Until the end of the 1970s, the Bank's high-ranking officials had been heavily interrogated on several widespread criticisms of the way in which it distributed aid, the illiberal regimes that it sustained, the way to target investment on basic needs, and its collaboration with the Brandt Commission, which could restore needed legitimacy to the Washington institution. In the midst of the second oil crisis, McNamara, who in 1981 would bring his mandate to a close, immediately intuited the potential economic consequences of the new situation and the revolution in store for the coming decade. He understood, before the new Republican administration in the USA or the leaders of western Europe themselves, the leadership role that international economic institutions could play once the criticisms of public opinion had been set aside and the pressures placed on the Bretton Woods institutions by the G77 nations had relented. The discussion that took place in the President's Council at the World Bank on February 11, 1980 is instructive, for it reveals—without any unnecessary diplomatic prudence—the reasons behind the new subaltern status of the developing world.[25] McNamara opened the meeting with the affirmation that the primary problem after the oil crisis was that deficits had not been financed, which had led to smaller investments, and thus fewer imports and smaller growth for the developing countries. The President stated that, after weeks of thought, he had come to the conclusion that what was needed was "structural adjustment" loans—that is, loans not for single projects, but to induce macroeconomic changes such as a reduction in spending or a rise in interest rates—in order to intervene rapidly in those developing countries that presented significant balance of payments deficits.[26] This was an innovation pregnant with future possibilities, that would definitely set aside the issues of basic human needs and agreements on commodities. This policy would permit close collaboration with the IMF, built primarily on the imposition of economic choices in line with the interests of the West's largest private creditors. Regarding the future role of the Bank in the 1980s, McNamara observed that all the discussions he had helped stimulate on the new economic order were now "last year's fashion." In light of more recent developments, the Bank would have to occupy itself only with financing the largest balance of payments deficits: "We will find ourselves faced with a new world." And it was no longer necessary to worry about the possible opposition of the developing countries because, to take the example of the Turkish government that, for all its shouting, was "flat on its back," and like the others was well aware of the unavoidable logic that would confront all those reluctant to follow Washington's

---

[25] WBGA, Office of the President, Records of Robert S. McNamara, Minutes 1976–1981, Box 2, "President's Council Meeting," February 11, 1980.

[26] On the way in which structural adjustments became the core business of the World Bank, see N. Woods, *The Globalizers: The IMF, the World Bank, and Their Borrowers* (Ithaca, NY: Cornell University Press, 2006).

prescriptions: "No letter [of intent] → no loan → no democracy → no economy." Even the *Financial Times*'s expert was surprised by the new spirit expressed by the World Bank in its 1981 report:

> Professional cynics might suspect that, in producing a Report which is so much more conservative in approach than some of its predecessors, and with so much emphasis on the need for developing countries to help themselves, the Bank is trimming its sails to the political wind in Washington, and is trying to persuade the Reagan team that 1818 H Street in Washington is not exclusively staffed by communists.[27]

And yet, if this revolution that occurred between 1979 and 1981 is quite evident with hindsight, it is equally clear that not all informed observers or even policymakers immediately understood its relevance.[28] Margaret Thatcher notes in her memoirs: "We were not to know it at the time, but 1981 was the last year of the West's retreat before the axis of convenience between the Soviet Union and the Third World."

THE EUROPEAN SINGLE MARKET PROJECT

Parallel with the disintegration of the united Southern front, a new current of thought was emerging in the United States that would soon reveal itself to be the most significant challenge to the socioeconomic structures developed by the industrialized countries since the Second World War.[29] "Neoconservatism," and the "neoliberalism" which informed its economic thinking, was born as a reaction against the sense of political degeneration and moral relativism that seemed pervasive in American society during the Nixon and Carter years. The new international economic order itself had contributed, according to neoconservatives, to a weakening of America's international prestige and economic strength. Moynihan noted how after the UN Special Session in 1974, "the United States was seen to be reeling back in compounded defeat, incapable of retaliation, unwilling even to contemplate retaliation."[30] In a few short years, this school of political thought would move from the margins to the center of the political stage, arguing against the role of the state, against international cooperation, against the multilateral and transatlantic lobbies represented by the Trilateral Commission and the Bilderberg Group, and proclaiming a "new beginning" in United States history.[31] The Heritage Foundation—a sort of Ford Foundation of the neoconservative movement—was established in 1973, and by 1985 had a staff of 105 and a US$11 million budget, and

[27] I. Davidson, *Financial Times,* July 20, 1981. Davidson also highlights a passage from the Report dedicated to industrial policy in western Europe: "For every $20,000-a-year job saved in Swedish shipyards, Swedish taxpayers pay an estimated $60,000 annual subsidy."

[28] One important book that shows the widespread belief, even among the finest analysists of international relations, in the future of Third World as an increasingly powerful actor of international cooperation at the beginning of the 1980s is H. Bull and A. Watson (eds), *The Expansion of International Society* (Oxford: Clarendon Press, 1984).

[29] M. Del Pero, *The Eccentric Realist. Henry Kissinger and the Shaping of American Foreign Policy* (Ithaca, NY: Cornell University Press, 2009).

[30] Moynihan, *A Dangerous Place,* p. 53.

[31] P. Gerbet, *Le rêve d'un ordre mondial: De la SDN à l'ONU* (Paris: Imprimerie Nationale, 1996), p. 326.

counted some 36 members in government positions.[32] Similarly, in Great Britain, where Margaret Thatcher had been elected in 1979, the think tanks that had supported her candidacy emphasized the need to revive free enterprise and international competition, instruments of liberation from the stranglehold of the unions, and to drive the state out of business and services—while at the same time both Reagan and Thatcher themselves actually increased budgets for security and defense, and were cautious in their approach to welfare.[33] In a speech to the Centre for Policy Studies, the most important intellectual center for British neoliberalism, Nigel Lawson—appointed Chancellor of the Exchequer in 1983—outlined how their epic challenge was to liquidate, along with the postwar social democratic compromise, the entire heritage of the Enlightenment: "The essential point is that what we are witnessing is the reversion to an older tradition in the light of the failure of what might be termed the new enlightenment."[34] Zeev Sternhell warns against underestimating this "anti-enlightenment tradition" that, in essence, called into question the very significance of the French Revolution:

> First of all, there is the classical Burkean critique of utopianism, the defense of the so-called Anglo-American tradition against the French tradition, the critique of egalitarianism, and an assertion of the importance of religion in the life of society and of the centrality of traditional moral values. And together with all this, there is a rejection of what is called the liberal "counterculture," which is held to be opposed to traditional "American values." Nationalism, which admires American power, also takes the form of an out-and-out war against international organizations (especially the United Nations, which endangers national sovereignty), against the dismantling of the nation-state within the framework of the European Union, and against the progressive disappearance of national characteristics. Here one can easily recognize practically all the major themes of Anti-Enlightenment thought from Burke to the mid-twentieth century.[35]

With the victory of Ronald Reagan in the presidential election, and especially after his inauguration in 1981, the United States moved swiftly to adopt a muscular and media-friendly foreign policy, taking a stance of open conflict with the Third World and the "Evil Empire" of international communism. In 1982 Washington finally rejected the UN Convention on the Law of the Sea, of extremely limited utility without American ratification.[36] In January 1985 the United States would formally withdraw from UNESCO, after previously having left and returned to the ILO. The Republican administration seemed initially to harbor the same lack of faith in international economic organizations such as the World Bank, accused

[32] S. Blumenthal, *The Rise of the Counter-Establishment: The Conservative Ascent to Political Power* (New York: Union Square Press, 1986), p. 33.

[33] D. Basosi, "The European Community and International Reaganomics, 1981–85", in K. Patel and K. Weisbrode (eds), *European Integration and the Atlantic Community in the 1980s* (Cambridge: Cambridge University Press, forthcoming 2013).

[34] R. Cockett, *Thinking the Unthinkable: Think-Tanks and the Economic Counter-Revolution, 1931–1983* (London: HarperCollins, 1994), p. 215.

[35] Z. Sternhell, *The Anti-Enlightenment Tradition* (New Haven, CT: Yale University Press, 2009), p. 433.

[36] Krasner, *Structural Conflict*, p. 11.

of wasting American contributions on lavish salaries for stateless civil servants. But the international economic institutions based in Washington would soon reveal themselves to be rather useful at preparing the ground for the revival of freedom of trade, investment, and capital movement.

With unstoppable force the political and economic climate rapidly shifted after 1980, and with it any opportunities for the structural modification of economic relations in favor of the Third World. As the social and cultural tides generated by the global 1968 slowly receded and transformed themselves into something new, the very legitimacy of the rights claimed by the Third World began once more to be called into question.[37] While it is true that 1979 witnessed the publication of Edward Said's *Orientalism*, a groundbreaking classic that would inaugurate an entirely new theoretical field studying Western cultural imperialism, it is equally true that such analyses seemed to be confined to new university departments and editorial houses focusing on "cultural studies" that seemed incapable of generating effective political action. Meanwhile, the 1983 publication of the French writer Pascal Bruckner's *The Tears of the White Man*—which equated European compassion with contempt, derided the notion of decolonization as the liberation of a mythical form of new man, and denounced the unjust and antidemocratic regimes of the Third World—enjoyed spectacular public success.[38] The following year marked the appearance of *La Pensée '68*, which would become a best-selling French diatribe against the "contemporary antihumanism" unleashed by 1968.[39] Such books called into question both Marxism and its philosophy of history, or more broadly any ideology that claimed the mantle of progress by virtue of immutable laws—from communism to socialism—in the name of a focus on the language of individual rights and freedoms.[40] This new language was less respectful of blocs, either that of the Soviets or that of the Third World, and the leadership it referred to no longer considered these blocs as immune from criticism or attack. The Helsinki process itself was by now seen in West Germany not as a guarantee of security or economic cooperation intended to slowly bring about the democratization of communist Europe,[41] but as an offensive weapon to bolster the room for maneuver of dissidents in the Soviet Union.

In 1980, an Italian entrepreneur careful to detect which way the political winds were blowing could allow himself to boast a little about the revival of the West and the need to overcome an otherwise useless sense of guilt at the fate of the poor nations of the world. Development, after all, was only achievable through integration into the capitalist system, with an acceptance of the rules and the political systems of the capitalist countries. Gianni Agnelli, the same

---

[37] K. Ross, *May '68 and Its Afterlives* (Chicago: University of Chicago Press, 2002), pp. 158–69.

[38] P. Bruckner, *The Tears of the White Man: Compassion as Contempt* (New York: Free Press, 1986).

[39] L. Ferry and A. Renaut, *La Pensée '68: Essai sur l'antihumanisme contemporain* (Paris: Gallimard, 1985).

[40] Judt, *Postwar*, pp. 559–66.

[41] T. Garton Ash, *In Europe's Name: Germany and the Divided Continent* (London: Jonathan Cape, 1993), pp. 258–79.

man who five years earlier had been forced to sign the humiliating agreement installing Italy's *scala mobile* (a system of wage and price indexing), declared with renewed faith that:

> [o]ur strongest weapon of attack is economic. But not the weapon of unconditional aid, which has only contributed to the weakness of our currencies, to the clouding of our vision, to the perpetuation of regimes contrary to our principles, to magnify the lack of self-confidence in many of us. Our weapon is the ability to include the South in our way of life...
>
> The foreign and military policy of the West and its industrial policy must be ever-more intertwined.[42]

This new and less conciliatory cultural awareness in the industrialized world did not mean, however, that Europe immediately renounced its intentions to play a role as the fulcrum of the global negotiations with the developing countries. Nor did this mean that western European governments, under strong pressure from internal pacifist movements, did not try to avoid the strong US stance against the Soviet "Empire of Evil" in favor of an approach based on the "interdependence" between capitalist and communist Europe.[43] And it is also true that, while political leaders were becoming ever more disinterested in the potential development of state-led mechanisms of international cooperation in favor of the poorest countries, within civil society an increasing number of citizens were getting involved in nongovernmental organizations (NGOs), hoping to engage in direct cooperation with the developing countries. In the words of the Italian historian Angelo Del Boca, whose many contributions to scholarship have aimed to demolish the myth of Italian colonialism and foreign policy in general as the benign work of "good people," this part of civil society:

> is an army of four million volunteers, who every day, in silence, almost in secret, walk the streets of Italy and the world to combat against suffering in all its guises. It is an army composed of 38,000 organizations...If there are Italians who merit the definition of "good people", in its authentic, non-self-exculpatory, non-mythologizing meaning, then it is these wonderful and humble volunteer workers.[44]

In the South itself, the European Community continued at the beginning of the 1980s to be identified as a privileged partner. In a conference at the Jawaharlal Nehru University in New Delhi organized by circles with ties to the Indian government, the keynote speaker K.B. Lall, former Secretary of Defense and Indian Ambassador to the European Community, reiterated:

> No other entity in the First World is as favourably situated to appreciate the impact of economics on politics or appraise the trade-offs between security and welfare. For this reason, it is the EEC's obligation to sharpen its perceptions, to share them with other industrial nations, and to use the leverage enjoyed by its member states to develop a

[42] G. Agnelli, *Una certa idea dell'Europa e dell'America* (Turin: Einaudi, 2005), pp. 171–2.
[43] Nolan, *The Transatlantic Century*, pp. 308–9.
[44] A. Del Boca, *Italiani, brava gente?* (Vicenza: Neri Pozza, 2005), pp. 303–4.

consensus within the Organization for Cooperation and Development (OECD) in favour of initiatives to spur the global negotiations to successful conclusion.[45]

Even Helmut Schmidt seemed to have understood the need for greater concessions to the Third World in order to resolve the economic emergency and head off a potential global recession created by the second oil crisis. Shortly before UNCTAD V in Havana, over the objections of the liberals in its coalition governing the Federal Republic of Germany, Schmidt presented a global plan for the stabilization of incomes from commodities to the World Bank Development Committee and the IMF: An international system similar to that already operating within Germany's borders, which guaranteed subsidies for unemployment during lean periods.[46]

The conciliatory attitude of European trade unions toward the Community's cooperation and development policy remained intact even in the immediate aftermath of the second oil shock. In a memorandum presented to the European Commission, one expert made note of the peculiarity of the unions' position with respect to development issues.[47] According to this analysis the unions defined development not only as a growth in productivity, but also as "an improvement of the material, moral and cultural resources of men and peoples, with the objective of their complete development as persons." The unions hoped to spare the marginalized classes of the developing countries from the inhumane exploitation suffered by the workers of Europe in the course of the nineteenth century. It was thus necessary to stimulate the workers of the South to build their own organizations and protective safeguards, combat military dictatorships, and push for greater attention to human rights in trade negotiations. Even more importantly, investments in the developing countries would have to be planned in such a way as to be structurally linked to the restructuring of industries in the Western world. With these recommendations in mind, it is not difficult to comprehend the rapid disillusionment with the "renegotiation" of the Lomé Convention. In 1980, after the signing of Lomé II, the ETUC decried the absence of a workers' rights clause in the new agreement, and argued that the goal of guaranteeing income from imports should be widened to include all the developing countries, without being limited to the former colonial nations.[48] The French communist union went much further in its criticism, arguing that the proceeds from stabilization programs had practically all returned to Europe, and that Lomé had finally revealed itself for what it was: A neocolonial scam.[49] The reality was that, even though the question had raised

---

[45] K. Lall, "The EEC, the Third World, and the New International Economic Order," in K. Lall and H. Chopra (eds), *The EEC and the Third World* (Atlantic Highlands, NJ: Humanities Press, 1981), p. xvii.

[46] L.L. Ortmayer, "West Germany and the Third World: Virtues of the Market or New Political Role?," in P. Taylor and G.A. Raymond (eds), *Third World Policies of Industrialized Nations* (Westport, CT: Greenwood Press, 1982), pp. 67–97.

[47] IISH, ETUC, Box 2934, J. Brück, Conseiller de la Dg VIII, "Les orientations fondamentales du mouvement sindacale," June 14, 1977.

[48] IISH, ETUC, Box 2934, "Trade Union Statement on the Lomé II Convention, Geneva," May 30, 1980.

[49] IISH, ETUC, Box 2983, "CGT Déclaration a l'occasion de la reunion du Comité Paritaire a Bordeaux," February 14, 1980.

debates in the European Parliament, Lomé II had confirmed the absence of political conditionality and of human rights clauses in the EC aid scheme.

European labor organizations wanted to influence the Community's policy toward the South, but above all they hoped to have a preponderant voice in the restructuring of European industry. While it was true, as the European Commission led by Roy Jenkins had predicted, that the emerging countries of the South would represent a crucial market for European exports, and would thus contribute to jump-starting growth on the continent, it was equally true that these countries would grab an important share of European manufacturing. There is plenty of evidence to suggest that within the Commission there were those who argued for closer collaboration with the unions in this regard.[50] But European governments never succeeded in putting into practice a common industrial policy. Such efforts went up in smoke at the end of the 1970s, along with the Vredeling directive on workers' participation and information in large-scale industry.[51] Workers employed in manufacturing industries that competed with the South were essentially left to the mercies of international competition.

In June 1980, at the European summit in Venice, the Ten—Greece would officially join in 1981—took a surprisingly innovative position on both recognition of the rights of the Palestinian peoples and the need to revive the North–South dialogue, dormant after the conclusion of the CIEC. They requested an analysis of the conclusions of the Brandt Commission. On the eve of the Tenth Special Session of the UN General Assembly in December 1980, which was set to reopen the as-yet unproductive discussions on the Common Fund for Commodities, the Community was still divided on which strategy to take:

> The fierce insistence with which certain delegations that have not accepted the "consensus" have defended the Bretton Woods institutions from having their autonomy called into question, is not only revealing of the weight of the finance ministers in the governments of the nations in question, but also of the fact that these countries do not accept the idea of the "globality" of negotiations, and that the new North–South dialogue is understood rather as a way to achieve certain very specific adjustments.[52]

The Socialist International, for its part, pursued direct connections with the countries of the Non-Aligned Movement, raising more than a few concerns in Moscow regarding the potential attractive power of a personality like that of Brandt in Latin America.[53] At the conference of socialist party leaders in May 1981, however, the atmosphere was rather tense. The Reagan administration and its new policy of "counterinsurgency" was pushing the world toward a new Cold War. Events in Afghanistan and El Salvador, combined with the Euromissiles crisis, were margin-

---

[50] IISU, ETUC, Box 3009, EC Commission, "Reciprocal implications of the Community's development cooperation policy and its other policies," June 14, 1977.

[51] Francesco Petrini, "Demanding Democracy in the Workplace: The Trade Union Confederation and the Struggle to Regulate Multinationals," in W. Kaiser and J.H. Meyer (eds), *Societal Actors in European Integration 1958–92: From Polity Building to Policy Making*, Basingstoke, Palgrave, 2012.

[52] IISH, ETUC, Box 3011, Commission, DG1, "Onzième session extraordinaire de l'Assemblée générale, New York, 25 Aout–15 Septembre, 1980."

[53] R. Allison, *The Soviet Union and the Strategy of Non-Alignment in the Third World* (Cambridge: Cambridge University Press, 1988), p. 57.

alizing the Socialist International and making its politics of détente seem ever more hollow. The Belgian Karel van Miert underlined how conservative politicians were now comparing détente to the disastrous policy of appeasement at Munich that had failed to halt the spread of Nazism. The conference minutes carefully danced around the issue: "Under the current circumstances it would be imprudent to accentuate any antagonism toward the United States."[54]

The failure of European socialism's internationalist strategy was evident at Cancun, in the meeting held there at the end of 1981. The summit had been organized by the Mexican President Lòpez Portillo, the Canadian Prime Minister Pierre Trudeau, and the Austrian President Bruno Kreisky with the firm intention of reviving the North–South dialogue at the highest levels and of discussing the future concrete reforms inspired by the Brandt Commission. All of the world's most powerful leaders were present at the seaside resort meeting, twenty-two heads of state or government in total, including Reagan and Thatcher. Mitterrand with his cries against "international economic Darwinism" and his call for expansion in international aid and commodity agreements was, with Trudeau, the only hope for the success of global negotiations.[55] But France's position was not a majority one among industrialized countries, many of which by then shared the World Bank's new position that developing countries should open up and help themselves and that decreasing trade barriers and open capital markets would be the best means to favor global growth. In fact, the Cancun summit marked the end of debate on a new international economic order. The primary roadblock was Reagan, not only for his personal ideological aversion to the United Nations, but because solutions on commodities or questions of international debt would be expensive for, and call into question the centrality of, the international economic institutions based in Washington, in which the United States had a much stronger position than in other international forums.[56]

In 1981, the Commission's delegation to Washington reported that the American strategy in the North–South dialogue had changed, from "talking them to death" to "making a stand."[57] For their part the Community nations, after having promoted the Lomé Convention in 1975 and the Paris conference until 1977, appeared in the following years to have lost the ability and the desire to act under the auspices of the UN, concentrating primarily instead on the protection of Western economic institutions. The 1981 report clarified the new European strategy, which was fixed on the more modest goal of influencing the American position: "We must maintain pressure on the Americans to favor cautious progress on North–South affairs, strong international economic institutions, and real multilateral assistance."

[54] IISH, SI 976, Ger Verhoeve, "Report on Party Leaders' Conference in Amsterdam," May 26, 1981.

[55] 5 AG 4, 4273, Note, "Préparation du sommet de Cancun; aspects commerciaux," September 28, 1981.

[56] Interview with Henri Nau (Senior Staff Member of the NSC in the White House responsible for Economic Affairs from 1981–3). Available online at <www.g7.utoronto.ca/oralhistory/nau040507.html>.

[57] IISH, ETUC, Box 2934, Washington Delegation, "North–South Policy: A Source of EC–US Friction," May 1, 1981.

In a 1982 meeting of the Presidium of the Socialist International, Brandt spoke explicitly of an *impasse* on three fronts in the elaboration of the socialists' strategy.[58] First, there was no agreement on how to behave toward the emergent anticommunist *Solidarnosc* (Solidarity) movement in Poland; pressures were strong to adopt a pro-Western stance. In Latin America, many were asking themselves how credible the International could be in its efforts to overcome its predominantly Eurocentric stance. And finally, on the North–South dialogue:

> The fundamental message of my Report, which was published two years ago now, and led to the Cancun meeting last October, has not yet led to any concrete action. The global negotiations in the United Nations have not yet begun. In the meantime, the situation of many citizens in many countries has become almost hopeless.

The memorandum presented in 1982 by the Development Commissioner Edgar Pisani can thus be considered a kind of eulogy for the EC's global cooperation policy. Pisani argued that global North–South negotiations were being blocked by renewed interest in the Cold War, and that a new, regional, political dialogue should have been set up between the EC and the ACP countries participating in Lomé. The debates over the memorandum proved that while there was no agreement on which path to take—and that British opposition to any role for the EC in political negotiations with the Global South (which could lead to impossible financial commitments) would be outspoken—the only idea that could receive approval was that of rendering aid to Lomé countries conditional upon some form of political cooperation. This signaled a definitive break with the position the EC had held since the 1970s of the unconditionalility of European aid, and the opening of an entirely different era in development and cooperation politics.[59]

By the middle of the 1980s, Europeans had to face several fresh challenges from a new kind of modernity:

> Immigration began to outpace emigration. Secularization jumped forward. Women turned from the married kitchen to the labor market and to individual emancipation. Labour demands expanded and contracted. Industrial employment peaked and descended. The working class reached its strongest position ever, and soon lost it. The boom culminated and went into its first crises. Socialist radicalism exploded and imploded. Post-war right-wing liberalism and moderate conservatism were discredited by the left, and re-emerged, invigorated, in a much more militant form.[60]

---

[58] IISH, SI 977, Willy Brandt, "Introductory Remarks at the Presidium Meeting of the Socialist International in Bonn on April 1, 1982," April 2, 1982.

[59] For the debates on the Pisani memorandum, see G. Migani, "Les Accords de Lomé et les relations eurafricaines: Du dialogue Nord–Sud aux droits de l'homme," in G.H. Soutou and E. Robin-Hivert (eds), *L'Afrique indépendante dans le système international* (Paris: PUPS, 2011). The increasing role of multilateral aid as a proportion of total western European aid halted at the beginning of the 1980s (quando si introducono le cluaole . . .).

[60] G. Therborn, *European Modernity and Beyond: The Trajectory of European Societies, 1945–2000* (London: SAGE Publications, 1995), p. 351; cited in C. Crouch, *Social Change in Western Europe* (Oxford: Oxford University Press, 1999), pp. 44–5. On the changes to European society from the 1970s to the 1980s see H. Kaelble, *Sozialgeschichte Europas. 1945 bis zur Gegenwart* (Munich: C.H. Beck Verlag, 2007), pp. 414–15.

European integration was going through one of its worst crisis: "Eurosclerosis" did in fact set in from 1979 to 1984. In the preceding decade the Nine's efforts to reinforce a European identity and develop a new institutional model had been continuous, and not without success. Conversely, in the early 1980s the countries of western Europe, France above all, were beset by strong protectionist pressures, such that they were willing to postpone indefinitely the entry of Spain and Portugal into the Community. Schmidt considered the admission of Greece, the cradle of Western democracy and civilization, so "important" that in a meeting with Jenkins he voiced his wish to impede the free circulation of Greeks into other Community nations: "there should never be full freedom of access... He did not consider Germany to be a country of immigration."[61] Thatcher had very quickly demonstrated the characteristics that made her the "Iron Lady." At the first European Council in which she took part, she harangued her European colleagues for four consecutive hours with demands and accusations, finally obtaining acknowledgment that the question of Britain's contribution to the Community budget would be among the first to be resolved at the earliest possible opportunity.[62] Thatcher had been prepared to block any Community decision until her demands were satisfied. Mitterrand's France seemed committed to advancing the progress of a European social agenda, in parallel with its internal efforts at socialist planning and strengthening of the public sector. This strategy went against the political currents then sweeping Europe, defying international monetary speculation and contrasting sharply with the reality of the shifting balance of power among social forces, which saw workers' organizations suffering dramatic defeats: In Italy, with the breaking of the Fiat strike in 1980, in Britain in 1984, and Sweden, with the failure of the Meidner plan in 1983. It was a period of intense conflict between two different concepts of Europe, the British and the French, as evidenced by the Dutch Prime Minister Ruud Lubbers's recollection of the Copenhagen summit of 1982:

> Right from the start of that meeting, there was this incredible tension between Thatcher and Mitterrand. The crux of Mitterrand's arguments was that investing in Europe meant turning our back on America, discovering our own strengths, protecting ourselves. After that, and on that basis, one could start initiating dialogues outside Europe. His story, in short, was an anti-American one. Our own strengths first. Thatcher said: "Rubbish. Rot. Open the doors. Free trade."[63]

Once France—with its choice of monetary "discipline" in 1983, and consequent renunciation of its plans to build "socialism in one country"—had taken a series of steps to re-enter the European Monetary System, moving in the direction of traditional Europeanism and reviving its axis with Germany, all of Europe's leaders

---

[61] HAEU, EN 1148, Commission of the European Communities, Office of the President, Crispin Tickell, "Call by the President of the European Commission on the Federal German Chancellor, Chancellor's Office," Bonn, October 27, 1978.

[62] Young, *This Blessed Plot*, pp. 306–74.

[63] G. Mak, *In Europe: Travels Through the Twentieth Century*, trans. Sam Garrett (New York: Pantheon Books, 2007), pp. 727–8.

committed themselves to finding a new project behind which to align the process of European integration.[64]

The great idea behind which Europe's leaders hitched the carriage of integration was that of the Single Market. This new concept permitted them to align the ambitions of those who hoped to strengthen the Brussels institutions to manage European economic stagnation and respond to the challenge of international economic competition, with the more widely diffuse desires of those who pushed for a revival of the "animal spirit" of freedom of enterprise and the market. The business world was in fact applying intense pressure, especially those industries facing a stiff challenge from more technologically advanced competitors in Japan and the United States.[65] These forces pushed for a revival of the internal market, against that inert mass of regulations that severely restricted the movement of capital and services, and against the paralyzing presence of the public sector in the economy.[66] It was in 1983 that seventeen businessmen, among them Visse Dekker of Philips and Umberto Agnelli of Fiat, met in Volvo's boardroom in Paris to create the European Round Table (ERT) of industrialists. Their objective was to promote wider opening of the market as well as increase investment in infrastructure and technology at the European level. Their catchphrase was "modernization" to "break the stagnation of the European economy." It was not so much the creation of an exclusive salon of high-level authorities from the business world that made the ERT innovative; we have already noted the origins of the Bilderberg Group and the Trilateral Commission. The novelty was that, in contrast to these transatlantic associations, the ERT emphasized the coherence of producers' and European business's interests. Keith Middlemas has noted how Jean Monnet's Action Committee was refounded in 1979 to include for the first time a number of industrialists, and how pressures from various industrial lobbies were central to the revival of European integration in the mid-1980s.[67] In support of such initiatives, in 1983 the European Parliament formed a working group that, with the name of the Kangaroo Group, gave itself the specific goal of promoting the removal of trade barriers—thus permitting goods to hop across Community borders more quickly. This impulse toward freedom of commerce and of investment would eventually guarantee that by the year 2000 the growth of exports would reach some 40 percent of Germany's GDP and 29 percent of that of France. Trade increases were accompanied by a parallel rise in financial transactions to the point that, where they had represented only 3 percent of global GDP in 1973, they reached a massive 149 percent only fifteen years later.[68]

---

[64] G. Saunier, "The Place of Vocational Training in François Mitterrand's Idea of a European Social Space (1981–1984)," in (2004) 32 *European Journal of Vocational Training* (May–August), pp. 77–83.

[65] K. Seitz, *Die japanisch-amerikanische Herausforerung: Deutschlands Hochtechnologieindustren kämpfen ums Überleben* (Stuttgart: Bonn Aktuell, 1990).

[66] Many studies highlight how the Single Market agenda was headed principally by global private enterprise. See J. Gillingham, *European Integration, 1950–2003: Superstate or New Market Economy?* (Cambridge: Cambridge University Press, 2003), pp. 231–49; B. van Apeldoorn, *Transnational Capitalism and the Struggle over European Integration* (London: Routledge, 2002).

[67] K. Middlemas, *Orchestrating Europe: The Informal Politics of the European Union 1973–1995* (London: Fontana Press, 1995), p. 102.

[68] Berend, *Economic History of 20th Century Europe*, pp. 290–1.

The other important piece in this revival of European integration was the choice of Jacques Delors as President of the Commission in 1985. An accomplished trade-unionist and politician, he understood firsthand the internal dynamics of organized labor and the contradictions within the socialist archipelago. With the help of the British Commissioner for the Internal Market, and in a college in which no socialist held a high-profile post, he emphatically placed at the center of his agenda the Single Market project, the enlargement to include Spain and Portugal, and the increase of aid disbursements to the poorest regions within the European Community.[69] In his memoirs, Delors explained his strategy thus:

> The growth of markets and deregulation will happen with or without us. The wind blowing in that direction is strong. It is a question of whether the pilot of the ship can react to the wind and find a course that will be a good compromise between the evolution of the international environment and ideas, on the one hand, and the defense of our interests and the European model, on the other.[70]

So it was in the middle of the 1980s that—to borrow Lucien Febvre's concept of the broad-shouldered European striding forward by flaunting his "civilization" and "organization"—the European Community took another step forward with a dramatic "organizational push": Widening to include the countries of southern Europe (Spain and Portugal joined in 1986); committing itself to the fiscal and economic discipline of the EMS; perfecting an internal market without customs barriers and with more limited room for state intervention. This new organizational impulse, made concrete by the Single Market project and signature of the Single European Act in 1986—the first reform of the Treaties since 1957—would contribute to profound changes in the daily lives of European citizens. These changes finally confirmed both Aldo Moro's concerns regarding the technocratic nature and ambiguous identity of the integration process, and Ambassador Henderson's warnings about the strength of the Common Market as an indispensable instrument to foster economic competitiveness and technological advancement.

On May 29, 1986 at the Berlaymont Palace, Jacques Delors, the President of the European Commission, unveiled the Community's new flag—with its circle of twelve golden stars on a blue background—while Beethoven's "Ode to Joy" rang out for the first time as Europe's new anthem. At the end of the ceremony, Delors addressed the European media with proud and almost defiant words: "Europe has acquired a size that will allow it to face the modern world and maintain its proper status."[71] Only one year earlier, all the original founders of the EC except Italy had signed the Schengen Agreement allowing for the free movement of people among the participating countries. On a more symbolic level, Schengen also represented the first official divide between citizens of the European Community and those who the Italians, with a subtle note of contempt, would soon define as *extracomunitari* (illegal aliens).

---

[69] C. Grant, *Delors: Inside the House that Jacques Built* (London: Nicholas Brealey Publishing, 1994), p. 70.
[70] J. Delors, *Mémoires* (Paris: Plon, 2004), p. 203.
[71] C. Lager, *L'Europe en quête de ses symboles* (Berne: Peter Lang, 1995), p. 57.

Toward the end of the 1980s Mikhail Gorbachev launched his project for a "Common European Home," implicitly renouncing global ideological competition and calling for greater strategic and economic collaboration with western Europe. In a 1988 speech to eastern European leaders, he admitted: "To the west of our borders there is a new giant developing, one with a population of 350 million people, which surpasses us in its level of economic, scientific and technological growth."[72] A year later, in his speech at the Council of Europe, that embodiment of the idea of Europe from the Atlantic to the Urals, Gorbachev spoke about European unity along the lines of Victor Hugo and of the need to defend national sovereignty:

> Let us not forget, however, that the curse of colonial slavery spread worldwide from Europe. Fascism was born here. The most devastating wars began here. Europe may take legitimate pride in its accomplishments, but it has far from paid all its debts to humankind. This is yet to be done. This is to be done by pressing for changes in international relations in the spirit of humanism, equality and justice and by setting an example of democracy and social achievements in their own countries.[73]

But by that point, there was no room for collaboration between two different social and economic systems in Europe. The nations of the European Community had decided to launch their own new strategy as a response to the explosive structural changes in international economic relations and within European politics and society at the end of the 1970s. This strategy allowed for less economic sovereignty for nation states and asked for more homogeneity. Antifascism and "the burden of colonialism" were concepts entirely out of tune with the revisionistic cultural and political atmosphere prevailing in western Europe.[74]

The audacious project of the Single Market that contributed to changing so dramatically the everyday lives of ordinary European citizens, as well as broader European social and political structures, would soon demonstrate all its appeal and challenging force: For trade unions and political parties, for those university students enthusiastically enrolled in study abroad through the Erasmus program,[75] and even for those living in the communist countries of eastern Europe. At the same time, from a longer-term perspective, it is justifiable to retain doubts about whether Europe—a civilization in continuous expansion since the sixteenth century, which in 1939 still directly controlled somewhere between 60 and 70 percent of the globe—would recover its cultural vitality, faith in progress, and popular appeal, after its defeat in the Second World War and the further contraction of

---

[72] M. Cox, "Who Won the Cold War in Europe? A Historiographical Overview," in F. Bozo, M.P. Rey, N.P. Ludlow, and L. Nuti (eds), *Europe and the End of the Cold War: A Reappraisal* (London: Routledge, 2008), p. 14.

[73] "Document No.73: Address by Mikhail Gorbachev to the Council of Europe in Strasbourg, July 6, 1989" in S. Savranskaya, T. Blanton, and V. Zubok (eds), *Masterpieces of History: The Peaceful End of the Cold War in Europe, 1989* (Budapest: Central European Univerity Press, 2010), p. 493.

[74] For some insightful comments on the cultural changes in the "core" European countries during the 1980s, see P. Anderson, *The New Old World* (London: Verso, 2009).

[75] S. Paoli, *Il sogno di Erasmo. La questione educative nel processo di integrazione europea* (Milan: Franco Angeli, 2010).

decolonization, that would allow it to construct a new—and this time peaceful—model for the rest of the world.[76] Certainly the European Community had strengthened itself, but it had not managed to become the center of a new universalism, in a world with new regional actors that were now imposing themselves on the two superpowers of the Cold War. This was perhaps a task beyond Europe's reach, which only the optimism that followed the social explosion of the global 1968 had made seem possible and which had inspired the optimistic declarations of the 1972 Paris Summit.[77] In his book *Capital Rules*, Rawi Abdelal describes the struggle between "ad hoc" and "managed" financial globalization in the 1980s. The US, and to a certain extent the UK, preferred an "ad hoc" approach based on hands-free for their rich financial institutions so that they could operate freely on the international markets. Their underlying idea was that, eventually, profit-making by private banks would prove beneficial to the home country. The French, on the other hand—especially after Mitterrand's failed efforts in establishing "socialism in one country"—started to support the free movement of capital, but within the rules set by multilateral institutions such as the IMF. In fact three or four of the main "globalizers" of finance in the 1980s were French.[78] The Single Market project was based on the same idea: a reversal of the "embedded liberalism" of the first Bretton Woods era. It implied deregulation and reduction of the role of the state within the Single Market area, and at the same time an effort to impose an EC point of view in the international economic institutions that set the rules of globalization.

[76] See S. Lucarelli, "The EU in the Eyes of Others: Towards Filling a Gap in the Literature," in (2007) 3(20) *European Foreign Affairs Review*, pp. 249–70.

[77] E.W. Said, *Reflections on Exile, and Other Essays* (Cambridge, MA: Harvard University Press, 2000), p. 432.

[78] Rawi Abdelal, *Capital Rules. The Construction of Global Finance* (Cambridge: Harvard University Press, 2007).

Bibliography

ARCHIVES CONSULTED

Algeria
Archives Nationales d'Algérie (ANA), Algiers
   Fond Abdessalam

France
Archives Ministère des Affaires Etrangères Français (AMAEF), Paris
    Direction des affaires économiques et financières
    Nations Unies et Organisations Internationales (NUOI)
Centre Historique des Archives Nationales (CHAN), Paris
Fond François Mitterrand (5AG4)
Fond Giscard d'Estaing (5AG3)

European Union
    Comité Economique et Sociale Européen (CES), Brussels
Union of Industrial and Employers' Confederations of Europe (UNICE)
Council of the European Union (CEU), Brussels
    Conference for International Economic Cooperation (CIEC)
Historical Archives of the European Commission (HAEC), Brussels
    Bureau Archives Commission (BAC)
    Cabinet Cheysson
Historical Archives of the European Union (HAEU), Florence
    Edoardo Martino (EM)
    Emile Nöel (EN)
    Franco Maria Malfatti (FMM)
    European Commission (BAC)
    High Authority of the European Coal and Steel Community (CEAB)
    Organization for Economic Cooperation and Development (OECD)
    The Council of Ministers (CM)

Italy
Archivio Centrale dello Stato (ACS), Rome
   Fondo Moro
Archivio Storico della Banca d'Italia (ASBI), Rome
   Direttorio Carli
Fondazione dell'Istituto Gramsci (FIG), Rome
   Archivio Partito Comunista Italiano (APC)

United Kingdom
National Archives (NA), London
   Board of Trade (BT)
   Foreign and Commonwealth Office (FCO)
   Foreign Office (FO)

United States
Gerald R. Ford Library (GFL), Ann Arbor, MI
    Country Files
    National Security Advisor (NSA)
    Office of Economic Advisors (OEA)
Jimmy Carter Library (JCL), Atlanta, GA
    National Security Advisor (NSA)
    White House Central Files (WHCF)
National Archives and Records Administration (NARA), Washington, D.C.
    Central Intelligence Agency (CIA)
    Central Policy Files (CPF)

Venezuela
Archivos Histórico Ministerio Poder Popular para Relaciones Exteriores (AHMPPRE),
Caracas

International Economic, Political, and Social Organizations
Archivio Ente Nazionale Idrocarburi (ENI), Pomezia
    Estero
Archives du Groupe Total (TOTAL), Paris
Food and Agriculture Organization (FAO), Rome
    Economic and Social Committee (ESC)
International Institute of Social History (IISH), Amsterdam
    European Trade Union Confederation (ETUC)
    Socialist International (SI)
United Nations Office in Geneva (UNOG), Geneva
    United Nations Conference for Trade and Development (UNCTAD)
World Bank Group Archives (WBGA), Washington, D.C.
    Records of George Woods
    Records of Robert S. McNamara

Internet Sources:
    Archive of European Integration in Pittsburg:
    <http:// aei.pitt.edu>
    Cold War International History Project:
    <http:// http://www.wilsoncenter.org/program/cold-war-international-history-project>
    European Oral History (European Commission 1958–72)
    < http://www.eui.eu/HAEU/EN/OralHistory.asp>
    European Navigator:
    < http://www.cvce.eu/>
    G8 Information Centre:
    <http://www.g7.utoronto.ca>
    Margaret Thatcher Foundation:
    < http://www.margaretthatcher.org/archive/default.asp>
    National Security Archive:
    <http://gwu.edu/~nsarchiv/>
    Open Society Archives:
    <http://files.osa.ceu.hu/holdings/>

NEWSPAPERS AND PERIODICALS

The Black Dwarf (London)
Corriere della Sera (Milan)
The Courier (Brussels)
The Daily Telegraph (London)
Financial Times (London)
The Guardian (London)
The Independent (London)
La Libre Belgique (Brussels)
Le Monde (Paris)
Le Nouvel Observateur (Paris)
La Repubblica (Rome)
Le Soir (Brussels)
Newsweek (New York)
Politica Internazionale (Rome)

SECONDARY WORKS

Abdelal, Rawi, *Capital Rules. The Construction of Global Finance*. Cambridge: Harvard University Press, 2007.

Abernethy, David, *The Dynamics of Global Governance: European versus Overseas Empires 1415–1980*. New Haven, CT: Yale University Press, 2001.

Abrahamian, Ervand, *A History of Modern Iran*. Cambridge: Cambridge University Press, 2008.

Adda, Jacques, and Marie-Claude Smouts, *La France face au Sud*. Paris: Karthala, 1989.

Ageron, Charles Robert. *La décolonisation française*. Paris: Armand Colin, 1991.

Ageron, Charles Robert and Marc Michel (eds), *L'ère des décolonisations* (Paris: Editions Karthala, 1995).

Agnelli, Giovanni, *Una certa idea dell'Europa e dell'America*. Turin: Einaudi, 2005.

Aissaoui, Abdelkader, *Algeria. The Political Economy of Oil and Gas*. Oxford: Oxford University Press, 2001.

Alacevich, Michele, *The Political Economy of the World Bank: The Early Years*, trans. The World Bank. Palo Alto, CA: Stanford University Press, 2009.

Albers, Detlev, Werner Goldschmidt, and Paul Oehlke, *Lotte sociali in Europa 1968–1974*. Rome: Editori Riuniti, 1976.

Aldcroft, Derek, *The European Economy 1914–2000*. London: Routledge, 2001.

Allen, David, "Political Cooperation and the Euro-Arab Dialogue," in David Allen, Reinhard Rummel, and Wolfgang Wessels (eds), *European Political Cooperation*. London: Butterworth Scientific, 1982.

Allison, Roy, *The Soviet Union and the Strategy of Non-Alignment in the Third World*. Cambridge: Cambridge University Press, 1988.

Al-Rasheed, Madawi, *A History of Saudi Arabia*. Cambridge: Cambridge University Press, 2002.

Anderson, Perry, *The New Old World* (London: Verso, 2009).

Andrew, Christopher, *The World Was Going Our Way: The KGB and the Battle for the Third World*. New York: Basic Books, 2005.

ARA, *Atti del convegno Quale socialismo, quale Europa*, November 1975. Milan: Feltrinelli, 1977.

Ardant, Gabriel, "La réforme des échanges internationaux par la création d'un fonds de stabilization des matières premières," in (1962) 9–10 *Tiers Monde*.

Arens, E.H., "Multilateral Institution-Building and National Interest: Dutch Development Policy in the 1960s," in (2003) 12(4) *Contemporary European History*, 457.

Arfè, Gaetano (ed.), *Brandt, Kreisky, Palme: Quale Socialismo per l'Europa*. Cosenza: Lerici, 1976.

Arndt, H.W., *Economic Development. The History of an Idea*. Chicago: University of Chicago Press, 1987.

Aron, Raymond, *Plaidoyer pour l'Europe décadente*. Paris: Robert Laffont, 1977.

Asor Rosa, Alberto, *Storia europea della letteratura italiana*, vol. III. Turin: Einaudi, 2009.

Attiga, Ali A., *Interdependence on the Oil Bridge: Risks and Opportunities*. Kuwait: Petroleum Information Committee of the Arab Gulf States, 1988.

Bade, Klaus, *Migration in European History*. Basingstoke: Palgrave, 2003.

Bagnato, Bruna, "Alcune considerazioni sull'anticolonialismo italiano," in Ennio Di Nolfo, R.H. Rainero, and Brunello Vigezzi (eds), *L'Italia e la politica di potenza in Europa (1950–60)*. Milan: Marzorati, 1992, 289.

Bagnato, Bruna, *Mattei in Morocco*. Florence: Edizioni Polistampa, 2004.

Bagnato, Bruna, *L'Europa e il mondo. Origini, sviluppo e crisi dell'imperialismo coloniale*. Milan: Le Monnier, 2006.

Bairoch, Paul, *Rivoluzione industriale e sottosviluppo*. Turin: Einaudi, 1967.

Bairoch, Paul, *Storia economica e sociale del mondo. Vittorie e insuccessi dal XVI secolo ad oggi*. Turin: Einaudi, 1999.

Ballini, Pier Luigi, and Antonio Varsori (eds), *L'Italia e l'Europa*, vol. 2. Rubbettino: Soveria Mannelli, 2004.

Bamberg, James, *British Petroleum and Global Oil, 1950–1975: The Challenge of Nationalism*. Cambridge: Cambridge University Press, 2000.

Banchi, Sara, "Intergovernmental confrontation in the UN framework: How many 'Europes'!," in Michele Affinito, Guia Migani, and Christian Wenkel (eds), *Les Deux Europes/The Two Europes*. Brussels: Peter Lang, 2009.

Barraclough, Geoffrey, *An Introduction to Contemporary History*. London: C.A. Watts, 1964.

Basosi, Duccio, *Il governo del dollaro. Interdipendenza economica e potere statunitense negli anni di Richard Nixon (1969–1973)*. Firenze: Polistampa, 2006.

Bayley, C. A., *The Birth of the Modern World 1780–1914: Global Connections and Comparisons*. Maldon: Blackwell Publishing, 2004.

Bedjaoui, Mohammed, *Towards a New International Economic Order*. Paris: UNESCO, 1979.

Bello, Walden, *Deglobalization: Ideas for a New World Economy*. London: Zed Books, 2002.

Benn, Tony, *Arguments for Socialism*. Harmondsworth: Penguin, 1980.

Bennoune, Mahfoud, *The Making of Contemporary Algeria 1830–1987*. Cambridge: Cambridge University Press Middle East Library, 1988.

Berend, Ivan, *An Economic History of Twentieth-Century Europe*. Cambridge: Cambridge University Press, 2006.

Bergère, Marie Claire, *Storia della Cina dal 1949 ai giorni nostri*. Bologna: Il Mulino, 2003.

Berghahn, Volker R., *America and the Intellectual Cold Wars in Europe. Shepard Stone Between Philanthropy, Academy and Diplomacy*. Princeton, NJ: Princeton University Press, 2001.

Bergmann, Uwe (ed.), *La ribellione degli studenti*. Milan: Feltrinelli, 1968.

Berlinguer, Enrico, *La political internazionale dei comunisti italiani*. Rapporto al XIV Congresso del PCI, 18 marzo 1975. Rome: Editori Riuniti, 1976.

Bhagwati, Jagdish (ed.), *The New International Economic Order: The North–South Debate*. Cambridge, MA: MIT Press, 1977.

Bitsch, Marie-Thérèse, *Histoire de la construction européenne de 1945 a nos jours*. Paris: Ed. Complexe, 2004.

Blanchard, Francis, *L'Organisation internationale du travail. De la guerre froide à un nouvel ordre mondial*. Paris: Seuil, 2004.

Block, Fred, *The Origins of International Economic Disorder: A Study of United States International Monetary Policy from World War II to the Present*. Berkeley: University of California Press, 1977.

Blumenthal, Sidney, *The Rise of the Counter-Establishment: The Conservative Ascent to Political Power*. New York: Union Square Press, 1986.

Boesche, Roger (ed.), *Alexis de Tocqueville: Selected Letters on Politics and Society*, trans. James Toupin. Berkeley: University of California Press, 1985.

Borring Olesen, T., "Between Words and Deeds: Denmark and the NIEO agenda 1974–1982," in H. Pharo and M. Pohle Fraser (eds), *The Aid Rush, Aid Regimes in Northern Europe during the Cold War*, vol. I (Oslo: Unipubl, 2008), 145.

Bösch, Frank, "Umbrüche in die Gegenwart. Globale Ereignisse und Krisenreaktionen um 1979" in (2012) 1 *Zeithistorische Forschungen*.

Bossuat, Gérard, "French Development Aid and Cooperation under de Gaulle," in (2003) 4 *Contemporary European History* 431.

Bossuat, Gérard, and Marie-Thérèse Bitsch (eds), *L'Europe unie et l'Afrique. De l'idée d'Eurafrique à la Convention de Lomé I*. Brussels: Bruylant, 2005.

Boué, Juan Carlos, "OPEC at (More Than) Fifty: The Long Road to Baghdad, and Beyond," (2010) 83 *Oxford Energy Forum*.

Bracke, Maud, *Which socialism, whose détente? European Communists and the 1968 Czechoslovak Crisis*, Budapest, Central University Press, 2010.

Brandt Commission, *North–South: A Program for Survival*, The Independent Commission on International Development Issues (Cambridge, MA: MIT Press, 1980).

Braudel, Fernand (ed.), *La Méditerranée. L'Espace et l'Histoire*. Paris: Flammarion, 1985.

Braudel, Fernand, *Civilization and Capitalism, 15th–18th Century*, Vol. II: *The Wheels of Commerce*. Berkeley: University of California Press, 1992.

Braunthal, Gerard, *The West German Social Democrats, 1969–1982. Profile of a Party in Power*. Boulder, CO: Westview Press, 1983.

Braunthal, Julius, *History of the International 1943–1968*. London: Victor Gollancz, 1980.

Brogi, Alessandro, *L'Italia e l'egemonia Americana nel Mediterraneo*. Florence: La Nuova Italia, 1996.

Bruckner, Pascal, *The Tears of the White Man: Compassion as Contempt*. New York: Free Press, 1986.

Brzezinski, Zbigniew, *Power and Principle*. London: Weidenfeld & Nicolson, 1983.

Bull, Hedley and Adam Watson (eds), *The Expansion of International Society* (Oxford: Clarendon Press, 1984).

Burke, Roland, "From Individual Rights to National Development: The First UN Conference on Human Rights, Tehran, 1968," in (2008) 19(3) *Journal of World History*.

Burke, Roland, *Decolonization and the Evolution of International Human Rights*. Philadelphia: University of Pennsylvania Press, 2010.

Byrne, Jeffrey James, "Our Own Special Brand of Socialism: Algeria and the Contest of Modernities in the 1960s," in (2009) 33(9) *Diplomatic History* 427.

Calandri, Elena, "Europa e Mediterraneo tra giustapposizione e integrazione," in Massimo de Leonardis (ed.), *Il Mediterraneo nella politica estera italiana dal secondo dopoguerra.* Bologna: Il Mulino, 2003, 47.

Calandri, Elena, "Italy's Foreign Aid Policy 1959–1969," in (2003) 12(4) *Contemporary European History* 509.

Calandri, Elena, "La CEE et les relations extérieures 1958–1960", in Antonio Varsori (ed.), *Inside the European Community. Actors and Policies in European Integration 1957–1972.* Baden Baden: Nomos/Bruylant, 2005, 399.

Calandri, Elena, "L'Italia e l'assistenza allo sviluppo dal neoatlantismo alla Conferenza di Cancun del 1981," in Federico Romero and Antonio Varsori (eds), *Nazione, inter-dipendenza, integrazione. Le relazioni internazionali dell'Italia (1917–1989)*, vol. 1. Rome: Carocci, 2005, 253.

Calchi Novati, Gian Paolo, *Decolonizzazione e Terzo Mondo.* Rome and Bari: Laterza, 1979.

Calchi Novati, Gian Paolo, *Storia dell'Algeria indipendente: Dalla guerra di liberazione al fondamentalismo islamico.* Milan: Bompiani, 1998.

Calchi-Novati, Gian Paolo and Lia Quartapelle, *La conferenza afro-asiatica di Bandung in una prospettiva storica.* Rome: Carocci, 2007.

Calleo, David P., "America, Europe and the Oil Crisis: Hegemony Reaffirmed?" in James Chace and Earl C. Ravenal (eds), *Atlantis Lost: US–European Relations after the Cold War.* New York: New York University Press, 1976.

Calvocoressi, Peter, *World Politics Since 1945.* London: Longman, 1996.

Camus, Albert, *American Journals*, trans. Hugh Levick. New York: Paragon, 1987.

Carli, Guido, *Cinquant'anni di vita italiana.* Bari: Laterza, 1996.

Carr, E.H., *What is History?* New York: Vintage, 1961.

Casadio, G.P., "Presente e futuro delle materie prime," in (1974) 3 *Politica internazionale* 36.

Castro, Fidel and Ignacio Ramonet, *My Life: A Spoken Autobiography*, trans. Andrew Hurley. New York: Scribner, 2008.

Cavallari, Alberto, *La Francia a sinistra.* Milan: Garzanti, 1977.

Caviglia, Daniele and Giuliano Garavini, "Generosi ma non troppo. La Cee, i Paesi in via di sviluppo e i negoziati sulla riforma del Sistema monetario internazionale (1958–1976)," in Elena Calandri (ed.), *Il primato sfuggente. L'Europa e l'intervento per lo sviluppo (1957–2007).* Milan: Franco Angeli, 2009, 53.

Caviglia, Daniele and Antonio Varsori (eds.), *Dollari, petrolio e aiuti allo sviluppo. Il confronto Nord–Sud negli anni '60–'70.* Milan: Franco Angeli, 2008.

Centro di Informazioni Universitarie (ed.), *Documenti della rivolta studentesca francese.* Bari: Laterza, 1969.

Cesari, Laurent, "Que disait la Trilatérale?," in (2000) 1 *Revue d'histoire diplomatique* 80.

Chaban-Delmas, Jacques, *Mémoires pour demain.* Paris: Flammarion, 1997.

Chassaigne, Philippe, *Les années 1970. Fin d'un monde et origine de notre modernité.* Paris: Armand Colin, 2008.

Chenaux, Philippe, "Les democrats-chrétiens au niveau de l'Union Europèenne," in Emiel Lamberts (ed.), *Christian Democracy in the European Union 1945–1995.* Leuven: Leuven University Press, 1997.

Chevalier, Jean-Marie, *Les grandes batailles de l'énergie.* Paris: Gallimard, 2004.

Chipman, John, *French Power in Africa.* Oxford: Blackwell, 1989.

Ciampani, Andrea, *La Cisl tra integrazione europea e mondializzazione. Profilo storico del "sindacato nuovo" nelle relazioni internazionali: Dalla Conferenza di Londra al Trattato di Amsterdam*. Rome: Edizioni Lavoro, 2000.

Cockett, Richard, *Thinking the Unthinkable: Think-Tanks and the Economic Counter-Revolution, 1931–1983*. London: HarperCollins, 1994.

Cohen, Samy and Marie-Claude Smouts (eds), *La politique extérieure de Valéry Giscard d'Estaing*. Paris: Presses de Science Politiques, 1985.

Cohn, Theodore, *Governing Global Trade. International Institutions in Conflict and Convergence*. Burlington, VT: Ashgate, 2002.

Cohn-Bendit, Daniel, *Forget 68*. Paris: Editions de l'Aube, 2008.

Colard, Daniel, "Le mouvement des pays non-alignés," (1981) 4613 *Notes et études documentaires*.

Colitti, Marcello, "Lo sviluppo condizionato dalla logica del profitto," in (1974) 9 *Politica internazionale* 42.

Colitti, Marcello, *Energia e sviluppo in Italia: La vicenda di Enrico Mattei*. Bari: De Donato, 1979.

Colucci, Michele, *Lavoro in movimento. L'Emigrazione italiana in Europa 1945–57*. Rome: Donzelli, 2008.

Commoner, Barry, *The Closing Circle: Nature, Man and Technology*. New York: Knopf, 1971.

Comte, E., "La formation du régime de migrations de l'Europe communautaire," doctoral thesis presented to the Sorbonne, 2009.

Connelly, Matthew, *A Diplomatic Revolution: Algeria's Fight for Independence and the Origins of the Post–Cold War Era*. New York: Oxford University Press, 2002.

Connelly, Mathhew, *Fatal Misconception. The Struggle to Control World Population*. Cambridge: Belknap Press, 2008.

Coolsaet, Rik, *Histoire de la politique étrangère belge*. Brussels: Vie Ouvrière, 1988.

Cooper, Frederick, "Writing the History of Development," (2010) 8(1) *Journal of Modern European History*, 5.

Cooper, Richard N., *The Economics of Interdependence: Economic Policy in the Atlantic Community*. New York: Council on Foreign Relations/McGraw Hill, 1968.

Coppolaro, Lucia, "US Payments Problems and the Kennedy Round of GATT Negotiations 1961–1967", in David M. Andrews (ed.), *Orderly Change: International Monetary Relations Since Bretton Woods*. Ithaca, NY: Cornell University Press, 2008, 120.

Corea, Gamani, *Taming Commodity Markets: The Integrated Program and the Common Fund of the UNCTAD*. Manchester: Manchester University Press, 1988.

Corm, Georges, *Fragmentation of the Middle East: The Last Thirty Years*. London: Hutchinson, 1988.

Corm, Georges, *Il Libano contemporaneo. Storia e società*. Milan: Jaca Book, 2006.

Cortázar, Julio, *Fantomas contra los vampiros multinacionales*. Buenos Aires: Ediciones Destino, 1965.

Cortese, Luisa (ed.), *Il Movimento studentesco, Storia e documenti 1968–1973*. Milan: Bompiani, 1973.

Cox, Michael, "Who Won the Cold War in Europe? A Historiographical Overview", in Frédéric Bozo, Marie-Pierre Rey, N. Piers Ludlow, and Leopoldo Nuti (eds), *Europe and the End of the Cold War: A Reappraisal*. London: Routledge, 2008.

Crainz, Guido, *Il paese mancato. Dal miracolo economico ali anni Ottanta*. Rome: Donzelli, 2003.

Crouch, Colin, *Social Change in Western Europe*. Oxford: Oxford University Press, 1999.

Crozier, Brian, *The Struggle for the Third World: A Background Book*. London: The Bodley Head, 1966.

Cruciani, Sante, *L'Europa delle sinistre. La nascita del Mercato comune europeo attraverso i casi francese e italiano (1955–1957)*. Rome: Carocci, 2007.

Cuevas, Alberto, "Salvador Allende," in Alberto Cuevas (ed.), *America Latina. Uomini e idee*, vol. 2. Rome: Edizioni Lavoro, 1995.

Cumings, Bruce, "The Origins of the North-Eastern Political Economy: Industrial Sectors and Political Consequences, 1900–1980", in (1984) 38 *International Organization* (Winter).

Dannehl, Charles, *Politics, Trade, and Development: Soviet Economic Aid to the Non-Communist Third World, 1955–1989*. Dartmouth: Ashgate, 1995.

Darwin, John, *After Tamerlane. The Rise and Fall of Global Empires 1400–2000*, (London: Penguin, 2008).

Darwin, John, *The Empire Project. The Rise and Fall of the British World System 1830–1970*, Cambridge, Cambridge University Press, 2009.

David, Paul A. and Melvin Reder (eds), *Nations and Households in Economic Growth: Essays in Honor of Moses Abramovitz*, New York, Academic Press, 1974.

Davies, Norman, *Europe East and West*. London: Jonathan Cape, 2006.

Davies, Norman, *Europe: A History*. New York: Harper, 2007.

de Bernis, Gérard, "Deux stratégies pour l'industrialisation du tiers-monde. Les industries industrialisantes et les options algériennes," in (1971) *Revue du Tiers-Monde* (July–September) 68.

De Giuseppe, Massimo, "Quei ponti sospesi (attraverso l'oceano). Giorgio La Pira e le voci dell'America latina," in (2004) 236 *Italia Contemporanea* 385.

De Grazia, Victoria, *Irresistible Empire: America's Advance through Twentieth-Century Europe*. Cambridge, MA: Harvard University Press, 2005.

de Vries, Margaret, *The IMF in a Changing World 1945–85*. Washington, DC: International Monetary Fund, 1986.

Debray, Régis, *Conversaciòn con Allende*. Buenos Aires: Siglo XXI Editores, 1971.

Dehousse, Fernand, *L'Europe et le Monde. Recueil d'études, de rapports et de discours 1945–1960*. Paris: Librairie Générale de Droit et de Jurisprudence, 1960.

Del Biondo, Ilaria, *L'Europa possibile. La Cgt e la Cgil di fronte al processo di integrazione europea*. Rome: Ediesse, 2007.

Del Boca, Angelo, *Italiani, brava gente?* Vicenza: Neri Pozza, 2005.

Del Pero, Mario, "I limiti della distensione: Gli Stati Uniti e l'implosione del regime portoghese," in Antonio Varsori (ed.), *Alle origini del presente. L'Europa occidentale nella crisi degli anni Settanta*. Milan: Franco Angeli, 2007, 39.

Del Pero, Mario, *Libertà e impero. Gli Stati Uniti e il mondo 1776–2006*. Rome & Bari: Laterza, 2008.

Del Pero, Mario, *The Eccentric Realist. Henry Kissinger and the Shaping of American Foreign Policy* (Ithaca, NY: Cornell University Press, 2009).

Del Pero, Mario, V. Gavín, F. Guirao, and Antonio Varsori (eds), *Democrazie. L'Europa meridionale e la fine delle dittature*. Florence: Le Monnier, 2010.

Dell, Sidney, *A Latin American Common Market?* Oxford: Oxford University Press, 1966.

Dell, Sidney, *Trade Blocs and Common Markets*. London: Constable, 1967.

Delors, Jacques, *Mémoires*. Paris: Plon, 2004.

Delureanu, Stefan, *Les Nouvelles Equipes Internationales. Per la rifondazione dell'Europa (1947–1965)*. Soveria Mannelli: Rubbettino, 2006.

Devin, Guillaume, *L'Internationale socialiste. Histoire et sociologie du socialisme international*. Paris: Presse de la FNSP, 1993.

Devin, Guillaume, "L'Internationale Socialiste face à la guerre du Vietnam," in Christopher Goscha and Maurice Vaïsse (eds), *La guerre du Vietnam et l'Europe (1963–1973)*. Brussels: Bruylant, 2003, 215.

Dhar, P.N., *Indira Gandhi: The "Emergency" and Indian Democracy*. Oxford, New Delhi: Oxford University Press, 2000.

Dimier, Véronique, "L'institutionnalisation de la Commission Européenne (DG Développement): Du rôle des leaders dans la construction d'une administration multinationale, 1958–1975," in (2003) 34(3) *Etudes Internationales (Canada)* 401.

Di Nolfo, Ennio, *Storia delle relazioni internazionali 1918–1999*. Bari: Laterza, 2000.

Dirlik, Arif, "The Third World," in Carole Fink, Philipp Gassert, and Detlef Junker (eds), *1968: The World Transformed*. Cambridge: Cambridge University Press and German Historical Institute, 1998.

Dobrynin, Anatoly, *In Confidence. Moscow's Ambassador to America's Six Cold War Presidents (1962–1986)*. New York: Random House, 1995.

Dosman, Edgar J., *The Life and Times of Raúl Prebisch, 1901–1986*. Montreal: McGill–Queen's University Press, 2009.

Droz, Bernard, *Histoire de la décolonisation au XXe siècle*. Paris: Seuil, 2006.

Droz, Bernard, and Anthony Rowley, *Storia del XX Secolo. Sviluppo e independenza (1950–1973)*. Florence: Sansoni, 1989.

Duchêne, François, "The European Community and the Uncertainties of Interdependence," in Wolfgang Hager and Max Kohnstamm (eds), *A Nation Writ Large? Foreign-Policy Problems before the European Community*. London: Macmillan, 1973.

Dumas, Roland, *Affaires Etrangères 1981–1988*. Paris: Fayard, 2007.

Dumoulin, Michel (ed.), *The European Commission 1958–72: History and Memories*. Brussels: European Commission, 2007.

Duroselle, J.B., and Andre Kaspi, *Histoire des relations internationales de 1945 à nos jours*. Paris: Armand Colin, 2004.

Eichengreen, Barry, *Globalizing Capital: A History of the International Monetary System*. Princeton, NJ: Princeton University Press, 1996.

Elkins, Caroline, *Imperial Reckoning. The Untold Story of Britain's <r>Gulag</r> in Kenya*. New York: Henry Holt and Company, 2005.

Emmanuel, Arghiri, *L'échange inégal. Essai sur les antagonismes dans les rapports internationaux*. Paris: François Maspero, 1969.

Engerman, David and Corinna Unger, "Introduction: Towards a Global History of Modernization," (2009) 33(3) *Diplomatic History*.

Enzensberger, Hans Magnus, "On Leaving America", in *The New York Review of Books* vol. 10, n. 4, February 20, 1968.

Eppler, Erhard, *Not Much Time for the Third World*. London: O. Wolff, 1972.

Evans, Martin and John Philips, *Algeria. Anger of the Dispossessed*. New Haven, CT: Yale University Press, 2007.

Fallaci, Oriana, *Interview with History*. New York: Liveright, 1976.

Fanon, Frantz, *The Wretched of the Earth*. New York: Grove Press, 1963.

Febvre, Lucien, *L'Europe: Genèse d'une civilisation*. Paris: Perrin, 1999.

Fejtö, François, *Chine–URSS: De l'alliance au conflit 1950–1972*. Paris: Seuil, 1973.

Feld, Werner J., *Multinational Corporations and UN Politics*. New York: Pergamon Policy Studies, 1980.

Ferguson, Niall, *The War of the World: Twentieth Century Conflict and the Descent of the West*. New York: Penguin, 2006.

Ferguson, Tyrone, *The Third World and the Decision Making in the International Monetary Fund*. London: Pinter Publishers, 1988.

Ferro, Marc, *Histoire des colonisations. Des conquêtes aux independences XIII–XX siécle*. Paris: Seuil, 1994.

Ferro, Marc, *Suez 1956: Naissance d'un Tiers Monde*. Brussels: Complexe, 1995.

Ferry, Luc and Alain Renaut, *La Pensée '68: Essai sur l'antihumanisme contemporain*. Paris: Gallimard, 1985.

Fielding, Steven, *The Labour Party. Socialism and Society since 1951*. Manchester: Manchester University Press, 1997.

Fitoussi, Jean-Paul, *Il dibattito proibito. Moneta, Europea, Povertà* (Bologna: Il Mulino, 1997).

Fontaine, André, *La guerre civile froide*. Paris: Fayard, 1969.

Foreign and Commonwealth Office, *Documents on British Policy Overseas*, Series III, Volume IV. London: Routledge, 2006.

Foreign Relations of the United States, 1964–1968, (FRUS) vol. VIII. Washington, DC: US Government Printing Office, 1998; vol. XXIV. Washington, DC: US Government Printing Office, 1999.

Foreign Relations of the United States, 1969–1976, vol. I. Washington, DC: US Government Printing Office, 2003; vol. III. Washington, DC: US Government Printing Office, 2001; vol. IV. Washington, DC: US Government Printing Office, 2002.

Foreman-Peck, James, "L'Europa conquista il mondo", in *Storia d'Europa*, vol. V. Turin: Einaudi, 1996.

Frankel, Francine, *India's Political Economy, 1947–1977*. Princeton, NJ: Princeton University Press, 1978.

Fraser, Robert, *The World Financial System*. London: Longman, 1994.

Freeman, Gary, *Immigrant labor and racial conflict in industrial society: The French and British experience: 1945–1975*. Princeton, NJ: Princeton University Press, 1979.

Frieden, Jeffrey, *Global Capitalism: Its Fall and Rise in the Twentieth Century*. New York: W.W. Norton & Co., 2006.

Frisch, Dieter, "La politique de development de l'Union européenne. Un regard personnel sur 50 ans de coopération internationale," in (2008) 15 *Rapport ECDPM*.

Fursenko, Aleksandr and Timothy Naftali, *Khrushchev's Cold War: The Inside Story of an American Adversary*. New York: W.W. Norton & Co., 2006.

Furtado, Celso, *Economic Development of Latin America: Historical Background and Contemporary Problems*. Cambridge: Cambridge University Press, 1976.

Gaddis, John Lewis, *We Now Know: Rethinking Cold War History*. New York: Oxford University Press, 1997.

Gaddis, John Lewis, *The Cold War. A New History*. New York: Penguin, 2005.

Gaja, Roberto, *L'Italia nel mondo bipolare. Per una storia della politica estera italiana*. Bologna: Il Mulino, 1995.

Galbraith, J.K., *The Affluent Society*. London: Hamish Hamilton, 1958.

Galbraith, J.K., *The New Industrial State*. Princeton, NJ: Princeton University Press, 1967.

Galbraith, J.K., *The Nature of Mass Poverty*. Cambridge, MA: Harvard University Press, 1979.

Galbraith, J.K., *A Life in Our Times: Memoirs*. New York: Ballantine, 1981.

Galeano, Eduardo, *Open Veins of Latin America: Five Centuries of Pillage of a Continent*. New York: Monthly Review Press, 1973.

Galeazzi, Marco, *Il Pci e il Movimento dei non allineati, 1955–1975.* Milan: Franco Angeli, 2011.

Gallagher, John and Ronald Robinson, "The Imperialism of Free Trade," (1953) 6(1) *Economic History Review* 1.

Gallino, Luciano, "Introduzione," in Herbert Marcuse, *L'uomo a una dimensione.* Turin: Einaudi, 1999.

Garavini, Giuliano. "L'Europa occidentale e il Nuovo Ordine economico internazionale (1974–1977)", in (2006) 6 *Ventunesimo Secolo* (March).

Garavini, Giuliano, "The Battle for the Participation of the European Community in the G7 (1975–1977)", in (2006) 12(1) *Journal of European Integration History* 141.

Garavini, Giuliano, "Completing Decolonization: The 1973 'Oil Shock' and the Struggle for Economic Rights," in (2011) 33(3) *The International History Review* 473.

Gardner, Richard N., *Sterling–Dollar Diplomacy in Current Perspective: The Origins and the Prospects of Our International Economic Order.* New York: Columbia University Press, 1980.

Gardner, Richard N. and Max Millikan, *The Global Partnership: International Agencies and Economic Development.* New York: Praeger, 1968.

Garthoff, Raymond L., *Détente and Confrontation: American-Soviet Relations from Nixon to Reagan.* Washington, DC: The Brookings Institution, 1994.

Garton Ash, Timothy, *In Europe's Name: Germany and the Divided Continent.* London: Jonathan Cape, 1993.

Geddes, Andrew, *Immigration and European Integration. Beyond Fortress Europe.* Manchester: Manchester University Press, 2008.

Gemelli, Giuliana, *Fernand Braudel e l'Europa universale.* Venice: Marsilio, 1990.

Gentile, Emilio, *L'apocalisse della modernità. La Grande Guerra per l'uomo nuovo.* Milan: Mondadori, 2008.

Gerbet, Pierre, *Le rêve d'un ordre mondial: De la SDN à l'ONU.* Paris: Imprimerie Nationale, 1996.

Gfeller, Aurelie Elisa, "Imagining European Identity: French Elites and the American Challenge in the Pompidou–Nixon Era," in (2010) 19(2) *Contemporary European History*.

Gillingham, John, *European Integration, 1950–2003: Superstate or New Market Economy?* Cambridge: Cambridge University Press, 2003.

Gilpin, Robert, *The Political Economy of International Relations.* Princeton, NJ: Princeton University Press, 1987.

Girault, René, "La France entre l'Europe et l'Afrique," in Enrico Serra (ed.), *La relance européenne et les traités de Rome (Actes du colloque de Rome, 25–28 mars 1987).* Milan: Giuffré, 1989, 351.

Giscard d'Estaing, Valéry, *Il potere e la vita.* Milan: Sperling & Kupfer, 1993.

Gliejeses, Piero, *Conflicting Missions: Havana, Washington and Africa, 1959–1976.* Chapel Hill: University of North Carolina Press, 2002.

Glyn, Andrew, *Capitalism Unleashed: Finance Globalization and Welfare.* Oxford: Oxford University Press, 2006.

Gomes, Bernardino and Tiago Moreira de Sá, *Carlucci Vs. Kissinger: Os EUA e a Revolução Portuguesa.* Capa Mole: Dom Quixote, 2008.

Gonzalez, Norberto and David Pollock, "Del ortodoxo al conservador ilustrado: Raúl Prebisch en la Argentina, 1923–1943," (1991) 30(120) *Desarrollo Economico: Rivista de Ciencias Sociales* 455.

Gosovic, Branislav, *UNCTAD: Conflict and Compromise: The Third World's Quest for an Equitable World Economic Order through the United Nations.* Leiden: A.W. Sijthoff, 1972.

Grant, Charles, *Delors: Inside the House that Jacques Built*. London: Nicholas Brealey Publishing, 1994.

Gray, William Glenn, *Germany's Cold War. The Global Campaign to Isolate East Germany, 1949–1969*. Chapel Hill: The University of North Carolina Press, 2003.

Grosser, Alfred, *Les Occidentaux. Les pays d'Europe et les États-Unis depuis la guerre*. Paris, Fayard, 1978.

Guasconi, Maria Eleonora, *L'Europa fra continuità e cambiamento: Il vertice dell'Aia e il rilancio della costruzione europea*. Florence: Edizioni Polistampa, 2004.

Guevara, Che, *Global Justice: Liberation and Socialism*. New York: Ocean Press, 2002.

Guevara, Che, *Che Guevara Reader*, 2nd edn. New York: Ocean Press, 2003.

Guitard, Odette, *Bandoung et le réveil des peuples colonisés*. Paris: PUF, 1969.

Gwin, Catherine, *US Relations with the World Bank 1945–1992*. Washington, DC: The Brookings Institution, 1993.

Habermas, Jürgen, *The Postnational Constellation*. Cambridge, MA: MIT Press, 2001.

Hall, I., "The Revolt against the West," (2011) 33(1) *International History Review*.

Hall, Samuel, Richard Williams, and E.P. Thompson, *New Left. May Day Manifesto*. London: New Left, 1967.

Halliday, Fred, "The Middle, the Great Powers and the Cold War", in Yezid Sayigh and Avi Shlaim East (eds), *The Cold War and the Middle East*. Oxford: Clarendon Press, 1997, p. 19

Harrod, Roy, *The Life of John Maynard Keynes*. London: Macmillan, 1951.

Hart, Jeffrey A., *The New International Economic Order*. London: Macmillan, 1983.

Hart, Michael, *Also Present at the Creation: Dana Wilgress and the United Nations Conference on Trade and Employment at Havana*. Ottawa: Center for Trade Policy and Law, 1995.

Harvey, David, *A Brief History of Neoliberalism*. Oxford: Oxford University Press, 2005.

Haslam, Jonathan, *The Nixon Administration and the Death of Allende's Chile: A Case of Assisted Suicide*. New York: W.W. Norton & Co., 2005.

Hayter, Teresa, *Aid as Imperialism*. London: Penguin, 1971.

Heath, Edward, *Old World, New Horizons. Britain, Europe, and the Atlantic Alliance*. Cambridge, MA: Harvard University Press, 1970.

Heath, Edward, *The Course of My Life. My Autobiography*. London: Hodder & Stoughton, 1988.

Heather, P., *Empires and Barbarians. The Fall of Rome and the Birth of Europe*. Oxford: Oxford University Press, 2010.

Heffer, Simon, *Like the Roman. The Life of Enoch Powell*. London: Weidenfeld & Nicolson, 1998.

Hege, Julien, "Editori di sinistra e lotta armata in Italia (1966–1979)," in M. Lazar and M.A. Matard-Bonucci (eds), *Il libro degli anni di piombo. Storia e memoria del terrorismo* (Milan: Rizzoli, 2010).

Hellema, Duco, Cees Wiebes, and Toby Witte, *The Netherlands and the Oil Crisis: Business as Usual*. Amsterdam: Amsterdam University Press, 2004.

Hill, Christopher and Karen E. Smith (eds), *European Foreign Policy. Key Documents*. London: Routledge, 2000.

Ho Chi Minh, "The Path Which Led Me to Leninism," in *Selected Works of Ho Chi Minh*, vol. 4 (Beijing: Foreign Languages Publishing House, n.d).

Hobsbawm, Eric, *The Age of Extremes: A History of the World, 1914–1991*. New York: Vintage, 1994.

Hobsbawm, Eric, *Interesting Times: A Twentieth Century Life*. New York: Random House, 2002.

Hobson, John A., *Imperialism*. Ann Arbor: University of Michigan Press, 1965.

Hochschild, Adam, *King Leopold's Ghost*. New York: Houghton Mifflin, 1908.

Hoffmann, Stefan-Ludwig (ed.), *Human Rights in the Twentieth Century*. New York, Cambridge University Press, 2011.

Hogan, Michael J., *The Marshall Plan: America, Britain, and the Reconstruction of Western Europe 1947–1952*. New York: Cambridge University Press, 1987.

Hopwood, Derek, *Egypt, Politics and Society 1945–1984*. London: Allen & Unwin, 1985.

Horn, Gerd-Rainer, *The Spirit of '68. Rebellion in Western Europe and North America 1956–1976*. Oxford: Oxford University Press, 2007.

Horne, Alistair, *A Savage War of Peace: Algeria, 1954–1962*. New York: New York Review of Books, 2006.

Huntington, Samuel P., *The Clash of Civilizations and the Remaking of World Order*. New York: Simon & Schuster, 1996.

Illich, Ivan, *Tools for Conviviality*. New York: Harper & Row, 1973.

Illich, Ivan, *Energy and Equity*. New York: Harper & Row, 1974.

Institut du Droit de la Paix et du Développement, Institut Charles de Gaulle, *De Gaulle et le Tiers Monde*. Paris: Editions Pedone, 1983.

Jalée, Pierre, *Le pillage du tiers monde*. Paris: François Maspero, 1965.

James, Harold, *International Monetary Cooperation Since Bretton Woods*. Washington, DC: International Monetary Fund and Oxford University Press, 1996.

James, Harold, *Rambouillet, 15 novembre 1975. La globalizzazione dell'economia*. Bologna: Il Mulino, 1999.

Jenkins, Roy, *European Diary: 1977–1981*. London: Collins, 1989.

Jha, Prem Shankar, *The Twilight of the Nation State: Globalization, Chaos, and War*. Ann Arbor, MI: Pluto Press, 2006.

Jobert, Michel, *Ni dieu, ni diable: Conversations avec Jean-Louis Remilleux*. Paris: Albin Michel, 1993.

Johnson, Harry, *Economic Policies Toward Less Developed Countries*. Washington, DC: Brookings Institution, 1967.

Judt, Tony, *Reappraisals. Reflections on the Forgotten Twentieth Century*. London: Vintage Books, 2008.

Judt, Tony, *Postwar: A History of Europe Since 1945*. New York: Penguin, 2006.

Juliá, S., "Né riforma, né rottura: Solo una transizione dalla dittatura alla demcorazia," in (2010) 9 *Ventunesimo Secolo* October 2010, 72.

Julien, C.A., J. Brohat, G.Bourgin, M.Crouzet, and P.Renouvin, *Les politiques d'expansion imperialiste. J. Ferry, Leopold II, F. Crispi, J. Chamberlain, Th. Roosevelt*. Paris: PUF, 1949.

Kaelble, Hartmut, Sozialgeschichte Europas. 1945 bis zur Gegenwart. Munich: C.H. Beck Verlag, 2007.

Kaiser, Wolfram, *Christian Democracy and the Origins of European Union*. Cambridge: Cambridge University Press, 2007.

Kaiser, Wolfram and Antonio Varsori, eds, *European Union History. Themes and Debates*. (London: Palgrave, 2010).

Kaiser, Wolfram and J.H. Meyer (eds), *Societal Actors in European Integration 1958–92: From Polity Building to Policy Making*, Basingstoke, Palgrave, 2012.

Kapur, Devesh, John P. Lewis, and Richard Webb, *The World Bank: Its First Half Century*. Washington: Brookings Institution Press, 1997.

Kemp, Tom, *Theories of Imperialism*. London: Dobson, 1967.

Kennan, George, *Democracy and the Student Left*. Boston: Little, Brown and Co., 1968.

Kennedy, Paul, *The Rise and Fall of the Great Powers*. New York: Vintage, 1989.

Kennedy, Paul, *The Parliament of Man: The Past, Present, and Future of the United Nations*. New York: Random House, 2006.

Keylor, William R., *The Twentieth Century World: An International History*. Oxford: Oxford University Press, 2001.

Kiernan, V.G., *From Conquest to Collapse: European Empires from 1815 to 1960*. New York: Pantheon Books, 1962.

Killick, Tony, *Development Economics in Action: A Study of the Economic Policies of Ghana*. London: Heinemann, 1978.

Kindelberger, Charles, *Europe's Postwar Growth. The Role of Labour Supply*. Cambridge, MA: Harvard University Press, 1967.

Kissinger, Henry, *Years of Renewal*. New York: Simon & Schuster, 1999.

Knowles, Caroline, *Race, Discourse and Labourism*. London: Routledge, 1992.

Knudsen, Ann-Christina, "Creating the Common Agricultural Policy. Story of Cereal Prices," in Wilfried Loth (ed.), *Crises and Compromises: The European Project 1963–1969*. Baden-Baden: Nomos Verlag, 2001, 131.

Krasner, Stephen, *Structural Conflict: The Third World Against Global Liberalism*. Berkeley: University of California Press, 1985.

Kreisky, Bruno, "Social Democracy's Third Historical Phase," in (1970) 5 *Socialist International Information* 65.

Kula, Witold, *The Problems and Methods of Economic History*, 2nd edn. Burlington, VT: Ashgate, 2001.

Kuroda, T., "Instauration du Système de preferences généralisées de la Communauté européenne, 1968–1971," in (2011/12) 34 *Bulletin de l'Insitut Pierre Renouvin* 137.

Kutler, Stanley, *The Wars of Watergate: The Last Crisis of Richard Nixon*. New York: W.W. Norton and Co., 1992.

Lacoste, Yves, *Unité et diversité du Tiers Monde*. Paris: La Découverte-Hérodote, 1984.

Lager, Carole, *L'Europe en quête de ses symboles*. Berne: Peter Lang, 1995.

Lagrou, Pieter, *The Legacy of Nazi Occupation. Patriotic Memory and National Recovery in Western Europe, 1945–1965*. Cambridge: Cambridge University Press, 2000.

Lall, K.B., "The EEC, the Third World, and the New International Economic Order", in K.B. Lall and H.S. Chopra (eds), *The EEC and the Third World*. Atlantic Highlands, NJ: Humanities Press, 1981.

Landolfi, Antonio, *Storia del PSI. Cento anni di socialismo in Italia da Filippo Turati a Bettino Craxi*. Milan: SugarCo, 1990.

Laschi, Giuliana and Mario Telò, *Europa potenza civile o entità in declino? Contributi ad una nuova stagione multidisciplinare di studi europei*. Bologna: il Mulino, 2007.

Laurens, Henry, "1967: A War of Miscalculation and Misjudgment," trans. Krystyna Horko, in *Le Monde Diplomatique*, English edn (June 2007).

Ledda, Romano, *L'Europa fra Nord e Sud*. Rome: Editori Riuniti, 1989.

Lee, Christopher J. (ed.), *Making a World after Empires: The Bandung Moment and Its Political Afterlives*. Athens: Ohio University Press, 2010.

Leffler, Melvyn P. and Odd Arne Westad (eds), *The Cambridge History of the Cold War: Origins, 1945–1962*, Cambridge, Cambridge University Press, 2012.

Lenci, Marco, "Dalla storia coloniale alla storia d'Africa," in Agostino Giovagnoli and Giorgio Del Zanna (eds), *Il Mondo visto dall'Italia*. Milan: Guerini e Associati, 2004.

Leuliette, Pierre, "Aventures d'un parachutiste," in *Esprit* (April 1959).

Levinson, Marc, *The Box: How the Shipping Container Made the World Smaller and the World Economy Bigger*. Princeton, NJ: Princeton University Press, 2006.

Lewis, Arthur, *The Evolution of the International Economic Order*. Princeton, NJ: Princeton University Press, 1978.

Lewis, John L., *Walking with the Wind: A Memoir of the Movement*. New York: Harcourt Brace, 1998.

Liauzu, Claude, *L'enjeu tiermondiste*. Paris: L'Harmattan, 1987.

Litvin, Daniel, *Empires of Profit. Commerce, Conquest and Corporate Responsibility*. New York: Texere, 2003.

Livi Bacci, Massimo, *La populazione nella storia d'Europa*. Bari: Laterza, 1998.

Lorenzini, Sara, *Due Germanie in Africa. La cooperazione allo sviluppo e la competizione per i mercati di materie prime e tecnologia*. Florence: Polistampa, 2003.

Loth, Wilfried (ed.), *Experiencing Europe: 50 Years of European Construction, 1957–2007*. Baden-Baden: Nomos, 2007.

Louis, William Roger, *Ends of British Imperialism: The Scramble for Empire, Suez, and Decolonization*, London, IB Tauris, 2006.

Lucarelli, Sonia, "The EU in the Eyes of Others: Towards Filling a Gap in the Literature", in (2007) 3(20) *European Foreign Affairs Review* 249.

Lucassen, Leo, *The Immigrant Threat. The Integration of Old and New Migrants in Western Europe Since 1850*. Chicago: University of Illinois Press, 2005.

Ludlow, N. Piers, *The Making of the European Monetary System*. London: Butterworth Scientific, 1984.

Ludlow, N. Piers, *The European Community and the Crisis of the 1960s: Negotiating the Gaullist Challenge*. London: Routledge, 2006.

Lundestad, Geir, *East, West, North, South*. Oxford: Oxford University Press, 1999.

Lussana, Fiamma, "Il confronto con le socialdemocrazie e la ricerca di un Nuovo socialismo nell'ultimo Berlinguer", in (2004) 2 *Studi Storici* (April–June) 568.

Macmillan, Harold, "The Wind of Change: Speech by the Rt. Hon. Harold Macmillan, Prime Minister, to both Houses of Parliament of the Union of South Africa, Cape Town, February 3, 1960," in *British Imperial Policy on Decolonization: 1938–1964*, vol. 2 (London: Macmillan, 1980).

Maggiorani, Mauro and Paolo Ferrari (eds), *L'Europa da Togliatti a Berlinguer. Testimonianze e Documenti 1945–1984*. Bologna: Il Mulino, 2005.

Magone, José Maria, *The Politics of Southern Europe. Integration into the European Union*. Westport, CT & London: Praeger, 2003.

Magrini, Liliana, "La V Unctad e le prospettive del dialogo Nord–Sud," in (1979) *Politica internazionale* (August–September).

Maier, Charles S., "Secolo corto o epoca lunga? L'unità storica dell'età industriale e le trasformazioni della territorialità," in Claudio Pavone (ed.), *'900: I tempi della storia*. Rome: Donzelli, 1997, 29.

Maier, Charles, "Consigning the 20th Century to History: Alternative Narratives for the Modern Era", in (2000) 105(3) *The American Historical Review*, 807.

Maier, Charles S., *Among Empires: American Ascendancy and its Predecessors*. Cambridge, MA: Harvard University Press, 2006.

Mailer, Norman, *The Armies of the Night*. New York: Penguin, 1994.

Mak, Geert, *In Europe: Travels Through the Twentieth Century*, trans. Sam Garrett. New York: Pantheon Books, 2007.

Malcolm X, *By Any Means Necessary*. New York: Pathfinder Press, 1970.

Malik, Yogendra and Dhirenda Vaspeyi, *India: the Years of Indira Gandhi*. New Delhi: E.J. Brill, 1988.

Mammarella, Giuseppe, *Storia d'Europa dal 1945 ad oggi*. Bari: Laterza, 1995.

E. Mandel, "Editorial," in *Black Dwarf*, June 1, 1969. Available online at <http://www.ernestmandel.org/en/works/txt/1969/black_dwarf.htm>.

Manto, Saadat Hasan, *Letters to Uncle Sam*. Islamabad: Alhamra, 2001.

Masmoudi, Mustapha, "The New World Information Order," in *Le Monde*, October 26, 1978.

Mason, Edward and Robert Asher, *The World Bank Since Bretton Woods: The Origins, Policies, Operations, and Impact of the International Bank for Reconstruction and Development, and the other Members of the World Bank Group*. Washington, DC: The Brookings Institution Press, 1973.

Mattelart, Armand, *Histoire de l'utopie planétaire: De la cité prophétique à la société globale*. Paris: La Découverte, 2000.

Maugeri, L., *The Age of Oil: the Mythology, History, and Future of the World's Most Controversial Resource*. Westport: Praeger, 2006.

Mazower, Mark, *Dark Continent: Europe's Twentieth Century*. New York: Vintage, 2001.

Mazower, Mark, *No Enchanted Palace. The End of Empire and the Ideological Origins of the United Nations*. Princeton, NJ: Princeton University Press, 2009.

Mazower, Mark, *Governing the World. The Rise and Fall of an Idea, 1815 to Present*. New York: Penguin, 2012.

Mazower, Mark, Jessica Reinisch, and David Feldman (eds), *Post–War Reconstruction in Western Europe. International Perspectives 1945–1949*. Oxford: Oxford University Press, 2011.

McLuhan, Marshall and Quentin Fiore, *The Medium is the Message*. New York: Bantam, 1967.

McNeill, William H., *The Rise of the West: A History of the Human Community* (Chicago: University of Chicago Press, 1963).

McTurnan Kahin, George, *The Asian-African Conference: Bandung, Indonesia, April 1955*. Ithaca, NY: Cornell University Press, 1956.

Meadows, Donella, *et al. The Limits to Growth: A Report for the Club of Rome's Project on the Predicament of Mankind*. New York: Universe Books, 1972.

Mechi, Lorenzo, "Le questioni sociali nel processo d'integrazione europea," in *La cittadinanza che cambia. Radici nazionale e prospettiva europea*, Annali della Fondazione Giuseppe Di Vittorio (Rome: Ediesse, 2005), 241.

Mechi, Lorenzo and Francesco Petrini, "La Comunità europea nella divisione internazionale del lavoro: Le politiche industriali, 1967–1978", in Antonio Varsori (ed.), *Alle origini del presente. L'Europa occidentale nella crisi degli anni Settanta*. Milan: Franco Angeli, 2007, 251.

Meimon, Julien, "L'invention de l'aide française au développement: Discours, instruments et pratiques d'une dynamique hégémonique," in (2007) 21 *Questions de recherche/Research in Question* 1.

Melotti, Umberto, "Migrazioni internazionali e integrazione sociale: il caso italiano e le esperienze europee," in Marcella Delle Donne and Umberto Melotti (eds), *Immigrazione in Europa*. Rome: Centro europeo di studi sociali, 1993.

Michel, Marc, *Décolonisation et émergence du Tiers monde*. Paris: Hachette, 1993.

Middlemas, Keith, *Orchestrating Europe: The Informal Politics of the European Union 1973–1995*. London: Fontana Press, 1995.

Miège, Jean Louis and Colette DuBois, *L'Europe retrouvé. Les migrations de la décolonisation*. Paris: L'Hamattan, 1995.

Migani, Guia, "La Communauté économique européene et la Commission économique pour l'Afrique de l'ONU: La difficile convergence de deux projets de développement pour le continent africain (1958–1963)," (2007) 13 *Journal of European Integration History* 133.

Migani, Giua, *La France et l'Afrique sub-saharianne, 1957–1963. Histoire d'une décolonisation entre idéaux eurafricains et politique de puissance*. Brussels: PIE Peter Lang, 2008.

Migani, Giua, "Les Accords de Lomé et les relations eurafricaines: Du dialogue Nord–Sud aux droits de l'homme," in G.H. Soutou and E. Robin-Hivert (eds), *L'Afrique indépendante dans le système international* (Paris: PUPS, 2011).

Migani, Guia, "Rediscovering the Mediterranean: first tests of coordination among the Nine", in Elena Calandri, Daniele Caviglia, and Antonio Varsori (eds), *Détente in Cold War Europe. Politics and Diplomacy in the Mediterranean*. London: IB Tauris, 2012.

Milward, Alan. S., *The European Rescue of the Nation-State*. Berkeley: University of California Press, 1992.

Milward, Alan. S., *The Rise and Fall of a National Strategy, 1945–1963*. London: HMSO, 2002.

Mishra, P., *From the Ruins of Empire: The Revolt Against the West and the Remaking of Asia*. London: Allen Lane, 2012.

Mitchell, Timothy, *Carbon Democracy. Political Power in the Age of Oil*. New York: Verso, 2011.

Mittelman, James H., *Out from Underdevelopment. Prospects for the Third World*. New York: St. Martin's Press, 1988.

Möckli, Daniel, *European Foreign Policy During the Cold War: Heath, Brandt, Pompidou and the Dream of Political Unity*. London: IB Tauris, 2008.

Mommer, Bernard, *Global Oil and the Nation State* (Oxford: Oxford University Press, 2002).

Monnet, Jean, *Mémoires*, trans. Richard Mayne. London: Collins, 1978.

Montani, Guido, *Il Terzo mondo e l'unità europea*. Naples: Guida Editori, 1979.

Moore, R. Laurence and Maurizio Vaudagna (eds), *The American Century in Europe*. Ithaca, NY: Cornell University Press, 2003.

Moravcsik, Andrew, *The Choice for Europe. Social Purpose and State Power from Messina to Maastricht*. Ithaca, NY: Cornell University Press, 1998.

Moravia, Alberto, *Which Tribe Do You Belong To?*, trans. Angus Davidson. New York: Farrar, Straus, and Giroux, 1974.

Moro, Aldo, *L'Italia nell'evoluzione dei rapporti internazionale*. Brescia: Ebe Moretto, 1986.

Moro, Aldo, *Ultimi scritti 16 marzo–9 maggio 1978*. Casale Monferrato: Piemme, 1998.

Moro, Aldo, *La democrazia incompiuta. Attori e questioni della politica italiana 1943–1978*. Rome: Editori Riuniti, 1999.

Morone, Antonio, *L'ultima colonia. Come l'Italia è tornata in Africa 1950–1960*. Bari: Laterza, 2011.

Morrison, Rodney J., *Portugal: Revolutionary Change in an Open Economy*. Boston, MA: Auburn House, 1981.

Moynihan, Daniel Patrick, *A Dangerous Place*. Boston: Little, Brown and Co., 1978.

Mulas, Andrea, *Allende e Berlinguer: Il Cile dell'Unidad Popular e il compromesso storico italiano*. Lecce: Manni, 2005.

Mwakikagile, Godfrey, *Nyerere and Africa: The End of an Era*. Atlanta, GA: Protea Publishing, 2002.

Myrdal, Gunnar, *The Challenge of World Poverty. A World Anti-Poverty Program Outline*. New York: Pantheon Books, 1970.

Naipaul, V.S., *Half a Life*. New York: Vintage, 2002.

Natta, Giulio, "Nuovi sviluppi della chimica macromolecolare nel campo degli elastomeri," in (1963) 1 *Materie plastiche ed elastomeri* 1.

Nehring, Holger and Helge Pharo, "Introduction: A Peaceful Europe? Negotiating Peace in the Twentieth Century, " (2008) 17(3) *Contemporary European History* 277.

Nehru, Jawaharlal, *Glimpses of World History*. Delhi: Oxford University Press, 1980.

Nkrumah, Kwame, *Neo-Colonialism: The Last Stage of Imperialism*. London: Thomas Nelson & Sons, 1965.

Noelke, Michael, *Europe–Third World Interdependence: Facts and Figures*. Brussels: Commission of the European Communities, 1979.

Nolan, Mary, *The Transatlantic Century. Europe and America, 1890–2010*. Cambridge: Cambridge University Press, 2012.

Northedge, Frederick Samuel, *Descent from Power: British Foreign Policy, 1945–1973*. London: Allen & Unwin, 1974.

Nossiter, Bernard, *The Global Struggle for More. Third World Conflicts with Rich Nations*. New York: Harper & Row, 1987.

Nugent, Paul, *Africa since Independence*. New York: Palgrave, 2004.

O'Brian, Patrick, "L'Europa e il Terzo Mondo", in *Storia d'Europa*, vol. V. Turin: Einaudi, 1996.

O'Hagan, Andrew, "Back in the US of A," in (2004) 51(9) *The New York Review of Books*.

Olivi, Bino, *Carter e l'Italia*. Milan: Longanesi, 1978.

Olivi, Bino and Roberto Santaniello, *Storia dell'integrazione europea*. Bologna: Il Mulino, 2005.

Ortmayer, Louis L., "West Germany and the Third World: Virtues of the Market or New Political Role?", in Gregory A. Raymond and Philip Taylor (eds), *Third World Policies of Industrialized Nations*. Westport, CT: Greenwood Press, 1982, 67.

Ortoleva, Peppino, *I movimenti del '68 in Europa e in America*. Rome: Editori Riuniti, 1998.

Packenham, Robert A., *Liberal America and the Third World*. Princeton, NJ: Princeton University Press, 1973.

Padgett, Stephen and William E. Paterson, *A History of Social Democracy in Postwar Europe*. London: Longman, 1991.

Padoa Schioppa, Tommaso, *L'Europa forza gentile*. Bologna: Il Mulino, 2007.

Paggi, Leonardo, "Un secolo spezzato. La politica e le guerre", in Claudio Pavone (ed.), *'900. I tempi della storia*. Rome: Donzelli, 1997.

Palayret, Jean-Marie, "'A Great School in the Service of a Great Idea.' The Creation and Development of the European University Institute in Florence," in (1997) 1(3) *EUI Review*, 1.

Palayret, Jean-Marie, "Il Comitato economico e socialize e le relazioni con i paesi e i territori associati e gli ACP (1958–1985)," in Antonio Varsori (ed.), *Il Comitato economico e sociale nella costruzione europea*. Padua: Marsilio, 2000.

Palayret, Jean-Marie, "Mondialisme contre régionalisme: CEE et ACP dans les negotiations de la Convention de Lomé", in Antonio Varsori (ed.), *Inside the European Community. Actors and Policies in European Integration 1957–1973*. Baden-Baden & Brussels: Nomos–Bruylant, 2006.

Panikkar, K.M., *Asia and Western Dominance: A Survey of the Vasco Da Gama Epoch of Asian History (1498–1945)*. London: Allen & Unwin, 1953.

Paoli, Simone, "La politica comunitaria in materia di istruzione nel corso degli anni Sessanta," in Laura Leonardi and Antonio Varsori (eds), *Lo spazio sociale europeo. Atti del convegno internazionale di studi, Fiesole 10–11 ottobre 2003*. Florence: Firenze University Press, 2005.

Paoli, Simone, "La geografia mentale del Sessantotto italiano 1967–1969," in (2007) 22 *Annali della Fondazione Ugo La Malfa*, 73.

Paoli, Simone, *Il sogno di Erasmo. La questione educative nel processo di integrazione europea* (Milan: Franco Angeli, 2010).

Papini, Roberto, *L'Internazionale DC. La cooperazione tra i partiti democratici cristiani dal 1925 al 1985.* Milan: Franco Angeli, 1986.

Parboni, Riccardo, *Il conflitto economico mondiale.* Milan: Etas Libri, 1985.

Parti Socialiste, *Les Socialistes et le Tiers Monde. Elements pour une politique socialiste de relations avec le Tiers monde.* Paris: Berger Levrault, 1977.

Pasolini, Pier Paolo, *Scritti Corsari.* Milan: Garzanti, 2006.

Peemans, Jean-Philippe, "Imperial Hangovers: Belgium—The Economics of Decolonization," (1980) 15 *Journal of Contemporary History* 257.

Pells, Richard, *Not Like Us. How Europeans Have Loved, Hated and Transformed American Culture since World War II.* New York: Basic Books, 1997.

Peluffo, Paolo, *Carlo Azeglio Ciampi. L'uomo e il presidente.* Milan: Rizzoli, 2007.

Pérez Alfonzo, Juan Pablo, *Hundiéndonos en el excremento del Diablo.* Caracas: Editorial Lisbona, 1976.

Petrini, Francesco, "Demanding Democracy in the Workplace: The Trade Union Confederation and the Struggle to Regulate Multinationals." in W. Kaiser and J.H. Meyer (eds), *Societal Actors in European Integration 1958–92: From Polity Building to Policy Making,* Basingstoke, Palgrave, 2012.

Petrini, Francesco, "Il '68 e la crisi dell'età dell'oro," in (2007) 12 *Annali della Fondazione Ugo La Malfa* 47.

Piccioni, Luigi and Gorgio Nebbia, "I Limiti dello sviluppo in Italia. Cronache di un dibattito 1971–74", in (2011) 1 *Altro 900. I quaderni di Altronovecento.*

Pisani, Edgar. "Communication to the Council, North–South dialogue on the eve of the conferences of Ottawa, Cancun, Nairobi and Paris," in *The Courier* n. 69 (September–October 1981).

Pisani, Edgar, *Un vieil homme et la terre.* Paris: Seuil, 2004.

Plana, Manuel and Trento, Angelo, *L'America Latina nel XX secolo.* Florence: Ponte alle Grazie, 1992.

Pons, Silvio, *Berlinguer e il fine del comunismo.* Turin: Einaudi, 2006.

Ponting, Clive, *A Green History of the World: The Environment and the Collapse of Great Civilizations.* New York: Penguin, 1991.

Popham, Peter, "How Britain plotted *coup d'état* to topple Italy's Communists," in *The Independent,* January 14, 2008.

Porter, Andrew, and A.J. Stockwell, *British Imperial Policy on Decolonization: 1938–1964,* 2 vols. (London: Macmillan, 1980).

Posner, Alan R., "Italy and the Third World: Response by an Intermediate Economy", in Gregory A. Raymond and Phillip Taylor (eds), *Third World Policies of Industrialized Nations.* Westport, CT: Greenwood Press, 1982.

Prashad, Vijay, *The Darker Nations: A People's History of the Third World.* New York: The New Press, 2007.

Prebisch, Raúl. "Sobre desarrollo y politica commercial internacional," in *Justicia Economica Internacional: Contribucion al estudio de la Carta de Derechos y Deberes Economicos de los Estados.* Mexico: Fondo de cultura economica, 1975.

Prebisch, Raúl. "Towards a New Trade Policy for Development. Report by the Secretary General of UNCTAD 1964," in Philippe Braillard and M.R. Dyalili (eds), *The Third World and International Relations.* London: Frances Pinter, 1986.

Puchala, D.J., "Western European Attitudes on International Problems, 1952–1961", (1964) 1 *Yale Research Memoranda in Political Science,* 266.

Qureshi, Lubna K., Nixon, Kissinger, and Allende: *US Involvement in the 1973 Coup in Chile.* Lanham, MD: Lexington Books, 2009.

Ragionieri, Ernesto, "Prefazione", in Jan Romein, *Il secolo dell'Asia. Imperialismo occidentale e rivoluzione asiatica nel secolo XX.* Turin: Einaudi, 1969.

Rainelli, Michel, *Le Gatt.* Paris: Editions La Découverte, 1993.

Reinhard, Wolfgang, *Storia del colonialismo.* Turin: Einaudi, 2002.

Remacle, Éric and Pascaline Winand, *America, Europe, Africa. L'Amérique, l'Europe, l'Afrique 1945–1973*. Brussels: P.I.E. Peter Lang, 2009.

Rémond, René, *Notre siècle, 1913–1988*. Paris: Fayard, 1988.

Reynolds, David, *One World Divisible: A Global History since 1945*. London: Penguin, 2000.

Riccardi, Luca, "Sempre più con gli arabi. La politica italiana verso il Medio Oriente dopo la guerra del Kippur (1973–1976)", in (2006) 6 *Nuova Storia Contemporanea* 57.

Richer, Philippe, *Cina e Terzo Mondo*. Milan: Mazzetta, 1972.

Ricupero, Rubens, *Beyond Conventional Wisdom in Development Policy. An Intellectual History of UNCTAD (1964–2004)*. Geneva: United Nations, 2004.

Rifkin, Jeremy, *The European Dream: How Europe's Vision of the Future is Quietly Eclipsing the American Dream*. New York: Penguin, 2004.

Rist, Gilbert, *The History of Development: From Western Origins to Global Faith*. London: Zed Books, 1997.

Rocard, Michel, *Le marché commun contre l'Europe*. Paris: Seuil, 1973.

Rodrik, Dani, "Globalization, Social Conflict and Economic Growth," UNCTAD, 8th Raúl Prebisch Lecture, October 24, 1997.

Rodney, Walter, *How Europe Underdeveloped Africa* (Dar-Es-Salam: Tanzanian Publishing House, 1973).

Rogan, Eugene, *The Arabs. A History*. New York, Basic Books, 2009.

Romano, Angela, *From Détente in Europe to European Détente. How the West Shaped the Helsinki CSCE*. Brussels: Peter Lang, 2006.

Romein, Jan, *The Asian Century: A History of Modern Nationalism in Asia* (Berkeley: University of California Press, 1962).

Romero, Federico, *Emigrazione e integrazione europea 1945–1973*. Milan: Edizioni Lavoro, 1991.

Rosen, George, *Western Economists and Eastern Societies: Agents of Social Change in South Asia 1950–1970*. Baltimore, MD: Johns Hopkins University Press, 1985.

Rosanvallon, Pierre, *L'âge de l'autogestion: Ou la politique au poste de commandement*. Paris: Seuil, 1976.

Ross, Kristin, *May '68 and Its Afterlives* (Chicago: University of Chicago Press, 2002).

Rossanda, Rossana, *L'anno degli studenti*. Bari: De Donato, 1968.

Rossanda, Rossana, *La ragazza del secolo scorso*. Turin: Einaudi, 2005.

Rostow, Eugene V., "The Multinational Corporation and the Future of the World Economy", in George W. Ball (ed.), *Global Companies: The Political Economy of World Business*. Englewood Cliffs, NJ: Prentice-Hall, 1975.

Rostow, Walt, *Gli stadi dello sviluppo economico*. Turin: Einaudi, 1962.

Rostow, Walt and Max Millikan, *A Proposal: Key to an Effective Foreign Policy*. New York: Harper and Brothers, 1957.

Rothstein, Robert L., *Global Bargaining: UNCTAD and the Quest for a NEIO*. Princeton, NJ: Princeton University Press, 1979.

Rubenstein, Alvin, *Moscow's Third World Strategy*. Princeton, NJ: Princeton University Press, 1998.

Ruggie, John G., "International Regimes, Transactions, and Change: Embedded Liberalism in the Postwar Economic Order," (1982) 46(3) *International Organization* 379.

Sabahi, Farian, *Storia dell'Iran*. Milan: Bruno Mondadori, 2006.

Said, Edward, *Orientalism*. New York: Vintage, 1979.

Said, Edward, *Reflections on Exile, and Other Essays*. Cambridge, MA: Harvard University Press, 2000.

Sandri, Renato, *La sfida del Terzo mondo*. Rome: Editori Riuniti, 1978.

Sangiovanni, Andrea, *Tute blu: la parabola operaia nell'Italia repubblicana*. Rome: Donzelli, 2006.

Santoni, Alessandro, *Il PCI e i giorni del Cile. Alle origini di un mito politico*. Rome: Carocci, 2008.

Saresella, Daniela, "La vocazione terzomondista del mondo cattolico degli anni Sessanta e il giudizio sulla politica internazionale statunitense," in Piero Craveri and Gaetano Quagliariello (eds), *L'antiamericanismo in Italia e in Europa nel secondo Dopoguerra*. Rubbettino: Soveria Mannelli, 2004.

Sassoon, Donald, *One Hundred Years of Socialism: The West European Left in the Twentieth Century*. New York: New Press, 1988.

Saunier, Georges, "The Place of Vocational Training in François Mitterrand's Idea of a European Social Space (1981–1984)", in (2004) 32 *European Journal of Vocational Training* (May–August), 77.

Sauvant, Karl P., *The Group of 77*. London: Oceana Publications, 1981.

Savranskaya, S., T. Blanton, and V. Zubok (eds), *Masterpieces of History: The Peaceful End of the Cold War in Europe, 1989* (Budapest: Central European Univerity Press, 2010).

Schildt, Axel, and Detlef Siefried (eds), *Between Marx and Coca-Cola. Youth Cultures in Changing European Societies 1960–1980*. Oxford: Berghahn Books, 2006.

Schlesinger, Arthur M., *A Thousand Days: John F. Kennedy in the White House*. New York: Fawcett Premier, 1966.

Schmidt, Heide-Irene, "Spinti in prima linea: La politica di cooperazione allo sviluppo della Repubblica federale tedesca (1958–1971)," in Luciano Tosi and Lorella Tosone (eds), *Gli aiuti allo sviluppo nelle relazioni internazionali del secondo dopoguerra*. Padua: Cedam, 2006, 111.

Schmidt, Helmut, *Men and Powers: A Political Retrospective*, trans. Ruth Hein. New York: Random House, 1989.

Schonfield, Andrew, *Modern Capitalism: The Changing Balance of Public and Private Power*. Oxford: Oxford University Press, 1965.

Schulz, M. and T. A. Schwartz, *The Strained Alliance. US–European Relations From Nixon to Carter*, New York, Cambridge University Press, 2010.

Schulze, Reinhard, *A Modern History of the Islamic World*. New York: New York University Press, 2002.

Schumacher, E.F., *Small is Beautiful: Economics as if People Mattered*. New York: Harper & Row, 1975.

Scott, Franklin D., *Sweden. The Nation's History*. Minneapolis: University of Minnesota Press, 1977.

Scott, Richard, *The History of the International Energy Agency—The First Twenty Years*, vol. I: *Origins and Structures of the IEA*. Paris: OECD/IEA, 1994.

Scott-Smith, Giles, *Networks of Empire. The US State Department's Foreign Leader Program in the Netherlands, France and Britain*. Brussels: Peter Lang, 2008.

Seitz, Konrad, *Die japanish-amerikanische Herausforerung: Deutschlands Hochtechnologieindustren kämpfen ums Überleben*. Stuttgart: Bonn Aktuell, 1990.

Selser, Gregorio, *Alianza para el Progreso. La Mal Nacida*. Buenos Aires: Ediciones Iguazú, 1964.

Servan-Schreiber, Jean-Jacques, *The American Challenge*. New York: Atheneum, 1968.

Service, Robert, *Comrades! A History of World Communism*. Cambridge, MA: Harvard University Press, 2007.

Seyd, Patrick, *The Rise & Fall of the Labour Left*. London: Macmillan Education, 1987.

Sheehan, James, *Where Have All the Soldiers Gone?: The Transformation of Modern Europe*, New York, Houghton Mifflin Harcourt, 2008.

Shepard, Todd, *The Invention of Decolonization. The Algerian War and the Remaking of France*. Ithaca, NY: Cornell University Press, 2006.

Shihata, Ibrahim F.I., *The Other Face of OPEC. Financial Assistance to the Third World*. London: Longman, 1982.

Shipway, Martin, *Decolonization and its Impact: A Comparative Approach to the End of the Colonial Empires*. Oxford: Blackwell, 2008.

Shlaim, Avi, *The Iron Wall: Israel and the Arab World*. New York: W.W. Norton & Co., 2001.

Silver, Beverly J., *Forces of Labor: Workers' Movements and Globalization since 1870*. Cambridge: Cambridge University Press, 2003.

Simonian, Haig, *The Privileged Partnership*. Oxford: Clarendon Press, 1985.

Sirinelli, Jean-François, *Mai 68. L'événement Janus*. Paris: Fayard, 2008.

Skeet, Ian., *OPEC: Twenty-Five Years of Prices and Politics*. Cambridge: Cambridge University Press, 1988.

Skidmore, Thomas, *The Politics of Military Rule in Brazil, 1964–1985*. London: Oxford University Press, 1988.

Soutou, Georges-Henri, *L'alliance incertaine. Les rapports politico-stratégiques franco-allemands 1954–1996*. Paris: Fayard, 1996.

Soutou, Georges-Henri, *La guerre de Cinquante Ans. Les relations Est–Ouest 1943–2000*. Paris: Fayard, 2001.

Spaak, Paul-Henri, *Combats Inachevés. De l'Indépendance à l'Alliance*. Paris: Fayard, 1969.

Spinelli, Altiero, *Diario europeo 1970–1976*. Bologna: Il Mulino, 1991.

Stein, Judith, *Pivotal Decade. How the United States Traded Factories for Finance in the Seventies*, New Haven, CT, Yale University Press, 2010.

Sternhell, Zeev, *The Anti-Enlightenment Tradition*. New Haven, CT: Yale University Press, 2009.

Stoffaës, Christian, *La grande ménace industrielle*. Paris: Calman-Lévy, 1977.

Stora, Benjamin, *Histoire de la guerre d'Algérie*. Paris: La Découverte, 2004.

Streeck, Wolfgang and Philippe Schmitter, "From National Corporatism to Transnational Pluralism: Organised Interests in the Single European Market," in Emilio Gabaglio and Rainer Hoffmann (eds), *The ETUC in the Mirror of Industrial Relations Research*. Brussels: European Trade Union Institute, 1998.

Suri, Jeremi, *Power and Protest: Global Revolution and the Rise of Détente*. Cambridge, MA: Harvard University Press, 2003.

Suri, Jeremi, "The Cold War, Decolonization, and Global Social Awakenings", in (2006) 3 *Cold War History* 353.

Sutcliffe, Anthony, "Cold War and Common Market: Europe, 1945–1973," in Derek Aldcroft and Anthony Sutcliffe (eds), *Europe in the International Economy 1500 to 2000*. Cheltenham: Edward Elgar, 1999.

Szàzs, André, *The Road to European Monetary Union*. London: Macmillan, 1992.

Tarrow, Sidney, *Democracy and Disorder. Protest and Politics in Italy, 1965–1975*. Oxford: Clarendon Press, 1989.

Tatò, Antonio, *Caro Berlinguer. Note e appunti riservati di Antonio Tatò a Enrico Berlinguer: 1969–1984*. Turin: Einaudi, 2003.

Teodori, Massimo, *Le nuove sinistre in Europa: 1956–1976*. Bologna: Il Mulino, 1976.

Thatcher, Margaret, *The Downing Street Years*. London: Harper Collins, 1993.

Therborn, Göran, *European Modernity and Beyond: The Trajectory of European Societies, 1945–2000*. London: SAGE Publications, 1995.

Thomas, Michael (ed.), *European Decolonization*. Aldershot: Ashgate, 2007.

Thomas, Michael, B. Moore, and L.J. Butler, *Crises of Empire. Decolonization and Europe's Imperial States, 1918–1975*. London, Bloomsbury, 2010.

Thompson, E.P., K. Alexander, S. Hall, R. Samuel, and P. Worsley, *Out of Apathy*. London: Stevens, 1960.

Thorpe, Andrew, *A History of the British Labour Party*. London: Palgrave, 2001.

Tinbergen, Jan (ed.), *Reshaping the International Order*. New York: E.P. Dutton Co., 1976.

Tomlinson, Jim, "The Commonwealth, the Balance of Payments and the Politics of International Poverty: British Aid Policy 1958–1971", in (2003) 4 *Contemporary European History*, 413.

Tosi, Luciano, "La cooperazione allo sviluppo della *Pacem in Terris* alla *Populorum Progressio*," in Agostino Giovagnoli (ed.), *Pacem in Terris*. Milan: Guerini e Associati, 2003, 147.

Touraine, Alain, *Vie et mort du Chili populaire: Juillet/Septembre 1973*. Paris: Seuil, 1973.

Toynbee, Arnold J., *Civilization on Trial*. New York: Oxford University Press, 1948.

Trentin, Bruno, *Autunno caldo. Il secondo biennio rosso 1968–1969*. Rome: Editori Riuniti, 1999.

Trentin, Massimiliano, *Engineers of Modern Development. East German Experts in Ba'athist Syria: 1965–1972*. Padua: Cluep, 2010.

Triffin, Robert, *Our International Monetary System: Yesterday, Today, and Tomorrow*. New York: Random House, 1968.

Tripp, Charles, *A History of Iraq*. Cambridge: Cambridge University Press, 2002.

Trouvé, Matthieu, *L'Espagne et l'Europe. De la dictature de Franco à l'Union européenne*. Brussels: Peter Lang, 2008.

Turpin, Frédéric, "Alle origini della politica europea di cooperazione allo sviluppo: la Francia e la politica di associazione Europa-Africa (1957–1975)", in (2007) 6 *Ventunesimo Secolo* (October 2007).

UNCTAD, *The History of UNCTAD 1964–1984*. Geneva: United Nations, 1985.

Vaïsse, Maurice, *La grandeur: Politique étrangère du général de Gaulle 1958–1969*. Paris: Fayard, 1998.

van Apeldoorn, Bastiaan, *Transnational Capitalism and the Struggle over European Integration*. London: Routledge, 2002.

van der Harst, Jan (ed.), *Beyond the Customs Union: The European Union's Quest for Deepening, Widening and Completion 1969–1975*. Brussels: Nomos Bruylant, 2007.

Van Kemseke, Peter, *Towards an Era of Development: The Globalisation of Socialism and Christian Democracy, 1945–1965*. Leuven: Leuven University Press, 2006.

Van Merriënboer, J., *Mansholt. A Biography*. Brussels: PIE Peter Lang, 2011.

Varsori, Antonio, *L'Italia nelle relazioni internazionali dal 1943 al 1992*. Bari: Laterza, 1998.

Varsori, Antonio, "La questione europea nella politica italiana", in Agostino Giovagnoli and Silvio Pons (eds), *L'Italia repubblicana nella crisi degli anni Settanta. Tra guerra Fredda e Distensione*. Rubbettino: Soveria Mannelli, 2003, 331.

Varsori, Antonio, "Puerto Rico (1976): le potenze occidentali e il problema comunista in Italia," in (2008) 16 *Ventunesimo Secolo* (June) 89.

Varsori, Antonio, *La Cenerentola di Europa. L'Italia e l'integrazione europea dal 1947 ad oggi*. Soveria Mannelli: Rubbettino, 2010.

Vernon, Raymond, *Storm over the Multinationals. The Real Issues*. New York: Macmillan, 1977.

Vinen, Richard, *A History in Fragments: Europe in the Twentieth Century*. London: Abacus, 2000.

Volpi, Franco, *Introduzione all'economia dello sviluppo*. Milan: FrancoAngeli, 1994.

Von Albertini, Rudolf, *La decolonizzazione: Il dibattito sull'amministrazione e l'avvenire delle colonie tra il 1919 e il 1960*. Turin: Società editrice internazionale, 1971.

Voorhoeve, Joris, *Peace, Profits and Principles. A Study of Dutch Development Policy*. The Hague: Nijhoff, 1979.

Waldheim, Kurt, *In the Eye of the Storm*. Bethesda, MD: Adler and Adler, 1986.

Walker, Martin, *The Cold War: A History*. New York: Henry Holt and Co., 1995.

Wallerstein, Immanuel, *L'histoire continue*. Paris: Editions de l'Aube, 1999.

Ward, Barbara, *The Widening Gap. Development in the 1970s*. New York: Columbia University Press, 1987.

Weiler, J.H.H., *The Constitution of Europe. "Do the New Clothes Have an Emperor?" and Other Essays on European Integration*. Cambridge: Cambridge University Press, 1999.

Wesseling, H.L., "Les Pays-Bas et la decolonization: Politique extérieure et forces profondes," in *Opinion publique et politique extérieure, III 1945–1981. Actes du colloque de Rome* (17–20 February 1982) Rome: Ecole Française de Rome, 1985.

Westad, Odd Arne, *The Global Cold War*. Cambridge: Cambridge University Press, 2005.

White, John, *The Politics of Foreign Aid*. London: The Bodley Head, 1974.

Wilford, Hugh, "CIA Plot, Socialist Conspiracy or New World Order?", in (2003) 3 *Diplomacy and Statecraft* 70.

Williams, Allan and Gareth Shaw, *Tourism and Economic Development. European Experience*. Chichester: John Wiley & Sons, 1998.

Wilson, Harold, *The War on World Poverty*. London: Gollancz, 1953.

Winand, Pascaline, *Eisenhower, Kennedy, and the United States of Europe*. London: Macmillan, 1993.

Wionczek, Miguel (ed.), *Economic Cooperation in Latin America, Africa, and Asia*. Cambridge, MA: MIT Press, 1969.

Wood, Robert E., *From Marshall Plan to Debt Crisis: Foreign Aid and Development Choices in the World Economy*. Los Angeles: University of California Press, 1986.

Woods, Ngaire, *The Globalizers: The IMF, the World Bank, and Their Borrowers*. Ithaca, NY: Cornell University Press, 2006.

Worsley, Peter, *The Third World*. London: Weidenfeld, 1964.

Yergin, Daniel, *The Prize: The Epic Quest for Oil, Money, and Power*. New York: Simon & Schuster, 1991.

Yew, Lee Kuan, *From the Third World to the First: The Singapore Story: 1965–2000*. New York: Harper Collins, 2000.

Young, Harold, *This Blessed Plot: Britain and Europe from Churchill to Blair*. London: Papermac, 1998.

Young, Nigel, *An Infantile Disorder? The Crisis and Decline of the New Left*. London: Routledge & Kegan Paul, 1977.

Young, Robert. *Postcolonialism: An Historical Introduction*. Oxford: Blackwell, 2001.

Zagari, Mario, *Superare le sfide. La risposta dell'Italia e dell'Europa alle sfide mondiali*. Milan: Rizzoli, 2006.

Zanatta, Loris, *Storia dell'America Latina contemporanea*. Bari: Laterza, 2010.

Zanchettin, Claudio, "Il Black Panthers Party. La rivoluzione internazionalista negli Stati Uniti", in (1972) 15 *Terzo Mondo*.

Zeiler, Thomas W., *Free Trade Free World: The Advent of GATT*. Chapel Hill: University of North Carolina Press, 1999.

Ziegler, Jean, "L'Internationale Socialiste. La reconquête de l'Amérique," in *Le Nouvel Observateur*, October 11, 1979.

Ziegler, Philip, *Wilson. The Authorised Life*. London: Weidenfeld & Nicolson, 1993.

Zimmermann, Hubert, "Western Europe and the American Challenge: Conflict and Cooperation in Technology and Monetary Policy, 1965–1973," in Marc Trachtenberg (ed.), *Empire and Alliance*. Lanham, MD: Rowman & Littlefield, 2003, 127.

Zubok, Vladimir, *A Failed Empire: The Soviet Union in the Cold War from Stalin to Gorbachev*. Chapel Hill: University of North Carolina Press, 2007.

Index

Printed and bound by CPI Group (UK) Ltd, Croydon, CR0 4YY